Groping for Ethics in Journalism

SECOND EDITION

Drawings by Fran Goodwin

Groping
for Ethics
in
Journalism

H. EUGENE GOODWIN

IOWA STATE UNIVERSITY PRESS / AME

GOODWIN, winner of the Kappa Tau Alpha-Frank Luther Mott award for the best re-
about journalism published in 1983 for the first edition of *Groping for Ethics*, became
itus of journalism in 1985 after twenty-eight years on the faculty of Pennsylvania State
ng the past two years he has served on the faculty of four Gannett-Foundation workshops
of Kentucky on the teaching of journalism ethics in American universities.

Peter Koeleman

University Press, Ames, Iowa 50010
ate University Press
bries of America

First e
Second ed

Library of Con

Goodwin, H. Eugene,
Groping for ethics   ng-in-Publication Data

1. Journalistic ethics
PN4888.E8G66   1987
ISBN 0-8138-0818-9
ISBN 0-8138-0819-7 (pbl   s.   I. Title.
                                        87-2753

CONTENTS

PREFACE

When I told people I was doing a book on journalism ethics, I got some interesting reactions. Like:

"What ethics?"

"Well, at least the bibliographic search will be short."

"Will it be a comic book?"

"Will the right people read it?"

I do not agree with the attitude toward journalism expressed in those only half-kidding reactions, but I understand it. Journalism is not held in high esteem by many people in this country, some of whom are journalists. Many see journalism as a tawdry calling, practiced often by unprincipled boors.

Actually journalism has gotten to be quite respectable these days. With the advent of cold type and computers, newspaper newsrooms are indistinguishable from insurance offices: rugs on the floor, no typewriters or teletypes clacking away, no glue pots, no green eyeshades, no shouts of "Hold the presses, I've got a story here that's gonna bust this town wide open!" Decorum rules. Television newsrooms tend to be more cluttered; but with makeup rooms, instant public recognition for its on-camera stars, and annual salaries of more than a million dollars for top anchors, TV journalism is nothing if not respectable. But try as it may, journalism cannot completely shake its Bohemian traditions. Hard-drinking, hard-smoking, hard-living, hard-nosed types still find news work compatible with their bad habits.

I have been observing journalists at work and play for many years. I was in what used to be called "the newspaper game" for about a dozen years; and as a teacher of journalism for more than twice that long, I have continued to watch the game being played. I like news people, scoundrels and saints alike. They do interesting things, some of which have to do with their work, and they tell interesting stories, some for public consumption. I love their irreverence and their skepticism, and admire their ability to get at the core of things in a world in which obfuscation and beating around bushes seems more highly revered.

But for a long time I have been bothered by some of the things journalists and news media proprietors do. They do not always seem to have a strong sense of morality, of what is right and wrong. Even news people I know to be honest and decent folks do wrongful things in pursuit of a story (I did the same myself and feel the shame to this day). My feelings about the occasional but serious moral lapses of journalists and of the news business as a whole began to jell when I took over the news media ethics course at Penn State that John Harrison, another newsman-turned-teacher, had taught for many years before his retirement. And as I organized my thoughts and files and dug into what had been written about the rights and wrongs of journalistic practice, I came to see a place for a book that would try to assess the current status of ethics in the field and present it in a way that might help journalists think through their ethical problems.

That is what I have tried to do with this book. It is not a philosophical book. I am not qualified by training or inclination to write a philosophical book. I did this book the only way I know how – the way I learned to report: Do your homework and then ask the questions. After reading all I could get my hands on that might be relevant, I interviewed about 150 working journalists and a few media watchers for the first edition and then another 20 or so for the second edition. More than 100 of those I interviewed on tape are quoted in this book. I am grateful – both to those who were and those who were not quoted – for sharing their knowledge and views with me. I learned from all of them.

In this second edition, I have tried to respond to the criticisms the first edition received – the most substantial one being that the book was not normative or prescriptive enough. In reworking and updating the original material and adding a wealth of new cases and insights, I have tried to be more judgmental. I trust that readers will easily distinguish between my facts and my judgments and will exercise their own judgments about mine.

Another thing this book is not is a report on the ethics of all mass communicators. It does not deal with the ethics of advertising or public relations practitioners or entertainers. Their standards are important but come from different roots and have, in my opinion, less bearing on the general welfare than do those of our principal information processors.

In considering the ethics of journalistic practice in this book, my focus is on newspaper, wire service, and television journalism. That is where most journalists ply their trade. When you study the ethics of a profession or business, you have to study the people who are in it; the channels and technology of communication with which they deal are secondary.

In addition to the journalists and observers I interviewed, a lot of people helped me with this book. My friend, Fran Goodwin, who is also my wife, edited and typed the manuscript through its various versions and did the cartoons that make their points more tellingly than my words. She and Sally Heffentreyer dug out important articles, books, and facts for me from libraries and other sources. Colleagues on the journalism faculty at Penn State – Tom Berner, Vince Norris, John Nichols, Don Smith, Bill Dulaney, Dan Pfaff, and John Rippey – contributed valuable criticisms and suggestions. Research papers by former graduate students Jack Tobias, Robert W. Hollis, Michael Salwen, George Osgood, Neil Genzlinger, Deborah Benedetti, Kathleen Pavelko, Donald Sneed, Charles Brewer, and Patrick McFadden; and by honors undergraduates Laura Rehrmann, Donna Shaub, and Robert King expanded my knowledge of matters dealt with in these pages. Former graduate student Robert LaBarre of the Riverside, California, *Press-Enterprise,* helped me collect West Coast material. I am also grateful to the Pennsylvania State University for the sabbatical leave that enabled me to complete research for and write the first edition of this book. My Iowa State University Press editor, Suzanne Lowitt, gently contributed scores of suggestions that improved both editions.

Finally, I wish to dedicate this book to my wife, whose encouragement and support made the work possible and whose companionship made it fun.

H. EUGENE GOODWIN
Professor Emeritus of Journalism
Pennsylvania State University

ACRONYMS

ABC = American Broadcasting Company
AFL-CIO = American Federation of Labor-Congress of Industrial Organizations
AIM = Accuracy in Media
ANPA = American Newspaper Publishers Association
AP = Associated Press
APME = Associated Press Managing Editors Association
APSE = Associated Press Sports Editors Association
ASNE = American Society of Newspaper Editors
BGA = Better Government Association
CBS = Columbia Broadcasting System
CIA = Central Intelligence Agency
FCC = Federal Communications Commission
GAO = Government Accounting Office
GNS = Gannett News Service
IRE = Investigative Reporters and Editors Association
NBC = National Broadcasting Company
NCAA = National Collegiate Athletic Association
NCEW = National Conference of Editorial Writers
NLRB = National Labor Relations Board
NPPA = National Press Photographers Association
ONO = Organization of News Ombudsmen
OWAA = Outdoor Writers Association of America
RTNDA = Radio-Television News Directors Association
SATW = Society of American Travel Writers
SPJ-SDX = Society of Professional Journalists, Sigma Delta Chi
UPI = United Press International

Groping for Ethics in Journalism

1 The Search for Standards

"I said they had a right to publish—but that doesn't mean I want you to read it!"

If you have ever dented a parked car, did you leave a note?

If a clerk gives you too much change, do you give the money back?

When you are asked to give a job recommendation for an acquaintance with less than average ability, do you tell the truth?

Those are the kinds of ethical questions most of us have to face more than once in our lives. They are not in the same league with such questions as: Should Truman have authorized the dropping of atomic bombs on Japan? Should Nixon have ordered the cover-up of the Watergate burglary? Should decisions about abortions be left to the women involved and their doctors? Yet how we answer such questions, whether mundane or cosmic, determines how ethical we are as individuals and how civilized our society is.

Sometimes economic factors dictate our ethics. Remember Alfred Doolittle, the dustman in George Bernard Shaw's *Pygmalion,* who tried to get Prof. Henry Higgins to pay for the "use" of his daughter Liza? Shocked by Doolittle's effrontery, Higgins's friend Colonel Pickering asks, "Have you no morals, man?"

"Can't afford them, Governor," Doolittle replies unabashedly. "Neither could you if you was as poor as me."[1]

Sometimes our upbringing—what we have learned from parents, pastors, and police – guides us through our ethical thickets. But many believe the guidelines of upbringing are less influential these days, that the moral codes of society are breaking down.

"The belief in authority disintegrated in this century, particularly the latter part of the century, the sixties being the best example of that," says James Wall, editor of *Christian Century*. "There's no 'sacred' anymore." Gone is "the assumption of the community, the family, and the individual that there are standards handed down to us from the authorities, the sacred holders of the Truth, or the government."[2]

Wall believes this disintegration of authority has made codes of morals, ethics, and standards obligatory in the professions. "When there's chaos in the land, somebody's got to have some kind of order."

Whether all or most journalists in the United States see this need to establish professional ethical standards to compensate for the disintegrating morals of the larger society is uncertain, but journalists have undoubtedly become more conscious of ethics in recent years.

David Shaw, media reporter-critic for the *Los Angeles Times,* views journalism's increasing emphasis on ethics as a "positive consequence of Watergate." He finds that "journalists have been forced to be more ethical because it is very difficult to expose politicians for lying and then turn around and lie yourself in exposing them." The combination of "the deceit that went into the Vietnam War build-up" and "the abuses of the Nixon administration culminating in Watergate . . . forced the press to clean up its act."[3]

Any careful investigator can find plenty of evidence of what Shaw is talking about. Journalists in all our news media – newspapers, television, magazines, and radio – seem to be more conscious of ethics today than in the past. But you can also find cases that seem to show journalism has a long way to go before it can claim to be an ethical calling.

This book is a report on the state of ethics in journalism in the United States, with some recommendations for improvement. It is based on an analysis of hundreds of interviews and discussions with print and broadcast journalists at all levels, and on the writings of ethicists, journalists, and others concerned about ethics in this vital field.

AGREEING ON GUIDING PRINCIPLES

Journalists in the United States have some major problems in coming to grips with their ethics. One has to do with their difficulty in dealing with the contrasting and often conflicting pulls of journalism the profession and journalism the business. Unlike most lawyers and physicians, the people we think of as journalists – reporters, writers, photographers, editors, news directors, and news producers who report and interpret the news – are mostly hired hands. They are not completely in control of their own methods and products. (This problem is dealt with in Chapter 2.)

Another major problem is the strong feeling throughout American journalism that First Amendment freedom is paramount, even if it means protecting bad journalism.

The First Amendment

Congress shall make no law respecting an establishment of religion, or prohibiting the free exercise thereof; or abridging the freedom of speech, or of the press; or the right of the people peaceably to assemble, and to petition the Government for a redress of grievances.

That guarantee of freedom in the First Amendment to the U.S. Constitution, and similar guarantees in the constitutions of the fifty states, provides the legal basis for press freedom in this country. That freedom in turn has had a powerful influence on the ethics of journalists and the news media, principal beneficiaries of the First Amendment.

It must be understood that the First Amendment does not literally mean that no laws whatever can be passed abridging freedom of the press. Like all provisions of the Constitution, the free press provision has been interpreted and reinterpreted by the courts over the years, so that several restrictions on absolute freedom – libel and slander, for example – have been permitted. The courts also have granted somewhat less freedom to broadcast journalists than to print journalists, although that discrimination seems to be disappearing.

In addition to the court decisions on press freedom, the interpretations that journalists give to the First Amendment shape their attitudes toward ethics and ethical standards. Some view this freedom in absolutist terms and therefore resist efforts to impose any universal standards on journalism and the news media, whether by government or by journalism itself.

"The strength of the American press is its diversity," insists Abraham M. Rosenthal, associate editor of the *New York Times.* "There are publishers I wouldn't dirty my hands with, but I don't want a code that would exclude them."[4]

Jack Landau, former director of the Reporters Committee for Freedom of the Press, fears that the courts will impose the "moral framework of the establishment press" on the alternative press, "all the little publications, some of which are creepy and way-out." They will do this, he believes, through the calling of expert witnesses from the larger newspapers and by applying the codes of the larger news media and of journalistic organizations as standards for all. He contends that the smaller newspapers and broadcast stations cannot live up to the standards of the *New York Times* because they do not have the staffs and resources to be as accurate and thorough as large metropolitan newspapers can be. Besides, many of the alternative publications do not buy all of the standards of the establishment press, Landau argues. "They say, 'Why should we be fair? Fairness is your white, middle class, male, Ivy League value. We have a right to put our own views across.' " Landau does not want "courts telling these people what is right and wrong."[5]

Because he is "an extremist about the First Amendment," Lyle Denniston, U.S. Supreme Court reporter for the Baltimore *Sun,* cannot accept a universal ethical code for journalists. He believes the First Amendment states "a social value preference for an open society, in which there cannot be any governmental restraints on the communication of ideas." An industrywide ethics code "is alien to my basic notion about the free communication of ideas: it is law or regulation in another format." Ethics for the journalist, Denniston holds, have to be individual, "based on some kind of internal moral-ethical perception."[6]

Although they share the absolutists' fear of government interference with news media freedom, many other journalists seem to infer from the First Amendment the notion that standards and responsibility are a sort of payment for freedom. They support greater efforts by journalists, often with the help of nongovernmental outsiders, to improve the ethics and standards of the news media and to be accountable to the public for their acts.

"We vigorously oppose any government interference in the gathering and disseminating of information," says Paul Janensch, general news editor for the Gannett group. "But we think it's wrong for the news media to wrap themselves in the First Amendment whenever someone challenges what we do and how we do it." The news media should be receptive to criticism from within and without, and "operate within written codes so that everyone involved in the news process knows what is permitted and what is out of bounds."[7]

Another who speaks for the moderate view of the First Amendment is Paul A. Poorman, former editor and vice-president of the *Akron Beacon Journal.* "Our skirts have to be clean. We have to be above suspicion . . . if we're to, first, make money, be a profitable institution, and second, fulfill the social role guaranteed to us in the Constitution," Poorman contends. The First Amendment does not talk about confidentiality, honesty, and the many ethical problems journalists face today because its framers could not anticipate what the press has become, he adds. Poorman has compiled a list of thirty-four broad areas, including interstate commerce and labor-management relations, in which Congress has made law impinging on the absolute freedom of the press. "Anytime I hear people waving the First Amendment," he says, "I remind them of the Twenty-first Amendment – the short one that abolished prohibition and says simply that the Eighteenth Amendment is hereby repealed."[8]

Social Responsibility. Many who have studied journalism and mass communications in America since World War II have looked to the social responsibility theory of the press as a possible basis for a system of journalism ethics. This theory was described but not labeled in the work of the so-called Hutchins Commission on Freedom of the Press and was brilliantly articulated by Theodore Peterson in *Four Theories of the Press* in 1956. Peterson, professor and former dean of the College of Communications at the University of Illinois-Urbana, wrote that the "major premise" of the social responsibility theory is that "freedom carries concomitant obligations; and the press, which enjoys a privileged position under our government, is obliged to be responsible to society for carrying out certain essential functions of mass communications in contemporary society."[9]

The social responsibility theory was seen by Peterson as replacing the traditional libertarian theory, which had guided those who established our press system when this country was founded. Libertarianism, a composite of ideas of such thinkers as John Milton, John Erskine, Thomas Jefferson, and John Stuart Mill, holds that the press and other media should be privately owned and as free as possible from government so they can pursue the truth as they see it and be a check on government. The press can be irresponsible as well as responsible, printing falsehoods as well as truth, because the citizens are rational and can separate one from the other. The important thing under libertarian theory is for there to be a free marketplace of ideas, because if all voices can be heard the truth will surely emerge.

"But somewhere along the way, faith diminished in the optimistic notion that a virtually absolute freedom and the nature of man carried built-in correctives for the press," Peterson maintained.[10]

He argued that social responsibility as a theory for the press was born out of several changes in the world. One of these was the technological and industrial revolution that changed "the American way of living," added movies, radio, and television to the media system, and encouraged concentration of media ownership in a few hands.

Another change "was a new intellectual climate in which some persons looked with suspicion on the basic assumptions of the Enlightenment," Peterson wrote. "And finally there was the development of a professional spirit as journalism attracted men of principle and education, and as the communications industries reflected the growing sense of social responsibility assumed by American business and industry generally."

Peterson did not try to build ethical standards from the theory he described. In fact, he cautioned his readers to "remember that the social responsibility theory is still chiefly a theory. But as a theory it is important because it suggests a direction in which thinking about freedom of the press is heading."

Interviewed twenty-five years after publication of *Four Theories of the Press,* Peterson points out that he never advocated anything in his chapter on social responsibility, although he is often accused of doing so. He believes the chapter had a great impact on schools of journalism and their curricula—"at least it introduced the notion of social responsibility"—and that may have in turn influenced the growth of a professional ethic in the practice of journalism. "But, unfortunately," he continues, "the ethic that has developed is an unreasoned ethic without a philosophical base."[11]

Although he believes most of the media codes of ethics and standards that have emerged in this century came in response to public criticism, Peterson "has a very strong respect for the ethical behavior" of the newspaper and magazine people he knows, at least those among his generation. He maintains they have a "very strong sense of rightness."

Peterson's Illinois colleague, Clifford G. Christians, notes somewhat sadly that the social responsibility theory "has not generated seasoned ethical standards." He adds that the decreasing numbers of information channels:

> remind us that the public good may be our only valid guideline for choosing which information to transmit. And certainly social responsibility is much more compatible with public ownership of the electromagnetic spectrum. For all that, as noted, principles based on this ideology remain undefined and its ethical sophistication limited.[12]

Another academic, John L. Hulteng of Stanford University, concedes that a majority of editors and educators and many working journalists believe that in this period of shrinking numbers of channels of information "social responsibility is the only valid and acceptable guiding theory for the press." But an ethical framework does not logically evolve from that theory, Hulteng writes, arguing that "the principles and standards that are influential in the workings of the mass media today stem from many sources and a variety of theories," including the more traditional libertarian ideology and "folkways of the news business."[13]

These less than optimistic assessments of the social responsibility theory's impact on journalistic practice should not be taken to mean that the theory is dead. It has had some influence and it may have more in the future. And although the theory lacks a full-blown philosophical base for a system of ethics in journalism, its central principle that journalists are obliged to be responsible to society still has great appeal.

The Public's Right to Know. Although the social responsibility theory may not be familiar to many journalists, a slogan that came along about the same time certainly is. "The public's right to know" (or "people's right to know," if you prefer) has been a chant of American journalists in the period since World War II as they fought to expand their access to news of government, business, and other areas of the society that have found ways to hide from public scrutiny.

The phrase seems to have started with Kent Cooper, former top executive of the Associated Press (AP), and then became cemented into the conventional wisdom of journalism when Harold Cross used it as a title of a book he wrote for the American Society of Newspaper Editors (ASNE) in 1953. The general theme of his book and of the doctrine the slogan represents is that the public has a legal right to know what its government is doing and the press is the representative of the public in finding that out.[14] Thus "the public's right to know" became a flag for those many journalists who infer from the roots of press freedom a special responsibility to be watchdogs of government, to protect the people from abuses of government.

From this doctrine also has come a long and reasonably successful campaign by journalism to get most of the states to adopt open meetings and open records laws and to get the federal government to enact the Freedom of Information Act in 1967. None of these laws has worked to the complete satisfaction of most journalists, but they have been useful in opening up more of the activities and records of government to the news media and to the public.

There has been an ethical dimension to the public's right to know movement. It has stimulated journalists, somewhat arrogantly in some cases admittedly, to see themselves as representatives of the people. Many a reporter has sensed a special responsibility when covering some important public meeting with no members of the public present except perhaps an observer for the League of Women Voters and a couple of lawyers representing some special interest or other. The reporter in that all-too-common circumstance usually makes a special effort to report actions that might affect those absent citizens—not to sell more papers or increase his or her station's audience, but out of a sense of duty. This same sense of representing the public at large has spurred journalists as they have tried to throw light on the less obvious activities of business and other areas of the private sector in which the public has an interest.

The Baltimore *Sun*'s Denniston sees a Catch 22 in Harold Cross's doctrine. He does not "buy former Justice Potter Stewart's view that the free press clause was put in the Constitution to give the press some kind of peculiar role in monitoring government. If you follow that to its logical conclusion, you end up with the concept of the press as a public utility." That notion has encouraged "the developing idea that the press is part of the government machine," Denniston believes. This means "we get access when we are necessary in the governmental process – and only when we are."[15]

One of Denniston's ethical premises "is that you really owe your reader nothing." He tries to reach readers but that differs from being obliged to reach them, as the public's right to know doctrine implies. "I do not work for a public utility," he insists. "I don't have to pick up everybody who wants to get on my bus. I'm in the business of gathering and selling ideas. If somebody wants to buy them, fine, but don't come to me and tell me you have a right to be told."

Denniston's concern about the public's right to know doctrine may not be shared by most journalists, many of whom see the press as a public utility in the sense that it has responsibilities to the public it serves. But for some reason the slogan itself has been used less and less often by those who speak for journalism in this country. The general public, on the other hand, seems to have taken to the slogan, some treating it as if it's their natural and constitutional right to be told what they want to be told.

And journalists, too, have tried to turn the doctrine to their own ends, invoking it, for example, as justification for questionable conduct; stealing or lying to get a story is often explained away by claiming that the public's right to know had to be served.

Journalists, limited by news space and time, have to decide every day what it is that the public has a right to know. A visit to any newsroom at the end of a working day shows even the casual observer how much news is left over, unused, apparently not material the public has a right to know. The point is not to make jest of the difficult news decisions that editors have to make but to argue that what the public has a right to know is determined by editors making subjective judgments and by managers who determine how much news space and time will be available. A doctrine so imperfect can hardly justify illegal and unethical behavior by any thinking journalist.

Accuracy and Fairness. Although American journalists have a hard time agreeing on many things, virtually all of them have come to accept accuracy and fairness as the most important of their professional standards. Both of these standards, of course, are ethical as well as professional or operational.

Accuracy has been a more troublesome ideal for journalists than it might appear. For one thing, journalists have to do their work under deadlines, very demanding deadlines at times. The pressure to get the news out to the public while it is still fresh causes errors. That is why many newsrooms in an earlier day posted the old International News Service admonition, "Get It First, But First Get It Right." Fine, but every journalist soon learns that getting it first sometimes means you don't get it right, and taking the time to get it right often means you don't get it first.

A second difficulty in achieving accuracy has to do with expectations. Most people outside of journalism, and even many journalists, expect journalism to produce the "truth," forgetting what Walter Lippmann tried to tell us years ago—that news and truth are not the same thing.[16] The facts that journalists *can* produce sometimes add up to the truth, but journalists are seldom able to put sufficient facts together at a given time to be able to tell the truth about some news subject. Reporting the Vietnam War gave us a good example of this problem: the journalists who covered that confusing and complicated conflict were never able to get at the truth about that war. They could report what U.S. generals said, what a portion of U.S. and South Vietnamese troops did that day, or what a segment of Vietcong troops did that day, but those were "facts" about the war. We are only now beginning to learn the "truth" about that war. On less complex news situations, of course, journalists can get closer to the truth. But the failure on the part of both journalists and the public to see journalism as a fact business and not a truth business has caused frustration among journalists and a general misunderstanding about journalism's function in our society.

This is not to say that journalists should not be and have not been truthful in their pursuit of facts. That is what the accuracy standard really means: being truthful both in the gathering and presentation of facts and information; not lying, not plagiarizing.

Although the history of American journalism contains some colorful lapses in the accuracy standard, accuracy has been an undisputed goal of virtually all journalists in this country for at least a century. But accuracy is not enough. You can be accurate and still be unfair. So thoughtful journalists seek fairness as well as accuracy in their journalism.

The standard of fairness is part of and in a way an offspring of objective reporting. Depending on which history or reporting books you read, objective reporting started in the nineteenth century with the growth of cooperative news gathering through the AP, or it developed in the twentieth century as journalists imitated the scientific methods of natural science. Whichever, the idea that news should be unbiased, balanced, and fair became and remains widely accepted in the field, even though the word "objectivity" has fallen into dispute.

One reason that objectivity in reporting got into trouble was the way it was interpreted and administered by many newsroom bosses, particularly those who ran the larger wire services. Too many of them defined objectivity in very narrow terms: just report what important people say and do; don't bother about the why's and don't worry about explaining anything; let the readers figure things out for themselves.

Michael J. O'Neill, former editor of the New York *Daily News,* learned about this narrow definition of objectivity when he went out to cover a meat packers' strike in Chicago about 1950 for United Press International (UPI). The union claimed the company had scabs working inside the plant, but management denied it. O'Neill climbed over the fence, ripping his suit on the barbed wire, and discovered nonunion workers living inside the plant and sleeping on 125 cots he counted. When O'Neill got back to his office, his editor told him he could not use what he had seen unless he could quote some company official. "Well, that's stupid," O'Neill says today, "because half the truth that you develop you're never going to get anybody to announce or to officially identify with."[17]

Demagogues have taken advantage of journalists who insisted that news was not news until somebody in authority said it. Senator Joseph McCarthy of Wisconsin helped bring about the decline of the old narrow view of objectivity by the way he twisted it and some other conventions of journalism to his own ends. Realizing that almost anything a U.S. senator said was news, McCarthy got the press to distribute his unsubstantiated charges about the large numbers of Communists who had supposedly infiltrated the government, even the military. This was in the 1950s when a lot of people were imagining Reds under their beds as the country went through one of its periodic scares about the Communist conspiracy. McCarthy would time his speeches, press conferences, and news releases so that they would just make the deadlines of the major news media, and so there was seldom time to check any of his charges for the same day's story, even if anybody had felt inclined to do so. After McCarthy's political bubble burst in 1954 when the Senate voted sixty-seven to twenty-two to censure him for his reckless and abusive conduct, many in the press took a hard look at how they had been used by this skillful abuser of truth. And one of the shibboleths of journalism they began to question was objectivity as it had been so narrowly defined.[18]

The notion of journalistic objectivity took a further beating during the Vietnam War and the domestic turmoil it produced through the 1960s and early 1970s. Critics blamed objectivity for journalism's failure to break out of the news management increasingly practiced by generals, presidents, and others in control of American life and institutions. Not only was it impossible for reporters to be unbiased, these critics argued, it was undesirable. And that line of criticism has persisted.

"It's stupid and dishonest for journalists to continue to insist that they are without gut feelings, values, politics, et cetera," declares Robert Scheer, a former editor of *Ramparts* and *New Times* and now a reporter for the *Los Angeles Times*. "And if they are, I want to know why and how did they get to be without those things and where have they been . . . . To me the more important question is not whether you can be neutral but how you do your job in a fair and honest way."[19]

Objectivity also has been criticized for producing a bland, almost ignorant, kind of news reporting that gives all facts and all views equal weight to the point of distortion. Critics argue that the many complexities in the world today require not neutral observers but journalists who educate themselves in the subjects they report so that they can interpret them from a point of view; only in that way can the public make sense out of the complexities.

Because of the barrage of criticism and questioning objective reporting has been under since the 1950s, it is no longer on every journalist's list of goals and ideals. Most journalists today, even those who still profess a belief in "objectivity," see fairness as the important principle to live by. Many still insist, however, that it is desirable and possible for reporters to be reasonably unbiased and to keep their own views out of their news stories. So objectivity has not died in American news work; it simply was so abused by some of its earlier adherents that many of today's journalists prefer the simpler standard of fairness.

The record here should also show that the public has been well served as well as poorly served by objective reporting. We have been well served when reporters, most of whom are generalists expected to be able to handle all kinds of news, sensed that they were dealing with subjects better left to others to judge and tried to be neutral and fair to all sides in their reporting of such subjects. Whenever reporters are in over their heads in reporting any complicated subject, we are probably better off with a report that simply lays out whatever facts are available without having them judged or interpreted for us.

We have been poorly served, on the other hand, when reporters in their striving for objectivity produced superficial reports—a string of quotes from various sources, for example, hung across the line like Monday's wash and making very little sense to anybody. We also have been poorly served when writers refused to abandon strict objectivity in reporting something as bewildering as the Vietnam War or the American public's reaction to it, phenomena that cried out for explanation and humanistic interpretation.

The main concern of this book about accuracy and fairness, however, is what these standards have to say about journalism ethics. In the sense that accuracy means being truthful in both the gathering and reporting of facts and information, it is a significant ethical standard, just as "Don't lie" is a principal warning in the everyday codes of ethics most of us carry around in our heads. Fairness in dealing with sources and in reporting also is a significant ethical standard when it is taken by journalists to mean that they should be fair and honest in news reporting, that they should not judge others prematurely and should instead exercise a bit of compassion. Objectivity has been defined in many ways, admittedly, but the ethical implications have always been there too and have dominated the work of many journalists. Objective reporting, with all of its imperfections, has by itself been a kind of ethic for U.S. journalists. (The "dispassion" of objectivity is discussed in Chapter 12.)

GROWTH OF CODES

The more formal agreement on ethical standards in journalism that has been achieved in this century has come mostly through journalism's professional organizations, such as the ASNE. In fact, adoption of a code of ethics was virtually the first action of the ASNE when it was organized in 1923.[20] Although some state press associations had by then adopted codes, the ASNE Canons of Journalism, as they were called, was the first national code of ethics and standards put forward by any organization of journalists. Since 1923, other national journalistic organizations, notably the Society of Professional Journalists, Sigma Delta Chi (SPJ-SDX), and the Radio-Television News Directors Association (RTNDA), have adopted such codes, and ASNE in 1975 thoroughly revised its canons and renamed them "The Statement of Principles of the American Society of Newspaper Editors."

Several of the 124 charter members of ASNE wanted to expel F. G. Bonfils, publisher of the Denver *Post,* for his role in the Teapot Dome scandal. Only a year after ASNE adopted its canons, Bonfils was accused of accepting a million dollars in bribes to suppress reports in his newspaper that government oil reserves in the Teapot Dome field in Wyoming were being sold illegally to private interests. But the debate about punishing the publisher for apparently violating virtually all of the canons ended in 1929 when the society voted that adherence to its code would be voluntary. The vote undoubtedly was influenced by Bonfils's threat to sue ASNE if it acted against him.[21]

Similar fears of litigation figured in the 1985 decision by the directors of SPJ-SDX against enforcing its code of ethics on individual members. The society's board of directors was advised by its counsel, Bruce W. Sanford, that if some punitive action were taken against a member for violating the code, that member could successfully sue. Also influencing the board's vote, according to Frank Sutherland, SPJ-SDX president at the time, was concern about code enforcement conflicting with First Amendment freedom and about the competency of officers of smaller SPJ-SDX chapters to "make judgments that could affect somebody's career forever."[22]

The lack of any machinery for enforcement characterizes all of the ethics codes that have been adopted by national and state organizations of journalists since ASNE agreed on its canons in 1923. The association codes are mostly statements of ideals and aspirations. RTNDA put together its code in 1966 and revised it in 1973. SPJ-SDX, which had endorsed the ASNE canons as its code of ethics in 1926, created its own code in 1973 and revised it in 1984 to condemn plagiarism. The Associated Press Managing Editors Association (APME) accepted a code of ethics in 1975. (The ethics codes of ASNE, SPJ-SDX, RTNDA, and APME are reprinted in the Appendix.)

The 1970s and early 1980s also saw the adoption or updating of codes by such smaller national news organizations as the Society of American Travel Writers (SATW), the Associated Press Sports Editors Association (APSE), the National Conference of Editorial Writers (NCEW), and the Society of American Business and Economics Writers.

The principal author of the SPJ-SDX code, Casey Bukro, environment editor of the *Chicago Tribune,* believes that code has had a positive impact on journalism, but he wishes the society would develop some mechanism to enforce it. As a member of the SPJ-SDX national board for eight years after the 1973 convention adopted the code, and more recently as the society's ethics committee chairman, Bukro has pushed for creation by local chapters of boards to hear complaints about ethics code violations. "But there is a fear that the local chapters will go on witch hunts—which doesn't give our members much credit for intelligence," Bukro says. "Our ethical problems are going to be greater if we ignore them."[23]

Not all journalists are so enthusiastic about written codes of ethics for the news media. "The journalism codes are so generalized as to be meaningless," says Leslie H. Whitten, novelist who was senior investigator for the Jack Anderson column for twelve years. "The few unethical journalists I've known are really flawed people. It's not that they don't follow any codes—they're not interested in codes. They were poorly brought up and they did dishonest things." Whitten believes the news business is "full of truly good people" who got into journalism "for vanity and the desire to do good for other people." The vanity is served through the by-line, he explains. "Journalism has always been a business of ethical people," Whitten says, "because they're poorly paid and they do it because it is a good thing to do and because of the by-line."[24]

Another prominent doubter about codes is Abe Rosenthal, recently retired as executive editor of the *New York Times,* who contends that most of the journalism codes "aim at the lowest common denominator" and are "too easy." Although he fears that national codes could be used against the press and jeopardize First Amendment freedoms, Rosenthal believes each individual newspaper has a right to adopt its own code if it wants one. He has standards for his newsroom, some of them in writing, but "we feel no necessity for gathering them together and putting them in a code," Rosenthal adds. "But if you're going to have a code, it has to be tough and it has to deal with questions of how much news, how much profit, how much space." He says that if he drew up a code of ethics for the entire newspaper business, "damned few would sign it."[25]

Rosenthal's distaste for an industrywide code of ethics that would be imposed on all journalists or on all journalists in a particular medium, such as newspapers, is shared by most leaders of the field. They accept or tolerate the existing codes of national and state associations of journalists because they apply only to the members of those associations, are very general in their strictures, and aren't enforced anyway. But the codes of ethics that have been adopted by individual news organizations—a newspaper like the *Philadelphia Inquirer* or the *Los Angeles Times,* for example—are another story.

Codes with Teeth. Although the *New York Times* news department in recent years has relied on memos and word of mouth rather than a more formal code for communicating its ethical standards, most of the major daily newspapers in this country have adopted written codes of ethics and standards. The picture is different in broadcast news. The major broadcast networks—ABC, CBS, and NBC—have detailed written codes for their news departments and those of the television and radio stations they own, but very few of the non-network broadcast stations have their own news department codes.

Many news organizations have shied away from writing codes of ethics on the advice of their lawyers who fear that such codes could be misinterpreted and used against them in court suits. Many smaller news organizations don't feel a need for a written code to convey ethical standards to their modestly sized staffs.

A few newsrooms prefer dialogue over documents when it comes to solving their ethical problems. One such is the *St. Petersburg Times,* whose editor and president, Andrew Barnes, conducts frequent staff meetings to discuss ethics and other newsroom problems. "In a way it seems to us that if you create a piece of paper in which you codify your morality, you almost do that instead of acting on it," Barnes believes. "When somebody says, 'I have this problem,' I would much rather have the response be, 'Let's talk about it,' . . . rather than 'Let's go look at the code.' "[26]

The "ongoing conversation" that Barnes prefers over a written code also occurs in some newsrooms that are governed by written codes. (And, in fact, the St. Petersburg operation does have a written policy on freebies and conflicts of interest.) But what Barnes is arguing against is a tendency in some shops to hang a code of ethics on the wall, declare yourself ethical, and go back to getting the paper out. That happens in far too many newsrooms, and the code that's hung on the wall is usually a localized version of some national code such as ASNE's, written in general language difficult to apply to specific local situations.

That's not the case with the written codes that have been put in effect at most major daily newspapers and at the ABC, NBC, and CBS network news departments. They are, for the most part, detailed and specific – and often enforced. A recent ASNE survey of the nation's twenty-five largest daily newspapers showed that the fourteen with written codes had dismissed eleven news staffers and suspended six others for code violations in the previous three years. The eleven big dailies without written codes said they had dismissed three employees and suspended five in that same period. The ASNE Ethics Committee said in its report on the survey:

> The reason most frequently cited by editors for the dismissal was lying. One editor said an employee was fired for falsely listing a college degree on the employment application. Three other employees were dismissed for falsification of expense accounts or time sheets.
>
> In another instance, a reporter used material obtained from a television interview without attribution. That act, the editor said, did not warrant dismissal. But the reporter insisted the material had been obtained independently, and a subsequent investigation proved otherwise. "The person lied to us," the editor said, "and was dismissed."
>
> Most of the other dismissals involved some form of outside em-

ployment that created a conflict of interest. For example, one reporter retained color transparencies and other materials that were
received for the newspaper job and used them in freelance work for
other newspapers and industry publications.[27]

The ASNE survey also included smaller dailies. Overall it showed
that the 226 editors who responded said they had dismissed or suspended
at least 78 news staffers for ethics violations in the previous three years.
When the survey results were separated by newspapers with and without
written codes of ethics, they indicated that "generally, editors
of . . . newspapers with ethics codes were more likely to take a stricter
view of what constitutes an ethics violation than newspapers without
codes."

One example of a newspaper that tries to enforce its tough ethics
code is the *Philadelphia Inquirer,* where a sports reporter once was taken
off the local college basketball beat when editors learned that his part-
time journalism teaching contract had been renewed only because the
college feared reprisals in his coverage of its basketball team. He was
reassigned to cover horse racing, but then it came out that he owned part
interest in a race horse. He was forced to sell the horse. Shortly after that
when he was assigned to cover the National Collegiate Athletic Association (NCAA) basketball tournament, it was discovered that he had written material for an NCAA brochure. All these outside activities in one
way or another violated the conflict of interest section of the *Inquirer's*
"Standards of Professional Conduct." The erring reporter finally had to be
told, according to managing editor Gene Foreman, that "if one more conflict developed, he would be assigned to the only job left in the sports
department – office clerk."[28]

Joseph W. Shoquist recalls that as managing editor of the *Milwaukee
Journal,* he had to suspend two staffers for short periods without pay for
violating the code that newspaper adopted in 1973. One suspension was
for a reporter who took part in a political demonstration. The second was
for a copy editor who surreptitiously produced campaign material for a
political candidate, a close friend.[29]

When he was managing editor of the *Democrat and Chronicle* in Rochester, New York, Richard B. Tuttle had to negotiate a resignation with a
veteran copy editor who was clandestinely doing public relations work for
several clients. The moonlighting was discovered when the editor accidentally left an opened letter from one of his clients on top of his desk.
"The guy's doing very well in PR now," Tuttle notes.[30] (Other cases of
disciplinary action against journalists by their own newspapers are reported and discussed throughout this book.)

When Tuttle left Rochester to become executive editor of another

Gannett Company newspaper, the *Star-Gazette* and *Sunday Telegram* in Elmira, New York, he persuaded his news staff to work with him in developing a fairly detailed code of ethics that ends with one of the strongest disciplinary clauses of any such code in the country: "Staff members violating this guideline are subject to discipline up to and including suspension without pay and dismissal."

Many of Tuttle's fellow newspaper editors reading that clause might remark: "Hell, it's easy to talk tough if you don't have the Guild!"

The Newspaper Guild. The Elmira *Star-Gazette* and about 1,520 of the 1,670 daily newspapers in the United States do *not* have contracts with the Newspaper Guild, AFL-CIO, a union representing editorial and commercial employees of newspapers, a few magazines, and wire services, including the two major ones, the AP and UPI. The Guild has contracts with only about 140 U.S. and Canadian newspapers, but they cover most of the larger dailies; Guild papers control about 31 percent of the total daily newspaper circulation in the United States and Canada.[31]

The Guild has gotten heavily involved in the ethics code movement in U.S. journalism because it opposes the imposition by management of ethics codes without their being bargained – like wages and hours – with employees. The Guild also does not like ethics codes in contracts for fear that they will be enforced like other working rules, resulting in suspension or dismissal of news workers for violating what the Guild believes should be ideals, not rules.

"Ethics codes should be advisory; they're not meant to be like criminal codes," says David J. Eisen, director of research and information for the Guild. Eisen and other Guild officials admit to some concern about the economic losses that occur to some news people when certain ethics code provisions are imposed. Freebies and junkets are regarded by many employees as "fringe benefits of the profession," Eisen observes. He argues that many publishers have encouraged the notion that although you have to put up with low salaries in news work, "you get free tickets to the movies and the ball game and you get to go here and there."[32] And Guild president Charles A. Perlik, Jr., points out that an ethics code clause preventing a sports reporter from serving as a major league baseball scorer at $50 a game could remove as much as $3,500 in annual income from that reporter's family.[33]

The question of whether gifts and favors to news employees are really wages, like tips received by waiters, was part of two controversial cases in which the Guild fought the imposition of ethics codes by publishers of the Madison, Wisconsin, *Capital Times* and the Pottstown, Pennsylvania, *Mercury*. In the *Capital Times* case taken to arbitration by the Guild in 1975, the first ruling in the complicated federal procedure was to the effect that freebies actually are wages, subject to collective bargaining. That decision by an administrative law judge was overturned in 1976 by the National Labor Relations Board (NLRB), which held that although an employer may put forth rules regarding free tickets, gifts, and the like, and require the reporting of outside activities that might cause conflicts of interest, that employer cannot attach penalties to such rules without first bargaining with the employees. Richard J. Ramsey, executive secretary of the Guild's national contracts committee, interpreted that NLRB decision as upholding the Guild's basic position "that an employer can have all the penalty-free guidelines it wants; but if it wants rules with penalties attached, the employer first must bargain at least about the penalty provisions."[34]

The NLRB took more or less the same position when the Guild brought the Pottstown case before it, eventually ruling in 1987 that the *Mercury* should rescind its ethics code.

The Guild's action in Madison and Pottstown was widely criticized by news executives. Probably the strongest criticism came from Norman E. Isaacs, retired editor of dailies in Indianapolis, St. Louis, and Louisville, and former editor-in-residence at the Columbia University School of Journalism, who said "the whole episode is a badge of shame" for the Guild. "I cannot fathom how it can stand apart while its locals indulge in the petty personal politics of defending free tickets, free travel, free meals, and free gifts as a matter of proper added compensation," Isaacs declared. "As with so many other facets in American life, what Heywood Broun launched as a crusade for more professional journalism has been turned into a chase for dollars and to hell with ethics."[35]

Isaacs testified against the Guild in the Madison case. "It was disgraceful to hear the Guild testimony," he contends. "One guy said he represented gays and the proposed code would impair his usefulness in getting things in the paper that represent gays at their best. The sports department did not want any impairment of their freebies . . . . The Guild people put the union movement ahead of the newspaper."[36]

Heywood Broun, to whom Isaacs referred, was a columnist for the old *New York World* and one of the founders and the first president of the American Newspaper Guild in 1933. There was a dispute among early Guild members as to whether the organization should have a professional or a trade union orientation, but Broun, according to an authoritative study of the Guild's early days, was "a pronounced unionist." He helped lead the Guild into what it has become—essentially a trade union affiliated with the AFL-CIO.[37]

Perlik, today's Guild president, sees two principal ingredients in "the

Guild's position on ethics codes whenever management takes them off the wall and attempts to transform them into office rules that can be transgressed only under penalty of dismissal":

> One is that employees, through their bargaining representative, must have some input into the code; virtue is one of the few things that newspaper publishers do not have a monopoly of. Some of the codes we have seen go far beyond the normal bounds of ethical considerations and seek to deprive employees of some of the basic rights of citizenship, such as involvement in political and community activity, while imposing no such restrictions on the publishers themselves. We think this is an appropriate area for negotiation, and two NLRB judges have agreed with us.
>
> The second main ingredient of our position is that, where a newly promulgated ethics code takes something of long standing and substantial value away from an employee, he or she should be compensated for it. Where is it written that employees should bear all the cost of a newspaper's sudden decision to be like Caesar's wife?[38]

Eisen and Ramsey note an irony in the Pottstown case. The code of ethics the now retired publisher of the *Mercury* sought to impose on the news staff is basically the SPJ-SDX Code of Ethics. There are two problems with that, they say. One is that it is virtually impossible to enforce the vague provisions of a code written as a statement more of aspirations than of specifics. The second is that SPJ-SDX itself does not try to enforce its code on its own members.[39]

The Guild has its own code of ethics, adopted by the organization's second convention in 1934. Leaders of the union today hold that this 1934 code and a 1933 statement in Article I of the Guild's constitution that one of the union's purposes is "to raise the standards of journalism and ethics of the industry" is evidence that the Guild has been working for ethics since its beginning.

The union that represents television and radio journalists—the American Federation of Television and Radio Artists—has not gotten involved in the ethics code controversy.

Before closing this discussion of journalism codes of ethics, it needs to be said that there is no proven relationship between ethics codes and ethical behavior. Everyone in the news business knows that the *New York Times* is an ethical newspaper run by journalists who try to act ethically. Yet that newspaper has no written code of ethics. Having a written code of ethics has not immunized other news organizations from ethical defects and violations. Written ethical standards are useful, perhaps essential, for communicating principles and guidelines to the large staffs of our major news organizations. They are also useful in telling outsiders, particularly aspiring young journalists, something about the ethical values held by top journalists. But determining which journalists and which newsrooms are practicing ethical journalism is much more complicated than simply asking, "Do you have a code?"

SITUATIONAL ETHICS

Journalists in this country tend to deal with their ethical problems case by case. They often answer questions about what they would do in particular ethical situations with, "It depends." Such situational ethics is bothersome because it suggests a lack of guiding principles. Yet, as discussed earlier in this chapter, journalists are not entirely lacking in such principles.

They seem to believe strongly in a free and independent press, free from government and other outside interests. There appears to be strong support for the idea that journalists should be responsible to society and that the public has a right to be informed. The standard of accuracy and fairness is about as universal as any standard could be. Some might also see the clear separation of news and advertising that exists most of the time in most journalistic media as a guiding principle. So there are some few principles that virtually all journalists seem to accept.

Why then are so many of the ethical problems in the field dealt with one case at a time? One reason is that, except for the simplest of ethical questions (Is it ethical to make up news? Should you be fair to people in the news?), there is considerable disagreement among journalists about what is right and what is wrong. Agreeing on broad and general principles still leaves great room for differing interpretations as to how those principles should be applied in particular ethical situations.

Principles, values, and goals often seem to conflict: For example, if you try to tell the whole truth about some newsworthy event, somebody in your story could get hurt. You may believe that the public has a right to know everything its government does, but what if that involves publicizing something that would threaten national security? You may believe that the public should know the sources of all the information you publish or broadcast, but what do you do then when the only way you can get certain vital information to pass on to the public is by agreeing not to identify certain sources in your stories? Most people in journalism put great stock in keeping themselves independent and avoiding conflicts of interest, but should that mean isolating yourself from other people and turning your back on the life of your community? An ethical decision often involves the weighing of conflicting principles and values.

The circumstances of each particular ethical problem do make a difference. Acceptable behavior in one circumstance becomes unacceptable in another. It might, for example, be very ethical for a court reporter trained in CPR to "participate in the news" by helping revive an attorney who collapses during a trial, but it would be unethical for a photojournalist to "participate in the news" by dropping his camera and tackling the visiting team's halfback.

Weighing of circumstances would be somewhat simpler if the body of "case law" weren't so slim. Because ethics is a relatively recent consideration in American journalism, the variety of possible circumstances surrounding the multitude of ethical problems journalists face has not been experienced enough times by enough journalists to bring about many "truths."

Another factor is the "open house" nature of the journalistic enterprise in our system: Anybody can play. The calling has virtually no admission standards. You don't have to possess special degrees or pass bar or medical exams to practice journalism. And you don't have to work for the *New York Times* or ABC News to be a journalist. You can declare yourself a journalist by starting up a newsletter or by creating and selling your own newspaper column. If you've got plenty of bucks, you can buy yourself into journalism by starting up or purchasing a publication or broadcast station. You don't have to work for establishment media to be a journalist; you can do your journalism on so-called alternative media, the little papers and magazines published and sold across this land. You can be a free-lance journalist, selling your taped or written stories or your photographs to the highest bidder. Free-lancers are numerically a small pimple in the total of American journalism, but they do exist, and in our free media system, they can legitimately claim to be journalists. The point is that an enterprise with so little control over its participants is apt to have difficulty agreeing on and adhering to shared standards, whether they be ethical or operational.

Thinking through Ethical Problems. Journalists are neither first nor alone in their struggle to be ethical. It is a struggle that occupies all of the professions and occupations, to one degree or another, and many individuals. Some have found help in the ethical theories developed by philosophers and thinkers, past and present, to guide humans in deciding moral questions. But ethical theory does not seem to interest most journalists. You don't see newsrooms cluttered with the works of Jeremy Bentham (1748–1832), the founder of utilitarianism, or Immanuel Kant (1724–1804), who professed, among other things, that the moral measure of an act is whether the maxim underlying it can be universalized—made a maxim for all persons, everywhere, for all time. It does not seem likely that journalists are going to turn to the classics for their ethical guides.

They might, however, turn to a simpler method for moral reasoning. One that I have used successfully in teaching journalism ethics to university students might work for working journalists as well. The method consists of seven questions that ought to be answered, either alone or in a conversation with others, before deciding how to handle a particular ethical problem or dilemma. Some of the questions are more pertinent than others in certain situations, but all of them need to be addressed. I suggest that when journalists are faced with an ethical problem, they should consider the following:

1. What do we usually do in cases like this? The way problems have been solved in the past is not always a good guide, but neither is ignorance of the usual response of a particular individual or organization to such problems. If policies for handling this kind of case have been established, they need to be considered.

2. Who will be hurt and who will be helped? Most ethical decisions in journalism involve some harm and some benefits, often harm to an individual or group of people that has to be weighed against benefits to the community or the public. Realizing who is apt to be hurt and whether the benefits can justify that hurt can help us make an intelligent decision.

3. Are there better alternatives? Often the harm that results from what we decide could be softened or even eliminated if another way could be found to achieve more or less the same goal. In any event, we should try to consider all of the alternatives before deciding on a particular course of action.

4. Can I look myself in the mirror again? One of the strong determinants in any ethical decision is quite personal. We have to be able to live with ourselves afterward. James D. Squires, editor of the *Chicago Tribune,* advises news people not to "do anything your momma would be ashamed of."[40]

5. Can I justify this to other people, the public? If we realize that we are going to have to justify our decision (explain it in an editor's note or column, for example), we're apt to be more careful in how and what we decide. In other words, we need to have good, understandable reasons for whatever we decide.

6. What principles or values can I apply? Certain principles or values—such as truth telling, the public's right to know, compassion, social responsibility, the Golden Rule, justice, fairness, and journalistic independence—might emerge as more important than others in a specific ethical decision. But the important thing is to try to use pertinent principles or values in the decision making.

7. Does this decision fit the kind of journalism I believe in? (Or does

it fit my general feeling about life and how people should treat one another?) Whatever we decide about a particular ethical question should fit our general philosophy of how journalism ought to be done and how people in a civilized society ought to behave.

The purpose of this seven-step process is not to get everyone to come up with identical decisions—that does not happen often in my experience with it in the classroom—but to encourage logical thought. This process does not conflict with ethical theory; rather, it is a way to apply ethical theories to practical decisions. If you believe, for example, in the utilitarian idea of the greatest good for the greatest number, you can express it (or even test it) through this process. And if you're not conscious of any ethical theory or philosophy that guides you, this process should at least help you to arrive at your ethical decisions in a thoughtful and logical way.

2 Business or Profession?

"If they're giving us eight papers in one, you'd think they could at least run Blondie."

Someone once described journalism as a profession grafted to a business. Leaving aside for a moment the question of whether journalism truly qualifies as a profession, that description accurately reflects the employee status of all but a handful of journalists. There are a few free-lancers around, but virtually all journalists ply their trade in the employ of others. Most full-time journalists work for daily and weekly newspapers, about 65 percent of the 116,000 employed by all news media. About 33 percent are broadcast journalists, doing news for local radio and television stations and national broadcast networks. The remainder work full time for the news services, chiefly the Associated Press, and for news magazines.[1] The organizations that employ these thousands of journalists are principally private companies that have to succeed in the marketplace just like other American businesses, seeking security and survival through profits.

No discussion of ethics in the journalism of this country can proceed very far without an understanding of how business considerations of the news media affect the journalism they present. Unlike most businesses, the media get most of their profits not directly from the consumer or the public, but indirectly through advertising, which contributes 60 to 100 percent of the revenue of most U.S. media. The consumer gets nothing free, of course, despite the absence of any direct payment for most television and radio programs and for some publications. You pay through your purchase of advertised goods and services, whose prices include the cost of advertising. It's like sales taxes, which you're not supposed to notice very much because you pay them in small amounts every time you buy things.

The secret of success in the media business is to gather an audience that at least some advertisers want or need to reach. It is not necessary or even desirable often to reach every person or household in a given community, region, or nation. If you have an audience of some sort that certain advertisers are willing to pay for access to, you can make a go of it in the media business. A larger audience may not be desirable if the additional members are people advertisers are unwilling to pay to reach.

So we have media, such as television networks, that try to be seen by or at least be available to almost everybody in the country. Newspapers and magazines tend to be more selective in the audiences they seek — newspapers in a geographic sense and magazines demographically. These are generalizations, of course. Local TV stations have local audiences, too, and they are limited to the area covered by the station's signal. Some magazines try to appeal more to a mass audience than a selective one, and some even try to do both. Some newspapers are abandoning their democratic traditions of trying to appeal to everyone in a given community or region and are seeking more affluent audiences better able to respond to advertising.

The facts of life about balancing audiences and advertisers have a lot to say about the kind of media we get in our system. And the kind of journalism we get.

BUSINESSES FIRST

Claude Sitton, editorial director and vice-president of the News Observer Publishing Company, Raleigh, North Carolina, contends that the decision about how much of the newspaper's budget should go to the news and editorial department "is not a simple matter. It's a hard balance to strike." If a newspaper is not doing well as a business, "it becomes weak and vulnerable to those people who would use the newspaper for their own purposes."[2]

Otis Chandler, chairman of the executive committee of the Times Mirror Company, Los Angeles, believes that "successful newspapers do not have to let the business side into the editorial arena. They have the luxury of letting the editorial department be completely independent to cover the news as it sees it." Chandler recalls working for a paper that was not successful financially, the old *Los Angeles Mirror-News,* which his corporation eventually folded. "Every line of advertising was so important," he says. "We really killed some news stories because we were trying to get the major department stores to advertise and we did not want to rock any boats."[3]

Another who believes that a newspaper has to succeed as a business in order to provide quality journalism is Donald Graham, publisher of the *Washington Post.* He sees the *Post* as testimony of that fact. "In the early 1950s," he recalls, "the *Post* aspired to be a world-class newspaper; its heart was in the right place, but it just didn't have any money. There's an old joke around the *Post* that in those days we could cover any international conference as long as it was in the first taxi zone." Noting with pride that although the *Post* had no foreign correspondents before 1960, it has bureaus all over the world today, Graham concludes, "Profits are not inconsistent with good journalism."[4]

Because the news media are businesses–and big ones at that–they are influenced by the same forces that bear on all American business enterprises. There is nothing intrinsically wrong or illegal about the media following the same economic Pied Pipers that motivate K-Mart, Mobil, United Technologies, IBM, and Crazy Joe's Used Cars, but news businesses differ from other businesses in one important way. Their constitutionally protected freedom is interpreted by most people to mean that they are a semipublic service as well as private profit-seeking businesses. As James C. Thomson, Jr., former curator of the Nieman Foundation, tells us, news organizations have to operate "both To Make Money (or at least not to lose it) *and* To Do Good (or to expose iniquity, and thereby improve society)." Because of this tension "between greed and idealism," Thomson believes every news organization has "two cultures, or at least outlooks, that are often at odds with each other: on the one hand, reporters and editors, who traditionally see their role as uncovering and disseminating the truth (or some approximation thereof); and on the other hand, owners, publishers, 'management,' who seek to stay in business and make a tidy profit."[5]

Although most news businesses are highly secretive about how much money they make, they make plenty. A. Kent MacDougall, in his prize-winning series on "Business and the Media" in the *Los Angeles Times,* tells us that the news business "is near the top of all industries in profitability." He maintains that "daily newspapers keep up to a quarter of every dollar they take in, even after taxes. *Time* and *Newsweek* are gold mines. And television, which has been likened to 'a license to print money,' is so lucrative that it bestows corporate presidents' salaries on many of its journalists."[6]

Ownership Trends. The most obvious indication of the business nature of the news media in recent years has been their tendency to be purchased and owned by groups and conglomerates. Just as small, independent grocery stores have all but disappeared from the American scene, the independent, family-owned newspaper has become the exception – only about 453 of the 1,670 daily newspapers were still in independent ownership in 1987. The others were owned by about 146 groups (also called chains when they got big enough), which gobbled up independent papers at the rate of about 50 per year in the late 1970s. The pace of acquisitions slowed in the 1980s, but it was relentless.

Although almost ninety of the newspaper groups (defined as two or more dailies in different cities, under the same ownership) publish four or fewer newspapers, group newspapers control about 80 percent of the total daily U.S. circulation of about 63 million. And some groups are very large by any measure.

In total circulation, the best measure of bigness, Gannett Company is the largest of the giants, owning 93 dailies with a combined circulation of more than 6 million in mid-1986. The only group close to Gannett in total daily circulation is Knight-Ridder Newspapers, whose 27 dailies circulated almost 4.5 million copies per day in 1986. Thomson Newspapers, a Canadian corporation specializing in buying up small dailies and converting them into unprovocative bulletin boards, was slightly ahead of Gannett in the number of dailies it owned, but their total daily circulation was only about 1.5 million. Other large newspaper owners are Newhouse Newspapers, Tribune Company, Times Mirror Company, and Dow Jones and Company.[7]

While the number of daily newspapers has been edging downward in recent years, television and radio stations have been growing like weeds. By 1986, the number of TV stations had gotten up to about 1,670, roughly the same as the number of dailies being published, and AM and FM radio stations had increased to about 10,000.[8]

But the acquisition fever that has characterized newspaper ownership in this country in the recent past has been slower to develop in broadcasting because of FCC limits on the number of stations that any one company can own. For thirty-one years, the FCC had permitted single owners to own no more than seven TV stations, seven AM radio stations, and seven FM radio stations. That limit was raised to twelve in each category in 1984, and acquisitions of broadcast stations began to increase almost immediately.[9] The raising of the limits by FCC reflected a trend in the federal government to deregulate private industry. Unless that trend changes, most observers expect the FCC to raise the owner-ship limits again in the near future or even eliminate them.

Some of the large owners of broadcast stations in the very fluid buying and selling climate right after the FCC's 1984 lifting were the three commercial networks (ABC, NBC, and CBS) and many of the big newspaper chains, such as Gannett, Knight-Ridder, Times Mirror, and the Tribune Company. They were joined by Australian media magnate Rupert Murdoch when he bought seven TV stations from Metromedia for $2 billion and got access to 24 percent of the nation's viewing audience.

Media ownership has been affected by another kind of FCC inter-ference in recent years. Its rules against a single person or firm owning TV stations and newspapers in the same city or market forced many newspapers to sell or trade their TV properties. The owners of the *Wash-ington Post* and the *Detroit News* gave us an example of this when they simply swapped the TV stations each had owned in its own city. And most of the TV stations sold by newspaper firms under FCC pressure were acquired by other newspaper firms. Criticized even by some FCC commissioners, the rule against cross-ownership could disappear one of these days if deregulation continues to be federal government policy, as it had been in the Carter and Reagan administrations.

Going Public. Otis Chandler of Times Mirror has often expressed the fear that some morning we could wake up to find an oil-rich sheik atop the Gannett media empire. That fear is plausible because of another busi-ness trend that media companies have joined. Most of the large media groups and conglomerates are public corporations whose shares of ownership are available for purchase in the stock market. Although fami-lies like the Sulzbergers of the *New York Times* and the Grahams of the *Washington Post* control and are not likely to sell the dominant shares of ownership in their news companies, many media companies are more vulnerable to the kind of acquisition Chandler fears.

Of more immediate concern, however, is the pressure from their stockholders for greater and greater profits and dividends that many public corporations experience. Treating a newspaper as just one more unit of production can be devastating to the quality of journalism in that newspaper. William B. Arthur, former executive director of the National News Council, believes groups such as Gannett, Knight-Ridder, and Times Mirror have improved the papers they have acquired. He is con-cerned, however, about newspaper conglomerates being run not by journalists but by "business school types" whose emphasis on the bottom line could damage journalism.[10]

Robert H. Giles, who edited the two Gannett dailies in Rochester, New York, before he was moved to Detroit to become executive editor after Gannett acquired the *Detroit News,* says he had complete freedom to run the Rochester papers as he saw fit. As editor of the *Times-Union* and *Democrat and Chronicle,* Giles reported to his publisher and also to the Gannett vice-president for news, both of whom gave him a free hand.

But Gannett influenced Giles's job in other ways. "The bottom line requirements limit what we want to do," Giles observes.

> The Gannett Company has very aggressive and ambitious profit goals. Anybody who wants to work for Gannett and be comfortable ought to understand that. Al Neuharth [then chairman and president, Gannett Co.] clearly sets the pace, and the standard is that our profits will be 15 percent better this year than they were last year. Everybody in the group, for the most part, is expected to contribute to that, which means that the kind of news hole I think we require here to put out absolutely first-rate newspapers is not available to me. That's a frustration because of my own standards for good newspapers and the standards of many of the people I've hired or promoted here.

Giles believes that Gannett has taken over many family-owned newspapers and "improved them enormously," but on a very good independent newspaper, such as the one in St. Petersburg, "the resources made available" to the editor by the owning family "are superior to what I have to work with in Rochester." Giles contends that Gannett wants to have it both ways—"put out good newspapers and continue to make a lot of money, and you can't always do that."[11]

The frustration Giles feels is shared by other editors of group- or conglomerate-owned newspapers. Group executives set profit goals that often mean less space for news, more advertising, and tighter budgets. Local publishers and editors who fail to meet those goals do not last long. The group accountants hold all the trump aces.

No one knows this better than Eugene L. Roberts, Jr., executive editor of the *Philadelphia Inquirer,* who has had a tough fight turning a once disreputable newspaper into a successful one, both journalistically and financially. Most people in journalism believe Roberts has succeeded spectacularly in the area of his prime responsibility—the news and editorial department. His staff in recent years has won all the top journalism awards: photographs in his crowded newsroom of the traditional champagne popping after Pulitzer Prizes are announced have become commonplace. But financially even Roberts's admirers wondered aloud whether Knight-Ridder didn't regret that it ever came into Philadelphia to run the *Inquirer* and the tabloid *Daily News,* two of the city's three dailies then.

Roberts's own analysis of the *Inquirer's* financial status is that although the newspaper was not an immediately pleasing investment, Knight-Ridder knew "right from the beginning that it was buying a sick newspaper that could be fixed." Roberts, who recently added the title of president of Philadelphia Newspapers to his executive editorship, believes the *Inquirer* will end up being one of the better investments Knight-Ridder has ever made. Knight-Ridder "has never been greedy about quick profits but it has never been tolerant of losses." Roberts claims the *Inquirer* stopped losing money for its owners after 1976, but it was tough going before that. In his first three or four years after joining the paper in 1972, he recalls that there were nine separate work stoppages by *Inquirer* unions.

Roberts does not complain about any pressure he might have been under to get the *Inquirer* into the black. Although Knight-Ridder "doesn't understand losing money" and "goes berserk with red ink," he feels the group "wants the *Inquirer* to be accurate, reliable, fair, and aggressive." In general, Roberts believes that "good journalism is amicable with good business."[12]

Knight-Ridder Newspapers and Times Mirror were most often mentioned by journalists interviewed for this book as companies that push for quality journalism in the news media they own. Gannett also got praise for improving the papers it buys. (Conversely, Thomson Newspapers comes in for the most criticism. Norman E. Isaacs, retired editor and press critic, calls the Thomson operation "a commercial printing establishment.")[13]

It is true that many family-owned newspapers, limping along under the lethargic management of third-generation sons or nephews who would rather be entomologists or merchant seamen, have been greatly improved after their sale by the imported skills of group executives. And many if not most of the dailies on anybody's "Ten Best" list are group-owned papers, such as the *Wall Street Journal,* the *New York Times,* the Louisville *Courier-Journal,* the *Washington Post,* the *Los Angeles Times,* the *Philadelphia Inquirer,* and *Newsday.* So it would be foolish to argue that group or conglomerate ownership results in bad journalism. Sometimes it does, but very often it does not.

Be that as it may, some journalists decry the loss of eccentricity and sacred cows they believe were more common when most newspapers were family owned. Norman C. Miller, national editor of the *Los Angeles Times,* holds that "eccentricity is a healthy thing" in the news business. "It tends to come from owner or independent editors," he contends. "Chains don't encourage that sort of thing. They encourage a certain conformity and mediocrity, a profit-line mentality, a shrinking from controversy." He concedes that some chains improve the newspapers they buy, such as Knight-Ridder did with the *Philadelphia Inquirer*, but other chains "are run by people for whom it doesn't make that much difference whether they're manufacturing shoes or newspapers."[14]

The Media Auction. Buying, selling, merging, and consolidating have characterized the media marketplace in recent years. And when media properties are sold they bring high prices.

General Electric paid $6.28 billion for RCA, which owns the NBC broadcast network. Capital Cities Communications acquired the ABC network for $3.5 billion. Lorimar-Telepictures Corporation had to put up $1.85 billion for seven big-city television stations. KTLA-TV in Los Angeles was sold to the Tribune Company of Chicago for $510 million, just a few days after the Hearst Corporation paid $450 million for WCVB-TV in Boston.[15]

The sale of the *Courier-Journal* and *Louisville Times* in Kentucky to Gannett for $307 million left the *St. Petersburg Times* standing alone as the last great independent family-owned newspaper in the country. Just before the Louisville purchase, Gannett acquired the *Detroit News,* along with several small papers, five TV stations, and two radio stations, for $717 million; and bought the *Des Moines Register,* the *Jackson* (Tennessee) *Sun* and two Iowa weeklies for $200 million.[16]

Times Mirror sold the *Dallas Times Herald* to William Dean Singleton's Media News Group for $110 million, just after buying the Baltimore *Sun* and *Evening Sun,* along with two television stations and some small magazines, for $600 million.[17]

Shortly after Australian-born Rupert Murdoch acquired the *Chicago Sun-Times* for $100 million, he moved boldly into movies and TV by gaining possession of Twentieth Century Fox Film Corporation for a total of $575 million and by purchasing seven large TV stations from Metromedia for $2 billion (he sold one, WCVB-TV, Boston, to Hearst for $450 million). Because the television purchases put his company in conflict with the FCC's ban on cross-ownership of both a newspaper and a TV station in New York and Chicago, Murdoch was given two years to sell his new TV stations there or sell the *New York Post* and the *Sun-Times*. The Chicago cross-ownership dissolved when the paper was bought for $145 million by an investor group headed by the man Murdoch had installed as publisher there, Robert E. Page. Although Page had made the *Sun-Times* more Murdoch-like by bolder headlines and increased crime news, he was proud that he had not turned the *Sun-Times* into a copy of Murdoch's sensational New York tabloid, the *Post,* as many had feared. As the new owner he said he plans to make the *Sun-Times* more serious again.[18] Murdoch, incidentally, would not have been able to buy the Metromedia stations as an Australian because federal law restricts an alien's share in the ownership of any American broadcast license to no more than 20 percent. He solved that problem by becoming a naturalized citizen on 4 September 1985.[19]

All those sales of recent years were stimulated by two economic forces. The groups and conglomerates were encouraged by federal tax penalties to keep reinvesting their accumulated earnings; also, they like to show earnings growth to attract investors.[20] Federal estate taxes encourage many families to sell their newspapers when the principal owner dies. J. Hart Clinton, publisher of the family-owned *San Mateo* (California) *Times,* explains that the bidding for independent newspapers by the chains drives up their values. When the major owner dies, the survivors are faced with a federal estate tax based on the market value of the paper that is so high they sell, and usually the best price is offered by a chain. "Considering that the federal estate taxes take 70 percent of an estate after the $5 million value is reached, and that newspapers in northern California have been selling for amounts in excess of $25 million," Clinton noted, "it is easy to understand why the owners have felt the only escape open to them is to sell to the highest bidder."[21]

Going back to 1900 and to 1940 gives us a picture of how newspaper ownership has changed. In 1900, 8 groups owned 27 of the some 2,200 daily newspapers in the United States, slightly more than 1 percent. In 1940, 60 groups owned 319 of the 1,878 dailies, or 17 percent.[22] In 1987, about 146 groups owned more than 1,200 of the 1,670 dailies, or about 73 percent.[23] (The downward trend in the total number of dailies leveled off after World War II. The total stood at about 1,750 from 1945 through 1980 when it began a new although slight downward trend.)

Group ownership has encouraged a trend toward monopolies that has left many cities without real newspaper competition. And recently two important cities – Washington, D.C., and Philadelphia – were added to that list, not by some group gobbling up the newspaper properties there, but by old-fashioned economic failure. The *Washington Star* ceased publication in August 1981 when its owner – Time, Incorporated – decided it could no longer afford to add to the $85 million it had poured into the *Star* in three and one-half years. ("Time has run out on the Star," the T-shirts soon said.) That left the nation's capital with only one daily, the morning *Post,* until the Rev. Sun Myung Moon's Unification Church started a new daily, the *Washington Times,* in the spring of 1982. Charter Company, a Florida-based oil and insurance conglomerate, closed the 134-year-old Philadelphia *Bulletin* in January 1982; at the time, it was losing $60,000 a day. The *Bulletin*'s disappearance left Philadelphia with two dailies, the *Inquirer* and the *Daily News,* both owned by Knight-Ridder and published out of the same plant. For a period just before the *Bulletin* closed, Philadelphia had four dailies – more than any U.S. city – but the *Philadelphia*

Journal, a sort of local *National Enquirer* that emphasized sports and sex, bit the dust in late 1981.

Owners of both the *Star* and the *Bulletin* tried to sell their papers and keep them alive, but no buyer was interested in bucking the malaise that has come over many big-city afternoon newspapers in modern times. Morning papers have always had a better break on the news (most of which tends to occur during daytime hours) and on delivery (having all night to get their papers out to the customers). But readers, until recent years, seemed to prefer evening newspapers, so the big afternoon dailies kept moving their deadlines forward to allow their traffic-slowed trucks more time to deliver their wares to customers who kept moving farther and farther out into the suburbs. Then people began to turn away from afternoon papers—or lots of them did anyway—preferring to get their evening news from television. In addition, many former metropolitan afternoon newspaper readers in the suburbs have switched to the dailies and weeklies that serve their suburban communities. Not all big-city afternoon papers are in trouble, but economic forces and changing lifestyles of readers do appear to be ganging up on them.

Before she became a news executive with *USA Today,* Nancy Woodhull served at different times as managing editor of both Gannett dailies in Rochester, New York—the morning *Democrat and Chronicle* and the afternoon *Times-Union.* She believes morning papers have an advantage over afternoon papers today because of the way most readers live. "You feel you have to read a morning paper because you're in a certain business and you don't want to look like an asshole; you want to know what's going on." The afternoon papers, on the other hand, "don't have the latest news because it takes so long to get them to your house," she adds. "And TV is so easy, you can chop wood and still listen to it."[24]

Rochester, with two Gannett dailies operating out of the same plant, is one of a number of cities in the United States with two jointly owned daily newspapers. Woodhull claims the competition between the *Times-Union* and the *Democrat and Chronicle* "is very serious," and that seems to be the case in other cities where both dailies are under the same ownership. But there has been a disturbing trend in such cities for owners to cut costs by consolidating their two "competing" dailies, as has happened in Minneapolis and Duluth, Minnesota; Allentown, Pennsylvania; Salem and Portland, Oregon; Des Moines, Iowa; and New Orleans, Louisiana, to mention just a few. (For a while at least, readers in New Orleans could subscribe to the morning or afternoon editions of a paper with the mouthful title of New Orleans *Times-Picayune/States-Item.*) These consolidations, more than any other factor, have been responsible for the drop in total number of dailies to about 1,670 in mid-1987.

About twenty U.S. cities still have separately owned dailies because their owners have been allowed under a special federal law called the

Newspaper Preservation Act to merge all but their news and editorial departments. Most readers have difficulty finding any major differences between two dailies in one city produced by the same company and two privately owned dailies under a joint operating arrangement being produced out of the same plant with shared business, advertising, circulation, and printing departments.

There are still about thirty cities in the country—like New York, Chicago, and York, Pennsylvania—that have at least two separately owned competing daily newspapers. That is quite a comedown from 1923 when there were about five hundred such U.S. cities. And New York at one time had twenty-three dailies; Chicago had eight, and Los Angeles, seven.[25]

The number of nondaily papers has also declined, but less dramatically than did the dailies between 1900 and 1940. There were 7,711 nondaily newspapers being published in the United States in 1986, with a total circulation of more than 50 million. In 1960 the country had 8,174 nondailies but total circulation was only 21 million.[26]

Although the pace of news media sales slowed in 1981, partially because many of the major groups began investing heavily in cable television systems, it perked up again in 1985 after the FCC raised the limit on the number of broadcast stations any one company can own. Big groups began swallowing up smaller groups, as happened when Gannett bought the Evening News Association in Detroit and the Des Moines Register and Tribune Company. The trend toward more group- and conglomerate-owned newspapers and broadcast stations does not seem reversible. It is possible that no independent or family-owned daily newspaper will be left in the United States by the year 2000. A company like Gannett might own as many as 150, plus as many broadcast stations as the law will allow.

"A tremendous amount of what happens to a community is in the hands of those family publishers when they decide to sell," *Washington Post* publisher Donald Graham comments. "It's not just a question of who you sell to but at what price. Invariably if you auction off a newspaper like a side of beef, the highest bidder is likely to be a person who wants to take the most money out of the paper."[27]

THE ROLE OF ADVERTISING

The heavy dependence on advertising as the financial base of our media system can also affect the quality of journalism we get. This is not to say that advertisers are allowed to dictate what goes into news columns or newscasts, although unfortunately this does sometimes happen, particularly on smaller or competitively inferior newspapers or broadcast stations. But advertising has a more subtle and indirect effect on the nonadvertising content of our news media.

When advertisers cut their advertising budgets as they do in hard times, or switch their ads from one medium to another, or go out of business, commercial media companies have to pull in their belts. These economies, including elimination of jobs, often make it difficult for news departments to do quality journalism. All three of the big broadcast network staffs were trimmed in the mid-1980s because of advertising losses caused by what a CBS executive called a "disinflation that is affecting all American industry in general and advertising in particular."[28] The dimunitions in quality that are bound to result from such cuts are probably more noticeable in small news organizations, where smaller staffs often mean less local coverage. The space or time that should be devoted to informing the public about their own communities is then filled with canned, syndicated, or news service material that costs a lot less each week than paying a hungry journalist.

The importance of advertising is illustrated in the difficult struggle the New York *Daily News* has had trying to stay alive despite having the largest circulation of any general interest daily in the country (1.35 million weekdays and 1.66 million on Sundays). The *News* was losing $30 million a year in 1982 when its owner, the Tribune Company of Chicago, despaired of all that red ink and put it up for sale. But the sale offer was withdrawn after the paper's unions agreed to accept elimination of 1,000 jobs. A new management team, headed by publisher James F. Hoge, turned the paper around financially so that it earned a profit of $20 million in 1984. But the closing of Gimbels and Ohrbach's department stores in Manhattan in 1986, causing the loss of almost $11 million in advertising in the *News*, prompted the publisher to put out a letter to his 2,800 employees warning that he was going to have to cut staff and other operating costs. "Survival is at stake," Hoge wrote.[29]

Another way that advertising affects the journalistic content of our news media is in the way it determines how much space and time journalists have for their news and commentary. Open, adless pages are rare on most U.S. newspapers (the *New York Times* even allows advertisers on its front page, although it restricts them to extraordinarily small type at the bottom of news columns). Editors often have to treat news as fillers to stuff around the ads. Newspaper pages with ads occupying three-quarters to five-sixths of the space, quite common proportions, leave editors with virtually no opportunity for displaying news in an appealing way or for illustrating news with photographs or other graphics. And many Sunday newspapers are so crammed with ads and so stuffed with advertising supplements (preprints is what the industry calls these inserts that used to come to us as "junk" mail) that they almost have to be forklifted off the porch. Publishers usually impose a formula for how much advertising the average day's newspaper should carry, and the proportion of ads to non-ads has been growing. It used to be close to 55 percent ads, 45 percent nonads in the late 1940s; today the ratio is more like 65 percent ads, 35 percent news on the average.[30] What happens most days on most U.S. newspapers is that the advertising department lays out its ads on the pages available and the news department gets what's left. The size of the paper most days depends not on that day's news but on that day's advertising.

In broadcast news, editors also have to shape their newscasts around the commercials, so there is always a limit on how much continuous time can be devoted to a single story or piece of audio or video tape. The average 30-minute newscast on network or local TV is divided into four or five chunks, never adding up to more than 24 minutes of news.

Soft News Sells. At the same time that the proportion of advertising to nonadvertising has been going up in most American newspapers, an increasing share of that nonadvertising space has been turned over to "soft news" or features. In addition to devoting more space to neighborhood activities, clubs, chicken dinners, three-foot-long zucchinis, and the like, most newspapers today run special sections devoted to such subjects as food, homes, education, life-styles, people, and recreation. Although the subject matter varies from paper to paper, these new and emerging sections have in common content that is designed to appeal not only to special segments of the audience, but to advertisers interested in reaching people with such interests. That same marriage of interests was seen, of course, in more traditional sections dealing with travel, real estate, and business. It is just that today's daily newspaper is devoting a much greater share of nonadvertising space to what people in the news business call "features."

Are these new specialized sections more evidence of advertiser influences on news? Many editors, particularly those atop newspapers that have gone in for the new sections, would defend them as legitimate journalism. Although he concedes that the *New York Times* started its special sections in the late 1970s for commercial rather than journalistic reasons (to attract more readers and advertisers), then executive editor Abe Rosenthal is proud of them because "they have strengthened the paper, have made it more interesting." His newspaper in 1976 was just barely out of the red. "We wanted to keep the *Times* as it was, but to stay the same we had to change," Rosenthal explains.[31]

In his history of the *New York Times,* Harrison E. Salisbury writes that Rosenthal stole the idea for the special sections from the old *New York* magazine that editor Clay Felker had developed. Salisbury quotes Rosenthal as saying, "I'll steal any idea from anybody as long as it's not nailed down." His cannibalized special sections did not go down well with all *Times* readers, Salisbury tells us:

> And there were those who criticized the new incarnation saying that *The Times* must now invent another section and label it "News." To this Abe's answer was that the new sections had given the paper a financial floor that made its position virtually unassailable, and this at a moment when the *News* and the *Post* [the *Times's* two New York competitors] were foundering. Now, unlike any other paper in the country, *The Times* could and did throw $30,000 a month, maybe $50,000 a month, over and above salaries and staff into covering the fall of Iran, the money was there, no strain. Abe could maintain forty correspondents in Europe without looking over his shoulder at the auditors.[32]

Some media watchers criticize the special feature sections for directing the energies and talents of journalists just to subjects that attract the kind of readers advertisers want. You don't see special sections appearing each week with labels like "Poverty," "Ghetto Life," "Hard Times," "Living Off The Land," or "Making It On Welfare." Nothing personal, but advertisers don't find poor folks very interesting.

Another extending of the definition of journalism to attract more or special kinds of readers and perhaps sell more advertising is apparent in the increasing chunks of space and time devoted to what one editor has called "celebrity journalism." Eugene Patterson, chief executive officer of the *St. Petersburg Times,* has said that the press has gotten so involved with celebrities he can no longer tell it from show business.[33]

Tabs. Another example of advertising's subtle influence on the news content of newspapers is the special theme supplement seen in virtually all daily papers and common in medium and small dailies. Often called "tabs" because they are printed tabloid size, these special sections are built around some theme like cars, brides, house and lawn care, football, business progress, restaurants, or some holiday. They are loaded with ads but they also contain what looks like news and informational material. Some of it is legitimate and useful information, but lots of it is simply puffery to wrap around the ads. The ideas for these tabs usually originate in the newspaper's advertising department, but the news department often has to write or edit the nonadvertising material and lay out the pages. This irks many editors and reporters because it takes time away from covering and processing serious news they feel would be more useful to the readers than the advertising-support material found in most tabs.

The *Philadelphia Inquirer*'s Roberts cancelled such tabs whenever they were proposed after he joined that paper in 1972. But he recalls letting one on savings and loan institutions survive because he feared that the advertising department was getting fed up with what must have seemed like an antiadvertising attitude. Then he discovered the reporter who traditionally had done this particular tab was working with the ad salesman to the extent of promising each potential advertiser that such and such a story would accompany each ad. Another *Inquirer* tab went down the drain.[34] But the *Inquirer* has not done away with tabs. As is the case at many newspapers, the *Inquirer* tabs are now produced by the paper's advertising department and labeled as advertising.

Some editors are not so lucky. James A. Dunlap, editor of the *Herald* in Sharon, Pennsylvania, has had to tolerate such supplements since his paper became part of the Ottaway group a few years ago. "We object to news theme tabs . . . but they're a fact of life of newspapers." Ottaway is a good group with high editorial standards, he adds, but "they want revenue and this is a way of getting some ad linage." Dunlap wishes, however, that the paper did not publish tabs "because of the junk that's run as news and of the time it takes" overworked news people to produce them.[35]

Newspapers have always published a lot of soft news – information of less than life-and-death importance but interesting to many or at least some readers. What is a more recent development is the addition of special sections, tabs, and features, not out of editors' beliefs that the readers need this additional information but because the supplements might attract a new audience to sell to advertisers.

More Direct Pressures. Some advertisers seek preferential treatment in the news media in which they buy advertising space and time. Nobody gets too excited about advertisers attempting to position their ads in certain parts of the newspaper or magazine, or at certain times of the broadcast day. But what does disturb journalists and observers is allowing advertisers to dictate or influence what passes for untainted news. The news columns and newscasts are not supposed to be for sale. And, generally speaking, they aren't.

But some advertisers have been allowed by weak publishers and broadcast managers to invade the news area. In Philadelphia recently, an FM radio station, WXTU, stopped playing a satirical song criticizing imported cars when a local Hyundai dealer heard it and complained. The song, "Hyundai, Hyundai," was distributed by the American Comedy Network, which provides material to 143 radio stations. A sample lyric: "Those low-priced imports look real good, but they're all doggie doo.

They're held together with paper clips, rubber bands and glue."[36]

Xerox Corporation invaded the editorial tent of *Esquire* magazine a few years back, but cancelled plans for further excursions into "sponsored journalism" after a scolding from essayist E. B. White, now dead but then living in retirement in North Brooklin, Maine. When the former *New Yorker* magazine writer heard that Xerox had paid $55,000 in fees and expenses to Harrison Salisbury for a twenty-three page article (evaluating the state of the country in its bicentennial year) and $115,000 in advertising to *Esquire,* which published the article in its February 1976 issue, he wrote a critical letter to his hometown newspaper, the *Ellsworth American.* A fascinating exchange of letters between White and W. B. Jones, director of communications operations for Xerox, ensued. Jones explained that Xerox merely wanted to extend what it had been doing for years on television—"sponsoring programs of substance that might not otherwise have gotten on the air." But White saw it as "sponsorship" that was "an invitation to corruption and abuse." He argued:

> A funded article is a tempting morsel for any publication—particularly one that is having a hard time making ends meet. A funded assignment is a tempting dish for a writer, who may pocket a much larger fee than he is accustomed to getting. And sponsorship is attractive to the sponsor himself, who, for one reason or another, feels an urge to penetrate the editorial columns after being so long pent up in the advertising pages. These temptations are real, and if the barriers were to be let down, I believe corruption and abuse would soon follow. . . . Buying and selling space in news columns could become a serious disease of the press. . . . I don't want IBM or the National Rifle Association providing me with a funded spectacular when I open my paper. I want to read what the editor and the publisher have managed to dig up on their own—and paid for out of the till.[37]

Two letters later, Jones wrote to White that Xerox had aborted two other *Esquire*-like projects "and although that process involved some discomfort, we now feel better for it. Your correspondence was a primary factor in our reconsideration, and we do appreciate your help in reaching what I am convinced is the right decision."[38]

Advertisers less thoughtful than Xerox still try to influence the selection and play of news, not by buying their way into the news columns, but by threatening to cancel or actually cancelling their ads. Car dealers seem unusually sensitive to news stories they feel will hurt sales, and they often boycott papers that run such stories. They did that in Charleston, West Virginia, when the *Gazette* published a series of seven articles detailing consumer complaints against area car dealers in 1978. The withdrawal of auto ads from the *Gazette* and the *Daily Mail,* linked under a joint operating agreement, so angered *Gazette* publisher W. E. Chilton III that when the dealers dropped the boycott, he wouldn't let them back in the paper at first, although he relented eventually.

Fred Vandegrift is another publisher who struck back when his paper, the *Salina* (Kansas) *Journal,* was boycotted by car dealers for six weeks in 1980. The dealers pulled their ads after the paper endorsed a city sales tax the dealers opposed. The *Journal* informed its readers of the boycott and then published a series of editorials criticizing it. "I think we should let the public know what organizations are trying to impose their will on us, trying to drive us out of business because we don't agree with their point of view," Vandegrift said. "That's trampling on freedom of speech."

A similar boycott against the *Centre Daily Times* of State College, Pennsylvania, in 1983 lasted for five months. But after informing readers that the boycott had begun, the *Times* never mentioned it again, even when it ended. Executive editor William Blair said the paper decided not to editorialize against the boycott because it would appear to be a conflict of interest—"it would look like we were crying for our own interests."

Boycotts by car dealers also have been carried out recently against newspapers in Danbury, Connecticut; Tucson, Arizona; and Jackson, Tennessee. But the *Trenton* (New Jersey) *Times* seems to have been hardest hit. It suffered a series of boycotts by car dealers in the 1970s sparked by several articles, including one by CBS economics reporter Jane Bryant Quinn about an agency in New York City that made it possible for people to buy cars at wholesale prices, and another by a columnist who wrote that the high price of a new car made him keep his clunker. The dealers even pulled their ads when the *Times* published editorial cartoons against the federal bailout of the ailing Chrysler Corporation. Don Lippincott, then managing editor of the paper, estimates that the boycotts cost the paper about a million dollars.[39]

The *Trenton Times* became friendlier with its advertisers after Joseph Allbritton bought the paper from the *Washington Post* in 1981 and almost immediately dismissed twenty-four people from a news staff of eighty. Fourteen other news staffers soon left the paper, complaining that the business office was taking over the newsroom and catering to advertisers. One who left, business editor Perri Foster-Pegg, said she had been told to include in an annual business supplement some flattering articles submitted by advertisers in the section. The advertisers complained after Foster-Pegg shortened or rewrote their news releases, unlike the rival *Trentonian,* which had published them as submitted. Shortly after that incident, which prompted Foster-Pegg to flee to a public relations job, the *Times* fired a new young business section reporter who added some clarifying information to a news release from an advertiser after he had been told by his editor to type it verbatim into the paper's computer system.[40] Allbritton, Texas financier who owned the old *Washington Star* from 1974 to 1978, claimed in a signed editorial in the *Times* that it was not the policy of "Allbritton Communications to allow the interests of our advertisers to influence the news." He said the management of the *Times* had erred when it ordered the news release to be used verbatim, but the dismissed reporter also had been wrong in defying the orders of his editor. Rem Reider, who was forced out as managing editor of the *Times* after the Allbritton takeover and who became associate news editor of the *Miami Herald,* said the new management Allbritton installed had "great sensitivity" about "pleasing the advertisers."[41]

Editor Dunlap of the Sharon, Pennsylvania, *Herald* has experienced advertisers who have withdrawn ads because of news stories that reflected adversely on them in some way, but that has not changed his policy of not allowing advertisers to influence news. He does not believe, however, that his news staff should go out of its way to offend advertisers. He objected, for example, to a travel feature in his paper that "played up one bus company that doesn't advertise and ignored another that does, that mentioned three travel agencies but omitted one that is an advertiser." If a story needs to be illustrated with local examples, Dunlap says, "our policy is to use the ones who advertise. I don't think that's compromising anything. . . . If you're going to pick only a few people to talk to, pick the ones who spend money with us."[42]

Sometimes the news content affects what is in the ads. What do you do, for example, when your news staff comes up with a story that contradicts what some of your advertisers are saying in their ads? Many publishers would simply look the other way, and run both. Back in the days before Murdoch bought it in late 1983, the *Chicago Sun-Times* had such a problem when its investigative reporting team came up with a major series on abuses and profiteering in abortion clinics. Pamela Zekman, who headed the team that produced the series, recalls that a week before the articles were to appear she pointed out to her editors that "people were coming into those clinics on the basis of ads we were running." She claims that "without a moment's hesitation," the paper cancelled contracts with the clinics that were worth $600,000 a year in advertising revenue.[43]

PROFESSION, TRADE, CRAFT?

What is this thing called journalism? A lot of people in it refer to it as a business. And it certainly is a business, as this chapter has tried to argue. But it's more than that. Some journalists say it's a profession; others prefer words like trade or craft.

Journalism is not a profession under the traditional definition of that word, mostly because it does not require advanced knowledge or a specialized university education. Although the traditional definition has been used by government in enforcing fair labor standards, the Labor Department began a review in 1986 of the whole matter of whether it should continue including news reporters, photographers, and editors as workers who need the protection of the Fair Labor Standards Act. Professionals such as physicians, lawyers, and some teachers are specifically exempt from that act and therefore unable to claim such benefits as overtime pay. Not surprisingly, the American Newspaper Publishers Association (ANPA) is urging that reporters, editors, and photographers be recognized as exempt professionals under FLSA, and the Newspaper Guild is fighting for the status quo.

Journalists are not, to a man or woman, clamoring for professional status. Many see journalism as a craft—perhaps an honorable one—but not a profession. Some even remember the old, old definition of a journalist as "a reporter who wears spats." But the strongest objection to labeling journalism a profession comes from those who fear that it would lead to licensing. Being licensed by government or by an organization of peers, the way lawyers and physicians are, is abhorrent to most journalists.

"We should admit to ourselves and to others that we are not professionals in the sense that doctors, lawyers and accountants are professionals," says John Seigenthaler, president, editor, and publisher of the Nashville *Tennessean.*

> We do not license. We do not disbar or defrock as a profession. Candidly, we must acknowledge that to try to do so would offend the basic and precious constitutional concept of free expression. Journalists, editors and publishers who bear and share the responsibility for presenting the news must never surrender their understanding of their ultimate responsibility to other judgments.[44]

Lyle Denniston of the Baltimore *Sun* contends that journalism cannot be a profession "because a profession has common universally accepted ethical laws and a system of sanctions to enforce them—like law, medicine, architecture, and accounting. . . . We are communicating ideas for sale, and so the ultimate restraint on us is the commercial one: will it sell? I don't apologize for working for a profit-making organization."[45]

On the other hand, some journalists believe they are working in a profession. One of these is William E. Deibler, managing editor of the *Pittsburgh Post-Gazette,* who maintains he is not worried about journalists having to be licensed "because, unlike other professionals, we have a constitutional protection in the First Amendment."[46]

And Ralph Otwell, former editor of the *Chicago Sun-Times,* believes you cannot mandate that journalism will be a profession and he hopes "there will never be a licensing requirement that will professionalize us in the way that medicine, law, and some other fields have been professionalized." But he thinks of journalism as a profession, which to him means that "in your job you have an obligation to the public that transcends mere business, commerce, or trade." Unfortunately, according to Otwell, journalism is not widely perceived as a profession by the public or by "a lot of people who are in it."[47]

Professor Edmund B. Lambeth argues that journalism is "a craft with professional responsibilities." Agreeing that licensing journalists "would violate the First Amendment to the Constitution by involving government in abridging the rights of some persons to publish or to enter journalism and practice it," Lambeth writes that "the service function of journalism in a democratic society is so important and its ethical component so imperative that to expunge journalism from the ranks of the professions would be folly."[48]

James W. Carey, dean of the College of Communications at the University of Illinois-Urbana, calls journalism "a profession by fiat." He believes journalism has been made a profession "without meeting the historic canons by which professions are identified" because of the "status and prestige" it has achieved "as the media have become more central and more centrally visible in the life of society." Carey is not cheered by the growth of professionalism in journalism and other fields:

> The principal effect of professionalism is to erode the moral basis of society. It does this because the professions insist that each inhabits a particular moral universe, peculiar unto itself, in which the standards and judgments exercised are those not of the general society and its moral point of view, but of a distinctive code. The professions divide up the moral universe in highly self-conscious ways, reorganize it through the explicit formulation of codes of ethics, and prosecute their distinctive moral claims with judicial, financial and authoritative power. . . . Moreover, the narrowness of the moral claims asserted by the professions have two confounding results. First, it means that professionals are privileged to live in a morally less ambiguous universe than the rest of us; they are able to treat as matters of principle what most of us must struggle with situationally and in terms of fine gradations of ethical judgment. Professionals are so busy standing on principle that there is no room left for the rest of us to stand. Secondly, the professions regularly conflate their own moral claims into principles that are binding upon the society for the welfare of everyone independent of their concrete relevance to particular situations. For example, the professions, and journalism is a leading case, often treat the Constitution as a suicide pact, as if it were written on Masada and not in Philadelphia, as if the entire social world must hinge on the sanctity of professional privilege.[49]

Journalism Education. The founders and organizers of the nation's journalism schools, which began in American universities shortly after the turn of the century, were boosters of professionalism. They hoped to provide the educational prerequisite for professional status. Elevating newspaper work to the level of a profession also added support and justification for having journalism courses and faculty in the first place. But acceptance by news media employers of a university journalism degree as the best preparation for work in journalism has been slow in coming. Only in recent years have newsrooms begun to be dominated by journalism school graduates, and most of these graduates have completed only a baccalaureate program. Graduate degrees in journalism or communications, or in subjects important to the understanding of news and people — such as history, political science, economics, literature, philosophy, science, or sociology — are rare in U.S. newsrooms.[50] And on the other side of the coin, it is still possible to begin in news work with no college degree: even the prestigious *Wall Street Journal* does not require one. So journalism appears to be a long way from meeting the educational criterion of the traditional definition of a profession.

Explanations for the slow retreat by U.S. news executives from what must strike most outsiders as an idiotic prejudice against an educational program designed to serve them are not easy to come by. One explanation must be in the inability of news executives to agree on what kind of education they want their prospective employees to have, so that disparate signals are sent to the universities. Some of the smaller newspapers and broadcast stations want people who can come in and go to work with little if any instruction. They want technicians. Yet it is obvious to most journalists, and even to journalism students who clamor for more and more instruction in technical skills so they can get and hold those beginning jobs, that a broad and general education is what is needed for success over the long haul. Journalism schools try to give their students both a technical and a general education to serve both their short-range and long-range interests, but that is not a simple task, and to most thoughtful journalism educators four years hardly seems enough time. Yet requiring advanced degrees for news work does not have widespread support among journalism employers, some of whom must realize that more and more educational prerequisites would mean that the news media would have to do something about their generally low beginning salaries.

It is true that the stars of journalism — TV anchors for network and metropolitan station newscasts; top writers, reporters, and editors of the large newspapers; executives of *Time* and *Newsweek* — are well paid. But beginning salaries in the field have been disgraceful. Maybe it is because journalism has always appealed to people who were willing to work without pay, as many newspaper and broadcast interns do today. Jack McKinney thought he was working for pay when at the age of 20 he talked the *Philadelphia Daily News* into letting him submit some music reviews. Now a columnist for that paper, McKinney recently wrote about how gratified he had been that most of his reviews were published but how bewildered he was when after his first two months as "music critic" he still had not been paid. One night he screwed up enough courage to awaken the managing editor, Dean McCullough, who was napping curled up in his roll-top desk:

> The slats rolled up and there, lying on his side all tucked up in a fetal position with a dead cigar in his mouth, was McCullough.
>
> "Yeah, what is it?" he demanded, blinking.
>
> "I guess you don't remember me, sir," I said. "I'm Jack McKinney. . . ."
>
> "Oh, yeah," said McCullough. "Good stuff, kid. Reads real good. Keep it coming."
>
> Feeling more confident now, I told him I was sorry to disturb him but I thought something must have gone awry in the *Daily News* accounting system.
>
> "Why do you say that?" McCullough asked.
>
> "Because I haven't been paid yet for any of my reviews," I told him.
>
> "No kidding!" he roared, swinging his short legs around to sit up in the desk. "Who hasn't been paying you?"
>
> "Why, uh, the *Daily News* hasn't been," I said.
>
> McCullough laughed heartily at this.
>
> "You don't understand, kid," he said. "You're supposed to get the money from them."
>
> Puzzled, I asked him who he meant by "them."
>
> "The people you write the reviews about," the managing editor explained.
>
> "But, sir," I protested. "That wouldn't be ethical."
>
> "Well, if that's the way you feel about it, suit yourself," said McCullough, returning to the fetal position and reaching up for the roll-top slats. "At least you're getting in to hear all that stuff for free."[51]

Pay is better for beginners now, but not much. The Dow Jones Newspaper Fund, which surveys university journalism and communications graduates each year, reported that 1986 graduates who took jobs on daily papers started at an annual average of $13,900, or $267 a week. Graduates who took television or radio jobs started at $12,600, or $241 a week, the same survey revealed.[52]

Another study by ASNE in 1986 pointed up the differences in beginning salaries paid by smaller and larger daily newspapers. It showed that beginning reporters were paid an annual average of $10,816, or $208 a week, on papers under 5,000 circulation; $13,312, or $256 a week, on papers with circulations of 18,000 to 25,000; and $22,984, or $441 a week, on papers of over 250,000 circulation. Beginning school teachers in those same three categories of cities were paid $15,514, $15,690, and $17,671 per year on the average.[53]

A study of salaries on smaller papers in one state painted the same gloomy picture. When Steve Nash surveyed 44 under-21,000 circulation dailies and weeklies in Virginia in 1985, he found beginning news salaries averaged just over $11,000 a year.[54]

At the time those 1985 graduates were entering the job market, the U.S. Postal Service was advertising for clerk carrier trainees at $9.48 an hour, which amounts to $379.20 for a 40-hour week, or $19,718.40 a year. So much for the rewards of professionalism.

3 Conflicts of Interest

"You know I'd marry you if I could, Suzie, but my editor says it would create a terrible conflict of interest."

As editor of this 98,000-circulation daily newspaper in the mid-South, you learn that your only black reporter has filed to be one of three candidates for two seats on the nonpartisan school board in the small town where she lives. The reporter is the mother of three sons. She's been with you about two years as a general assignment reporter covering events in your city. The school board she is seeking to join is in another county about 15 miles from your city and your newspaper covers it only occasionally and usually with a part-time stringer, rather than a staff reporter. Your paper has a policy, which has been posted on bulletin boards, that prohibits "participation of an employee in any political activity that could raise questions as to the newspaper's objectivity." Although you serve by appointment of the mayor as a member of a city parking authority, you do not consider this to be violating your policy because the authority has only advisory functions. But the question before you now is whether your reporter's candidacy for this nonpartisan school board 15 miles away violates your policy and if it does, what are you going to do about it?

What editor Ralph L. Millett, Jr., did about it was to wait until reporter Jacqueline B. McClary was elected and then tell her she'd either have to give up her seat on the school board or her job. When McClary refused to resign from the board, Millett fired her. The dismissal lasted less than a year, however, because a labor arbitrator ordered the *Knoxville* (Tennessee) *News-Sentinel* to reinstate her with back pay.

The arbitrator, upholding a grievance filed on McClary's behalf by the Newspaper Guild, found the paper's policy against political involvements to be reasonable but not enforced uniformly. McClary went back to her job and continued to serve out her four-year term on the Alcoa School Board. Millett quit the parking authority and retired a few months after the arbitrator's ruling.[1]

Although this case, like most, is far from a pure example, the ethical issue it points up is conflict of interest. What that means, in a dictionary sense, is a situation in which you find that one of your jobs, interests, activities, or duties can be advanced only at the expense of another of your jobs, interests, activities, or duties.

Most American news executives worry a lot these days about conflicts of interest because they fear that the public will question their news reports if they are produced by people whose independence is not obvious. If the public knows or suspects, for example, that a reporter is working on the side for a political candidate or cause, it might not believe what that reporter writes about that particular candidate or cause. The credibility of the reporter, and perhaps the entire news organization is threatened. In this way of thinking, the appearance of a conflict of interest can be just as serious as a real conflict: If the public believes that some journalist is in the vest pocket of some politician, credibility suffers even if the journalist is not, indeed, in anybody's vest pocket.

The rub comes in deciding when a real or apparent conflict of interest is serious enough to result in the feared loss of credibility. Reporter McClary did not see any serious conflict of interest in her being a reporter in Knoxville and serving on a nonpartisan school board 15 miles away in another county. Her editor apparently did. The arbitrator found it "farfetched" to believe that the public would question the newspaper's objectivity because of a reporter serving on a board that the paper covered only with stringers.

Although many in and out of journalism might argue that school boards, because they collect and spend big tax dollars, are just as political as city councils and boards of county commissioners, McClary makes a distinction. She does not see how it would be possible for a journalist "to serve on the city council or run for mayor" in the same city he or she covers. But serving on a nonpartisan school board would be all right, particularly if that board is some distance from the newspaper for which the journalist works.[2]

After three years in office—for which she gets paid $25 a month—McClary has seen none of the conflict-of-interest problems that were the concern of her editor. She says that her newspaper has covered her board with a stringer and often not even that. The only big news that her board made in those three years was when it elected a new superintendent for the small district of but three schools. The *News-Sentinel* used a stringer to cover that election.

McClary felt compelled to run for the board because her participation in school meetings showed her that although the school system had a good reputation, it also had some serious problems. "I thought that because I am a journalist that I could make a positive contribution," McClary explains. "I've covered city council, county commissioners and those kinds of public governing bodies, and I know how to ask questions and get information." She deplores journalists who are cynical about people who serve on public bodies and believes "people should do their civic duty and get involved however they can." Although race was not primary in her decision to run, McClary was aware that blacks who constitute 25 percent of the Alcoa school district population had no representative on the five-member school board.

McClary recalls reading her paper's outside activities policy on a bulletin board when she first joined the staff in 1981. But "when they changed it—I guess they posted it—I didn't really pay any attention to it," she concedes. "There was no emphasis put on it." Because she was aware of Millett's service on the parking authority and of a former staffer who had served as a county commissioner while he was working for the paper, she says she "certainly did not anticipate the storm of controversy that came up over my running for the school board in Alcoa."

Since returning to the paper after her nine-month layoff, McClary has been allowed to specialize in health and medical news. She says she is happy with her new editor, who is changing the paper for the better, and is particularly pleased that the news staff now includes four black reporters.

Jacqueline McClary was not the first American reporter to get into trouble because of a news organization's policy against certain or all conflicts of interest. She was luckier than most, in part because she had a union behind her. But her case illustrates the problems that arise when employer organizations, even for understandable reasons, demand that their employees turn their backs on civic responsibilities and participation. It also illustrates the double standard that often exists between owners or managers and working journalists in defining and punishing so-called conflicts of interest.

AT THE WORKING PRESS LEVEL

Rod Nordland got more respectable when he became a foreign correspondent first for the *Philadelphia Inquirer* and then for *Newsweek*. But back in the days when his specialty was covering and evading motorcycle gangs, he came into the presidency of a rejuvenated drinking and social organization in Philadelphia known as the Pen and Pencil Club. One of his first irreverent acts as leader of that group was to establish the Harry J. Karafin Award to memorialize that city's worst journalist. Harry who? Karafin, Harry Karafin. He was a reporter who was fired by the *Philadelphia Inquirer* in 1967 after *Philadelphia Magazine* exposed how he used sources and his access to the news columns of the *Inquirer* to build up his public relations business sideline. Karafin would prey on shady businesses under investigation by some legal agency or other and get them to buy his public relations services. Then he would turn the publicity faucets on and off in the *Inquirer* to suit his clients. He died while serving time in prison for blackmail. It is interesting that his unethical career was exposed by *Philadelphia Magazine,* not by his own newspaper (then owned by Walter Annenberg) nor by the town's leading paper at that time, the since deceased *Bulletin.*[3]

Eleven years later, however, the *Inquirer,* now under the new management of the Knight-Ridder chain, broke the news when it had to reassign its nightlife columnist because of a conflict of interest.[4] The columnist, Bill Curry, left the paper. Gene Foreman, managing editor of the *Inquirer,* reports that Curry had "disturbed us by business investments that were close to a conflict of interest, but when he went into business with a restaurant he had promoted in his column, a resignation was negotiated."[5]

If Nordland had been able to continue the Harry Karafin awards, one might well have gone to R. Foster Winans, a *Wall Street Journal* reporter who was found guilty of securities fraud. At his trial, Winans admitted that he had leaked information to a couple of hungry stockbrokers about what was to be published in the *Journal*'s "Heard on the Street" column, many of which Winans wrote. The stockbrokers then bought or sold the stocks they thought would be affected by what the columns said, transactions that earned them a profit of about $700,000, only $30,000 of which went to Winans and his roommate, David Carpenter. Winans was sentenced to eighteen months in jail for violating federal securities laws, but his lawyers have appealed the conviction to the U.S. Supreme Court after losing their initial appeal to the federal Appeals Court in Manhattan. Carpenter was sentenced to three years' probation. One of the stockbrokers got six months, which he was allowed to serve on weekends; the other stockbroker was never charged because he became the government's chief witness against the other three.[6]

The *Wall Street Journal,* which has for years had one of the strongest conflict-of-interest policies in the news business, did not wait for the courts to make their final ruling on Winans. He was fired from his $610-a-week job as soon as the *Journal* learned that the Securities and Exchange

Commission was investigating him. The *Journal* explained in an editorial that leaking market-sensitive information from coming columns was specifically prohibited by its policies, which were "especially stressed to writers of market columns." The credibility of the newspaper "could not be long sustained if readers come to believe that our articles are tainted by some hidden agenda other than informing the public," the editorial added. In an article reporting on its own investigation of Winans's "unethical behavior," the *Journal* said that when Winans had worked for the *Trentonian* in Trenton, New Jersey, before coming to the *Journal,* he had taken unpublished information from the computer files of fellow reporters and used it in free-lance stories he sold to the *New York Times* and other newspapers.[7]

Most of the conflicts of interest that mar American journalism are not as blatant as the Karafin, Curry, and Winans cases, but some journalists do get involved outside their newsrooms with friends, causes, organizations, activities, and sidelines that constitute possible or real conflicts of interest.

Outside Jobs. Moonlighting, or holding down a second full- or part-time job, has become common in acquisitive modern society. Other than possible damage to health, moonlighting seems to present few serious problems to its participants. But if you are a young reporter making less money than your moonlighting neighbor, a store clerk who drives a cab on the side, you risk your job and your reputation unless you choose your second occupation with great care. Writing a book is fine. It might make you some money and bring credit to you and your news organization. Writing a promotion booklet for a local developer can get you fired. Doing an article for a national magazine is permissible. Doing an article for another newspaper in your area can get you fired. Doing a piece for a program put out by a professional team you cover can get you in trouble.

Selling your writing skills to the highest bidder may not be wise if you wish to survive as a reporter. Increasingly, U.S. news organizations have taken a dim view of outside jobs and activities that might cause the public to smell a conflict of interest.

Many of the contracts that the Newspaper Guild has with newspapers include so-called outside activities clauses, restricting what news department employees can do with their off duty hours. David J. Eisen, director of research and information for the Guild, claims that these clauses are "not ethical provisions: the public doesn't give a damn about them. They're publishers' interest provisions" that serve the economic interests of the employers.[8] Eisen and other officers of the union obviously believe that newspaper managers have used conflict of interest as a justification for extending their authority over their employees. And this restricts reporters and editors from obtaining maximum economic benefit from their skills and talents.

As it has often done, the Guild went to arbitration when the Rochester, New York, *Times-Union* and *Democrat and Chronicle* refused permission for one of their photographers to work for a short period for the Lake Placid Olympic Organizing Committee. Robert H. Giles, the executive editor then, said that working for a news source while employed by his newspapers was a conflict of interest, even if photographer Talis Bergmanis took vacation or leave to do it. (The Olympic Committee invited Bergmanis and nine other photographers to illustrate a proposed book on how to organize a winter olympics and also to provide news photos to smaller papers unable to staff the 1980 competition at Lake Placid, New York. Most of the invited photographers were free-lancers, but some were newspaper photographers, and one of those who accepted was Joe Traver, who got permission from the Buffalo *Courier Express* to do so.) After two hearings, the arbitrator, Joseph Shister of Buffalo, ruled in essence that the company had not proved a real conflict of interest. He made the company pay Bergmanis a total of $1,850 – the $600 he would have been paid by the Olympic Committee (twelve days at $50 per day) and $1,250 for the free-lance photographs he might have sold if he had been allowed to work the olympics for the committee.[9] Bergmanis left the Rochester papers after winning his grievance.

Giles believes his organization was "the victim of an arbitrator who does not understand the newspaper business." He explains that his newspapers did not appeal to the NLRB because the decision did not set a precedent and arbitrator's decisions are usually upheld by the NLRB and the courts.[10]

Giles made it clear to the news staffs of his two newspapers that the arbitrator's decision had not changed the editor's attitude about conflicts of interest. "Our readers must have absolute trust in the independence and the integrity of our newspapers and the journalists who work for them," Giles stated in a staff memo. "We must avoid activities that can cause suspicion among readers about our ability to report the news in a fair and balanced way. Our relationships with news sources, promoters, advertisers and public relations people must be kept at arm's length." He said the Olympic Committee that wanted to hire Bergmanis "was, at once, a news source, a sports promoter, an advertiser, a fund raiser, and a public relations organization. Part of its mission was to influence the news." Giles wrote:

> The idea that potential conflicts of interest should be avoided is not intended to prevent members of our news staffs from doing volunteer work in the community or pursuing leisure activities or even some work related to their professional lives. The test is whether the

readers of our newspapers could reasonably assume that there was a conflict. In some cases, the presence of a conflict is clear. In others, it might be a close call. Responsibility for making those calls is mine. The arbitrator's ruling has not changed the rules here. They require that any outside activities have the advance approval of the executive editor.[11]

Another arbitrator in a *Boston Globe* case similar to that in Rochester upheld the newspaper's right to prohibit a staff photographer from working on his own time for the Boston Red Sox. The photographer, who had been with the *Globe* for nineteen years, was denied permission to take a part-time job as backup to the team's official photographer. His role would have been to shoot pictures for the Red Sox yearbook, score cards, and promotional materials without being credited by name. Arbitrator Sharon H. Ellis saw the part-time job as violating the "outside activities" provision in the agreement between the newspaper and an independent union representing news employees. She noted that the *Globe* did not want "its journalists working for and receiving remuneration on a continuing basis from one of its major news sources. It fears that notwithstanding the absence or presence of actual conflict of interest, the type of outside employment sought in this case could be seized upon by competing media and used to cast suspicion upon the *Globe*'s objectivity and freedom from bias or interest."[12]

The *Boston Globe* also disapproved of the outside activities of political columnist David Farrell, so much so that it asked for and received his resignation. Farrell was discovered to be working part time for two companies—doing public relations for Merkert Enterprises, a food brokerage firm, and as a news writer for a New Hampshire television station. *Globe* editor Michael Janeway said that if Farrell had asked permission in advance, as *Globe* policy requires, it would have been denied. The *Globe* usually grants permission only for certain kinds of outside work, such as teaching journalism courses or writing books, the editor added.[13]

Editors may differ on what constitutes a conflict of interest for their staffs—and some have them written down and some have not—but the requirement of advance approval for outside activities is approaching universality in U.S. newsrooms. Working for a competing news medium, usually defined as one aimed almost exclusively at the same or part of the same audience as that of the employing medium, is on almost every editor's taboo list. So is working for any public relations firm or department, or for any political or governmental agency. Free-lancing on your own time that results in a book, an article in a national magazine, or an exhibition of photographs is usually not considered a conflict. In fact, such activities often bring prestige to the employer as well as the employee. Teaching part time at a university or other respectable school is usually no problem if the schedule can be arranged. Investing in stocks and bonds or in business is usually approved unless the investments are tied too closely to your regular assignment or to something you have published or broadcast or intend to. Volunteer or unpaid work is also generally verboten if it links the journalist too closely with news sources and subjects: writing speeches, news releases, or ads for political candidates; taking part in a controversial demonstration; holding office in a political party or an unpaid position in government; heading a local pro or antiabortion group. Editors usually do not object to staff members affiliating with conventional churches and other reasonably noncontroversial organizations (Girl Scouts, Kiwanis, Rotary, and the like), but they might prevent staff members from holding office in those organizations, especially those involving any responsibility for publicity or public relations. Registering with one of the major parties in order to vote in primaries is not taboo, but many reporters and editors still choose to register as independents.

The extrajournalistic opportunities available to photographers have brought about some special policies on many newspapers. Most editors do not allow their photographers to sell any photos taken for their newspapers for fear that some photographers might be tempted to put marketability above journalistic value in the pictures they take. Some newspapers give away prints of the photos that have been published if family members or others ask for them. More newspapers, however, seem to be charging for such prints, and the *Philadelphia Inquirer* shares the revenue from such sales with its photographers. Photographers who want to freelance or take photographs for pay during off-duty hours are usually subject to the same advance permission and other restrictions applied to writers.

Newspaper and magazine journalists usually avoid anything to do with advertising in deference to long-standing rules about keeping news and advertising separate. But radio and television news people, particularly but not exclusively at the local level, feel less constrained. Making commercials, even testimonial commercials, seems to be part of the job in the news departments at some radio and TV stations. This may add to the income of newscasters who do commercials, but it certainly detracts from their credibility as reporters and presenters of news. A news director whose testimonial for a local tire dealer ("These tires get me where I need to go in my job as news director at WJAC") is inserted in his station's evening newscast is begging for the public to lose its trust in him and his staff. And Gene Shalit's credibility as the theater-movie critic on NBC's *Today* show is not enhanced when he all but drools over a dog food.

When the *New York Times* revealed that Hodding Carter III was being paid for appearances on ABC News at the time he was anchoring

"Inside Story," a public television program that criticized news media performance, he said he didn't see that as any big deal. "Inside Story," which often examined the ethics of various news organizations when it appeared regularly on many PBS stations, had done several pieces on ABC News, including a generally positive one on Peter Jennings, anchor of ABC's evening newscast. When the *Times* asked Carter about his receiving $1,000 apiece for more than 25 appearances on the Sunday David Brinkley show, Carter said, "This issue really doesn't trouble me." He said that in addition to being paid by ABC News, he had also been paid for columns in the *Wall Street Journal* and for speaking engagements. The important issue, Carter argued, is whether his journalism is fair and accurate. But his boss at "Inside Story," senior executive producer Ned Schnurman, said he wished they had included a disclosure of the ABC payments in the program on Peter Jennings. "We always said that if we did a series that was critical of the press, sometime we would slip up ourselves," Schnurman added. "This is one of those times."[14]

Another television journalist who doesn't see any conflict of interest in accepting money from a source he regularly covers is Bill Williams, news anchor for WBIR-TV in Knoxville, Tennessee. The *Knoxville Journal* reported that Williams had received $5,741.68 in talent fees and expenses for work he did for the Tennessee Valley Authority. In fact, he used pieces of a documentary he helped produce for TVA in a series on water quality that he did for his station. Neither Williams nor his news director, Jim Swinehart, saw anything wrong with Williams working on the side for TVA. "I can't see an ethical problem with what I did," is the way Williams put it. The *Knoxville Journal* article also quoted Fred Behringer, executive editor of some small newspapers near Philadelphia and then vice-chairman of the SPJ-SDX ethics committee, as being appalled at the "obvious conflict of interest" in Williams accepting money from a news source.[15]

Sometimes it's difficult to anticipate the kind of outside work and activities by news staffers that might cause a loss of public trust. Paul A. Poorman, former editor of the *Akron Beacon Journal*, recalls that one of his reporters was arrested as a client in a police sweep of prostitutes in that city. The reporter told police he was on assignment. He wasn't. Poorman could not fire the reporter for his false claim at that point, but the Guild later agreed to make such lying a dismissible offense.[16] When Eugene L. Roberts, Jr., first came to the *Philadelphia Inquirer* as executive editor in 1972, he heard sirens and screeching tires in the paper's parking lot late one night. He looked out the window to see police arresting a make-up editor and two other men for passing football parlay cards for gambling—cards that the editor was having printed on *Inquirer* equipment. "He took the opportunity to resign," Roberts recalls.[17]

Many editorial writers come down hard on Congress when it raises its limits on what members may acquire in fees for outside activities (in 1986 those limits were $30,040, or 40 percent of their annual salaries, in the Senate; and $22,530, or 30 percent of their annual salaries, in the House).[18] But many of the stars of journalism make plenty of extra bucks the same way senators and Congress members do—on the lecture circuit. Popular columnists like Art Buchwald and George F. Will and glamorous TV news stars like Ted Koppel and Sam Donaldson command up to $25,000 or more for speeches, but the average journalist gets paid much less than that. The problem is not so much the size of the fee as it is the quid pro quo—what is expected beyond the speech by the organization paying the fee. If a speaking fee dents in any way the independent judgment of that journalist-speaker, then it is a conflict of interest that ought to be avoided.

The Special Taboo of Politics. Of all the outside activities of journalists, politics seems to offer the greatest number of ethical pitfalls. Perhaps it is because of the vigilant attention news organizations pay to politics and government. Although this taboo gets broken every year— especially in the smaller communities around the country—it is inconceivable that a major journalist today would get involved in politics in the way that Warren G. Harding did, using his *Marion* (Ohio) *Daily Star* to launch a political career that got him elected to the presidency in 1920. A lot of people thought Walter Cronkite might go into politics when he relinquished the anchor position on "CBS Evening News" to Dan Rather in 1981, but he didn't. He feels strongly, he said in a recent interview, "that a person whose reputation has been based on a journalistic enterprise should not capitalize on that by getting into politics. Once that happens a lot, it's got to create a considerable doubt in the public's mind about the motivation of every other anchorperson who remains on the air. Are they attempting to tell you the truth, the news of the day, or are they building a political base for a future run at high office?"[19]

Cronkite's good advice either didn't reach or failed to impress Carol Stanton Granstrom, who quit after seven years as anchorwoman for WESH-TV in Orlando, Florida, and ran for Congress in 1984. She was defeated in the Democratic primary by sixteen-year incumbent Bill Chappell. After her defeat, she told an *Orlando Sentinel* writer that she did not intend to return to television news.[20]

Granstrom, at least, quit her TV job before seeking public office. Some journalists, like Jacqueline McClary, whose tale was told in the opening of this chapter, have run for office while continuing in news work. Julianne Agnew was dismissed as editor of the Today's Living section of the Knight-Ridder papers in Duluth, Minnesota, when she filed to run for the City Council. John McMillion, then publisher of the *Herald* and the *News-Tribune,* told her she had violated the conflict of interest policy that Knight-Ridder applies to its publishers and editors. Agnew lost her job and the election.[21]

Journalists don't always get fired when they run for public office, as McClary and Agnew did. At one time in 1985 the city council in Tyrone, Pennsylvania, had two working journalists as members. One was Dan Meckes, editor of the *Tyrone Daily Herald,* who continued to cover the council after he was appointed to it. The second was an elected member, Virginia Werner, a staffer at the nearby *Altoona Mirror,* who insisted that another reporter for her paper cover the meetings of her council.[22] The Washington, Pennsylvania, *Observer-Reporter* also had a reporter who was covering himself as a member of the borough council in Waynesburg, a few miles from Washington, and a news editor who was an appointed member of a county planning commission. Both resigned after the little daily in Waynesburg, the *Democrat Messenger,* criticized the *Observer-Reporter* for allowing its staff members to work in governing roles. Although *Observer-Reporter* publishers John and William Northrop agreed in a letter to the editor of the *Democrat Messenger* that reporters should not hold elective office, they also argued that "newspapers should be community leaders." It is not surprising, they added, "that a community should turn to newspaper people for some of its leaders, or that the individual newspaper people would feel an obligation to respond."[23]

Eugene Patterson, chief executive officer of the *St. Petersburg Times,* was once asked by one of his news staffers if she could work publicly in George McGovern's 1972 campaign for president. "I told her and the staff I could not infringe on their civil right as citizens to participate freely in politics," Patterson says. "But I appealed to their professionalism, as bearers of a special constitutional right, in expressing my hope that they would voluntarily forego partisan political activity in public. Staffers must have thought it a fair request because not one has embarrassed the *Times,* then or since."[24]

Conflicts in Sports. The sports departments of daily newspapers run into some conflicts of interest by their very nature. In the first place they have a hard time deciding whether they are covering entertainment, business, or athletic wins and losses. Most days they do all three. But their major conflict of interest comes mostly from another schizophrenia—whether to promote sports or cover them.

Most sports pages until recent years seemed to be more interested in promoting sports, being cheerleaders for the coaches and players, often to the detriment of the facts and the readers. That is still the case on many smaller and medium-sized dailies and in many of the newspapers published in university communities. Rick Starr, sports editor of the *Valley News Dispatch* in New Kensington, Pennsylvania, admits that he and his small staff do not do much critical reporting. For example, they gave routine coverage to three separate incidents in his area of high school football players who broke their necks and were paralyzed for life. "We should have investigated these incidents more thoroughly," Starr now believes. "We should have tried to find out why these things happen and what the coaches were doing that might have caused them to happen." Another example, he says, is the way high school sports is reported, with the emphasis on the home team, and little if any critical material. The ideal, Starr believes, is to be entertaining and cover sports as entertainment, "but also be able to put the toys away when necessary and go after the substance."[25]

Bill Lyon, sports reporter and columnist for the *Philadelphia Inquirer,* believes that twenty-five years ago every newspaper sports department in the country "was a 'homer'—an arm of the local team's public relations staff." But sports reporting has improved, he argues. "If Babe Ruth played today, you'd know he was a heavy drinker and a womanizer."[26]

The maturing of sports journalism has been hard on some club owners, coaches, and players who really want scrapbook material and have been conditioned in many cases to get it. Alan Robinson, sports editor of the AP in Charleston, West Virginia, was rudely awakened to this attitude when he wrote a story quoting a college basketball player who had become so disillusioned with the University of West Virginia's athletic program that he was considering going into the hardship draft. A West Virginia coach threatened to cancel Robinson's press credentials, charged that the editor was trying to hurt the school's athletic program, and told a television audience that Robinson was angry at the university because he had flunked out of journalism school. Actually, Robinson had transferred from West Virginia after making straight A's in his journalism courses. Relating this incident to the 1979 convention of the APSE, Wick Temple, then AP sports editor, charged that the coach "was trying to intimidate the reporter and make him a cheerleader for the basketball program." Temple urged sports editors not to be discouraged by news sources who get upset, "and while we don't want to pick fights, we must make the sports establishment understand that at long last it is going to be covered—really covered—by the press."[27]

Both the risks and rewards of critically covering sports the way good news organizations cover government were brought home to the *Lexington* (Kentucky) *Herald-Leader* when it published articles about cash payments by boosters to University of Kentucky basketball players. The paper was besieged with hate mail, bomb threats, and 400 cancelled subscriptions. "It seemed as if the entire state decided we had violated a sacred law and needed to be punished," wrote Michael York, one of the two reporters who did the articles that so offended Kentucky basketball fans.[28] It is interesting that the *Herald-Leader* exposé was not produced by the paper's sports department, but by York, a Washington correspondent called in for this task, and a young cityside reporter, Jeff Marx. The articles won a coveted Pulitzer Prize for investigative reporting in 1986.

George Langford, former sports editor of the *Chicago Tribune*, sees sports pages today as being a combination of news and entertainment. Langford's paper is one of the few in the country with an investigative reporting team in sports, digging into such matters as the academic machinations that otherwise respectable universities go through to make or keep athletes eligible to play. He believes newspaper sports departments have to be watchdogs over the sports establishment. "TV and radio won't do it," Langford feels. "The Cubs and the White Sox, like most professional teams, hire the announcers. They're not journalists—most of them are just shilling for the franchise."[29] He is referring here to the veto power most professional teams and many college teams have over the play-by-play and color announcers who cover games for radio and TV, so that the coverage is almost always positive for the image of the clubs being covered. But even radio and TV sports reporters not tied so closely to the teams seldom do any critical reporting of the sort you associate with news coverage of government, by either print or broadcast journalists. Boosterism still exists on newspaper sports pages, but it is a much greater problem—almost an incurable disease—in broadcast sports reporting.

A more direct conflict of interest in sports journalism has been the fifty-year-old custom of having newspaper baseball writers in major and minor league cities serve as official scorers at home games. After the *Milwaukee Journal* decided in 1962 that its baseball writers should no longer serve as official scorers, daily newspapers in major and minor league cities have increasingly prohibited the practice as a conflict of interest because: (1) the scorers get paid by the leagues, $50 a game in the two major leagues, making it possible for a writer to get as much as $3,000 to $4,000 in extra income from the sport he or she covers; and (2) scorers make decisions that affect statistics of individual players, such as whether a batter got on base as the result of a hit or an error, and that sometimes upsets the players to the point that the scorer has a more difficult time doing the job of reporting the game. Just one example from the 1979 season serves to illustrate the second conflict problem: *Pittsburgh Press* sports reporter Dan Donovan, serving as a scorer, ruled a ball a hit and cost pitcher Bruce Kison a no-hitter. When Donovan went to the

Pittsburgh Pirates' locker room after the game to talk to players for his story, Kison berated him. The *Press* decided to join the lengthening list of papers pulling their writers out of the scorer's seat.[30]

Because more newspapers are prohibiting their baseball writers from serving as official scorers in major and minor league cities, the leagues often turn to sports reporters from suburban and nearby city newspapers to do their scoring. So in some cities, even though all of the daily newspapers published there have withdrawn their writers from scoring, active baseball writers from elsewhere are still doing the job and the conflicts of interest continue.

Some critics see a conflict of interest in the way most daily newspapers publish betting odds and other information that contributes to illegal gambling. "I wonder if such listings do not swell the betting pot so that there is more incentive to bookmakers or gamblers to find ways to convert their bets to sure things," Sam Zagoria wrote when he was ombudsman of the *Washington Post.* "In my opinion, gambling is not a victimless crime, because for some it is a sickness, and newspapers should not be cooperating in the illicit conduct. As one sports editor put it, 'Should we publish the phone numbers of prostitutes?'"[31]

A related ethical question has to do with sports reporters betting on the sports they cover. Most seem to feel that such wagering is apt to negatively affect the way the betting journalist looks at the event he or she is covering. But most horse racing reporters and columnists regularly bet on the races they cover. Almost all major race tracks have pari-mutuel windows in their press boxes, and at a Kentucky Derby the journalists wager as much as $100,000. Such betting is legal, of course, but is it a conflict of interest? No, says Andrew Beyer of the *Washington Post,* one of the writers who makes heavy use of the press box betting windows. He contends that playing the horses makes him a better reporter. "When you study horses as much as I do, you acquire a greater knowledge of the technical side of racing, which the casual player doesn't have," he says.[32]

Although the jury may still be out on the ethics of sports reporters betting on the events they cover, there seems little question about sports staffers who leak information to gamblers. That obviously unethical practice cost three sports department clerks their jobs at the *New York Times* when they were caught in 1970. Another obviously unethical, as well as illegal, practice is for a sports staffer to run a bookmaking operation from his paper's sports department. The 1982 APME Sports Committee claimed that the assistant sports editor of a daily it declined to name, at the request of its editor, was actually doing that. The bookie-editor, whose bookmaking income exceeded and often tripled his weekly salary, was fired, of course.[33]

Contests. It seemed like a good idea at the time. Hold a little contest for reporting or editorial writing. Then get some respected editors to judge them. And the winners can be models for everybody, thus improving the breed.

That was years ago. Today U.S. journalists have more than 400 contests they can enter, and leaders of the field are wondering aloud whether a good idea has not been carried too far. Three main problems result from the proliferation of journalistic awards: The first is that there are so many of them that all but a handful have lost significance as improvers of the breed. Second, the competition for the few prestigious journalism awards, such as the Pulitzer Prizes, is often so intense that journalists have been known to hype their articles in hopes of winning one of the big prizes. A third problem arises from a growing minority of the contests that are sponsored by vested interests who seem to be trying to get the news media to present material that might not otherwise get in print or on the air and to reflect a slant favored by the sponsor. The National Association of Realtors, for example, offers $5,000 in prizes for "articles dealing with real estate development, property tax relief, etc."[34]

The *Milwaukee Journal* did not have award winning in mind when it assigned reporter Don Bluhm to check out major Mexican resorts after the 1985 Mexico City earthquake. But two months after Bluhm's articles were published, a flyer came to his desk announcing a contest to reward "outstanding press reports abroad which aided in clarifying the image of Mexico" after the quake. Since the *Journal* had paid his way and he obviously had not written his articles to win any prize, Bluhm saw nothing in his paper's ten-year-old policy on contests to prevent his entering this one. So he entered, and he won a $12,500 second prize. The size of the award—twelve and a half times what Pulitzer prize winners get—concerned *Journal* editors, who looked into sponsorship of the contest and found that it had been organized by, among others, Mexico's secretary of tourism, the presidents of two national travel organizations, and the president of a chain of Mexican hotels. The editors concluded that acceptance of such a prize "in a contest intended to promote tourism in Mexico gives the appearance of a conflict of interest that compromises the newspaper's credibility." Concurring with his editors, Bluhm returned the money.[35]

Other newspapers, such as the *Philadelphia Inquirer,* the Louisville *Courier-Journal,* and the *Roanoke Times and World News,* also have written rules about which contests their news staffs are allowed to enter. And the 1983 convention of the Society of Professional Journalists adopted guidelines for determining which contests fell within the society's code of ethics. Basically, the SPJ-SDX guidelines reject contests that "state or imply favorable treatment of a cause or subject," insist that judging panels be "dominated by respected journalists or journalism educators," and tolerate cash awards only in contests wholly sponsored by professional journalism organizations, journalism foundations, or universities.[36]

Many of the hundreds of contests listed in the directory of journalism competitions published each year by *Editor and Publisher* magazine would not pass muster with SPJ-SDX. The biggest plums in the directory used to be seven much-criticized contests sponsored by outdoor sports and recreation firms and open only to members of the Outdoor Writers Association of America. But the 1985 directory listed only one such plum, the $2,000 award from Evinrude for OWAA members who excel in "reporting on the sport of boating and preservation of the waterways."[37]

The other category of vested interest awards severely criticized in recent years—those given for travel articles—continues to be well represented in the *E and P* directory. The Korea National Tourism Corporation offers something called the "Heavenly Horse Award" for travel writing about the Republic of Korea. Similarly, the Pacific Travel Association recognizes the best articles and pictures about travel in the Pacific area each year. Travel writers can also win $500 from the Greater Las Vegas Chamber of Commerce for stories about that entertainment and gambling center; $500 from South Carolina "for articles promoting travel in South Carolina"; $1,000 from the Travel Industry Association of America "for articles explaining the travel industry's role in the U.S. economy"; and the La Pluma de Plata Mexicana Awards, $2,750, plus silver trophies and trips, from the Mexican National Tourist Council for articles "that promote travel to Mexico."

"I doubt if a story on how to deal with Montezuma's revenge would win the La Pluma de Plata award," says Paul Poorman, former editor of the *Akron Beacon Journal,* expressing the reservations that he and many journalists have about vested interest contests. "Nor is an exposé of the guy who put too much sand in the concrete when he built Interstate 90 around Erie apt to win the lucrative cash award for best writing about highways and highway problems sponsored by the National Highway Contractors' Association and the Cement Institute."[38]

Spouses and Kin. Sometimes conflicts of interest in journalism, real or apparent, are caused by the activities or jobs of the wives, husbands, or children of journalists.

In Seattle recently, Elaine Bowers, the new bride of *Seattle Times* Managing Editor Mike Fancher, quit her job as press secretary to the mayor after only a day. Her job qualifications were not in doubt. She had been a reporter for the *Kansas City Star* and the *Houston Chronicle* and had worked as press secretary to Missouri Gov. Kit Bond for two years.

But if she stayed on in her new job in the mayor's office, her husband was going to lose his. *Seattle Times* management informed him that because his wife's new job put him in violation of the paper's ethics code provision that staffers are not to make news judgments about individuals they are related to by blood or marriage, he would be transferred out of the newsroom. Bowers ended up taking a public relations job with the Seattle Public Health Hospital. Fancher still has to remove himself from any news involving the hospital, but he was allowed to continue as managing editor, and later he was promoted to executive editor.[39]

When Charles W. Bailey was editor of the *Minneapolis Tribune,* his paper reported that his wife had made a large contribution to the campaign of a U.S. senatorial candidate. This prompted Bailey to get out a memo to his staff which read:

> The contribution may be a matter of some embarrassment to me. I hope it will not be a source of embarrassment for the *Tribune.* It didn't seem to me that I had any business trying to tell my wife what she could do with her money as long as what she proposed to do was legal and would be a matter of public record.[40]

Mike Wallace of the CBS "60 Minutes" show, one of television's most aggressive reporters, tried to kill an update on conditions in Haiti because of pressure from his wife, Lorraine. Wallace had done a tough report on the Caribbean island in 1972 that caused, he claimed, "an infinite amount of distress" to his wife's relatives in Haiti. "They asked me, candidly, please not to do another story." So when Morley Safer, fellow star of "60 Minutes," proposed to take another look at the poverty-stricken dictatorship of that small country in 1981, Wallace asked Safer not to do it—for his wife's family's sake—and Safer agreed. But columnist Jack Anderson broke the story, which put "60 Minutes" on the spot. Executives of the show announced that the Haiti report would be done after all.[41]

Most news executives agree they have no legal right to influence the activities of spouses. So when a conflict of interest does arise because of a spouse, all the news organization can do is reassign the journalist if the conflict is serious enough or assure in some other way that this journalist does not handle any news involving the spouse. "Journalists have to be mindful of the problems their spouses can cause," says Phil Currie, vice-president/news staff development for Gannett, "but we have to let each person live his or her own life."[42]

The children of journalists can also raise conflict-of-interest problems. Bill Endicott resigned as Sacramento bureau chief for the *Los Angeles Times* after his editors told him that he would be transferred unless his 23-year-old daughter quit her entry-level secretarial job with Willie Brown, speaker of the California Assembly. Endicott, who was hired almost immediately by the *Sacramento Bee* to be its chief correspondent at the capital, said he could see no moral or legal basis for the request that he ask his daughter to quit her job. "My daughter is an independent adult," he added. "I can't tell her where to work, nor would I if I could."[43]

Stuart Bykofsky was removed from the television column he was writing for the *Philadelphia Daily News* and put back on general assignment features after he tried to help his daughter get a job in broadcasting. When he was dining one day with Paul Yates, general manager of the NBC-affiliated station in Philadelphia, Bykofsky mentioned that his daughter had graduated from the Broadcasting Institute of Maryland but couldn't even get an interview for a job in broadcasting. Yates, who had recently worked for the NBC-affiliated station in Baltimore, offered to help arrange some interviews, which he apparently did. The Baltimore interviews did not lead to a job, however, and Bykofsky's daughter ended up as a rock disc jockey in Harrisburg. Unfortunately for Bykofsky, his editor, Zachary Stalberg, picked up rumors that Paul Yates was bragging to colleagues that his station, KYW, didn't have to worry about any harsh criticism from Bykofsky's column because he had gotten Bykofsky's daughter a job at the Baltimore affiliate. "The impression was that Bykofsky had compromised himself," Stalberg said.[44]

Many newspapers in the old days had nepotism policies that prevented spouses from working in the same newsroom. Young journalists sometimes postponed their marriages and simply lived together to get around such rules. That may be one reason those rules are disappearing. But it is common today to find husbands and wives both doing journalism, sometimes for the same employer but often for different news organizations. Sometimes they're on the same beat, as was the case with Charles Bierbauer and his wife, Susanne Schafer. Both covered the Reagan White House, she for the Associated Press and he for Cable News Network. A cursory survey Susan Page did for an article on journalist couples in the *Washington Journalism Review* turned up more than three dozen such couples in Washington, not counting the metropolitan staffs of the city's newspapers or local TV stations. Page herself is half of a journalist couple, she working in the Washington bureau of *Newsday* and her husband, Carl Leubsdorf, as bureau chief there for the *Dallas Morning News.* Most of these couples have such different assignments that they never run into conflicts of interest, but even those who cover the same stories seem to keep their conflicts under control. Al Hunt, chief of the Washington bureau of the *Wall Street Journal,* who is married to Judy Woodruff, chief Washington correspondent for the "MacNeil/Lehrer NewsHour," contends that "good reporters can compete against their spouses during the day and sleep with them at night."[45]

ACTIVISM AT THE TOP

Extrajournalistic activities by the owners and publishers of American news media have more serious implications than those of so-called working journalists. When a proprietor or top executive has a conflict of interest, it can affect the credibility and independence of the entire news organization. Yet news media VIPs still seek and hold public office as high as the U.S. Congress, get involved in all sorts of civic and community affairs, and work behind the scenes with other "kingmakers" to see that the "right people" run government.

The tradition in American journalism of newspaper publishers and executives playing active roles in community, state, or national affairs is dying, but it's dying slowly. In a 1984 survey, Don Sneed of Texas A & M University turned up more than a hundred newspaper publishers and editors who have held or now hold public office.[46] In President Reagan's 1984 campaign, a group of about fifty smaller newspaper publishers joined "Newspaper Friends of Reagan/Bush" to distribute materials supporting their candidates to other small dailies and weeklies. "Freedom of the press is for he who owns one," one of the "newspaper friends" maintained.[47]

John Cowles, Jr., was very active in civic, political, and business affairs when he ran the *Star* and the *Tribune* in Minneapolis until 1983. His activism became so controversial, both in Minneapolis and in journalism generally, that forty-five of his own news employees took an ad in their paper to protest his "leadership role in sensitive political and economic issues," because it caused the public to doubt their ability "to be dispassionate and fair."[48]

The kind of civic activities that John Cowles, Jr., got involved in probably would have earned him praise and esteem, especially from his own employees, if he had been any kind of president except the president of a newspaper publishing company. He put his energies and his company's money into building the famous Guthrie Theater, the Walker Art Center, and the orchestra hall for the Minnesota Symphony. During the racially tense sixties, he led the formation of a coalition of business leaders and public officials to provide communication with blacks and other minorities.

His father had been principal purchaser of the bonds floated to build the stadium in suburban Bloomington used by the professional football and baseball teams in that area. When the two teams, the Vikings and the Twins, threatened to leave the Minneapolis area if they did not have a larger, weather-protected facility, John Cowles, Jr., set out to give them what they required to stay, the new domed stadium in downtown Minneapolis that opened in 1982. It was his push for a new stadium that brought about the unusual publication in the *Tribune* of an ad by some of its news staffers protesting the extrajournalistic activities of their boss.

What Cowles did to promote the controversial stadium was to take the lead in raising funds, in lobbying necessary legislation through the state legislature, and in negotiating with the city government. Cowles contributed "something like $4.9 million in cash and land to make it happen," according to Stephen D. Isaacs, CBS News producer, then editor and senior vice-president of the *Minneapolis Star* before it was merged into the present *Star and Tribune*. The deal that was finally made with the city allowed the principal donors certain rights to develop the land around the new stadium. To accomplish this, Cowles and other business leaders formed Industry Square Development Corporation and "limited themselves to a 6½ percent profit," Isaacs reports.[49]

The Minnesota News Council looked into the coverage of the stadium controversy by the two Minneapolis dailies after Minnesotans Against the Downtown Dome complained that the reporting was biased. Backing away from outright condemnation of Cowles for his leadership role in the stadium project, the council concluded that readers of the *Star* and *Tribune* received "a reasonably fair, accurate and balanced report of events surrounding the stadium decision." The council said it found no evidence that Cowles had "attempted to influence coverage," nor that reporters and editors had "experienced subtle pressure to inhibit aggressive coverage of the stadium issue as a result of Cowles' involvement."

But Isaacs is not happy that his corporate owner involved himself in the stadium fight the way he did. "John didn't just contribute to the cause . . . ," Isaacs says. "He was the principal negotiator with our city government: He was not *a* player, he was *the* player." Isaacs recalls that his staff had to overcover Cowles, had to lean over backwards to show "that we were not in fact distorting our coverage because of John's involvement."

"The greatest contribution an owner can make to his community is by putting out a quality newspaper that has a high standard of integrity and ethics," Isaacs argues. "The claim of owners that they need to put something back into the community is hypocritical and a lie. If they wanted to make a generous contribution, they could put it in a noncontrolled trust and turn over all the revenues they wanted to some kind of institution that would use them in an honorable way. . . . But I don't know a single owner who would do this, because what they're really after is power." Newspaper publishers and owners getting involved in community affairs is counter to their most important commodity—credibility—and therefore counter "to the essence of their business," Isaacs maintains.

Cowles, of course, disagrees with Isaacs. He believes "publishers have a positive obligation to engage in the important activities of the community." He says the "whole notion that newspaper publishers and owners, as well as newspaper editors and reporters, should isolate themselves, sanitize themselves, from the community is a kind of recent idea, developed mostly by the biggest papers in communities so large that it is not clear and easy to see how an individual publisher can make a lot of difference." Cowles is sympathetic to the developing view that newspapers have to be "neutral bystanders," but he maintains that such neutrality should apply only to the news departments. "Publishers should be able to express their views not just through their editorial pages but through their efforts and work in the community," he contends. In most places in America, it is not seen as "improper behavior" for a publisher to lead a fund-raising drive for a new hospital, or similar projects, he adds.

Cowles does draw the line at newspaper proprietors and publishers running for partisan political office "because that makes life more difficult for their reporters and editors." But he sees nothing wrong in a publisher running for nonpartisan office, such as the school, park, or library board. Nor does he see any reason for publishers to refrain from making personal financial contributions to political campaigns. But "generally, high-profile, politically partisan activities should be avoided in the city where you publish your paper," he concludes.[50]

Cowles is right that the trend for top news brass to avoid real or even apparent conflicts of interest is relatively new. There has been until recent years a strong tradition of political activism among newspaper publishers and some editors. Cowles was in that fading tradition. What seems to be happening today is that editors and news executives, except in a few small towns, are staying out of politics and avoiding any outside activity that would make it seem that they favored some group or cause over some other. Owners, publishers, and executives responsible for the business side of the news media, regardless of size, feel less restricted in their outside activities. Most do not get as involved as Cowles did in Minneapolis, but many feel they have to pitch in to do their share as heads of major businesses in their communities.

Perhaps the modern concern about the extrajournalistic projects of news media owners and managers has something to do with the decline since World War II in competitive newspaper markets and in locally controlled, family-owned news organizations. The big, less personal corporations that own most of our news media today seem more threatening, less susceptible to local influence, less sensitive to local needs. And in an earlier time community and political activism was more acceptable because there was always a competing voice offering an alternative view.

Donald Graham, who sits in the publisher's chair at the *Washington Post* that was occupied before him by his grandfather, his father, and his mother, maintains that the "whole conception of what a publisher should do has changed." He believes the basic responsibility of a newspaper owner "is reporting the news rather than making it." While he hesitates to condemn what other newspapers do, because "the health of a given community is of vital importance to the newspaper," Graham says that like his mother, Katharine Graham, now chief executive of the Washington Post Company, he chooses to do his job as a newspaper person, staying out of politics "or any action that could be said to be political."[51]

Julius Duscha, director of the Washington Journalism Center, covered politics for the *Post* when Donald Graham's father, Philip Graham, was publisher and later when Katharine Graham held that position. Although he was aware of Phil Graham's activities as a political ally of Lyndon Johnson, Duscha believes it did not affect his reporting of such presidential candidates as John F. Kennedy. "It's probably harder for reporters to cover things when their owners or publishers are involved, but it's still possible to do a fair job," Duscha says. He believes a newspaper publisher should be "on the scene and involved in his town, not antiseptic, but willing to accept the presidency of the chamber of commerce one year, and be on the redevelopment committee, the new city committee, or whatever."[52]

Charles Seib, retired ombudsman of the *Washington Post* and former managing editor of the old *Washington Star,* sees considerable pressure on publishers – especially in smaller communities – to be active. Although it might be all right for publishers in these smaller communities "to get involved in some outside activities," Seib concedes, "editors and reporters must avoid any significant outside involvements."[53]

That distinction between publishers, who reign over the newspaper as an important business in the community, and the editors and reporters, who do the daily work of reporting and commenting on the news, is commonly made by those concerned about conflicts of interest. Gannett's Currie believes reporters and editors should avoid even registering to vote as Democrats or Republicans, but "publishers have to represent the newspaper in the community," even if that sometimes puts the newsroom in an awkward position.[54]

Richard Smyser, who edits a small newspaper in a small community (the 11,800-circulation Oak Ridge, Tennessee, *Oak Ridger*) seems to agree with both Seib and Currie. "Each city, each community needs within it certain role players," he has written:

> There must be doctors. There must be lawyers, unfortunately. A minister or two is helpful. . . . Of course, we need a plumber. And each city needs at least one editor. One editor who is an editor and nothing else. . . . Having chosen the role of editor, he doesn't muck up that role – confuse it, complicate it, contradict it, and most of all, take time away from it – by being an industrial promoter, a school

board member, a United Way campaign chairman or even publicity advisor to the local little theatre.[55]

A newspaper that still encourages nonpolitical community involvement, even for reporters and editors, is the Sharon, Pennsylvania, *Herald*. "We're still a part of the community and have community responsibilities," observes *Herald* editor James Dunlap. "You cannot be part of your community and know what's going on in your town unless you are involved. You learn about things a reporter or editor would have no way of knowing without that contact with the power faction in the community." Dunlap notes that his publisher belongs to the country club, one news executive is on the board of the chamber of commerce, another is on the board of United Way, and still another is on the local hospital board. Dunlap is active in Rotary and the Boy Scouts; other members of the staff are involved in other service organizations. "These are basically noncontroversial organizations that rarely make the news in any significant way," Dunlap maintains, "but if there was a scandal or something in United Way, we'd report it."[56]

Community involvement by newspaper executives can be carried too far, of course. The monopoly paper in Flint, Michigan, the Newhouse-owned *Flint Journal*, was headed in 1985 by a publisher and editor who sat on the boards of seventeen community and business booster organizations. The publisher, Robert D. Swartz, had chaired the Flint Chamber of Commerce, and was publicity chairman of the fund-raising campaign for AutoWorld, a theme park built in Flint. The editor, Alfred L. Peloquin, founded something called the Alliance for a Greater Flint and was marketing chairman of the Flint Convention and Visitors Bureau. In addition, the metro editor, Allan Wilhelm, was a member of the Mayor's Committee to Improve Flint's Image.

This superinvolvement by *Journal* brass seems to have been calculated. Although Flint was in deep economic trouble – its 26 percent unemployment rate was the highest in the nation in 1983 – the paper's executives downplayed such bad news as the closing of a General Motors plant and pursued a policy of cheerleading. "The *Journal* is in bed with the very institutions it should be covering," said Al MacLeese, a feature writer on that paper for seventeen years who was looking for another job. "The paper has begun to resemble a community newsletter."[57]

A kind of community involvement that was applauded by many in journalism resulted in a Pulitzer Prize in editorial writing for the *Miami Herald*. The *Herald* editorialized strenuously against a Reagan administration policy of detaining illegal aliens indefinitely, a policy that caused hundreds of Haitians in south Florida to be locked up in a harsh detention center in Miami. But the paper went beyond editorializing. Jim Hampton, editorial page editor, and Howard Kleinberg, another *Herald* editor, joined other Miami leaders on an ad hoc committee organized to fight the detention policy. "We weren't getting anywhere with our editorials, and they weren't getting anywhere with their efforts," Hampton said in justifying the involvement. The consolidation must have worked because the committee eventually succeeded in getting a federal judge to overturn the detention policy and release the Haitians. The *Herald* did not hide the paper's participation with the committee in its submission of editorials to the Pulitzer board. In fact, the submission emphasized what the *Herald* had done to get the Haitians freed, stating that members of its editorial board not only visited the detention center, "but met with federal officials and enlisted as many local persons as possible in pushing the paper's protest against the detention policy and conditions in the center." Some journalists felt that the *Herald* went too far in participating in the news it was covering, but a majority of editors on the Pulitzer jury and board were impressed that the paper's editorials had achieved a concrete result.[58]

Corporate and Conglomerate Conflicts. The growth of corporate and conglomerate control of news organizations raises conflicts of interest that some critics see as destructive of the entire information system of the country. Ben Bagdikian in his 1983 book *The Media Monopoly* claimed that fifty corporations controlled most American media—newspapers, magazines, radio, television, books, and movies. And he predicted that the number of controlling corporations would continue to decrease. "Conflicts of interest between the public's need for information and corporate desires for 'positive' information have vastly increased," Bagdikian wrote. Many directors of media corporations also serve as directors of nonmedia corporations. Bagdikian noted, for example, that "a dozen of the country's largest multinational banks hold significant voting shares in many of the fifty largest media companies, control their debts, or exchange directors with them."[59]

When media companies become conglomerates by investing in firms outside the information business, or when nonmedia companies buy and own news organizations, serious conflicts of interest arise when those news staffs have to cover the other interests of their owners. The Tribune Company buying the Chicago Cubs is a case in point. That company also owns the *Chicago Tribune* and WGN-TV and WGN-AM in Chicago, as well as five other daily newspapers and eight other broadcast stations around the country.

James D. Squires, who became editor of the *Chicago Tribune* the same day the parent company bought the Cubs, saw immediately the problem the paper would have convincing the public that the Cubs would not be favored in *Tribune* coverage. The first thing Squires did was to hire Jerome Holtzman from the rival *Sun-Times,* "a baseball writer who had the history of being the most independent, uncompromising, ethical reporter in sports. His word and his background were just impeccable," Squires maintains.[60]

But covering the ball team was only part of the problem. The paper also had to cover the controversy that arose when the Tribune Company sought a city permit to put lights in Wrigley Field, where the Cubs play. Some people who live around the stadium fought the move but the major problem for the newspaper was the opposition that came from city and state politicians who apparently saw an opportunity to buy some editorial good will from the *Tribune.*

"When the corporation's lawyers go to Springfield to try to get lights in their ballpark," Squires says, "all the politicians down there say, 'Well, can I get the *Tribune*'s endorsement?'" The editor claims that his publisher, Stanton R. Cook, "does not monkey around with the editorial end of the newspaper. And my deal is that if you guys are going to play with baseball teams, television stations, and movie stars, you can't have a damned thing to do with the editorial page. And they observe that." But Squires fears that a lot of people outside the company do not believe that the *Tribune*'s journalists can be that independent from the company's other interests.

"If corporate managers understood what makes a newspaper successful with readers, they wouldn't buy baseball teams or anything else in the same city as the newspaper," Squires insists. "But people who make these decisions are not editors. If we're going to act like conglomerates, we're going to be perceived as conglomerates and treated by courts and legislatures as conglomerates indistinguishable from others."[61]

That same warning was voiced by the late National News Council after it looked into the propriety of several news organizations in Florida kicking in $180,000 to fight legalization of casino gambling in Miami Beach and other nearby resorts. A related conflict of interest question was raised by the leadership of the anticasino forces by the governor of the state, Reubin Askew, who personally solicited the contributions from many of the media companies. Florida voters eventually rejected legal casinos in 1978 by a margin of 72 to 28 percent.

Almost every major media company in the state responded favorably to the governor's plea to help him stop what he saw as a disaster for Florida. He raised a total of $1.7 million. Hotel owners in the Miami Beach area, who were pushing for legal casinos, raised $600,000 to underwrite the petition drive that resulted in 420,000 signatures and put the issue on the ballot, and they ended up contributing almost 90 percent of the $2.9 million collected by the procasino side. The casino backers also hired Sanford Weiner of San Francisco, who organized the successful campaign that brought legal casinos to Atlantic City, New Jersey.

Among the media company contributors to the anticasino campaign were the *Miami Herald,* principal newspaper of the Knight-Ridder group, and three other Knight-Ridder dailies in Florida; Cox Newspapers, publishers of the *Miami News* and *Palm Beach Post-Times;* the *St. Petersburg Times;* Wometco Enterprises, parent company of WTVJ in Miami; the *Orlando Sentinel* and the *Fort Lauderdale News,* owned by the Tribune Company; the *Tampa Tribune;* and the *Florida Times-Union* of Jacksonville. Two Knight-Ridder executives gave almost $20,000 in personal funds. (Notably missing from the list of contributors was the New York Times Company, which then owned eight dailies and one weekly in Florida, and Gannett, which had four dailies and two weeklies in the state.) The only media company that gave money to the casino side was the Miami Beach *Sun Reporter,* which contributed $5,000 to underwrite a feasibility study.

The National News Council investigated the *Miami Herald's* involvement and coverage of the casino fight after receiving a complaint from Jim Bishop, author and syndicated columnist. Apparently unconcerned about his own conflict of interest, Bishop chaired the statewide steering committee of "Let's Help Florida," the group that put the issue on the ballot through petition, and fought for legalizing casinos along Florida's so-called Gold Coast. Bishop, whose column appeared in the *Herald,* among other newspapers, challenged the news council to determine if financial contributions from the *Miami Herald* and solicitation of other contributions from other publishers by its president, Alvah H. Chapman, did not constitute, when linked to its hostile editorial stance, "an unprecedented influence of the media in a people's referendum campaign." Bishop also raised questions about the objectivity of the news coverage by media whose corporate owners had put money in the campaign.[62]

The council found no evidence of unfairness in the way the *Miami Herald* reported the referendum battle. In fact, the council concluded that "the Herald acquitted itself with distinction." Although the financial contributions by Chapman put the reporters and editors assigned to this story in an uncomfortable spot, "they decided, in the best tradition of journalism, that the only response they could in conscience make was to strive even harder than they normally did to be fair," the council said. "They succeeded admirably in that effort." The council did not examine coverage of the issue in other Florida media.

On the appropriateness of the media company contributions, the news council did not specifically condemn what the Florida media executives had done, but it warned other news organizations that the Florida example may not be a good one to follow. Media executives who "decide that the business interests" of their organizations require similar financial contributions in public policy issues up for decision by voters face three serious risks, the council concluded:

1. "First, they run the risk of undermining public confidence in the fairness of their news columns." It noted that a *Herald* poll during the campaign showed that a majority both of those favoring casinos and those opposed believed that newspapers contributing financially to the referendum could not be fair in their news columns. Among the anticasino respondents, 59 percent said financially contributing papers could not be fair, as against 25 percent who felt they could be fair, and 16 percent who said they did not know. In the procasino group, 58 percent said they thought such papers could not be fair, 33 percent thought they could, and 9 percent were on the fence. (Of the 701 persons in the sample, roughly two-thirds were anticasino.)

2. A second danger lies in the possible "blurring [of] the line of separation that should properly exist between the state and the media." Here the council referred to Chapman's conduct "as chief fund raiser for the governor . . . in a campaign that becomes the overriding preoccupation of both men" and in soliciting funds from bankers and other business leaders outside the media. Such behavior could raise questions in readers' minds "about how detached the press can be in covering news or making editorial judgments affecting the business community."

3. Another risk is created by the justification that proprietors often give when they get involved financially in extrajournalistic activities – the argument that they do it for the financial health of their own news organizations. "They may find themselves reinforcing the argument of those who contend that the assertiveness of the trend toward conglomerate ownership has made newspapers and other media corporations just another form of big business, indistinguishable from other large corporations in their right to claim special protection under the Constitution."

In one of two dissenting opinions from the council majority, council member William A. Rusher, publisher of *National Review,* disagreed that journalists face risks "if they participate, as citizens or civic-minded corporations, in forms of political activity that would be regarded as downright praiseworthy if engaged in by a non-journalist." Rusher said "the American people fortunately do not share the perception of journalists as priests." He argued that each journalist should be allowed to "be a fully rounded human being: faithful to his God if he has one, and loyal to whatever political creed attracts him. And if he cares enough to contribute financially to some cause he deeply believes in, most people won't think less of him for it, but more."

The news council staff's report on the Florida case included some statements from the principals. One of these was Eugene C. Patterson, then president of the *St. Petersburg Times,* which made a $25,000 contribution to the anticasino drive. "This was our first venture in contributing financially to support our editorial view on a public vote and I would expect it to be our last, since a question that would change the fundamental nature of a society rarely presents itself," Patterson observed. He saw the casino fight as one such question. "I would hate to think newspapers are neutered as citizens by a pacifist mentality when rape is threatened . . . ," Patterson added. "The magnitude of the gamblers' financing convinced me this was no time to be spooked by the hobgoblins of little minds. Advertisement of our own virginity scarcely responded to the threat. Wearing a chastity belt presupposes we'll resist the lock pickers."

The executive who made the decision not to put any *New York Times* money into the anticasino pot, John R. Harrison, said he got two personal pleas to do so from Governor Askew. Harrison, who as vice-president of the New York Times Corporation was in charge of its Florida papers, feared that financial involvement would compromise reader confidence.

Allen H. Neuharth, chief executive of the Gannett chain, the other major media company that did not contribute money to the anticasino fight, said the decision was made by the local managers of the Gannett papers in Florida, but he applauded it. "The whole question of press credibility is such a sticky one," Neuharth told council investigators, "that those of us who own media and identify ourselves financially with one side of a controversial issue, no matter how objective our reporting is, will be suspect."

Procasino forces got the issue on the Florida ballot again in 1986, and voters rejected it again by an overwhelming margin. Although most of the state's newspapers editorialized against legalizing casino gambling in this second referendum, none contributed money as most had done in 1978. Chapman and thirteen other Knight-Ridder executives made individual contributions totalling $53,000 to fight the casino invasion.[63]

AVOID OR DISCLOSE CONFLICTS

The phrase "conflict of interest" does not appear in the early codes of ethics adopted by the ASNE, various state press associations, and individual newspapers in the period just before and during the 1920s. Today it is a standard item in such codes. Some of the early codes – particularly that of the Kansas Editorial Association, adopted in 1910 and apparently the first such code in this country—expressed concern about undue influence on the press by outsiders who owned newspaper stock or who made loans to publishing companies, and a few of the early ethical statements warned against news people holding office or accepting side jobs that might affect the news.[64] But today's codes are much more explicit on this issue, reflecting the growing and general apprehension throughout American society about conflicts of interest in business, government, education, science, and virtually all aspects of modern life.

The journalism codes adopted by national organizations deal with the conflict problem in their typically more general language. The 1975 Statement of Principles of the ASNE, for example, states: "Journalists must avoid impropriety and the appearance of impropriety as well as any conflict of interest or the appearance of conflict. They should neither accept anything nor pursue any activity that might compromise or seem to compromise their integrity." Equally brief is the statement in the RTNDA Code of Broadcast Ethics: "Broadcast journalists shall govern their personal lives and such nonprofessional associations as may impinge on their professional activities in a manner that will protect them from conflict of interest, real or apparent."

A bit more explicit is the reference in the Code of Ethics of SPJ-SDX:

> ETHICS: Journalists must be free of obligation to any interest other than the public's right to know the truth. . . . Secondary employment, political involvement, holding public office, and service in community organizations should be avoided if it compromises the integrity of journalists and their employers. Journalists and their employers should conduct their personal lives in a manner which protects them from conflict of interest, real or apparent. Their responsibilities to the public are paramount. That is the nature of their profession.

The APME Code of Ethics declares:

> The newspaper and its staff should be free of obligations to news sources and special interests. Even the appearance of obligation or conflict of interest should be avoided. . . .
>
> Involvement in such things as politics, community affairs, demonstrations and social causes that could cause a conflict of interest, or the appearance of such conflict, should be avoided.
>
> Outside employment by news sources is an obvious conflict of interest, and employment by potential news sources also should be avoided.
>
> Financial investments by staff members or other outside busi-

ness interests that could conflict with the newspaper's ability to report the news or that would create the impression of conflict should be avoided.

Stories should not be written or edited primarily for the purpose of winning awards and prizes. Blatantly commercial journalism contests, or others that reflect unfavorably on the newspaper or the profession, should be avoided.

The Ethical Guidelines of the budding APSE organization deal with some of the special conflicts in sports journalism:

II. Participation. Writers should avoid involvement in outside activities that would create a conflict of interest or give the impression of one. . . .

Some papers and some sports editors have been prime movers in lining up potential franchises in cities. Our job is reporting developments, not serving on committees or getting involved in bringing in franchises or building stadiums or arenas.

It is in the best interest of journalism that there come an end to writers serving as official scorers. . . . It is not the fee attached to scoring which is at issue; it is the involvement of the reporter in an official role. . . . If the scoring function does not affect a journalist's ethical standards, it most certainly does create a question about his credibility as an independent sports analyst. . . .

Writers should not write for game programs or other league or team publications produced by teams or leagues the writers are responsible for covering.

Specifically, writers should not take pay from the sport they cover. . . .

VIII. Outside employment. In an era where various types of "moonlighting" have become prevalent, . . . frequently . . . staffers are offered outside employment during off-duty hours. Wherever such outside jobs affect anything the newspaper is covering, the sports editor should insist that his staffers not accept such positions. We face the age-old problem that financial involvement cannot help but affect news treatment and even the seemingly innocuous role of doing statistics for a baseball team carries with it the seed of inside-the-office pressure for favored treatment.

In addition to violating *Wall Street Journal* ethics policies, Winans, the fired reporter whose travesty was described earlier in this chapter, was way out of line with the code of ethics of the Society of American Business and Economic writers. That code holds, among other things, that a business writer should:

3. Avoid active trading and other short-term profit-seeking opportunities. Active participation in the markets which such activities

require is not compatible with the role of the business and financial journalist as disinterested trustee of the public interest.

4. Not take advantage in his personal investing of any inside information and be sure any relevant information he or she may have is widely disseminated before he buys or sells.

5. Make every effort to insure the confidentiality of information held for publication to keep such information from finding its way to those who might use it for gain before it becomes available to the public.

Conflicts of interest guidelines that have been adopted by some news media chains, by the CBS, ABC, and NBC broadcast networks, and by individual newspapers are more detailed and specific than those described above. Some of the larger news media companies—such as CBS, Gannett, and Knight-Ridder—require their executives to sign what amounts to pledges of conformance with company policies on avoiding conflicts of interest. But as this chapter has tried to make clear, there is still troubling disagreement among journalists as to what constitutes conflicts of interest and who is expected to avoid them.

It can easily be argued that conflicts of interest are unavoidable in modern society and that journalists, of all people, need to be part of—not aloof from—the main currents of life. And if that contention is reasonable, perhaps journalists need to insist not so much on avoiding many activities now regarded as conflicts of interest but on candidly disclosing their possible conflicts to the public.

"It may be less important to forbid an outside activity than to be sure it is fully publicized if it does occur," Charles W. Bailey concluded after a study of conflicts of interest for the now defunct National News Council. "Journalists prescribe full disclosure as a cure for many problems they see in political, governmental and business worlds; there is no good reason why it shouldn't be applied with equal enthusiasm to the news business."[65]

The concern about avoiding conflicts of interest in journalism has spurred some in the field to shun not just leadership roles in their communities but any participation at all. This sometimes leads to fortress newsrooms run by journalists woefully out of touch with what's really going on in the world outside. This hardly seems an appropriate posture for people we depend on to make sense out of the complexities of today's news.

4 The Seducers: Freebies, Junkets, and Perks

"So this is what they mean by a free press."

What if you are the chief editor of a metropolitan newspaper in mid-America and you get an anonymous letter, apparently from a Jeep dealer in town, charging that your popular outdoor editor has free use of an International Harvester Scout? The letter, which seems authentic, also charges that your editor mentions Scouts but never other brands of four-wheel-drive vehicles in his writings. You confront your outdoor editor and he admits that for almost a year he has been using a $10,000 Scout free of charge. Although accepting such a "gift" is prohibited in your paper's code of ethics, the outdoor editor, who to your knowledge has no blemish on his sixteen-year record with the paper, argues that he has done nothing wrong and that use of the free vehicle has not influenced what he has written. What do you do? Do you take him at his word and give him another chance? Do you throw him out of your office?

In Kansas City, Missouri, where this happened, Michael J. Davies, who was editor of the *Star* and *Times* newspapers, gave the outdoor editor another chance, but then fired him about a week later. Davies explains that he first decided to let the outdoor editor off with a stern warning, despite advice from supervising editors that the man should be dismissed, because he was new in the top editor's job at the *Star* and *Times* and uncertain about how strongly his predecessors had enforced the organization's ethics code. (Davies had only recently left the managing editorship of the Louisville, Kentucky, *Courier-Journal* to join the *Star* and *Times*.) So after warning the outdoor editor that he "was on the thinnest of thin ice," Davies posted notes on newsroom bulletin boards declaring "amnesty week" for all to come forward and be forgiven for past violations of the ethics code so that a fresh start could be made on Monday. Davies then discovered that the outdoor editor not only had held back part of the truth about the four-wheel-drive gift; he also failed to come clean about "a couple of other goodies." Davies fired the offending editor on the spot and assigned two reporters to look into the ethics of outdoor writers across the country.[1] The dismissed editor sued the newspaper company for $10 million, a suit still pending as this is written.

The two articles the *Star* and *Times* published on outdoor writers painted an ethically ugly picture. Reporters Rick Alm and Bill Norton interviewed about two dozen outdoor writers and editors, some other journalists, and some manufacturers of outdoor equipment. They found: widespread acceptance by outdoor writers of manufacturers' discounts of up to 50 percent; some acceptance of free goods (one fishing equipment company was giving away about $35,000 a year in free equipment to outdoor writers); and some acceptance by outdoor writers of boats and recreational vehicles on long-term loans from the manufacturers. Some outdoor writers were doing publicity for the same hunting lodges and fishing clubs they covered in their news columns. The ethics code of the Outdoor Writers Association of America (OWAA), which has manufacturers as "supporting members," states that loans, gifts, and discounts are "commonly accepted practices" in the trade but cautions that writers should not accept such favors for anything other than journalistic pursuits. The code also advises against accepting free room and board unless a salable story can be produced.

Alm and Norton reported that at least three newspapers had bought big equipment for their outdoor writers: the *St. Louis Post-Dispatch* provided its writer with a camper-truck and a fishing boat with trailer and motor; the *St. Louis Globe-Democrat* furnished a bass boat, motor, and trailer; the *Denver Post* provided each of its outdoor writers with a four-wheel-drive vehicle. Norton reported that the outdoor editor whom Davies fired for accepting a free four-wheel-drive vehicle had tried to get the *Star* and *Times* to buy him such a vehicle for his work but had been turned down. So he struck a deal with a friend at a local International Harvester factory outlet to get himself a free Scout, but insisted that he made no promise of free publicity. The Norton article revealed that the outdoor editor had an annual travel budget from the newspaper organization of $12,000, about $1,200 of which was set aside for equipment. The dismissed outdoor editor is quoted as saying that since his budget did not provide for major expenses, he had to "beg people" because he could not personally afford a boat, a motor, a trailer, or a vehicle. Alm in his article said manufacturers freely admitted that they gave discounts, favors, and freebies to outdoor writers in return for favorable publicity.[2]

The provision in the *Star* and *Times* ethics code that cost the outdoor editor his job states that "gifts of merchandise which might be construed as a reward for past coverage or an inducement to future coverage . . . are to be rejected." Virtually all news media ethics codes have similar provisions designed to combat the attempts by outside interests to buy favorable publicity through favors to journalists. These favors come in all sorts of packages—from free lunches to fur coats, from bottles of liquor at Christmas to free trips to Tahiti. Regardless of the value of the gifts, it is the motives of the givers that bother thoughtful journalists.

FREEBIES

The freebie—something given without charge or cost—was at one time commonly accepted in the newsrooms of America. Many journalists accepted Christmas presents from the people they covered. Taking free tickets to the theater, the circus, or the baseball game was a common occurrence. Traveling free of charge on the train or airplane with the political candidate or sports team you were covering was encouraged. Letting news sources pick up the tab for your drinks or meals was often done. Freebies went with the job, perquisites of a trade notorious for underpaying its apprentices. There was "a tradition in journalism of take what you could get," says Richard B. Tuttle, publisher and editor of the Elmira, New York, *Star-Gazette*.[3]

Freebies are still being accepted by journalists today, and the outside interests are still working hard to buy their way into the news columns with favors, but the practice is widely condemned in the field and may disappear entirely. As this chapter hopes to show, the freebie problem is greater on the smaller newspapers and broadcast stations and in some specialized areas of journalism, such as outdoor writing, travel, real estate, food, and sports.

Most of the written codes of ethics in journalism treat freebies as conflicts of interest. Freebies often are symptoms of conflict of interest and they can tempt a journalist into a conflict, but it's important to understand that conflicts of interest can exist without freebies and freebies don't always lead to conflicts of interest. For example, a reporter can usually accept a minor gift or favor from a news source without that leading to a conflict, say in the form of a story favoring that source. And when a journalist seeks public office, as some have done, unfortunately, that's a conflict of interest whether freebies were part of the picture or not.

Goodbye, Free Lunch. Efforts by public officials, politicians, and other VIPs to influence or at least gain favor with journalists through the "gifts" of free food and drink continue to be a problem.

Some news sources insist on picking up the tab whenever they have lunch or drinks with reporters; some like to wine and dine journalists at parties. They may not expect anything in return for such favors, but again they may. Most journalists these days insist on at least paying for their own meals and drinks, and some who work for big media often buy meals and drinks for their news sources.

David Shaw, media reporter-critic for the *Los Angeles Times,* started paying for lunches with news sources when he got his first full-time newspaper job on a small California daily in 1963 and was making $79.21 a week. "Other reporters couldn't believe I was doing it," Shaw recalls. "No one on my paper did that then." Shaw believes "the easiest way is to draw the line and take nothing from anybody, and as a result my expense accounts are enormous."[4]

Jack Nelson, chief of the *Los Angeles Times* Washington bureau, says it is common for his reporters to take their news sources to lunch. His bureau also regularly invites government officials and other news makers in for on-the-record, taped breakfast discussions that result in news stories.[5]

A reporter for the less affluent *San Francisco Examiner,* Lynn Ludlow, says he would rather pay $10 not to have meals with 90 percent of the people his job forces him to have meals with. "If somebody insists on picking up the tab, I'm not going to make a big production out of it," Ludlow adds. "My main goal is not to be pure ethically; my main goal is to get the news. If it calls for having dinner with somebody and letting him pick up the tab, fine."[6]

A New York City journalist recently went for five days with no other sustenance except press freebies. "Malnutrition was no problem," wrote Rhoda Koenig, literary editor of *New York* magazine. Her article, entitled "Diary of a Freeloader," describes a round of press lunches, cocktail parties, and suppers paid for by such would-be press seducers as American Express, Merrill Lynch, the Gucci Galleria, Columbia Pictures, the French Embassy, the German Information Center, Milton Bradley games,

Ketchum Communications advertising and public relations, Little Brown publishers, and *People* magazine. "On any weekday in New York City, uncountable numbers of journalists are gobbling and quaffing food and drink they have not paid for," Koenig reported. "Few journalists will admit to being influenced in what they write by the existence or quality of refreshments, yet the public relations people continue to provide so much food that a busy (or shameless) journalist never has to pay for his own meals."[7]

James Lowman, editorial page editor of the Elmira, New York, *Star-Gazette*, who spent four years as a one-person news bureau in two small communities near Elmira, believes it is permissible to accept "lunches, Cokes, beers and so on from sources" in rural settings, where "a different set of ethics" is at work. "You have to remember that the person offering the treat has a set of ethics, too," Lowman said. "The moment you turn him down, you are questioning his own ethics. It hurts people for the reporter to turn the treat down. People are grossly offended by that in the small community."[8]

George E. Osgood, Jr., who covered Wellsboro, Pennsylvania, for the Elmira paper, has written that the "metropolitan dog-eat-dog . . . philosophy doesn't hold water in most rural communities." People in rural communities "know and trust each other, for the most part," Osgood said, "and neighborliness gets more than just lip service." He concedes that a reporter accepting a loaf of homemade bread from some public official's wife can be used by critics, "but there is likely to be a greater clamor . . . if such an offer is refused by a reporter too 'big-headed' to accept simple friendship and too set in his city ways to understand rural hospitality."[9]

Lowman and Osgood make sense when they argue that what might be seen as a freebie in an urban journalism setting is often a friendly gesture in a small town. But rural reporters share with their urban colleagues the risk of being pulled across that thin line between a friendly, neighborly gesture and an attempt to influence news policy through gifts of food and drink. You have to be able to get inside the heads of the givers and receivers to understand whether that line has been crossed. Some observers thought it had been crossed when President Reagan in his first year in office invited the some seventy reporters, TV producers, and photographers who covered him during his vacation on his Santa Barbara, California, ranch to come with their families to a little "company picnic." As the president and his wife, Nancy, circulated through the crowd, making small talk (everything they said, by prearrangement, was off the record) and kissing cheeks of the journalists' children, the members of the prestigious White House press corps sipped drinks and munched from buffet tables "creaking under piles of smoked salmon, tenderloin fillets wrapped in bacon, escargots baked in French dough, oysters on the half shell, a glorious assortment of cheeses, fresh fruit and a jelly-bean cake. Chefs stood ready to cook scampi au Pernod and fettucini Alfredo to order."[10]

President Reagan continued such picnics for news people and their families into his second term in the White House, although the food got less continental and more Western barbecue. The picnics were not held on his ranch but on the nearby estates of friends, and they were paid for by Republican rather than White House funds. The President and Mrs. Reagan usually attracted a swarm of correspondents as they moved through the picnic crowd. Even the most aggressive members of the White House press corps purred at the opportunity to have their pictures taken with the Reagans, a service provided by White House photographers who distributed souvenir prints later. The president also invited the press in for Christmas parties and some small cocktail parties from time to time, all such socials being off the record, of course. In addition, the guest lists for White House parties during Reagan's reign always seemed to contain the names of a couple of journalists. The journalists who attended these various affairs apparently viewed them less as freebies than as one more rare opportunity to get a closer look at a president who was very closely guarded by the Secret Service after the 1981 assassination attempt and who kept the press at a distance throughout his tenure.

Merry Christmas! The gift givers can be a problem for journalists at any time of the year but Christmas really brings out their effusiveness. Here again, the Christmas presents to newsrooms and news people have decreased both in number and lavishness over the past two or three decades, but they still exist. Newspaper newsrooms of the 1950s often looked like the gift-wrapping sections of department stores as loot from all manner of givers would roll in. Some, like baskets of apples from a well-known Virginia senator, would be for everybody; others would be for specific writers or editors. Some of the gifts were sent to the journalist's home, or more often, to the bureaus and press rooms away from the main office. Tom Hritz of the *Pittsburgh Post-Gazette* tells how that worked at the press room of the City-County Building in Pittsburgh: "It would start with a trickle at the beginning of December. By Christmas week, the grungy little newsroom . . . was awash with the gratitude of the bench and bar: Scotch, bourbon, rum, rotgut—even champagne." The reporters would try to live by "The Rule" that you could accept it if you could eat or drink it on the premises, right then and there, Hritz wrote in his column.

But so much liquor would come in that, try as they might, they could not keep up with "The Rule." They would have to stuff gallons of gratitude and appreciation into shopping bags and take them home.[11]

Most public relations people have stopped sending gifts to newsrooms. Years of having them returned by the newspapers have discouraged the practice. Benjamin C. Bradlee, executive editor of the *Washington Post,* says that very few Christmas gifts are sent to the paper today and when they are, "they are turned away at the elevator and sent to Walter Reed Hospital and charity."[12] At the smaller-community level, James A. Dunlap, editor of the Sharon, Pennsylvania, *Herald,* remembers how the "sports editor's desk would be piled high with liquor at Christmas time, but no more." Dunlap believes that his policy against accepting such freebies has stopped the flow of gifts that used to be common in his newsroom.[13]

Super Sports. The professional sports organizations that come out on top in their sport each year usually have rings or some other mementos made for the players. They also offer them to the sports reporters who cover that team, or they may give the reporters a less expensive gift. For example, when the Pittsburgh Steelers won the 1979 and 1980 Super Bowls, the players got rings cast especially for the occasion. "But when the Steelers came to the reporters and asked us if we wanted rings, we said no," Rick Starr, sports editor of the New Kensington, Pennsylvania, *Valley News Dispatch,* recalls. "But they came up with alternative gifts – cuff links one time and a watch or something the second time – all engraved, of course." Starr accepted these alternative gifts, but he says now that he wishes he had not and he will not accept any more such gifts, even if his fellow reporters do.[14]

The public relations arms of the leagues and associations that run professional sports and put on the extravaganzas that decide the winners each year also try to take good care of the reporters. At the World Series, the Super Bowl, and other season-ending championship games, the leagues provide souvenir gifts, lots of free meals and drinks, elaborate press rooms, hospitality suites, and free video games, in addition to news releases and staged news conferences and interviews.

Ira Miller of the *San Francisco Chronicle* and Bill Lyon of the *Philadelphia Inquirer,* who have covered some Super Bowls and other championship finals, believe the gifts and freebies have decreased over the years. At the Super Bowl, for example, "all you get is coffee and a Danish" at the press room each morning, Lyon notes. "And they give you pens, brief cases and little plastic things." He says there's a free bar in the press room, but he doesn't drink.[15] Miller agrees that the gifts are much less lavish than they used to be. He sees the juice and coffee he takes at the press room as a real service because the buses for the training camps of the two teams involved leave at 7 A.M. or so, before the hotel coffee shops are open. As for the free bar in the press room, Miller says "the writers don't seem to hang out there a lot."[16]

Whether the spending on amenities for the press is lavish may depend on the eyes of the beholder. For example, the National Football League spent $4 million on entertainment during the 1982 Super Bowl in Detroit, much of it to keep the press happy. John Jacobs, a cityside reporter for the *San Francisco Examiner* who covered the press covering that Super Bowl, wrote that in addition to free brunches, lunches, and dinners, the media representatives were given:

> complete access to free drinks on what seemed like a 24-hour-a-day basis (next door to the press office), free use of a car, a free Louis Weitz carrying case with Super Bowl XVI shoulder patch, a free green Super Bowl XVI clipboard with a football field drawn in white (alas, no chalk), a free reporter's notebook encased in a blue plastic wraparound Super Bowl XVI cover, a free Super Bowl XVI canvas tote bag, and, oh yes, on game day, a free box lunch of roast beef on roll, fruit juice, sliced vegetables, fudge brownie and other assorted goodies.[17]

At the 1984 Super Bowl in Tampa, the press was "wined, dined and entertained, in the open and almost brazenly," said Tom Goldstein, who observed the week of press festivities prior to the game for his book *The News at Any Cost*. About 2,500 working and nonworking journalists and some of their spouses, children, and friends got press credentials for that event, Goldstein reported, but "it would be difficult to determine how many of these actually covered the game." In addition to the parties, sponsored by the NFL, Budweiser, and others, "there were free passes to Tampa Bay Downs, St. Petersburg Derby Lane and Tampa Jai Alai," Goldstein wrote. "The St. Petersburg Beach Area Chamber of Commerce offered the visiting press a cruise, entertainment, and meals. Walt Disney World, which often invites reporters as nonpaying guests, provided bus transportation and tickets to its theme parks seventy miles away."[18]

Because of such reports of lavish entertaining of the press covering sports extravaganzas, the APME Professional Standards Committee has from time to time monitored those events. That's what it did at the 1980 Winter Olympics in Lake Placid, New York. It should have been called the "Freebie Olympics," concluded the APME report by Richard Benedetto of Gannett News Service. "Any enterprising journalist armed with shopping bags and a cast-iron stomach could have carted home scores of free gifts every day and drunk more free booze every night than any human could handle, with a gratis meal now and then thrown in for good measure," Benedetto wrote. The gifts he reported did not sound elaborate, but they were numerous. Cocktail parties and dinners for the reporters were held by Eastman Kodak, Xerox, Canon Camera, *Ski Magazine,* Finlandia Vodka, Rossignol Skis, the state of New York, K2 and Elan skis, the Austrian National Board of Trade, Adidas sports equipment, and Mr. and Mrs. Cornelius Vanderbilt Whitney.[19]

The Los Angeles Summer Olympics of 1984 "may be remembered by the press as one of the biggest freebie opportunities in sports history," M. L. Stein wrote in *Editor and Publisher* magazine. Among the freebies given to all accredited journalists covering that event: an official duffel bag, pocket calculator, sun visor, Olympic medallion, Sanyo pocket radio, film processing from Fuji, camera repairs and loans from Canon, accessory vests from both firms, Olympic books, and a commemorative Coca-Cola bottle. "In addition, reporters were invited to numerous parties, including one by the LAOOC (Los Angeles Olympic Organization Committee) that featured free liquor, food and five live orchestras," Stein reported.[20]

Most members of the Associated Press Sports Editors Association do not object to sports staffers accepting souvenirs handed out at major sporting events. That was indicated in a 1985 poll by APSE–whose members come mostly from the country's larger newspapers–which showed that 92 out of 124 sports editors allow their reporters to accept such souvenirs. Interestingly enough, 86 of the same sample of sports editors reported that their papers had written policies forbidding staffers from accepting gifts.[21]

Convention Giveaways. The national organizations of journalists have been credited in this book so far with providing certain leadership in the development of ethical standards. But, unfortunately, they have also contributed to the notion that journalists are on the take, because of the way they used to run their national conventions.

The RTNDA was notorious in the news business at one time for filling its national conventions with freebies–cocktail parties, dinners, and entertainment sponsored and paid for by outside interests, such as automobile manufacturers. All that stopped about 1975, spurred by a CBS "60 Minutes" report on a salmon-bake party on a Puget Sound island that Chrysler threw for delegates to the 1973 RTNDA convention in Seattle. (That program, incidentally, embarrassed other journalists and some newspapers because it exposed freebies throughout U.S. journalism.) RTNDA has cleaned up its convention. Treasurer Lou Prato, former news director of WDTN-TV, Dayton, Ohio, reports that the organization now charges an exhibition fee to "anybody there to do business with our delegates," including sponsors of hospitality rooms. Prato says some outside interests, such as the tobacco and railroad industries, still run hospitality suites during the conventions, but he claims the exhibition fees have "made us strictly honest."[22]

The SPJ-SDX, perhaps the most idealistic of the national organizations of news people, had convention freebies in the old days. Old-timers in the society remember particularly the "Bloody Mary breakfasts"—booze, fruit juice, coffee, and Danish—sponsored every convention morning by the International Telephone and Telegraph Corporation. SPJ-SDX adopted a purity policy in the early 1970s, decreeing that convention support would be accepted only from media groups.

The ASNE and the APME also allowed auto manufacturers and other corporations to sponsor cocktail parties and buffets at one time. But they were eliminated sometime before 1970. The APME experienced some embarrassment, however, when the local organizers of its 1979 convention in Tulsa, Oklahoma, persuaded some big companies in the region to sponsor small dinner parties for all of the delegates and their spouses in various locations around Tulsa, including corporate dining rooms. "Tulsa Hospitality," they called it. Some of the editors had to "pay for their suppers" by listening to organized spiels from their sponsors, apparently hopeful of influencing national public opinion through the press. Embarrassed national officers made certain there was no "Phoenix Hospitality" night at the next convention.

Newspaper food editors keep the freebie tradition alive when they accept free travel and lodging to cover the annual conventions of the Food Marketing Institute. In recent years about half of the sixty to seventy newspaper food editors who attended took the free transportation and rooms; the other half had their expenses paid by their newspapers.[23] The annual Pillsbury Bake-Off also picks up travel and room tabs for newspaper food editors who attend. In 1984, three-quarters of the sixty food editors who covered that recipe contest took advantage of Pillsbury's freebies.[24]

Food editors seeking to gain respectability, and to free themselves from freebies by getting their newspapers to pay expenses for legitimate coverage, have formed the National Food Editors and Writers Association. Founded in 1974, the organization has a code of ethics prohibiting acceptance of gifts and free travel.[25]

Freebies have also been part of the conventions and meetings of state organizations of journalists, publishers, and broadcasters, some of which used to give full credit in programs and other convention literature to outside sponsors of convention events. And although purity policies have eliminated virtually all outside-sponsored events from state journalistic meetings, some outside companies still run hospitality rooms in the hotels where the meetings are held.

Free Tickets. Critics often question how the news media can be objective when their reporters are given free tickets to events they cover and review. It is true that the news media traditionally have accepted complimentary tickets for their reporters and photographers to cover sports events and to review plays, concerts, and movies. Whether getting in free has ever influenced the work of the reporter or reviewer is beyond the scope of this study, but it seems safe to say that it probably has not. Be that as it may, there is a definite trend for news organizations to pay to get their people admitted to events they are covering.

This trend is particularly visible in coverage of the arts. Except on smaller papers without arts critics on their staffs, news organizations today usually insist on paying the expenses of their reviewers of plays, concerts, exhibitions, and the like.

In sports, almost all newspapers and broadcast stations accept so-called press passes for reporters and photographers who cover sporting events. But there has been a definite trend away from taking free general admission tickets for staffers other than those covering the game. Although 118 of 124 newspaper sports editors polled by APSE in 1985 said staffers covering an event should be allowed to accept press passes, 103 of them said staffers *not* covering the event should *not* be allowed to accept free tickets.[26]

Accepting free general admission tickets smacks too much of the old days when the circus advance man would drop off several free tickets in every newsroom where the circus was scheduled to appear. The advance man hoped, of course, that the free tickets would stimulate a little favorable publicity, and they often did. But the practice left a bad taste in some mouths and that is one of the reasons that acceptance of free general admission tickets by the news media is frowned on today.

When she was business editor of the *Trenton Times,* Perri Foster-Pegg wrote a column about being offered a ticket to hear Bruce Springsteen from a private box in the sports arena where he was drawing capacity crowds. Much as she wanted to go to the concert, she turned down the ticket because it was offered by the vice-president for public relations for the Prudential Insurance Company. She said Prudential wanted her to join some other reporters and a few Prudential officials in the plush, glass enclosed box. When she objected to the invitation, she said, the PR man suggested she come anyway and contribute the $12.50 ticket price to some charity. But that was not the point, Foster-Pegg wrote. He was not "asking me to meet Prudential officials in the company boardroom. He was asking me if I wanted to be a privileged guest at a sold out, highly coveted concert. It was a gift, and it didn't matter what it cost." Foster-Pegg says her colleagues on the staff were "split over whether I was being too righteous, or had responded appropriately."[27]

Sometimes a decision to start paying for all tickets can be costly. Michael J. Davies recalls that someone once suggested that the Louisville papers, where he worked from 1968 until 1978, start paying for the seats they used to cover the Kentucky Derby. "We calculated it would cost us $50,000 to buy tickets for the seventy people we had covering it," Davies explains. "We decided we didn't want ethics that bad."[28]

JUNKETS

Perhaps the most serious freebie ethically is the junket, a free trip paid for by a news source or some vested interest who picks up the tab for the journalist's transportation and often for food and lodging as well. There seems to be no question that junkets are on the decline among the bigger media, best able to pay to send their journalists where they need to go. The ASNE, which represents about 500 of the 1,670 dailies (and they tend to be the larger ones), finds fewer and fewer junkets each time it surveys its members. When it did so in 1979, responses from 274 editors showed that 81 percent refused free air fare or expenses from foreign governments, 80 percent refused free transportation to cover athletic events, 74 percent did not accept free travel from state government, 64 percent paid a pro rata share of the cost of traveling with a sports team, and 62 percent would not accept free transportation from a business or industry group, even to visit a project of specific interest to their communities. Comparing the 1979 results with those from earlier surveys in 1972, 1974, and 1977, the ASNE Ethics Committee concluded that "there has been a steady drop in the number of newspapers willing to accept free trips for any reason."[29]

The smaller newspapers and broadcast stations get fewer offers to take free trips and tend not to cover many stories outside of their circulation areas. But when junket opportunities do come along at their level, there seems to be less hesitancy about accepting them, ethics notwithstanding.

Two special areas of journalism—travel and entertainment—have been especially susceptible to free rides. Free trips have also been a problem for sports and political reporters.

Travel Writers. As Americans have been able to travel and vacation more, the news media, particularly newspapers and magazines, have tried to provide information to serve those needs. They have also hit a rich lode of advertising in doing so; about $630 million was spent advertising travel services in U.S. newspapers in 1984.[30] Some parts of the travel industry – which includes private and government tourist agencies, airlines, cruise ships, and resorts – are willing to pay the expenses of travel writers to get publicity.

Robert W. Greene, assistant managing editor of *Newsday*, tells of the time he got called back from Rome because of a personal emergency. All he could get was a first-class ticket on a Pan American Airways 747. "I found myself surrounded by free-lance travel writers," Greene recounts. "All of them were either riding for nothing or were on a discount." Greene says he gave their names to the *Newsday* travel editor when he got back, to assure that their contributions either would not be used or their stuff would be edited very carefully. "They were going to these places for nothing or almost nothing and then after a couple of weeks of wining and dining and having a good time, they'd come back and write puff stories."[31] Greene put his finger on one of the principal problems in travel journalism: So much of it is done by free-lancers, out of the control to a degree of the editors who publish their material – and virtually all newspapers and magazines with travel sections do use free-lance stories.

Travel writers have a professional organization, the Society of American Travel Writers (SATW), but its code of ethics does not prohibit or even discourage accepting free transportation and accommodations. Like the outdoor writers' association, the travel writers' society accepts associate members from industry. It is another case of journalists being in bed with their news sources. In fact, the associate members in SATW are so numerous that when its code of ethics was recently revised by a special committee, "carefully selected to give equal representation" to active and associate members, industry representatives held half of the committee seats. The chairman of the committee was Glenn T. Lashley of the Automobile Association of America.[32]

"There's more freeloading, boondoggling, unprofessional, and unethical conduct in the travel field than in any other part of the industry," concludes John Bull, assistant to the executive editor of the *Philadelphia Inquirer*, who used to free-lance travel articles to other papers when he was on vacation. He took some free trips to do his free-lance stories, and he reveals he invariably would find people in the group who were not legitimate reporters or writers. "When the New York public relations agents for the foreign tourist agencies can't fill the spots with genuine travel writers, they dig down and produce bodies," Bull contends.[33]

Another insight into the travel junket business comes from David

Shaw, media reporter-critic for the *Los Angeles Times*. He reports that a friend in the public relations department of SAS Airlines "is always after me to take free trips." Whenever they have an inaugural flight, Shaw says, "they fill it up with the press who ride free, round trip, to places like Stockholm and Copenhagen."[34] Shaw does not take junkets, and neither do the people in the travel section of his newspaper. "We've been paying our own way in travel for years," says William F. Thomas, editor of the *Los Angeles Times*. "I don't know how you can make anybody think you're going to write an honest story about Bora-Bora when somebody spent $5,000 to fly you over there."[35]

Eugene L. Roberts, Jr., executive editor of the *Philadelphia Inquirer,* discovered that one of his writers had taken a free $8,000 cruise with his wife only a few weeks after the paper had declared a formal policy of paying its own way and not accepting freebies. The first thing the writer did when he got back from the cruise was to turn in a long article about it, complete with color photographs supplied by the steamship company. His resignation was requested and received.[36]

Although papers the size of the *Los Angeles Times* and the *Philadelphia Inquirer* can eschew junkets and still cover travel news, smaller papers seem to have a harder time doing so. The *Sacramento Bee,* with a circulation of about half that of the *Inquirer* and a quarter that of the *Times,* had gradually weaned itself away from taking travel junkets. But travel section budget cuts in 1981, according to *Bee* ombudsman Art Nauman, forced "the travel editor to swallow his pride and go back to the airlines and tourist agencies and say, 'Hey, I'd like to do a story about Bermuda, but I can't pay for it myself.'"[37]

A 1986 survey by *Editor and Publisher* magazine turned up a similar picture. About 48 percent of the travel writers and editors on more than 100 dailies polled said their papers prohibited junkets. Among the 38 percent who said they accepted complimentary trips, several claimed that they had to because their travel budgets were too limited for them to do a decent job. Virtually all of the admitted junket takers came from the smallest papers in the sample.[38]

As editor of the travel section of the *Chicago Tribune,* Alfred S. Borcover no longer has to accept free trips to cover travel, but he remembers when he did, and he doesn't believe taking junkets is as bad as some journalists think. He explains that "even back in the days when we were taking freebies, Kermit Holt (then senior travel writer at the *Tribune*) and I reported things as we saw them. Our responsibility was still to our readers." Borcover, who served two terms as president of the SATW in 1973 and 1974, believes that junket taboos have resulted in many newspapers not covering travel at all or cutting way back on what they do cover. He maintains it is still possible to go on a junket and write fair and honest stories about it. "If somebody's going to be influenced by a Bloody Mary, heaven help us!" Borcover says. "Some newspapers have taken the whole ethics thing and driven it to ridiculous ends."[39]

Covering the Entertainers. The American motion picture and television industry still likes the junket game, even though there are fewer players these days as more and more news organizations pay their own way. The three major TV networks and the top film studios, seeking advance publicity on new movies and TV shows, arrange special news media screenings, complete with interviews with stars, directors, producers, and others. To attract reporters, the networks and studios offer to pick up the transportation and on-site expenses of the journalists who attend the screenings. Many writers still accept such junkets, but the number of newspapers and magazines who reject them increases each year.

Back in the 1960s, the commercial TV networks started offering press tours of Hollywood studios to the thirty or so reporters covering television then. Not only would they pay full expenses, the networks would throw in side trips to Mexico, Hawaii, and San Francisco to interview "stars." About 1970, CBS, NBC, and ABC started coordinating their individual tours into the same periods of up to fourteen days every June and January, so that reporters could preview the new offerings of all three during one trip. More recently, PBS, the public TV network that is edging toward commercial status, joined in the coordinated tours. A survey in 1974 showed that about 70 percent of the journalists attending the Hollywood press tours had their transportation, hotel, and meals paid for by the networks, but a 1979 survey showed that the percentage had dropped to 30.[40]

While it is true that an increasing number of the some one hundred TV reporters who cover the preview tours pay their own transportation and hotel bills, almost all of the meals are provided by the networks. "And they are lavish," comments Sylvia Lawler, TV reporter-critic for the Allentown, Pennsylvania, *Morning Call.* She told her readers about one of the sponsored meals on the set of the "Little House on the Prairie" show:

> In the incongruous midst of the series' fictional pioneer town site of Walnut Grove, next to the Ingalls' parlor, dining room and the one-room schoolhouse and to the right of the town jail and Miss Nellie's Restaurant and Hotel, were two bars, a seven-piece band with singer and tables of mounded ice heaped with shrimp, West Coast Dungenness crab and planks of smoked salmon being sliced on the spot by waiters in black tie.
>
> Chasen's, the world-famous Beverly Hills restaurant, was caterer for the dinner of roast beef bordelaise, asparagus hollandaise, artichoke salad, and for dessert, Peach Melba. As a bonus, there was a

side dish of Chasen's renowned chili, the chili Elizabeth Taylor used to have shipped to her wherever on the globe she happened to be filming.

All served by waiters pouring Beaujolais wine at 18 round, red-clothed tables centered with bouquets of red roses and baby's breath.[41]

In addition to the lavish meals, the networks put on cocktail parties and run hospitality suites at which TV executives and personalities are usually available for interviews, Lawler notes. The hundred or so reporters who get invited to the press tours by the networks because they come from the larger TV markets organized themselves into the Television Critics Association in 1977 to provide a liaison with the powerful networks. Lawler believes that the association has also helped to "clean up" the tours, discouraging such practices as charging a fur coat to your hotel bill to be paid for by the networks, as some critic supposedly did in an earlier day.[42]

Like TV reporters, the movie critics get frequent offers to junket to Hollywood or to wherever the film is being made. Some magazine and smaller newspaper critics take the junkets, but most of the larger newspapers seem to be paying expenses when their critics go. "The trend in the major newspaper markets is toward paying rather than accepting the studio's free junkets," observes Al Newman, vice-president of publicity and advertising for Metro Goldwyn Mayer studios in Los Angeles. Newman told the ASNE Ethics Committee that he cheered the "younger generation of hard-hitting journalists who are more honest in their reporting. . . . Naturally, the older practices of courting the press left a stigma, but the trend away from junkets—and a new breed of writer with a more honest approach—will better serve all concerned."[43]

That trend away from junkets seemed to hit a snag when Disney World became Junket World for about 5,000 media people and their guests one weekend in 1986. The occasion was the fifteenth birthday party of Walt Disney World near Orlando, to which Disney brass invited about 14,000 media representatives—from small-town radio disc jockeys to big-time publishers. The invitations offered free airfare, hotels, meals, everything, to recipients and their guests. About 10,000 showed up, half of whom came at Disney's expense. Well, it wasn't all on Disney's tab. Of the $8 million that Disney figured the media party cost, Disney put up only $1.5 million. The rest came from airlines and central Florida hotels in the form of free transportation and rooms, and from tax-supported state and local tourist bureaus.

Most of the freebie riders seemed to be on the fringes of journalism rather than journalists—radio personalities, free-lance travel writers, editors of special interest magazines, radio and television station employees with little or no connection with news, and the like. But there were plenty of legitimate journalists there on the take, small towners mostly. "It's only the big metropolitan papers that get hung up" about such junkets, said Jerry Wise, publisher of small papers in Louisiana. "We take a more relaxed view in the weekly field." Lee Elby, an editor of the Connellsville, Pennsylvania, *Daily Courier,* who brought three other *Courier* employees with him, said that he saw no ethical problem in taking Disney's junket because he does not work in Florida. Radio station WBSB in Baltimore was represented by a dozen freebie riders. This kind of press representation may help explain a news conference question posed to Warren E. Burger, recently retired chief justice of the Supreme Court who was at the media party to promote the 200th birthday of the U.S. Constitution. "Could you tell us your favorite recipe?" Burger was asked.

The three-day party was also covered by legitimate journalists whose organizations paid their way. Most of their reports were not about the Disney anniversary so much as they were about the media junketeers. "The biggest story from Florida was the way the press debased itself," the *New York Times* editorialized, "and those who accepted Disney's gifts were the most likely to miss it."[44]

Sports and Politics. Sports and political reporters frequently have to travel around the country to cover out-of-town sports events and national political campaigns. In the old days, it was common for such reporters to ride free on the trains and planes of the teams and candidates. But the free rides have virtually disappeared in political journalism, and they seem to be on their way out in sports reporting.

Virtually all the news media sending reporters to cover the president and national campaigns for the presidency pay the full cost of transportation. When the transportation is a chartered airplane, as it usually is, the news media pay a proportionate share of the full cost, which amounted to more than the price of a first-class ticket for those reporters traveling with President Reagan. (Curt Matthews, former Washington correspondent for the Baltimore *Sun* who sometimes traveled with the White House press corps, says he is always "kind of shocked" when the president and the reporters land somewhere and he hears people standing at the fence saying, "It's outrageous that those reporters get to travel around with the president on my tax dollars."[45]) Sometimes on state campaigns, reporters will accept a free ride with a public official or a candidate, but here too the policy of paying your own way seems to be taking over.

It is difficult to pay for the plane ride when the aircraft is military, as is sometimes the case when reporters cover military projects or need to get some place where the U.S. military is present but commercial airlines are not. News executives say it's "a pain in the neck" to get a bill from the military, but most are finding ways to pay for such travel these days.

Sports reporters for the larger newspapers, magazines, and TV stations and networks usually pay their pro rata share when they travel on a plane chartered by the sports club they are covering. Many prefer to travel to out-of-town games on their own, however, giving up what advantage there is in being with the players and coaches to be able to travel on a schedule suited to the deadlines of the news organization they work for rather than those of the team.

When APSE in 1985 asked its members, most from larger papers, whether their organizations prohibited staffers from traveling at the expense of the teams they were covering, eighty said yes, thirty-nine no, and five didn't answer. That's about 65 percent whose papers are paying to send their sports people to away games, leaving about a third free to accept rides from the sports teams they cover.[46]

The percentage of smaller news organizations not represented in APSE paying their own way for sports travel has to be lower than 65 percent, given the economics of small vs. large. Unpretty as this picture is, it's a big improvement over the day when virtually all sports journalists had their travel and often their hotel bills picked up by the sports clubs.

The usual justification for taking sports junkets is that some games and sports events would not otherwise get covered by that particular news organization. If that's the case, then it would seem that news organizations accepting free rides would tell their audiences all about it. But that seldom if ever happens. Perhaps executives of those junket-taking sports departments suspect that the public might distrust articles written by reporters whose ability to get those stories depended on the largess of the teams they cover.

Junkets have been and are being offered to journalists other than those we have discussed so far in this section—travel and entertainment writers, and sports and political reporters. The top editors of daily newspapers also get invitations, particularly from foreign governments such as Israel and Taiwan, who apparently feel the way to influence the press is through the top. But the indications are that few editors are accepting such invitations today.

PERKS

As with congressmen and college professors, certain perquisites go with a journalist's job. Usually unspectacular, journalists' perks include such things as free or reserved parking, work space in pressrooms of government buildings, press cards from police and other governmental agencies to admit journalists to places the public cannot go, and (rarely) discounts at government stores.

Until recent years, the press galleries of the United States Congress, the pressroom at the White House, and the pressrooms in statehouses and city halls had one thing in common: the news media paid no rent for their use. That began to change in the 1970s, as the Watergate revelations sharpened sensitivities of both journalists and public officials about their relationships. Some of the larger news organizations are now paying for the space they use in government buildings. And in some state capitals, such as Sacramento, California, and Tallahassee, Florida, the news media have moved out of the statehouse and set up outside pressrooms of their own.

The movement to vacate or start paying rent for government pressrooms is still small, and it is more visible in the cities and state capitals than in Washington, D.C. Some news media have begun to make financial contributions to the U.S. Treasury for the facilities they use in the White House, Congress, and other government buildings, but the majority have not. Unlike some state governments, the federal government has declined to establish any sort of rent schedule. The *Wall Street Journal* and Knight-Ridder newspapers voluntarily contribute more than $1,000 a year to the U.S. Treasury to pay for the government pressrooms they use in Washington. "We don't have an inalienable right to those facilities," explains Norman C. Miller, former Washington bureau chief for the *Journal*.[47]

Like Miller, news executives who are concerned about rent-free pressrooms provided by government contend that pressrooms are just another freebie from a news source. They also worry about government officials using the pressroom as a weapon, as Mayor Jane Byrne of Chicago appeared to do once when she banned the *Chicago Tribune* from the City Hall pressroom in anger about something the *Tribune* had said about her. She thought better about it the next day and rescinded the ban, but many journalists shuddered at the thought that important work space could be removed at the flick of some politician's pique.

Claude Sitton, editorial director of the Raleigh, North Carolina, *News and Observer* and *Times,* objects to free parking space and telephones for reporters working in government buildings, but he sees a reason for government-provided work space. Noting that his papers tried to pay rent for the pressroom in the statehouse but the state government said it could not come up with a rent schedule, Sitton believes the press serves "as a public surrogate" when it covers government. "The legislature, like other public bodies, has a responsibility to report on its proceedings, and we're acting as a transmission belt," he adds.[48]

More Serious Perks. Another kind of perk that a few journalists have taken advantage of is that of using their positions for some sort of personal gain—accepting, for example, a discount price on a new car or a lower membership fee in a country club, offered to them because of the control they presumably have over publicity.

James Naughton, associate managing editor of the *Philadelphia Inquirer,* recalls that when he was a young reporter on the Cleveland *Plain Dealer* and in need of a new car, he asked around the office. "The auto editor told me to call General Motors PR in Detroit and get one at dealer cost," Naughton says. "You'd do the same thing when you needed new tires for your car. Nobody thought twice about it." Naughton believes today that he should not have done that.[49]

Jack Landau, former director of the Reporters Committee for Freedom of the Press, remembers that back in the late 1950s and early 1960s when he was working for the *Washington Post* "it was quite common for automobile company PR people to arrange factory-priced cars for journalists." Landau started to arrange such a discount for himself, but he backed away from the deal after mentioning it to his editor, J. Russell Wiggins. "Wiggins said he could get GM to let him use a Buick for a whole year just on the hope that he might write a story saying he liked the car, but that would be bribery," Landau recalls. Then Wiggins told him: "Don't do it; it's unethical."[50]

You do not hear much these days about such special deals on new cars for journalists, but as the report on outdoor writers in the opening of this chapter notes, the practice apparently still exists.

Another kind of perk, which some newspaper executives found out about when Gannett News Service (GNS) put the spotlight on it in 1979, is the sale of books sent to the papers for review. What many news executives apparently did not realize was that their book review editors were selling hundreds and thousands of books sent to them each year and pocketing the proceeds. The GNS story claimed that some editors were pocketing up to $1,000 a month selling books that did not belong to them to the Strand used book store in New York. This perk ended for some book review editors and at least two lost their jobs when the GNS exposé by Michael Cordts of the Rochester, New York, *Democrat and Chronicle* appeared. There were newspapers, however, that had already set up some system of disposing of the review books. The *New York Times,* for example, which probably receives more books for review than any other U.S. daily, sells most of the 37,000 books it gets each year, matches whatever proceeds result from that sale, and contributes the total to the New York Public Library. (A fuller account of Michael Cordts' investigation of the selling of review books appears in Chapter 6.)[51]

RESIST SEDUCTION, CODES SAY

The freebie problem is a comparatively new one in American journalism. At least, it was hardly mentioned in the early literature on journalism ethics in the 1920s. Today it is almost a fixture in the codes of ethics and standards of the news media and of journalistic organizations. This is not to say that would-be seducers of the press did not exist in the early years of this century. Obviously they did. But their efforts apparently were not perceived by press leaders as a serious threat to journalistic integrity. One theory as to why freebies came to be seen as a problem for journalism is that they grew out of public relations, which has developed in this country in this century, particularly since the 1920s. As government, business, and other segments of American society came to depend on the advice of professional propagandists and publicists, currying favor with the press soon came to be seen as a necessary or at least helpful step in communicating with the public at large. Currying favor has often translated into gifts, free tickets and trips, discounts, free drinks and dinners – the things newspeople call freebies.

If the history of freebies available to journalists could be graphed, the line representing the periods of greatest abundance would rise slowly through the 1930s and 1940s, reaching its highest point in the late 1950s and early 1960s, and would then drop slowly through the 1970s and 1980s. The problem is a long way from being licked, most thoughtful journalists seem to feel, but freebies are not running wild as they did thirty years ago.

Bill Lyon, sports reporter and columnist for the *Philadelphia Inquirer,* sees fewer journalists willing to take freebies today than in the past "and fewer overt attempts to influence the media through gifts, junkets and the like." But he believes the freebies are still out there for the asking. "An unscrupulous journalist can damned near open his own pawn shop," Lyon adds.[52]

One reason that freebies are decreasing as a problem in journalism is that news organizations, particularly the larger ones, are paying full expenses to send their reporters where the news is. Reporters do not need free tickets, meals, and rides to do their jobs. But some smaller newspapers and radio stations still count on some favors to get the news, particularly if it involves travel for their reporters.

Michael J. Davies, editor and publisher of the *Hartford Courant,* reminds metropolitan newspaper editors that it is easy for them to have high ethics, but it is tougher for the smaller papers. "The smaller paper editor has to say, 'If I don't take this freebie, then I don't cover the football game or I don't have a travel section,'" Davies holds. "The big guys should not be arrogant and look down their noses at the little guy who doesn't have many resources. Ethics are what you can afford."[53]

Of the codes of ethics of national journalistic organizations, only that of the RTNDA says nothing about freebies. All the others give freebies a good tongue lashing.

"Newspapers should accept nothing of value from news sources or others outside the profession," declares APME. "Gifts and free or reduced-rate travel, entertainment, products and lodging should not be accepted. Expenses in connection with the reporting of the news should be paid by the newspaper. Special favors and special treatment for members of the press should be avoided."

The SPJ-SDX states that "gifts, favors, free travel, special treatment or privileges can compromise the integrity of journalists and their employers. Nothing of value should be accepted."

And the ASNE warns that journalists "should neither accept anything nor pursue any activity that might compromise or seem to compromise their integrity."

Two of the areas in journalism singled out because of their special problems with freebies—sports and travel—have some ethical guidelines on this matter from their professional organizations.

Five of the eleven Ethical Guidelines of the APSE deal with some aspect of freebies as follows:

I. TRAVEL, OTHER EXPENSES

The basic aim for members of this organization and their staffs is a pay-your-own-way standard. It is acceptable to travel on charter flights operated by teams and organizations, but the newspaper should insist on being billed. The newspaper should pay for meals, accommodations and other expenses of its sports staffers covering stories.

If newspapers allow writers to dine and drink at special, nonpublic places provided by teams or colleges, the papers should pay for food and drink consumed. . . .

IV. GIFTS AND GRATUITIES

Gifts of insignificant value—a calendar, pencil, key chain or such—may be accepted if it would be awkward to refuse or return them. All other gifts should be declined.

A gift that exceeds token value should be returned immediately with an explanation that it is against policy. If it is impractical to return it, the gift should be donated to a charity by your company. . . .

VII. CREDENTIALS, TICKETS

As the result of untoward pressure by sports organizations, some newspapers advocate the payment of a reporter's admission to the event being covered. Where such overt pressures for favored treatment occur, the recommendation is that the newspapers adopt the firm policy of such payment. When there is a normal relationship, APSE considers acceptable standard press credentials and tickets, including parking, for those covering an event. However, sports editors should refuse to be placed in the demeaning position of requesting complimentary tickets for their relatives, friends or newspaper associates. . . .

IX. USE OF MERCHANDISE OR PRODUCTS

APSE members and their staffs should not accept the free use or reduced rate purchase of merchandise or products for personal pleasure when such an offer involves the staffer's newspaper position. This includes the loan or cut-rate purchase of such things as automobiles, boats, appliances, clothing and sporting goods.

X. MISCELLANEOUS

Free or reduced memberships or fees in clubs or similar organizations should not be accepted.

As mentioned earlier in this chapter, the SATW adopted a revised Statement of Ethics and Code of Professional Responsibility by mail ballot in the fall of 1981. The society has both travel editors and writers and free-lance travel writers as members, and about half of its membership has associate status and comes from the travel industry. The sections of the revised code that have to do with freebies in general and junkets (the society prefers "familiarization trips") follow:

1. SATW recognizes the need for annual and ongoing scrutiny of its membership, eliminating those dilettantes who merely engage in travel journalism as a hobby, and at the same time demanding ever higher professional standards of admission to membership.

2. SATW will work cooperatively with publishers, editors and broadcast media toward achieving higher rates of pay for articles, photographs, films and other travel-related materials, while stressing the economic necessity for reimbursement of legitimate travel expenses so that all members may function in travel journalism without even the appearance of compromising their integrity, so far as the public is concerned.

3. SATW will maintain liaison with those segments of the travel industry which sponsor familiarization trips, while at the same time underscoring the complete independence of the travel journalist in reporting on the negative as well as the positive results of such trips, or to decide that the material justifies no report of any kind. In this connection, SATW emphasizes the advisability of sponsors providing advance documentation as to the variety of potential story material that might be developed by a familiarization trip, and stresses the

negative impact on a journalist's productivity if too much time is devoted to unnecessary social events at the expense of free time to develop story materials. . . .

5. The sole responsibility of the SATW member is to provide his/her readers, listeners or viewers with objective and independent reporting. SATW calls direct attention to the fact that some members represent publications which do not accept complimentary transportation, accommodations or other necessities or amenities of travel. Prospective hosts sponsoring familiarization trips at no charge to invited journalists are requested also to state in the invitation what the full rate or the press industry rate would be for such trips, giving those members who must pay all or part of the cost of any trip the option to do so. . . .

7. Members shall not accept payment or courtesies for producing favorable materials about travel destinations against their own professional appraisal. . . .

11. Members shall regard press trips as working opportunities and make every effort to obtain and report travel news accurately, without imposing excessive demands upon the hospitality of hosts. Any services required by a member, over and above those provided on a hosted trip, shall be paid for by the member. . . .

13. Associate members shall neither accept nor pay money for acquiring new accounts, and shall not offer cash or any form of payment to editors and writers in return for editorial coverage.

The codes of individual news organizations are for the most part more specific in their freebie provisions, even spelling out the few minor gifts that staff members may accept.

Most American journalists can't be bought with a Gucci bag, or a bottle of booze, or even a free plane ride. So the problem for most journalists is not that they can be seduced by freebies but what accepting them says about journalism. What freebie-grabbing says is that here are a bunch of people on the take. A business in which credibility and public trust are indispensable can ill afford that kind of image.

"We pay our own way," is a clear standard that all journalists and news organizations ought to follow. But that should be a standard, not an unbending rule, because reporters should not be prevented from accepting occasional work-related meals or drinks if that helps them do their primary job of getting the news. White House reporters who accept an invitation in order to get a rare close-up of a shielded president come to mind. So does a picture of a city hall reporter having coffee with a brainy member of the mayor's staff, or a sports reporter having lunch with the top college coach in that area. Reporters in these and similar circumstances should try to pay their share, of course, but that's not always possible. And when it isn't possible, it's silly to make a fuss about it. The test has to be whether the freebie was in the line of duty, and whether it helped that particular journalist do a better job of reporting.

The "we pay our own way" standard should also apply to smaller news organizations who justify freebies by contending that they are necessary for them to do their jobs. The problem with that argument is in defining what that job is. Most of the small newspapers and radio stations who permit reporters to take free rides or junkets to cover sports events or do travel pieces would be serving the public better by keeping those reporters at home and doing more than most do now to cover their own backyards. Why should we expect our smaller news organizations to be inadequate reflections of the *New York Times* or NBC News? What the small newspaper or radio station can do that the big media cannot is tell me what's important to me in my town. If I want a travel section, I can buy a metropolitan newspaper or a magazine. If a small newspaper wants to give me a report on a distant sports event involving an area team, let it get that story from a wire service or news syndicate or hire a stringer. Those junketing reporters could do more for me by digging into local problems, and they wouldn't be tainted by their feelings of obligation to the sponsors of their free rides.

Many of the roughly 170 journalists interviewed for this study said they believe the field is more ethical today than in the past. When asked why, most based their optimism on the decline in freebies. Perhaps because it is so visible, this area of journalism ethics is one that many journalists use as a measure of progress. Some of those interviewed seemed unwilling or unable to envision ethical problems beyond freebies and conflicts of interest; that is what ethics in journalism means to them.

But, as this book will reveal in the remainder of its chapters, the ethical problems of the news business go far beyond the relative simplicity of conflicts and freebies. It is entirely possible for a journalist to avoid freebies and conflicts of interest and still be a patsy for the power structure, or hurt people by unduly invading their privacy, or use methods in gathering news that throw suspicion on the news gathered, or act irresponsibly and without compassion in presenting news, or lie.

5 Reporters and Their Sources

"I'll quote you as an unimpeachable source, and you can quote me as highly reliable."

What if you learn, as editor of a metropolitan newspaper, that a promising new reporter in your Washington bureau had been romantically involved with a state official while covering politics for her previous newspaper two years ago? You also learn that she received a fur coat, a sports car, and other expensive gifts from this politician and that they shared an apartment. Do you ignore it? Do you reprimand her? Do you fire her? What right do you have to tell her who her friends can be and what gifts she can accept from them? Besides, this all happened before she came to work for you.

That is the sort of decision that faced the news executives of the *New York Times* a few years back when they learned that Laura Foreman, a thirty-four-year-old reporter in their Washington bureau, had had an affair with a fifty-four-year-old state senator and south Philadelphia political leader when she worked as a political reporter for the *Philadelphia Inquirer.* Her editors apparently learned of her relationship with Pennsylvania State Senator Henry "Buddy" Cianfrani when the Federal Bureau of Investigation questioned her as they were checking out Cianfrani on income tax evasion charges. At about the same time, the *Inquirer* itself broke a story reporting that the FBI was investigating Cianfrani and that he had been romantically linked with Foreman, who had left the *Inquirer* staff seven months earlier to join the *Times* Washington bureau. The *Inquirer* also reported that Foreman, while covering local politics for the paper, had accepted about $10,000 (the paper raised this estimate to $20,000 in later stories) in gifts, including a fur coat, from Cianfrani, who was legally separated from his wife at the time. The *Inquirer* story did not dwell on what was most bothersome to editors of the *Times* and the *Inquirer:* Cianfrani was both a news source for Foreman and a subject of many of her articles.

Inquirer executive editor Eugene L. Roberts, Jr., said his paper had not confirmed the close relationship between the reporter and the politician until she had been taken off the local political beat, and he did not learn about the expensive gifts until after she had left the *Inquirer.* The *Inquirer* did not take any action against Foreman; she left the paper for a better job in the Washington bureau of the *Times.*[1]

The *Times* editors took a harder line when they learned what Laura Foreman had done. They forced her resignation. Abraham M. Rosenthal, then executive editor of the *Times,* reflects that the "penalty was severe but there was nothing else I could do." Foreman "violated a cardinal rule," Rosenthal says. "She could not continue covering things in Washington, everybody in the Washington bureau agreed. And nobody wanted her here in the main office; her name was an embarrassment." It made no difference to Rosenthal that Foreman's violation occurred on another paper. "We don't tell our readers that our reporters start being ethical only when they come to the *Times,*" he explains.[2]

Also involved in the decision to dismiss Foreman was David R. Jones, then national editor of the *Times,* who has no reservations about the action the paper took. "If we had known about it when she was hired, we would not have hired her," Jones maintains. "Therefore, she was really hired, in a sense, under false pretenses, false credentials." He reports that the paper "took some flak" from women, who charged, in effect, that if Foreman were a man, she would not have been forced out. Jones denies that any double standard was applied in this case. "I'm not foolish enough to think that reporters, both male and female, do not occasionally shack up with news sources, but I'm not aware of it, and I have better things to do than to run a sex squad on my staff." Besides, he doubts that any other reporter has been involved with a source the way Foreman was. "If I were aware of any similar conflict of interest with any reporter on my staff, male or female, the result would be the same," Jones contends. "A deep personal (particularly sexual) relationship with an important news source is a conflict of interest that merits dismissal."[3]

Not only women raised the double standard question in the Foreman case. Richard Cohen, *Washington Post* columnist known for uncovering the corruption that led to Spiro T. Agnew's resignation as vice-president, wrote that Foreman lost her job for breaking a rule made by men. The rule in her case was the "cardinal" one of not accepting "anything of value from anyone," Cohen said, but what "strikes you about the Foreman case is how it could not have happened to a man." Male reporters "have been having affairs with women they cover for as long as there have been reporters, women and spare time," Cohen observed. "It is somehow assumed that when a male reporter sleeps with a female source or with a woman connected with someone he is covering, he is using her–that along with her body, he gets, say, campaign secrets. In the Foreman case, we are assured she was not used by Cianfrani; that she could have been using him seems not to have occurred to many people. . . . The point is that for all Foreman may or may not have done, she is clearly being judged by standards that don't apply to men."[4]

Jay McMullen tells us about the way some male reporters have used female sources. In an *Esquire* article written by *Chicago Tribune* Washington correspondent Eleanor Randolph, McMullen is quoted as saying of his days covering city hall for the old *Chicago Daily News:* "I've screwed girls who worked at city hall for years. All those goddamn bluenoses who think you get stories from press conferences–hell, there was a day when I could roll over in the bed in the morning and scoop the *Tribune.* Anybody who wouldn't screw a dame for a story is disloyal to the paper." McMullen later married Jane Byrne, and he quit newspaper work when she became mayor of Chicago.[5]

Randolph, who later became a reporter for the *Washington Post* and who was a friend of Foreman, asked in her *Esquire* article: "What would have happened if Laura had been a man and Buddy had been a woman?" The answer is "a little muddy," she said:

> If a man took gifts valued up to $20,000 from a person he wrote about–love or no love–he would be in trouble. He would have a hard time convincing an editor that it was not a bribe, and in this area a man might have found himself in deeper difficulty than a woman.
>
> As for sleeping with the subject of stories, however, there is little doubt that until very recently a male reporter who took a female source or subject to bed had simply scored with more than a good story.[6]

After the *Times* dismissed Foreman and as the *Inquirer* became aware that most of the rumors staff members had heard about Laura and Buddy were true, *Inquirer* editor Roberts assigned his Pulitzer Prize-winning investigative reporting team of Donald L. Barlett and James B. Steele to look into the entire mess. They produced a 17,000-word article examining the Foreman-Cianfrani affair in meticulous detail and reporting how various *Inquirer* editors were ignorant of or duped or looked the other way while the conflict of interest developed. Their blockbuster report revealed how, over a year and a half, a romance blossomed between the reporter and her political friend, and that he gave her more than $20,000 in gifts, including a sports car, a fur coat, jewelry, a TV set, stereo equipment, furniture, and a brass bed. Although he was living with two other women when Foreman came into his life, Cianfrani was soon concentrating his attentions on her, and they eventually moved into an apartment together. After Foreman had been covering local politics for about eight months, rumors reached some of her editors that she was having an affair with Cianfrani, but when Roberts asked her about it, she denied it. Roberts, true to his long-standing policy, trusted his reporter. But the rumors persisted and soon the affair was an open secret around town. Roberts and two subeditors questioned her again. She replied by complaining about rumors she said were being spread by reporters in the *Inquirer*'s city hall bureau who envied her accomplishments as the first woman ever assigned by the paper to cover local politics. The three editors read her complaint as another denial. By the time top editors accepted the rumored affair as a fact, Foreman had been reassigned to the national presidential campaign. They did nothing more about it because they reasoned that since she no longer covered local politics, her relationship with Cianfrani was her own business. Cianfrani continued to be one of her sources, however, because he helped lead Washington Senator Henry M. Jackson's campaign in Pennsylvania for the Democratic presidential nomination, and Cianfrani was a delegate to the Democratic National Convention, which Foreman covered. Shortly after the presidential campaign ended, Laura Foreman left the *Inquirer* for the *New York Times*.[7]

Foreman would not allow Barlett and Steele to interview her, and she made virtually no public statement in her defense at the time she resigned. But later she wrote an article for the *Washington Monthly* in which she argued that getting close to subjects was a good way to get stories. She talked mostly about former Mayor Frank Rizzo of Philadelphia in this piece but she also dealt with her Cianfrani problem:

> I think it's probably right that I was too close to one politician I covered – Buddy Cianfrani, the man I fell in love with. . . . As soon as was practicable I got myself transferred so that I wouldn't have to cover him anymore, and in the interim I mentioned him as little as possible and stuck as much as I could to what was commonly known. I never slanted a story in his favor. If it was a bad situation, it was bad because we were in love, not because of the gifts Buddy bought me, which were the immediate cause of my downfall.

At another point in the article, in which she recounts several anecdotes about Rizzo that she learned about because of her closeness to him, Foreman wrote:

> Although my relationship with Buddy would never have started if I had been a standoffish, distance maintaining reporter, I wouldn't put it in the same category as my relationship with Rizzo. I think reporters should try to walk the narrow line of friendship with politicians they cover if it will help them write better stories. I don't think they should fall in love with them—that makes honest reporting well-nigh impossible.

Foreman does not say in this article that she ever told her editors she was having an affair with Cianfrani. But she concedes: "It was common knowledge around the *Inquirer* newsroom that Buddy and I were having an affair, and people may not have liked it, but there were no consequences for me professionally at that time. My editors continued to like my stories."[8]

While Laura Foreman was being let go by the *Times,* Cianfrani had his own troubles. He was arrested, tried, and sentenced to five years by a federal court for mail fraud, racketeering, and conspiracy. He pleaded guilty to accepting bribes to influence the admission of students to graduate schools and for arranging to place ghost workers on his state senate payroll. Shortly after serving twenty-seven months in the U.S. penitentiary at Allenwood, Pennsylvania, he and Laura Foreman were married.[9]

Looking back on the troublesome case, Gene Roberts is not sure he would do anything different. Foreman told him that "Buddy was just one other person she was dealing with." Checking out a complaint about the accuracy of a story is one thing, Roberts says, "but it's quite another matter to check out rumors about the romantic life of one of your reporters, staking out her apartment and all that. You have to have better ethics instruction for the staff before such things happen." He recalls that Foreman asked to be transferred from local politics, "but it was too late by the time she did." What Laura Foreman did "was a clear conflict of interest," Roberts says, that "grew with each passing month."[10]

Laura Foreman's conflict of interest is not the sort that happens every day in the newsrooms of this land, but it underscores the ethical pitfalls in the delicate relationships between reporters and their sources. It is obvious to even casual observers that reporters rely heavily on human sources, people they interview and ask questions of. Documents and observation of an event, such as a game or a court trial, also provide reporters with material for their articles and broadcasts, but they get most of their information from other people.

FRIENDLIES AND UNFRIENDLIES

A friendship between a reporter and a news source does not have to go as far as the Foreman-Cianfrani relationship before it becomes troublesome, particularly for the reporter. Reporters who develop friendships with their news sources, seeing them socially as well as professionally, can easily fall into the trap of favoritism. Sometimes without being aware of it, reporters start taking care of their friends, looking out for them: When you need a good quote or a new angle on your story, call old pal Joe. When your old pal gets into the news, make him look good if you can. When you catch old Joe with his hand in the till . . .? Sources can also take care of their reporter friends, feeding them news or tips exclusively or at least ahead of their competitors, or filling them in on the sort of background information that makes their stories sound more authentic. A kind of a mutual back-scratching pact can easily develop.

It is understandable how such friendships occur. Reporters and their sources often have a lot in common. In most cases, reporters share and know much more than the average person about the source's chief area of interest. It is no wonder that politicians and political reporters, police and police reporters, coaches and sports reporters sometimes become friends. And in smaller journalistic settings, reporters and their sources are more apt to see and be with one another socially because the social network in smaller towns offers fewer opportunities for them to avoid one another. Friendships can easily spring from the church dinners, the evening softball, the Independence Day parade, and the daily contacts that make up the social life in small towns. Nevertheless, many reporters in both rural and metropolitan environments try hard to avoid deep friendships with their sources for fear of relationships that would or might interfere with the reporter's perspective and ability to treat news subjects fairly. But some take chances.

Reporter Lorie Hearn admitted that she became personally involved with cerebral palsy victim Elizabeth Bouvia when she covered Bouvia's nationally publicized fight in 1983–1984 for the right to starve herself to death. Hearn covered Bouvia's struggle against hospital and medical officials for about eight months, first for the Riverside, California, *Press-Enterprise* and then the *San Diego Union*. Their friendship was such, Hearn wrote, that when the twenty-six-year-old patient cut off interviews with other reporters, "she clung to her relationship with me. She said she liked me, grew to trust me, and said she somehow felt safe when I was with her."[11]

Hearn got some interesting stories from Bouvia's battle–stories other journalists couldn't get–but her editor in San Diego took her off that assignment when he learned that the reporter had acquired exclusive book, movie, and television rights to the patient's life story. All of this was exposed by television station KCBS in Los Angeles, which reported that Hearn had been writing her newspaper articles about the case for three months after getting Bouvia to sign the contract. Hearn admitted that she had obtained such a contract on 30 January 1984, but said it had no bearing on her reporting of the case.[12]

Feeling compassion for an intelligent patient, paralyzed since birth, who said she didn't want to live if she had to be trapped in a useless body, is certainly understandable. It could even help a writer write more sensitively about that patient. But once Lorie Hearn entered into a business arrangement with that patient to merchandise her story, the reporter had a stake in fanning that story, keeping it alive, and controlling what parts to reveal now and what parts to save for the book or TV movie or what have you. The reporter was no longer the independent observer that quality and ethical journalism requires.

Hearn apparently learned from the criticism she got about the contract because she has not, as of this writing, tried to cash in on it. She has continued to work for the *Union* as a top general assignment reporter. As this was written, Bouvia was in the Martin Luther King-University of Southern California Medical Center in Los Angeles, still alive and still fighting for her right to die.

When Roger Mudd of NBC News was working at CBS he was known around Washington as a friend of the Kennedy family, Jack W. Germond and Jules Witcover tell us in their book on the 1980 presidential campaign. Mudd and his wife were good friends of Ethel Kennedy, Robert's widow, but not particularly close to Senator Edward Kennedy. Although the Mudds often went to parties and casual evenings at Ethel Kennedy's home, where the senator was sometimes present, they had been in Senator Kennedy's home "perhaps three times on social occasions." Mudd only had the kind of social relationship with Senator Kennedy "that many Washington reporters have with many members of Congress they have covered over the years," Germond and Witcover wrote.

His friendship with some members of the Kennedy family caused Mudd to hesitate about taking on the assignment of doing an hour-long documentary for CBS News on Senator Ted Kennedy as a candidate for president. He did do the documentary, of course, and it became a major political event that some saw as contributing to the senator's lack of success in obtaining the Democratic nomination in 1980. Mudd's tough questioning, spurred perhaps by his not wanting to be seen as a "Kennedy insider," and the senator's often incoherent replies created a furor. The program also killed the Mudds' friendship with Ethel Kennedy and caused "a great freeze" to descend on Mudd from Senator Kennedy and his immediate family and staff.[13]

When President Reagan almost fired his first budget director, David Stockman, it was because of what Stockman was quoted as saying in an *Atlantic Monthly* article by William Greider, then national editor of the *Washington Post*. The article related Stockman's personal doubts about his own budget estimates and about the Reagan administration's ability to balance the federal budget while cutting taxes. Stockman was quoted as saying that "we didn't think it all the way through" and "we didn't add up all the numbers" when the administration was trying to get Congress to pass its economic program in 1981. Stockman told a news conference that he understood the interviews by "an old friend of mine" were off the record, but that Greider understood them "to be off the record for use in the newspaper over the period in which our conversation occurred." Greider said his original understanding with Stockman was that he would not use any of the interviews immediately in the *Post* but would be free to write a longer, analytical article after the first phase of the budget battle was over.[14] Greider also explained that he and Stockman were "old friends" only in the "limited social usage of Washington, where anyone who has met someone twice at dinner parties is apt to call him an 'old friend.'" But they had known each other for several years, Greider admitted, because as a reporter he had sought out Stockman as "a bright young congressman from Michigan."[15]

"My rule is I try not to become friends with my sources," says veteran Washington reporter Mike Feinsilber of the AP. "It's asking too much of human nature to separate the reporting function from your social function. This is hard because many of my sources are about my age and are fine people I'd like to have as friends."[16]

Concerned that the press has become "a power-groupy institution," Lyle Denniston, who covers the U.S. Supreme Court for the Baltimore *Sun,* maintains that Washington reporters "have dinner all the time with their sources." He asks: "How can you have sources to your house and have intimate personal relationships and be their adversary the next day if you have to be?" He claims the same thing happens in state capitals. "There's too much intimacy between reporters and sources," Denniston charges. "The press is a captive of government almost everywhere it has a relationship with it."[17]

Ellen R. Findley worked in one of those state capitals as a reporter for the Baton Rouge, Louisiana, *Morning Advocate*. She recalls calling up an attorney "who was a very good friend" to ask him about the mayor's race. She was interviewing him for a story, but he thought they were talking as friends. When her story appeared, she says, "we both got a lot of flak—me from him, and him from the politicians he offended."

Women reporters often run into another kind of source problem. Findley, who later became a reporter for the *Sacramento Bee,* says that many of the male news sources she dealt with in Louisiana practiced the traditional charm of gentlemen of the Old South. This sometimes went beyond opening doors for a lady, inviting her to lunch, and helping her on with her wraps. "I got propositioned a whole hell of a lot," Findley says. She got out of it by "pretending to be dumb," rather than insulting the propositioner, she explains, "because 90 percent of the time he was a source I needed."[18]

Elaine Tait, food and restaurant writer for the *Philadelphia Inquirer,* should get the most-gracious-squelch award for the way she rejected a news source who was making advances to her. She told him, "You know, I'm a married woman and I don't fool around—but boy, if I did, you'd be the first one." Tait reports she and the source got along fine from then on.[19]

Broadcast journalists also may have a special source relationship problem, according to Brit Hume, Capitol Hill correspondent for ABC News, who has also worked for newspapers and the Jack Anderson column. He explains that in television reporting, because you often don't have as much time as you do in print, you "develop a handful of people who can help you . . . and you come to depend on them. Then it becomes tough to take a shot at them." Broadcast journalists need access, he says— "that shot of Reagan walking toward the helicopter, even if what he's saying is pure word salad, is important in television. We have to be able to get to people, to be in the main scheme of things, to be known by the VIPs." Hume sees the risks in such a dependence on certain top sources. "You have to make sure you are not compromised by this need for access," he warns.[20]

Some editors of larger newspapers rotate reporters on campaigns and beats, to minimize the "cozy" relationships that sometimes develop when reporters have to depend on the same sources again and again. But there are still reporters who have spent most of their professional lives covering one beat. They develop contacts from their long service covering the same area or subject, and that is often valuable. They also develop friendships, and that can get in the way. Editors acknowledge this problem when they, as they often do on the larger newspapers, assign reporters from outside a particular beat to move in on a special or negative story that the regular reporter could not do without losing some of his or her prize sources.

A police reporter for the *San Francisco Examiner* for thirty years got himself fired for doing what he called "a personal favor." Malcolm Glover's favor was for a self-acknowledged San Francisco madam named Marlene "Brandy" Baldwin, who he had known for about eight years. She called him at the press room in police headquarters one day and asked for some information on a missing persons report and a cocaine arrest. Glover got the information for her as a favor for a potential news source. "You talk to a lot of people without it developing into a story," he explained, "but you are building up contacts, you're gaining their confidence." In this case, "Brandy," who was under investigation for suspected prostitution, bragged around town about having a secret source in the policy department. So when police learned of Glover's favor, they notified his bosses at the *Examiner,* who fired the reporter for using his special position at police headquarters to get information not for the public but for a friend. The Guild took the case to arbitration and succeeded in getting Glover reinstated but with a six-month loss of pay, amounting to about $14,000. James I. Houck, who was news editor of the *Examiner* at the time, described the ethical issue raised by Glover's favor in terms of journalism's responsibilities under the First Amendment. "Why are we here?" he asked. "To gather information for our friends or to gather it for our readers?"[21]

Socializing with news sources, even if they are not close friends, can present difficulties for reporters. What do you do, for example, when some VIP, cocktail in hand, starts talking about the merger deal his firm is making, or the secret decision to force out the police chief? Some reporters say that anything they hear at a social gathering is fair game, but most figure it is fairer to call up the VIP or some other source the next day and try to get the "party talk" on the record in a more official way. Some avoid the problem by shunning such parties in the first place, or they socialize only with friends and have an agreement that reporting ends when the party begins.

Sources as Adversaries. A concept that has appeal for many journalists is that reporters are, or ought to be, adversaries of their sources, particularly political sources. An adversarial relationship between reporters and sources is necessary for the press to be a true watchdog of government and other important institutions of American life, this argument holds. We saw reporters as adversaries during the uncovering of the Watergate scandal that caused President Nixon to resign. The televised image of aggressive reporters like Clark Mollenhoff of the Cowles Newspapers and Dan Rather of CBS News pounding their tough questions at Nixon did not sit well with some viewers but many journalists cheered. They saw such aggressive reporting as necessary in fulfilling journalism's watchdog role, and appropriate because of the seriousness of the high-level government shenanigans the reporters were trying to expose. So journalists talk a lot about hard balls and soft balls when they discuss interviews and news conferences, hard balls being the kind of tough questions Nixon got from many reporters in those Watergate days and soft balls being the easy ones that any savvy source can duck or knock out of the ball park.

But treating all sources as adversaries can be just as unfair to them and to the public as treating them all as buddies. Reporters who act as if most public officials are crooks or potential crooks are not only wrong in that assessment of all but a handful of public officials; they are apt to let their prejudices dictate both their questions and their news stories. And it is distressing when some reporters give the adversary treatment to even ordinary people caught up in and unsophisticated about the news, browbeating them with questions in a manner more appropriate in Hollywood fiction. As reporter Robert Scheer of the *Los Angeles Times* reminds us, "You have to be more careful when you're interviewing someone not used to being interviewed. You need to be fair to them."[22]

SECRET SOURCES

Journalists in the United States have come to believe that certain kinds of information cannot be obtained unless some sources are kept secret. Some sources will not talk for the record for various good reasons: They might lose their jobs, be physically harmed or even killed, or lose the trust of those from whom they are getting the information they are passing on to the journalists. Some of the major exposés of modern journalism would not have been possible without information that was obtained by reporters only because they agreed to extend confidentiality to and protect the identity of some of their sources. Probably the most famous secret source in recent journalistic investigations was "Deep Throat," the name that Robert Woodward and Carl Bernstein gave to the anonymous insider who helped them break the Watergate cover-up for the *Washington Post*. But Deep Throat was only one of many secret sources Woodward and Bernstein used to develop their stories that contributed to the eventual resignation of President Nixon and the jailing of several White House aides.

Watergate is the kind of story journalists usually cite when they argue for their right to keep certain sources secret. Another is the exposé of organized crime, such as the series "Crime on the Waterfront" that the late Malcolm Johnson did for the *New York Sun* and that won him a 1948 Pulitzer Prize. His son, Haynes Johnson, reporter-columnist for the *Washington Post*, contends that if his father "had used the names of some of his sources, they would have been killed. It's that simple." Source protection also was essential in the Watergate investigation, he believes.

"People who told us things because they thought crimes were being committed that were literally destroying our democracy would have had their careers wrecked if they had been identified." (Malcolm and Haynes Johnson became the only father and son to have won Pulitzers for reporting when Haynes Johnson received one in 1966 for his coverage of civil rights clashes in Selma, Alabama.)[23]

Because secret sources are important if not essential in exposing some society- or life-threatening conditions, journalists have sought laws to give them the right to protect their sources if called into court. They have also argued that the First Amendment guarantee of freedom to publish or broadcast is meaningless if it does not also guarantee them the right to gather information, even if it comes from secret sources. Although the latter argument has not gained widespread acceptance by judges, about half of the fifty states have passed so-called shield laws extending to journalists and their sources the protection that the common law has traditionally afforded to the privileged or secret communications between lawyers and clients, doctors and patients, clergy and flock, and husbands and wives. There has been talk of a federal shield law as well, but journalists are divided on that question, many arguing that it would be undesirable to set journalists up as a special privileged class. Others are concerned that "what Congress giveth it can taketh away," that such a law could be amended in the future in ways detrimental to journalism and press freedom.

Many reporters have gone to jail or paid fines since 1958 because they refused to reveal their sources to a court. Many of these punishments occurred in states that had shield laws but courts did not uphold them, usually for the reason that the journalist's "shield" had to yield to the Sixth Amendment rights of accused persons to a fair trial. The first reporter in modern times to go to jail to protect a source was Marie Torre, then a radio-TV columnist for the old *New York Herald Tribune*. It seemed like a trivial case at the time. She refused to identify the unnamed CBS executive she had quoted in her column to the effect that Judy Garland was being dropped from a forthcoming program because she was too fat. For this stand on principle, she spent ten days in jail for contempt of court.

Since the Torre incarceration in 1958, a parade of reporters and even a few editors have done time rather than give in to some court's insistence that they expose secret sources. Two of the best-known cases involved Myron Farber of the *New York Times*, who resided in a New Jersey jail for forty days because he refused to turn his notes over to the court in the murder trial that ended in the acquittal of Dr. Mario E. Jascalevich, and the late William Farr, who spent forty-seven days in jail for refusing to reveal his sources for a story in the *Los Angeles Herald Examiner* that said the Charles Manson family had planned to kill a number of celebrities, including Elizabeth Taylor.[24] Although several other journalists besides Farber and Farr have been jailed for shorter periods of time, untold numbers of journalists have cooperated with courts to avoid being held in contempt. Since the stories of those who cooperate are not widely publicized, no one knows how many journalists have done so.

Once in a while a journalist is saved from a jail term by a secret source releasing the journalist from his or her pledge of confidentiality. Or, as was the case recently in Boston, saved by a secret source deciding to come forward and testify. WCVB-TV reporter Susan Wornick had been ordered jailed for three months by a judge who held her in contempt of court for defying his order to reveal the name of the sole eyewitness to a 1985 drugstore burglary. Wornick told the judge that she had promised confidentiality to the eyewitness because he feared retaliation by police since the burglary was allegedly committed by members of the Revere, Massachusetts, police force. After Wornick appealed, the man who was her source revealed himself to authorities and testified before a grand jury investigating criminal charges against the police department. The judge withdrew his contempt ruling against the reporter.[25]

Supporters of the principle of confidentiality for journalists argue that a reporter is no better than his or her sources of information. If you cannot promise protection, many people will not talk. And if you give in when a judge orders you to reveal a secret source, other sources will clam up when you or other reporters go to them for information.

The legal argument for giving journalists the same privilege enjoyed by doctors, lawyers, clergy, and spouses but denied to most citizens is rejected by William A. Rusher, publisher of the conservative *National Review* and a lawyer. He believes the analogy that would equate the so-called reporter's privilege with the four types of communication treated as privileged at common law just will not hold up:

> All four common law privileges protect the communication, not the communicator. In all four, the identity of the communicator is known, but the substance of the communication may be withheld at the instance of the communicator in order to serve a greater public good — for example, to encourage clients to speak freely with their lawyers. In the case of a reporter and an anonymous source, the substance of the communication, far from being kept confidential, is blared around the world; what is kept secret is the identity of the communicator — the dubious theory being that anonymous revelations will serve the best interest of the American public.[26]

While agreeing that reporter's privilege is "an ethically justifiable doctrine in a small number of cases involving the very future of society,"

James W. Carey decries turning it into "the very essence of the journalistic relationship." Carey, dean of the College of Communications at the University of Illinois-Urbana, said he finds journalist Renata Adler's conclusion about journalistic privilege to be compelling: "There should be only rare and well defined exceptions to the rule that a journalist always reveals his sources; secrecy and journalism are contradictions in terms."[27]

Two editors with impressive credentials as reporters see material gained from confidential sources as useful for leads to on-the-record information, but not as a basis for news stories. Claude Sitton, editorial executive of the Raleigh, North Carolina, *News and Observer* and *Times,* who distinguished himself covering civil rights and the South for the *New York Times,* observes that "once you go beyond using confidential sources for leads, you're on dangerous grounds." He believes that if a story based on information from secret sources gets into the courts, the reporter is either held in contempt for not disclosing the sources or "a judgment is awarded to the plaintiff on the grounds that you don't have any defense because you refuse to come clean with the court." At his newspapers, Sitton says, confidentiality is not given to any source until he and the editor and reporter involved "have prayer meetings," and sometimes not before he has conferred with his publisher and their libel lawyer.[28] Robert W. Greene, assistant managing editor of *Newsday,* generally recognized as one of the top investigative reporters in the country, argues that taking the easy route of building stories on confidential sources instead of using them merely as leads can bring big libel judgments that cause your paper to cease investigative reporting. "If you can't reveal your sources when you're hauled into a libel court," Greene explains, "it doesn't count as evidence on either side."[29]

The legal complications surrounding confidentiality and journalistic privilege are so interesting it is easy to lose sight of the ethical questions they raise: When, if ever, should a journalist agree to protect the identity of a source? How far should the pledge of confidentiality extend—just to publication or broadcast, or to court testimony as well? Is it ethical for a journalist to break a promise not to reveal a confidential source? Is a reporter violating a confidentiality pledge by disclosing such sources to his or her editor? How can we be sure that unscrupulous sources are not using confidentiality to avoid responsibility for passing on possibly damaging information? How can we be sure that reporters are not using "secret sources" to peddle their own opinions?

Editors Wary of Confidentiality. Editors of responsible news organizations have grown increasingly wary in recent years about the use of secret sources. Their concern seems to center on: (1) The possibility that the media are being used by sources who insist on secrecy, or by reporters who make up things and get them into stories by attributing them to so-called secret sources; (2) the possible loss of credibility when readers and viewers are not given specific sources of important information; and (3) the difficulties in defending against libel suits when judges refuse to consider proof of the accuracy of disputed stories if they are based on sources the media refuse to identify.

As with most things in this world, confidentiality in journalism has its degrees. Earlier in this chapter we discussed the top level of confidentiality—its use in a Watergate or organized crime sort of story that is of vital public interest and involves uncooperative and secretive people. Hardly anyone questions the use of secret sources by journalists trying to expose major cancers in the society. But secret sources are also used on less earthshaking stories, particularly those reporting on politics and government. Our newspapers are full of "administration officials said," "a White House source disclosed," "a source close to the governor said," "an authoritative source said," or simply "sources said." That is the way reporters fulfill the convention of attributing the information they have collected, without specifically naming their sources who, for one reason or another, have demanded secrecy (in the news business, such sources are called anonymous or "blind" sources).

Most journalists, even those who defend the use of secret sources on major and political stories, believe that too much reporting has been based on blind sources, particularly since Watergate. They see a mystique developing around the method as increasing numbers of reporters seem to think that their stories are more interesting and dramatic if they contain a secret source or two. There's also a suspicion among many editors that some reporters use anonymous sources because they are too lazy to pin down proper identification.

Norman E. Isaacs, retired newspaper editor and chairman of the National News Council until 1982, has been startled in recent years "by reporters calling up people and saying right away, 'If you don't want to be quoted, that's all right.' "[30] William J. Small, former president of UPI and NBC News, says he wishes he had a dollar for every time a reporter has called him and said, " 'Look, why don't we do this off the record?' They're always shocked when I say I never talk off the record."[31] When she was managing editor of the Rochester, New York, *Democrat and Chronicle,* Nancy Woodhull remembers, one of her reporters turned in a story without any specific identification of its sources. Asked about this, the reporter said, "Well, gee, I didn't think they'd want their names used," says Woodhull, who left Rochester to become a senior editor at *USA Today.*[32]

Greene of *Newsday* makes a more serious charge against the use of blind sources. "I've seen reporters who pass off their own ideas with anonymous sources," Greene declares. "I'm enormously suspicious of it."[33] And Richard Cunningham, veteran newsman who became a journalism teacher at New York University, opposes casual uses of confidential sources: "It annoys me to see some young reporter go off to the legislature or city council and start reporting 'observers said.' I know they haven't had time to develop good sources or a sense of what the consensus is among responsible observers."[34]

The loss of credibility when reporters are not able to name sources in their stories is the most bothersome aspect of confidentiality to some news executives. Attribution—telling the public where the information came from—is a cardinal principle of American journalism and one that obviously has to be bent when news comes from secret sources.

"Readers ought to know all you can tell them about where your information is coming from so that they can understand that information," says Donald Graham, publisher of the *Washington Post.* "If you can't tell the reader exactly who said it, you ought to tell them as much as you can about what sort of person said it so that the readers can understand, if possible, what the source's motives were." Graham believes that reporters have a duty to get their information on the record, but he says that is not always possible in Washington. "If we ran no unattributed information, we would be taking a high moral stance, but we would be denying information to our readers."[35]

Woodhull believes that when a source cannot be fully identified "we should say why. Was the person afraid of losing a job, afraid of taking sides? We should know the source's motive and share that with the reader as often as we can."[36]

What Graham and Woodhull advocate has been formal policy at the Louisville *Courier-Journal* since 1976. The Louisville guidelines on anonymous sources say in part: "The reason for the source's anonymity should be explained in the story as fully as possible without revealing the source's identity. (If the reason isn't a good one, then the source shouldn't be quoted.)" Many other papers, including the *Kansas City Star* and *Times,* follow more or less the same rule.

Many journalists are worried about sources using them when they refuse to be identified with the information they pass along. Basing stories on unnamed sources "always involves manipulation," says Charles Seib, retired ombudsman of the *Washington Post.* "And the reader is almost always misinformed."[37] Clark Mollenhoff, former investigative reporter who teaches at Washington and Lee University, has written that "any really experienced investigative reporter knows that many public officials who are quite reliable when speaking on the record will peddle a large amount of malicious misinformation when talking on a confidential basis. The investigative reporter must be constantly on guard against being used by clever informants who may make unjustified accusations against those whom the informants wish to damage."[38]

Secret sources have cost some newspapers when they were the basis of stories that brought on suits for libel. Some judges have demanded that the reporters of those stories disclose their sources, and when the reporters, as often happens, refuse to do so, the courts decline to listen to any proof that the story is true and accurate. Cognizant of this threat, the APME Freedom of Information Committee advised newspaper editors to take the following steps "in dealing with confidential sources":

> (1) In every investigative or sensitive story, make a serious effort at getting your sources on the record. Send the reporter back, and back again, even if it means warning the source that the newspaper might not use the story unless he is willing to go on record. Such a warning sometimes jolts a source into committing himself. After all, he usually wants to see the story in print or he wouldn't be talking with you in the first place.
>
> (2) If your source still refuses to go on the record, then ask if he would agree to being kept confidential EXCEPT in the event of a libel suit. You are only being fair to your source by explaining that a court could order you to name him.
>
> (3) If both these tacks fail, then it is time for a talk session with reporter, lawyer, and editors. Find out the trend of disclosure cases in your state. Weigh the measure of risk involved in doing the story against the compelling nature of the story itself. Bottom line: Is the story worth the risk? Are you willing to accept the consequences?[39]

Blind Source Rules Tightened. Journalism suffered a severe black eye in 1981 when the *Washington Post* had to return a Pulitzer Prize for feature writing when the prize-winning article, the story of an eight-year-old heroin addict, turned out to be fabricated. The fabricator, a young reporter named Janet Cooke, was fired after confessing her hoax. The incident was a great embarrassment to the *Post* and the news business in general. It stimulated agonizing discussions about journalism ethics and credibility, and raised several questions about journalistic practices, including the widespread use of anonymous sources. Before *Post* editors learned that Cooke's story was a fake, they had stood by her when outside critics demanded to know the identity of "Jimmy," the pseudonym she gave to the young addict. She had told her editors that the pusher who had gotten "Jimmy" hooked on heroin had threatened to kill her if she revealed who he was. And it was that issue—the anonymous source issue—that got the most attention in the wake of the *Post*'s humiliating return of Cooke's 1982 Pulitzer Prize for feature writing. (Other ethical questions evolving out of the Janet Cooke case are discussed in Chapters 7 and 12).

At the *Washington Post,* executive editor Ben Bradlee decreed that from then on, at least one editor would have to know the identity of any anonymous source used. "But you're kidding yourself if you think that's gonna stop another Janet Cooke," he warns. "It makes people feel better. If I feel I need to know a source, I'll ask, but there's no way to build an organization without trust. So I don't intend to spend a lot of time asking everybody the source of everything. But if I get in a shit sandwich again, I'm going to sure as hell know!" Bradlee also says the *Post* is "going to renew efforts that had probably lagged on maximizing attribution."[40]

Some observers believe the stage was set for a Janet Cooke incident at the *Post* by Deep Throat, the anonymous source Robert Woodward used in his Watergate investigation with fellow reporter Carl Bernstein in the early 1970s. One well-publicized fact about Deep Throat, certainly known to those who work in the *Post* newsroom, is that his identity was never made known to *Post* editors at the time. Bradlee now admits he knows who Deep Throat is, but he would not say just when he found out.[41] He does say that in his lifetime, Woodward (who is now an assistant managing editor in charge of a special investigative reporting team at the *Post*) will be able to tell the world in the *Post* who Deep Throat was.[42]

After the Cooke affair, many newspapers did what Bradlee did—required that at least one editor had to know their "Deep Throats." Other papers that already had such rules reaffirmed them.

At the Rochester, New York, *Times-Union,* where the policy is to name sources unless there is some overriding reason not to, Anthony Casale, assistant managing editor before he moved to *USA Today,* says he insisted on knowing the identity of every blind source before a story was published. Sometimes he even interviewed the blind source himself after the reporter had already done so. "Reporters don't push hard enough to get sources on the record," Casale believes. Casale conferred with every one of the confidential sources for a series on police informers that his *Times-Union* staff produced; he got them to sign affidavits attesting to what they had told his reporters and agreeing to come forth if the paper was sued for libel. "We had to allow confidentiality on that series because people's lives were in danger," Casale says, but he took the opposite tack on another investigation, one of police brutality. "We felt that if we used unnamed sources, our findings would be dismissed," he explains. "Some sources would not go on record, but enough did" for the *Times-Union* to produce a series of articles detailing examples of police brutality suffered by thirteen victims who were fully identified.[43]

Editors of three major American newspapers recently overruled pledges of confidentiality given by their reporters and published the identities of their anonymous sources. That's what happened in the Twin Cities when the *Minneapolis Star and Tribune* and the *St. Paul Pioneer Press* and *Dispatch* identified a Republican politician who gave reporters copies of documents revealing that a Democratic candidate for lieutenant governor had been convicted of shoplifting twelve years before. The man passed out his copies a week before the election with the understanding that he would not be identified as the source. All the newspaper and broadcast reporters agreed. And he was not identified by any of the TV and radio stations who broadcast the story nor by any of the several Minnesota newspapers that published it, except for the two dailies in Minneapolis and St. Paul. *Star and Tribune* assistant managing editor Mike Finney and *Pioneer Press* and *Dispatch* executive editor David Hall said they decided to identify the politician because they felt readers should know that the twelve-year-old shoplifting conviction was being made public by the supporter of a rival candidate. John R. Finnegan, vice-president and editor of the St. Paul paper, accused the politician, Dan Cohen, of "trying, in the most blatant way, to manipulate the Twin Cities media for maximum exposure with no risk to himself or his party." One of the reporters whose pledge of confidentiality was breached, Lori Sturdevant of the *Star and Tribune,* was so incensed when she learned that her editors were inserting Cohen's identity into her story that she refused to allow her by-line to go on it. "I did not like that my word was being broken," she said.

The Democratic candidate, Marlene Johnson, was elected lieutenant governor despite the shoplifting conviction. As a result of the bad publicity he got, Dan Cohen was fired as public relations director for a large advertising agency and he sued the two dailies for breach of contract, misrepresentation, and fraud. The suit was still pending as this was written.[44]

It was a similar political operative in Chicago who caused *Chicago Tribune* editor James D. Squires to overrule a pledge of confidentiality given by one of the paper's columnists. The pledge was given in exchange for a tape recording of a meeting between Mayor Harold Washington and two minor politicians. The tape contained some unflattering and potentially explosive remarks by the mayor about a controversial alderwoman, who was supposed to be one of his allies. The tape passer suggested to the columnist that since Mayor Washington had a history of denying most of that columnist's political gossip, "the columnist could write the story, wait for the denial and then spring the tape recording on Washington, publicly proving him a liar," Squires wrote.

Because it appeared that the Mayor had been taped without his knowledge, Squires first sent a reporter over to ask the mayor about the tape. Then the *Tribune* published a story that told not only what Washington had said about his alderwoman friend, but that he had been secretly taped "and the tape found its way into the hands of political enemies who were trying to use it to embarrass him," Squires said.

"Failure to include the motivation of the leaker would have misled the reader, left the story in an incomplete if not erroneous perspective desired by the leaker and further abused the system of protecting anonymous sources," Squires contended.[45]

Because many editors are taking a similar hard line against overuse of confidentiality, we are seeing fewer blind-sourced stories in our newspapers these days. Whether this means that we are getting more accurate or truthful information is another question. Reporter Robert LaBarre of the Riverside, California, *Press-Enterprise,* speaks for many reporters when he says, "I would hate to see the desire for putting everything on the record by name kill a complete and accurate story." He recalls covering a race riot between blacks and Mexican-Americans in a prison near Riverside:

> I obtained an interview with some of the participants on both sides who, to a man, did not want their names used. They feared retaliation for their outspokenness. The morning paper ran the story, but the afternoon paper declined. The editor of the afternoon paper simply would not run stories that were not attributed by name. Instead the afternoon paper ran an interview with the assistant prison commander in which he outlined race relation programs the prison had established. The prisoners considered the programs silly (although I believe they used language stronger than that).[46]

The policy at the *St. Petersburg Times* tries to walk a tightrope between abusing truth and abusing confidentiality. "We teach young reporters, 'Don't go off the record,'" says the editor, Andrew Barnes. "But we have a smaller group of very senior people who have a great deal of latitude." Barnes explains that it would be impossible to cover narcotics traffic, a big story in Florida, without reporters being able to accept off-the-record information and even do some information trading. But he emphasizes, "This is one of the things we give the right to do only to our very experienced people."[47]

Rituals of Confidentiality. Journalists have had to invent a variety of contracts with a confusion of labels to carry out their agreements of confidentiality with sources. They go by such names as "off the record," "without attribution," "on background," and "on deep background."

Although often misunderstood and misinterpreted, "off the record" is the most common contract made between reporters and sources. It is supposed to mean that the information so embargoed cannot be published or broadcast, but frequently sources use it to mean they do not want to be identified with the information, which is what "without attribution" means to most journalists. And if that were not confusing enough, sources sometimes say that things are off the record when it is impossible for them to be so—such as a speaker at a public meeting of scores of people who asks that his very public remarks be "off the record." That speaker obviously does not know the meaning of the term. Off the record has become fashionable, says Robert Scheer, *Los Angeles Times* reporter. "Ask a guy on the street what time it is and he says, 'Off the record, it's 4:30.'"[48]

That is why Scheer and most other reporters question sources when they ask for something to be off the record. Many times the source really means "Don't quote me" or "Don't use my name." And sometimes the source wants only part of what he or she is saying to be off the record.

Reporters who accept off-the-record information—some walk away if they are not able to get the source to cancel the embargo—usually honor it. But they generally find a way to get the information out. One way is to use it as a lead to ask questions of other sources who reply for the record. Another is to go back to the original source after circumstances have changed to see whether the information cannot now be put on the record.

Occasionally a journalist will violate an off-the-record pact, as did Claude Lewis, *Philadelphia Inquirer* editorial writer. The case involved Dom Manno, a twenty-three-year-old columnist for the student newspaper at the University of Pennsylvania, who shocked Philadelphia by writing that he hoped President Reagan would die from the shots he received in the 1981 assassination attempt. As associate editor of the late *Philadelphia Bulletin,* Lewis tried to reach Manno by telephoning the student newspaper but ended up talking "off the record" to another Penn student staff member who, in the course of the conversation, "expressed agreement with the proposition that 'President Reagan should be killed,'" Lewis wrote in his column. Lewis said he violated "this man's trust" because "I owe more allegiance to the president and the country than to people who hide behind the very freedoms we value, in order to express ideas that threaten us all."[49] Lewis said some months later he felt it would have been more unethical to have hidden from his readers what the Penn student told him than it was to break the off-the-record agreement.[50]

"On background" describes the arrangement when public officials or sources outside the government call in a group of reporters to brief them on some subject of public or at least news interest. The understanding in such briefing sessions can vary but it usually means that the briefer is not to be identified directly with the information. Congress, the State Department, and the White House use this device to provide background information to reporters. Under the rules, the "on background" source has to be identified as "a senior White House official," the "State Department advisor," the "key congressional aide," or some such concoction. The source usually dictates how he or she is to be identified. This briefing device is commonly used to background reporters on impending federal and state budgets. Sometimes reporters set up the "for background only" sessions and invite public figures as high as the president to meet with a group of them and talk "without attribution."

"On background" is what *Washington Post* reporter Milton Coleman understood Democratic presidential candidate Jesse Jackson to mean when Jackson said to Coleman, "Let's talk black talk." Coleman, who is also black, had heard that phrase before from Jackson, whose campaign for the Democratic nomination for president in 1984 was being covered by Coleman at the time. "I assumed that this conversation would not be one where the so-called amnesia rule applied, where you act like you never heard it," Coleman explains.[51] So the reporter signaled the candidate to go on.

"Jackson then talked about the preoccupation of some with Israel," Coleman wrote. "He said something to the effect of the following: That's all Hymie wants to talk about is Israel; everytime you go to Hymietown, that's all they want to talk about. The conversation was not tape recorded, and I did not take notes. But I am certain of the thrust of his remarks, and the use of the words, 'Hymie' and 'Hymietown.' I had not heard him use them before. I made a mental note of the conversation."[52]

Although Coleman did not write a story about the remarks right away, because he felt there was no context for them at the time, the words did get published shortly as the 37th paragraph of a 52-inch story by Rick Atkinson analyzing Jackson's difficulties with Jewish voters. By then, Coleman had learned that Jackson had used those same words in conversations with two or three other reporters. The paragraph Atkinson used based on what he was told by Coleman, who was credited at the bottom of the story as a contributor, read:

> In private conversations with reporters, Jackson has referred to Jews as "Hymie" and to New York as "Hymietown."

At first no one seems to have noticed that paragraph buried way down in Atkinson's article, but it became a major issue a few days later after the *Post* published an editorial calling on Jackson to explain his use of those "degrading and disgusting" words. Jackson, after first insisting that he could not recall using the words, finally conceded that his remarks were "insensitive" and denied that what he said "in any way reflects my basic attitude toward Jews or Israel."[53]

Coleman, who has since been named assistant managing editor for metropolitan news at the *Post,* defends his violating an "on background" agreement. Jackson "was presenting himself for the highest elective office in this land," Coleman said, and "he had said something that appeared to at least stereotype if not . . . denigrate a group of American electors. That statement ought to be brought to the public's attention. . . . The convention of background or nonattribution has never been intended to hide remarks that would denigrate a particular group of people."[54]

Coleman got a lot of flak from other journalists for what he did. Many of his critics are black. One of these, Les Payne, assistant managing editor of *Newsday,* does not believe the information "that Milton Coleman allowed to get out in another reporter's story was sufficient to trash his source," Jesse Jackson. Violating a promise to a source should be done only in very special cases, Payne argues. "If I gave (President P. W.) Botha my word in a background interview that I would not use his name and he told me that South Africa had the A-bomb, I probably would trash him," the *Newsday* editor adds, because "this information is so important that it should get out" with the source identified.[55]

But Coleman's behavior was also supported by journalists who feel that reporters covering big-league politics should not allow candidates to hide their real views of the world and other people behind off-the-record contracts. Unfortunately, political candidates have been doing that for years. Coleman's report inserted in Atkinson's story made it appear that Jackson not only was the first black candidate for president in modern times, he was also the first candidate to make ethnic slurs or exhibit prejudices. Coleman's adherence to his journalistic principles created a situation that was unfair to candidate Jackson.

Two of Coleman's colleagues at the *Post,* Woodward and Bernstein, the two reporters who exposed the Watergate scandal, gave journalism its most recent confidentiality agreement. They called it "on deep background." It was what Woodward used to persuade the source they referred to as "Deep Throat" to help them break that complicated story. Woodward promised Deep Throat that "he would never identify him or his position to anyone. Further, he agreed never to quote the man, even as an anonymous source. Their discussions would be only to confirm information that had been obtained elsewhere and to add some perspective."[56]

One offshoot of the background briefing is the "leak," the word applied to information given to journalists that is not available to them through ordinary channels. That sort of thing happens when some person who is privy to private information decides, for one reason or another, to share that information with the world by feeding it to a single journalist or a small group of them. Sometimes the leaker is a government or political employee upset about what his agency or organization is doing. Some of Woodward and Bernstein's sources were disgruntled employees. Sometimes the leaker is a public official of some stature, who wants certain information out without having to have its release pinned on him or her.

These rituals have more meaning in the journalism of the nation's capital than anywhere else in the country. They come out of the relationships that have developed over the years between high-level politicians and high-level journalists. The skill of participants on both sides may account for their complicated arrangements, as with chess players who no longer play checkers because the game is too simple.

Casey Bukro, who covers environment and energy for the *Chicago Tribune,* is incensed that Washington journalists take so much information that is not on the record. "I travel the country and talk a lot to science and government types," Bukro said. "In general, people outside of Washington talk for the record. But in Washington, all kinds of people want to give you backgrounders." That may upset Bukro, but Thomas J. Brazaitis, Washington bureau chief for the Cleveland *Plain Dealer,* says that "many reporters in Washington, like lifers in a leper colony, hardly seem to notice any more."[57]

One who does notice is James McCartney, veteran Washington correspondent for Knight-Ridder newspapers. He reminds his colleagues that "the responsibility of the press is to the public," not to government officials. "All of these reporting 'ground rules' are an outgrowth of a desire by public officials to protect themselves, and are acceded to by reporters, even good reporters, because they feel they have few alternatives," McCartney has written:

> It is my personal belief, after some 20 years of working in Washington, that perhaps the most salutory thing that could happen in the journalistic community would be if every reporter were required to take an oath that he would walk out of the office of any official who insisted on talking to him "off the record."
>
> The second most salutory, by only a small margin, would be if reporters flatly refused to accept routine information on a "background" basis—not for attribution to anyone, in other words, by name.
>
> And the practice of "deep background"—in which the reporter is granted permission to use the information, providing he use it with no attribution at all—ought to be forbidden by constitutional amendment. This is the rule in which the reporter can write "on his own authority," as though the information dropped from the sky.[58]

The *Washington Post* tried to get the Washington press corps to boycott backgrounders back in the early 1970s, but the *New York Times* would not go along. *Post* editor Bradlee believes "we could have shut them down," if the *Times* had joined in.[59] Today the *Times* Washington bureau has come closer to Bradlee's thinking and has instructed its reporters to resist backgrounders as much as they can. But their protests have caused only a few officials to call off their backgrounders and go on the record, and their protests have been criticized by other reporters. "It's frustrating," said Bill Kovach, former Washington bureau chief for the *Times.* "It looks as though the press, in Washington at least, doesn't have much problem with backgrounders. The *Post* fights it from time to time. There are a few reporters who resist backgrounders, but not many. The vast majority of reporters in Washington are very comfortable with that sort of relationship, very dependent on it."[60]

Former *New York Times* executive editor Abe Rosenthal agrees that reporters "can be taken advantage of by backgrounders," but he believes reporters should still go to them. "They should have no obligation to write about the backgrounders if they turn out to be self-serving," Rosenthal adds. "I profited from many of them when I was a reporter, but I'm sure I was used many times."[61]

Being used. That is what bothers journalists about arrangements that restrict their ability to tell the whole story—not just what was said, but who said it and why. As you can see from this discussion, however, journalists have entered into such arrangements, and some have even gone to jail rather than break their promises to keep certain sources secret.

WHAT THE CODES SAY

The codes of ethics of national journalism organizations do not have much to say about the kind of source relationship problem that Laura Foreman got involved in, although they undoubtedly assume that their conflict of interest prohibitions would include not sleeping with sources. Nor do many of the codes of individual media specifically discuss entanglements with news sources. Not surprisingly, one code that does deal with that problem is the one at Foreman's old paper, the *Philadelphia Inquirer,* which holds that "a staff member should not write about or photograph or make news judgments about any individual related to him or her by blood or marriage or with whom the staff member has a close personal, financial or romantic relationship." Among other newspapers with a similar provision in their ethics codes are the Elmira, New York, *Star-Gazette,* the Sioux Falls, South Dakota, *Argus Leader,* the San Jose *Mercury News,* the *Detroit Free Press,* the *Seattle Times,* and the Rochester *Times-Union* and *Democrat and Chronicle.* The only national organization code that even touches on the Foreman-type problem is the APME code, which says under its Conflicts of Interest section: "The newspaper and its staff should be free of obligations to news sources and special interests." All of the national organization codes do deal, however, with the secret source issue, and all support the need for confidentiality with various qualifications. Here are the appropriate provisions:

From the APME: "News sources should be disclosed unless there is clear reason not to do so. When it is necessary to protect the confidentiality of a source, the reason should be explained."

From the ASNE: "Pledges of confidentiality to news sources must be honored at all costs, and therefore should not be given lightly. Unless there is clear and pressing need to maintain confidences, sources of information should be identified."

From the RTNDA: "Broadcast journalists . . . acknowledge the journalist's ethic of protection of confidential information and sources, and urge unswerving observation of it except in instances in which it would clearly and unmistakably defy the public interest."

From the SPJ-SDX: "Journalists acknowledge the newsman's ethic of protecting confidential sources of information."

Among codes and policies adopted by newspapers, news services, and broadcast stations and networks, the policy on anonymous sources of the Louisville *Courier-Journal* has been copied by many in the field. Issued on 15 January 1976, that policy reads:

> There has been increasing concern recently, both in and out of the building, about the use of anonymous sources in news stories.
>
> The concern revolves around these points:
>
> 1. The practice can be unfair to the reader. He doesn't know how much faith he should put in what an anonymous source is saying. One possible result of this is the erosion of our credibility.
>
> 2. It can be particularly unfair if the anonymous source is allowed to attack the credibility, character or motives of someone named in the story. The person being attacked—by name—has little or no defense from his unidentified attacker.
>
> 3. A news source sometimes will say something under the cloak of anonymity which he would not have the courage to say if he was being quoted by name. In most cases, he shouldn't be allowed to do this.
>
> 4. Occasionally, the use of anonymous sources can be a shortcut for the reporter, although not necessarily a desirable one.
>
> There is no denying that under some circumstances the use of anonymous sources is a legitimate journalistic tool. There are stories, particularly investigative ones, that would not be published if it were not for anonymous sources. However, we must exercise extreme caution.
>
> From now on, these guidelines should be followed when a reporter wishes to use an anonymous source in a story. They refer primarily to staff-written stories but should be applied whenever possible to wire stories as well.

—The reason for the source's anonymity should be explained in the story as fully as possible without revealing the source's identity. (If the reason isn't a good one, then the source shouldn't be quoted.)

—Information from an anonymous source should ordinarily be used only if at least one other source substantiates the information.

—A supervising editor should be consulted every time an anonymous source is going to be quoted.

—We should avoid letting anonymous sources attack someone's character or credibility. If, in a rare instance, it is necessary to do so, we should not print the assertion without first giving the victim a chance to respond.

Because of Deep Throat and the Janet Cooke episode, it is interesting to note this attribution of sources section in the ethics and standards code executive editor Benjamin Bradlee has written for the *Washington Post:*

This newspaper is pledged to disclose the source of all information unless disclosure would endanger the source's security. When we agree to protect a source's identity, that identity will not be made known to anyone outside *The Post.*

Before any information is accepted without full attribution, reporters must make every reasonable effort to get it on the record. If that is not possible, reporters should consider seeking the information elsewhere. If that in turn is not possible, reporters should request an on-the-record reason for restricting the source's identity, and should include the reason in the story.

In any case, some kind of identification is almost always possible—by department or by position, for example—and should be reported.[62]

The Wilmington, Delaware, *News-Journal* shows concern about unsophisticated sources in its ethics code, which in general calls for all sources to be disclosed unless that would endanger the source or prevent getting a significant story. The provision on naive sources reads:

Reporters should not take advantage of unsophisticated sources not familiar with newspaper procedures. Reporters should clearly explain the difference at the outset between off-the-record, not-for-attribution, background and on-the-record remarks.

Because the use of unidentified sources raises questions about the paper's credibility and fairness, the code of the Rochester *Times-Union* and *Democrat and Chronicle* advises that:

Anonymous sources are to be avoided except as a last resort. Legitimate efforts must be made to get sources on the record: only when those efforts have been exhausted will the use of anonymous sources be considered.

The identities of all sources must be verified and disclosed to the editor responsible. . . . In case of a lawsuit, the identities of sources may also need to be disclosed, on a privileged, confidential basis, to the newspaper's lawyer. Sources should be advised of this practice as necessary. . . .

When an unidentified source must be used, the story should explain why the source's identity is being withheld. Enough information must be given to establish the source's authority to speak on the subject.

The *Detroit Free Press* code also shows concern about blind-sourced stories that end up in the courts. In its section on confidentiality, the *Free Press* code says:

Since the U.S. Supreme Court has ruled that the First Amendment does not extend to journalists the absolute right to protect the confidentiality of news sources, reporters on their own cannot guarantee sources confidentiality in a published story. If a demand is made after publication for the source's identification, a court may compel us to reveal the source. In circumstances where the demand for absolute confidentiality is made as a condition for obtaining the story, that situation needs to be discussed with a supervising editor before a commitment is made. Trust works both ways—the editor must be able to trust the reporter fully, and vice versa.

Of the ethics codes of the three commercial broadcast networks, that of CBS News is the only one pledging to stand behind news employees who choose to fight against being forced to divulge a secret source. CBS News says:

There may be occasions when a CBS News employee is threatened with legal action and/or jail for refusal to disclose a source. On such occasions, the employees of CBS News have, of course, the right to decide to reveal the source since it is their personal liberty which may be at stake and CBS cannot order them to risk going to jail or other punishment. But as a general principle, and one CBS endorses, journalists fight to avoid naming sources, and in such cases, employees will have the full support of CBS News. Our policy is to provide journalistic counsel from officers of the News Division, legal counsel from the CBS Law Department, and, if the individual involved wishes outside counsel as well, CBS News will pay those attorneys' fees after consultation and agreement on the necessity, appropriateness, qualifications and fee arrangements of such counsel.

Lou Boccardi, president of the AP, worries about the loss of credibility with the public when nameless sources are used. In a policy memorandum to all of the domestic and foreign bureaus on 27 February 1981, Boccardi told AP staffers: "When someone asks not to be identified, ask them why and say so in the story. This is one very effective way to curb a practice that has grown up at the expense of OUR credibility, not that of the sources."

Isolating the problems evolving from the relationships between reporters and their sources as we have done in this chapter, we can see that secret sources seem to be the thorniest. Journalists appear to agree that there are times when granting secrecy to certain sources is the only way to get vital information, but there is less agreement on what level of threat to an individual or to society is required before secret sources can be justified, or whether there has to be any threat at all. There is a widespread belief in the news business that confidentiality is being given too readily, and that the public suspects information that is not pinned to specific sources. For credibility's sake, journalists need to work harder to get all information on the record.

The other reporter-source problems this chapter has examined are also important. The conflicts of interest that arise when reporters and news sources become too friendly are obvious evils. Reporters have to be wary of falling into cozy relationships with sources that inhibit their ability to be truthful in what they report from and about such sources. And treating sources as adversaries may be necessary in a Watergate-type situation in which sources try to lie to the public, but reporters have to be cautious about loosing their aggression on sources not deserving of that treatment. Aggressive reporting does not require the abandonment of civility.

6 Deception, Misrepresentation

"Pretend you don't notice him—but make sure he knows how to spell your name right."

Imagine that you are executive editor of this metropolitan daily newspaper. A veteran reporter on your staff has been doing an exhaustive study of the prison system in the United States. Now he wants to pass himself off as a criminal and spend a few days in some big state penitentiary to find out what it's like from the inside. This, of course, will mean that he will have to deceive some people because if the warden knows who he is, he will get special treatment, and if the other inmates know who he is, his life may not be worth a plugged nickel. But the reporter believes he can arrange to get himself incarcerated without the people at the prison knowing he is really a journalist.

Do you approve of your reporter posing as a criminal for a few days? Assuming that you can be satisfied that his security will be assured, do you tell him to go ahead with his plan to get himself falsely committed to a state prison? Does it bother you that he will not be able to identify himself as a reporter, that he will be carrying off a masquerade?

That is the kind of problem that confronted the editors of the *Washington Post* in 1971 when Ben H. Bagdikian wanted to get inside the Huntingdon State Correctional Institution in Pennsylvania as a criminal, not as a visiting reporter. He had spent months investigating American prisons and jails, inspecting dozens of them and interviewing scores of prisoners, but he did not feel he could truly describe the psychological effect of being inside. Bagdikian did get himself committed as "Benjamin Barsamian," a prisoner awaiting grand jury action for murder, and he spent six days in the maximum security penitentiary in central Pennsylvania. It was not easy getting in. He arranged it through the state attorney general and only the attorney general, his deputy, and the head of a confidential state police unit knew Bagdikian was a *Washington Post* reporter. No one at Huntingdon prison knew him as anyone but the prisoner two state policemen delivered in handcuffs as a "transfer" from a distant county jail. Bagdikian knew that the false identification was essential because if other inmates suspected that he was not a real prisoner, they would automatically assume he was a planted informer, "an occupation with high mortality rates." The warden and Bagdikian's fellow inmates did not learn his true identity until five weeks after his release when he described his experiences inside Huntingdon in the second of eight articles published in the *Post* under the label, "The Shame of the Prisons."[1]

Ironically, the executive editor of the *Post* at that time was Benjamin C. Bradlee, who seven years later would lead the successful fight on the Pulitzer advisory board to deny a 1979 Pulitzer Prize to the *Chicago Sun-Times* because that paper's entry had used deception. Bradlee and other prominent editors who sided with him thus turned what is known in the news business as undercover reporting into a major ethical issue.

Bagdikian says that back in 1971 Bradlee "did not disapprove of my passing myself off as a criminal. . . . The chief concern was security not the ethics of it." And Bagdikian, who has taught journalism ethics as dean of the School of Journalism at the University of California at Berkeley, still believes there was nothing unethical in his undercover reporting of life inside Huntingdon prison. "I believe that testing institutions that affect the public is one of the legitimate functions of journalism, so long as the test is of something important and it is done honestly," Bagdikian contends.

> The important thing in this case was not to alter the scene I was reporting, and then report this normal scene as accurately as I could. . . . If the warden knew I was a reporter, there isn't any question that he would have taken pains to place me in an untypical position for what he would conceive to be my own safety. If the prisoners had known I was not a real prisoner, either they would have acted abnormally with me or killed me as a suspected informer.

When Bagdikian ran into the warden at a conference on prisons some months after his article was published, the warden accused him "of unethical behavior, of coming into his prison under false pretenses." Bagdi-kian says he tried to explain, but the warden was too angry. "No warden or administrator likes to think he was spied upon for public use," Bagdi-kian adds. "In fact, I was pretty uncritical of Huntingdon because I had, from my past research, known that compared to most maximum security prisons it was one of the better ones, except for its size."[2]

Bradlee's opposition to undercover reporting seems to have its roots in the exposure by the news media of the Watergate scandal of the Nixon era, an exposure in which his newspaper played the leading role. "In a day in which we are spending thousands of man hours uncovering deception, we simply cannot deceive," Bradlee has said. "How can newspapers fight for honesty and integrity when they themselves are less than honest in getting a story? When cops pose as newspapermen, we get goddamn sore. Quite properly so. So how can we pose as something we're not?"[3] Although the Bradlee-authored standards and ethics section of the *Washington Post Deskbook on Style* makes no mention of undercover reporting and does not specifically prohibit using deception or misrepresentation to get a story, Bradlee says that it is his paper's policy "not to deceive peo-ple." Then he qualifies that by adding, "We do not lie about our profession but we don't waste time telling everybody what our profession is."[4]

Bradlee, like many journalists, appears to make a distinction be-tween active and passive deception. He has approved the use of passive deception on the *Post* in recent years, particularly articles by Neil Henry. In 1981 Henry moved among the homeless in Washington and Baltimore, not as a reporter but as a fellow vagrant. Two years later he went south as a migrant worker to expose exploitation of jobless black men recruited from Washington soup kitchens with promises of big pay and good food and lodgings. In these investigations, Henry did not change his name, but he kept his reporter's status to himself. A similar approach was taken by *Post* reporter Athelia Knight in 1984 to investigate the smuggling of drugs into Lorton reformatory in Virginia by women visiting inmate rela-tives and friends.

Bradlee does not approve of active deception in the form that the *Chicago Sun-Times* employed in its articles that he helped keep from winning a 1979 Pulitzer Prize for local reporting. In order to find out about reported shakedowns of small businesses by government inspec-tors in Chicago, the *Sun-Times* went into the tavern business. Reporters Pamela Zekman and Zay N. Smith posed as a couple from out of town and bought a tavern they decided to call the "Mirage." With help from Chica-go's private, muckraking Better Government Association (BGA), Zekman and Smith operated the tavern in much the same way as the federal law enforcement agencies operate their so-called stings, providing opportuni-ties for lawbreakers to break the law under surveillance. It worked.

Scores of electrical and building inspectors were indicted for soliciting bribes to overlook deficiencies. The state set up a special tax auditing team, called the Mirage unit, to uncover tax fraud by accountants for restaurants, bars, and other cash businesses. The *Sun-Times* rocked Chicago with four weeks of exciting, dramatic articles by Zekman and Smith, illustrated with pictures taken by *Sun-Times* photographers from a concealed hideaway built above the ladies' and men's rooms. But the Pulitzer Prize went elsewhere – to reporters Gilbert A. Gaul and Elliot G. Jaspin of the *Pottsville* (Pennsylvania) *Republican* for a story about how a group linked to organized crime destroyed a coal operation. The Gaul-Jaspin effort did not involve any undercover reporting.[5]

Newspapers the size of the *Pottsville Republican* do not often do undercover reporting. The method is usually employed by reporters in larger cities, particularly those in competitive situations. The results of undercover reporting are often dramatic and exciting; they make good reading and viewing.

Undercover reporting – investigating something by having reporters pass themselves off as insiders – is but one form of deception practiced by journalists, past and present. Reporters sometimes feel it is necessary to make their sources believe they are people other than reporters. Such misrepresentation can be as innocent as not identifying yourself and letting your source assume you are just another member of the public (as consumer reporters commonly do when they are doing price comparisons). Or it can be as devious as misrepresenting yourself to a source as a police officer, a coroner, or some other official whose questions are more apt to be answered than those of reporters.

An Honorable Tradition? Undercover reporting was not invented by the *Chicago Sun-Times*. It goes back at least to the 1890s when Nellie Bly (her real name was Elizabeth Cochrane) pretended to be insane in order to find out how patients were treated in the Blackwell's Island Insane Asylum. Her three articles for the old *New York World* were headlined "Ten Days in a Mad-house."[6]

And it is easy to find all sorts of undercover reporting going on in the 1930s, perhaps stimulated by the competition for dwindling depression dollars. Nellie Bly's inside report on a mental institution was repeated by the old *Chicago Times* in 1933 when it allowed one of its reporters to pose as mentally ill so that he could be voluntarily committed to the state mental hospital at Kankakee, Illinois, by another reporter posing as his brother. When the reporter was released by his "brother" a week later, he wrote about the dreadful conditions he had seen inside. His article was headlined "Seven Days in a Madhouse." Silas Bent, writing about this undercover report, said that it caused the *Times*'s circulation to go up considerably "but that was of minor importance in comparison with a drastic cleanup of the institution."[7] One of Nellie Bly's modern-day copiers is Doug Struck of the Baltimore *Sun,* who conned his way into the Crownsville (Maryland) Hospital Center, a mental institution. He wrote about the jaillike conditions he found during his six days as a patient there in a series of articles in the Annapolis *Evening Capital* headlined "Inside Crownsville."[8]

When the *Chicago Sun-Times* in 1980 exposed so-called accident swindlers – victims who fake injuries to collect insurance damages that they share with lawyers, doctors, and nurses who aid them – it may not have been aware that a precedent for that type of journalistic investigation had been set by Hearst's *San Francisco Examiner* in 1933. The *Examiner* reporter posed as an automobile accident victim to collect damages, just as *Sun-Times* reporters did in their investigation. The *Examiner* reporter's fake spinal cord injury enabled him to expose a racket that cost two doctors and two hospital orderlies their jobs and brought suspensions of two other physicians and eleven ambulance drivers and hospital stewards.[9]

When journalism historian Frank Luther Mott started collecting the best news stories and publishing them in a book each year, undercover reports were frequently included. The best news stories of 1934, for example, contained an exposé of the Drake estate swindlers that Arville Schaleben of the *Milwaukee Journal* did by pretending he was a prospective investor, and a description of what it is like being a transient and spending the night in a shelter for homeless men that William M. Pinkerton wrote for the *Omaha World-Herald.*[10]

If the Mott collections had continued, they undoubtedly would have reprinted some later-day examples of undercover reporting. A couple of investigations by *Newsday* should have made it. Back in 1953, a *Newsday* reporter, with the help of a judge, got himself sentenced to the Suffolk County jail on Long Island as a "burglar." He spent three months behind bars and when he came out he wrote a series detailing life in that particular jail, and reporting on the bribery, drug sales, and other illegal activity that went on there. And in the early 1970s, Robert W. Greene headed an investigative team at *Newsday* that produced a series on heroin imports that is still a model of team and undercover reporting. Greene tells of posing in France as a lawyer, even forging business cards and files, "to track down a high-ranking official of the French secret service who had imported nearly ten tons of heroin into the United States." Greene says that what he did was the only and the most effective way to get his story, "and I'd do the same thing again tomorrow."[11]

The Pulitzer Prize, despite what happened in 1979, has gone to undercover reporters. Edgar May of the *Buffalo Evening News* won a Pulitzer in 1961 for articles based on his taking a job as a social worker. Ten years later, the *Chicago Tribune* won a Pulitzer for a series by William Jones reporting on collusion between police and private ambulance companies that he learned about by working as an ambulance driver.[12] The New York *Daily News* got a Pulitzer in 1974 for a series exposing doctors who were overcharging the Medicaid program that was done by a reporter and photographer posing as Medicaid patients with the knowledge and cooperation of New York Medicaid officials. Zekman, whose work on Mirage for the *Chicago Sun-Times* caused such a flap on the Pulitzer advisory board, shared in two Pulitzer Prizes for stories that were based on undercover reporting when she worked on the *Chicago Tribune*. The first of these was in 1973 for a series on vote fraud that was done by reporters who posed as election judges, and the second was in 1976 for an exposé of abuses in two area hospitals, which were closed down as a result. She and other members of the investigative team at the *Tribune* learned about the abuses by working incognito at the two hospitals.[13]

The Turnaround on Mirage. So why did the *Sun-Times* suddenly come up empty handed in Pulitzer competition for using methods that apparently had not handicapped entrants before 1979? The general answer seems to be that particularly since Watergate many of journalism's leaders have begun to question the use of deception and other "shady" methods to get news stories. They wonder aloud how journalists can point accusing fingers at the misbehavior of politicians and others in public life if journalism's own house is not in order. The more specific answer to the turnaround on the *Sun-Times* case is that there happened to be a number of those questioning editors among the fifteen on the 1979 Pulitzer advisory board, which makes the final selections after juries of journalists have narrowed the entries to the "best" in each of the various categories.

That predisposition against honoring undercover reporting continued to dominate the thinking of Pulitzer board members into the eighties. In 1982 the board again rejected the first choice of its jury in the public service category—a sixteen-part series by Merle Linda Wolin in the *Los Angeles Herald Examiner* that exposed sweatshop conditions and exploitation of illegal immigrants in the garment industry in southern California. Wolin went undercover as a Brazilian immigrant and worked in several shops to observe conditions firsthand. Shunning the recommendation of its jury, the board, as it has often done in the past, shifted an entry from another category and awarded the Pulitzer Prize for public service to the *Detroit News* for articles on brutality aboard navy ships. The *News* had entered the articles in the local investigative and special reporting category. The chairman of the public service jury that recommended the *Herald Examiner* series, John M. Lemmon, managing editor of the Baltimore *Evening Sun,* praised his jury's first choice as an "excellent piece of reporting." Although he has reservations about undercover reporting, Lemmon said that he believes there was no other way to get the story Wolin went after.[14]

The Mirage story was also the first choice of the special local reporting jury in 1979, according to Joseph W. Shoquist, who headed that jury when he was managing editor of the *Milwaukee Journal.* He says he saw "nothing unethical" in what the *Sun-Times* did. "It wasn't even deception in a literal sense," Shoquist adds, "because they owned and operated the bar."[15]

Zekman argues that "there was nothing we did in that project that I wouldn't do again. . . . We knew it might be controversial because it was advancing undercover reporting one step farther, in that instead of working in a business we were going to own a business. Working in a bar would not have told us what we sought. You had to own the bar to find out whether businessmen were being extorted by building inspectors."[16]

Ralph Otwell, who was editor of the *Sun-Times* before Australian media mogul Rupert Murdoch bought it in 1983, believes that the Mirage series was the most successful of the many undercover investigations the *Sun-Times* did for forty years before the Murdoch purchase. "It reached the most people in a way that they related to what we learned," Otwell says of Mirage, "and it documented something that had always been a truism in Chicago but yet had never been documented by anybody to the extent that we did it."[17]

Otwell credits the private, not-for-profit Better Government Association for stimulating many of the investigative and undercover projects in Chicago's news media. One of BGA's methods is to work with journalists to expose wrongdoing in the city; two BGA investigators ran the Mirage bar with Zekman and Smith, and the organization was fully credited in the *Sun-Times* articles.

One of the Pulitzer advisory board members in both 1979 and 1982, Eugene C. Patterson, views undercover reporting as "a fashionable trend I don't like to see encouraged." Patterson, chief executive officer of the *St. Petersburg Times,* said the Mirage series caused a debate on the Pulitzer board. "Some expressed concern that by honoring such reporting, encouragement to other journalists to do likewise would result," he said. "My personal feeling was that hard work and shoe leather could have unearthed the sources necessary to do the Mirage story, and most other such undercover stories. And I further feel that the press as a whole pays a price in credibility when a newspaper that editorially calls for government in the sunshine and candor in business shows itself disposed to shade the truth or mask its motives in its own method of operation, short of some extraordinary circumstance that would require a policy decision by the editor."[18]

After the Pulitzer board declined to give an award to an undercover reporting effort again in 1982, Patterson explained that he had made his position clear on that issue in 1979, and the majority of the board continued to agree with him.[19]

The revulsion against undercover reporting on the Pulitzer board undoubtedly has influenced the attitude of many news executives. And as a consequence, undercover reporting began to decline in the 1980s. Deceiving people, even for a good cause, began to turn off lots of journalists.

A CONTROVERSIAL METHOD

Journalists interviewed for this book were almost equally divided on whether journalists should report undercover. But hardly anybody endorsed or condemned the method without some qualification. Those who favor it do not believe that it should be done casually on virtually every story that comes along. Those who disapprove of it believe there might be some special and rare circumstance in which the method might ethically be used.

Newsday's Greene is a strong advocate of undercover reporting, although he would not pose as a cop and he believes reporters still have to get all the documents and statements they can "because that's complete reporting." But suppose "you get an indication that patients in a mental hospital are getting beaten senseless and are being robbed," Greene suggests. "You do not go to the public relations man for the mental institution and say 'Tell me the story.' And if you try interviewing the mental patients, you end up with thirty statements from people who have been adjudged mentally incompetent. The only way is to take the statements, because they are supportive, but also put somebody in there to observe what is going on."[20]

Zekman makes much the same point. Undercover reporting to her is "a much more valid way to get at the truth of things than any other technique there is." She contends she is

> much more comfortable about doing a series about a nursing home abusing patients on the basis of my own reporters' observations than on the basis of charges made by the families of the patients—who are not there, who have no way of knowing whether mother fell out of bed or was pushed out, whether mother was attacked and cut or

whether she fell or whether another patient cut her. The family can't possibly know. They may be willing to go on the record, but what kind of responsible operation is it to take such statements and go with them alone?[21]

Zekman, who has done undercover reporting for both Chicago dailies and at WBBM-TV, Chicago, where she heads up an investigative reporting unit, sees no great distinction between passive and active deception. When journalists let sources assume they're just members of the public and not reporters, "they're saying that as a member of the public they're entitled to know what any member of the public should know," Zekman says. But undercover reporters practicing active deception are merely trying to put themselves "into situations that other members of the public are in," she adds. "There is not a grave distinction."

Referring to the controversial Mirage case, Zekman maintains that all the *Sun-Times* team did was to "put ourselves in the bar just like thousands of people who own bars in Chicago. Just because we're reporters should not stop us from being able to see how the public is being abused."[22]

But what continues to bother many journalists about active deception is that the undercover reporters have to misrepresent themselves, pretend to be somebody other than reporters. Veteran reporter and editor Albert E. Fitzpatrick, director of minority affairs for Knight-Ridder newspapers, feels "misrepresentation is wrong." But he would go along with passive deception because "you're not really harming anybody." You use passive deception "because you want that information and you don't want to disturb the scene," Fitzpatrick explains. "In active deception, somebody's going to be harmed."[23]

Chicago Tribune editor James D. Squires admits that passive deception by "not declaring yourself" can be "as deceptive as lying." But he says, "I'm more comfortable if I can be deceptive by silence and not deliberately lie and misrepresent myself."[24]

Paul Janensch, general news executive for Gannett newspapers, does not regard the methods used on the Mirage project as "out and out unethical." What the *Sun-Times* did was "passive subterfuge as opposed to active," he concludes. "They didn't solicit bribes or other illegal acts." Another justification for the Mirage series, adds Janensch, who was a police reporter in Chicago in the early 1960s, was that "it exposed a system that had never been exposed that way before."[25]

Joining Bradlee and Patterson in opposing underground reporting is A. M. Rosenthal, associate editor of the *New York Times*. "Reporters should not masquerade," he said. "We claim First Amendment rights and privileges, and it's duplicitous for us to then pass ourselves off as something other than reporters. Saying you'll get a better story or perform a valuable public service doesn't change anything. It's still wrong."[26]

Maintaining that "you should never misrepresent yourself," Haynes Johnson, reporter-columnist for the *Washington Post,* believes there is "no need for masquerades" in American journalism. "You don't have to go undercover to uncover things," he holds. When he covered civil rights all through the South, Johnson recalls, he never felt (as some reporters did) that he had to pass for somebody he wasn't. "I dressed exactly the same as I always do for work, I told people I talked to exactly who I was," he explains. "If you want to establish trust with sources, you've got to be absolutely straight and not pretend you're somebody else. Tell them why you're there, what you're there for, what your purpose is, what you intend to do with it."[27]

The trouble with undercover reporting, in the view of Brit Hume, Capitol Hill correspondent for ABC News and former investigative reporter for columnist Jack Anderson, is that "the public sees it as dirty pool." Using a method that the public perceives as "dishonest or slippery" gives any offended subject "a powerful weapon with which to attack you."[28]

Another broadcast journalist, Bill Kurtis, anchorman at WBBM-TV, Chicago, worries about what underground reporting leads to. "You're working in this office incognito and there are these confidential medical documents in a file," Kurtis hypothesizes. "Do you take them out of the building—which is larceny—to keep or copy, telling yourself it's not really stealing because what you are taking are 'ideas,' not physical property? . . . What's next? Breaking and entering? Burglary? Going into a psychiatrist's files at night? It's the direction that this is all leading to that journalists should be worried about."[29]

David Shaw, media reporter-critic for the *Los Angeles Times,* is another who is bothered by undercover reporting. Conceding that there are times when there may be no other way to get a vital story, Shaw believes undercover reporting is sometimes used because "it's much easier to do it that way." He cites as an example of what is troublesome about this method a report on conditions in a mental hospital done by another *Los Angeles Times* staffer, Lois Timnick. She used a phony name and posed as a psychology graduate student to work for two weeks in the hospital. While there she signed an oath not to divulge information or records about patients, Shaw relates, but in her article she wrote about what was in patients' confidential records, using pseudonyms for their real names.[30]

Claude Sitton, editor of the Raleigh *News and Observer,* does not like undercover reporting or any kind of misrepresentation, but he "can see the necessity for it in rare circumstances." He tells of sending a reporter into the fields of eastern North Carolina to take a job as a migrant worker "because we had tried every other means of getting that story and hadn't succeeded." The reporter got the job and worked with a crew for a week, but "he went back to the crew chief before doing his story and told the crew chief who he was and got his comments."[31]

Reporter George Williams of the *Sacramento Bee* went undercover in the early 1970s and almost did not come back. As *Bee* ombudsman Art Nauman recalls, Williams got himself admitted to the state mental health system after considerable preparation, learning such things as how to act mentally ill and how to take pills but not swallow them. He used his own name but did not say he was a *Bee* reporter. After Williams had been in the receiving ward in Sacramento for three days waiting to be sent to the Napa Valley State Hospital, a new managing editor opposed to deception came aboard at the *Bee*. One of the new editor's first acts, Nauman recalls, was to cancel the assignment and chastise the city editor who had made it. "We had a hell of a time getting the reporter extricated," Nauman says. "Since then we haven't had any undercover projects at the *Bee*."[32]

Some Representative Cases. Although the *Chicago Sun-Times* specifically and Chicago journalism in general are what come first to the mind when undercover reporting is discussed, other newspapers have also added to the literature on this controversial subject. Here are some representative cases:

The *Washington Post*. A good example of the kind of passive deception the *Post* allows these days was a six-part series written by black reporter Neil Henry in 1983. Labeled "The Black Dispatch," Henry's remarkable articles described the exploitation of jobless and often homeless Washington blacks recruited for vegetable picking in the South. Each summer, vans or trucks would pull up to D.C. soup kitchens or shelters where their drivers would offer free but one-way rides to farms where pickers could earn $50 a day while paying only $3 a day for a bed and food—"Good food, too," Henry quotes one of the drivers as saying, "Niggah food. Poke chops, cone bread, collard greens."

Neil Henry hung around a soup kitchen for five weeks before he got a chance to be recruited. What he and the eight other men who signed on for a ride in Billy Bongo's van found when they got to their migrant camp in North Carolina was a far cry from what Billy Bongo had promised. The work was backbreaking, the bunkhouses were filthy and crawling with worms, and the food was $3 a meal instead of $3 a day and featured such morsels as "steaming pig ears with tiny whiskers still protruding from the flesh." Instead of $50 a day, they netted at most $1 an hour and at worst nothing. The only one in that van who made any money was Billy Bongo, who had been paid $150 to bring them to the camp. Most of the eight desperate men who were in the van with Henry left the camp within a week or so, almost penniless.[33]

Henry used his real name and his Social Security card; he also carried a *Washington Post* press card, but he never had to show it. "I was never asked exactly what I was," Henry recalls. "Usually with homeless and jobless people there's never any curiosity from people who deal with them about exactly who they are. . . . I was just another homeless man."[34] He dressed for the part, of course, and he had what he called "a scraggly beard."

Henry did more than go undercover to produce his articles. He went back to North Carolina in his reporter's suit with a *Post* photographer. They talked to the migrant camp operator where Henry had worked; to Billy Bongo, the van driver who recruited him; and to others who knew about the legal and illegal ways vegetable crops are harvested in that part of the world.[35] This kind of "return to the scene," identifying yourself this time as a reporter, is regarded as a way of balancing the earlier deception, as well as a way of getting a more complete story.

Why did he become a migrant worker to do his series? Henry explains that the only way you can really understand "this particular subculture is not by going through, say, soup kitchens or shelters in your usual middle-class duds, clean shaven, etc." If you do that, you'll be treated as an outsider. "The way to do it," he says, "is to become, as nearly as possible, one of these people, to suffer as they do, to yearn as they do. The only way to really get the story was to become a part of the story."[36]

The *Wilmington* (North Carolina) *Morning Star.* Remember back in 1984 when trucks full of sand were parked in front of the gates to the White House because of intelligence reports that terrorists were preparing to strike here in the United States? Three months before, a bomb-laden truck crashed through security barriers and exploded in a marine barracks in Beirut, killing 241 marines. The country was on edge. And that certainly included the staff of the *Morning Star,* whose managing editor and two other staffers had covered Beirut and were convinced that because marine commanders in Lebanon had not recognized the terrorist threat, they were responsible for the death of their men. So managing editor William J. Coughlin, Beirut bureau chief for the *Los Angeles Times* from 1971 until 1975, ordered his staff to look into security at Camp Lejeune marine base, fifty miles north of Wilmington. Although their investigation indicated that terrorists could infiltrate security at Camp Lejeune, Coughlin claimed that "if we published a story saying that, the Marine Corps would deny it and our readers would not believe us."[37]

What Coughlin decided to do instead was to send a team of reporters dressed and acting like terrorists to infiltrate the base. For six weeks the nine pseudo terrorists planned and rehearsed for what they called "Operation Heyjoe" (after the "Hey, Joe" that Beirut street vendors used to shout at marines there). "We had drawn up a five-page operations order that was mapped and timed like a D-Day assault," Coughlin wrote later. The team members were instructed to carry their press cards and to acknowledge their identities as soon as they were challenged. "If we were stopped," Coughlin said, "we would then write a story on the effectiveness of security at the base."

The team entered the base in three conveyances – two trucks and a seventeen-foot motor boat. The four team members on the boat drove it up the New River that flows through Camp Lejeune. Once inside the camp, they feigned motor trouble at a pier next to General's Row. While a photographer from the team took pictures of her, a woman reporter walked up to the home of General Alfred M. Gray, commanding officer of the Second Marine Division, and got Mrs. Gray to let her in to use the toilet. In the bathroom the reporter taped a message to the underside of the toilet tank top that said: "Operation Heyjoe was here. Everyone in this house could have been taken hostage. Think about it."

Meanwhile the two trucks, which were filled with empty boxes that could conceivably hold explosives, had gone unchallenged through two separate gates to the base. The trucks were driven by bearded reporters. One truck was photographed by a team member as it paused in front of base headquarters. Then both trucks pulled up in front of Second Division headquarters, Coughlin said, "in position to drive through the glass doors had this been, as in the Beirut bombing, a suicide mission." More photos were taken. Another woman reporter got into the headquarters, also by asking to use the toilet and by showing a supermarket check-cashing card with no photograph for identification. She also left a "Think about it" note on top of a locker in the women's toilet down the hall from the commanding general's office.

The final photos were taken in front of the base junior high school. For this one, the reporters donned ski masks and were photographed crouched by their trucks.

Coughlin showed the story and photos to General Gray and base commander General Donald J. Fulham before they were published. "They told us they had known we were coming and had used Operation Heyjoe to practice a counter-terrorist exercise," Coughlin reported. "Considering that our reporters and photographers had swarmed unchallenged over the base, their counter-terrorist exercise – if there was one – was not much of a success."

The managing editor said security was tightened at Camp Lejeune the day after the story was published. "Cars were stopped at base road-blocks, vans and trucks were searched at the gates and sentries peered into pizza boxes being delivered to the base." Although the Marine Corps did not connect the transfers to the paper's infiltration, both Generals Fulham and Gray were soon reassigned, Coughlin said.

Deceiving the marines did not seem to be the principal ethical issue in this case for editor Coughlin. He wrote about it later as a question of whether their stunt put them in a position of creating the news rather than reporting it. He concluded that "conducting the operation was the only way to show the precise state of security, or lack of security, at the base. If someone had shown the marines how easy it was to blow up the barracks in Beirut, the terrible tragedy of October 23 (1983) might not have happened."[38]

The *Albuquerque Tribune*. *Tribune* editors apparently liked the articles one of its reporters did in 1981 after spending some time as a substitute public school teacher. Headlined the "Undercover Teacher," her articles raised questions about discipline and educational quality in the city's schools.

Two years later they assigned a new reporter, Leslie Linthicum, twenty-four, to pose as a high school student and get inside Albuquerque's biggest high school. "The editor and I wanted an untarnished picture, one not colored by the public relations interest of school officials or the self-consciousness of teachers and students," Linthicum wrote.

Linthicum dyed her graying brown hair, plugged in some barrettes, nibbled down her fingernails, and put on some jeans and loafers to pass for a seventeen-year-old transfer student. She took the name Leslie Tay-lor, adopting the last name and address of a friend. She told the school's registrar that she had no transcript but was transferring from a Pennsyl-vania mining community she had chosen because its high school had been closed by a months-long teachers' strike. The registrar took her word for the courses and credits she claimed to have completed, but told her she was going to send for a transcript and immunization records. After sign-ing her fake name to a school identification card and a class schedule, Linthicum telephoned the Pennsylvania school and told them the request for a transcript was a bureaucratic mistake that they could ignore. That call, of course, required her to assume another pose – that of an official at the Albuquerque school.

What did she find on the inside? Her series of articles, labeled (you guessed it!) the "Undercover Student," told of what she saw as an overreliance by teachers on audio-visual aids, guest speakers, and in-class writing and reading assignments. She reported that two-thirds of her classes in the two weeks and a day of her masquerade did not require any lecturing and discussion-leading by the teacher. The articles named the teachers but not the students. Linthicum also reported on social divisions in the student body, illegal drug and alcohol use and sales of drugs in the school, and the general lack of interest in education among students.

The articles ran front-page for six straight days, kicked off by a teaser article that was headlined, "Reporter Poses as Student: What's It Like in City's Biggest High School?" That emphasis on how the reporter had deceived to get the story continued through the series.

"Students, teachers, parents and school administrators reacted with shock and anger, not to the meat of the articles but to the ethics of the method," Linthicum confessed. "They felt violated, intruded upon and tricked into trusting an individual who lied for no good purpose." But the reporter defended the methods she used, claiming that masquerading was the only way she could get this important story. She disagreed with critics who argued that the stories would have been no different if she had gone into the school with the permission of administrators and with the knowledge of teachers. "I am convinced the experience would have been very different," she said. If there were no other way to get an important story accurately, she added, "I would do it again."

If she does, it will have to be on another paper. Jack McElroy, assistant managing editor who was city editor when Linthicum did her investigation, said the *Tribune* "has decided against any future undercover reports because of the obvious questions about their credibility and fairness."[39]

The *Los Angeles Herald Examiner.* Merle Linda Wolin, Latin affairs reporter for the *Los Angeles Herald Examiner,* transformed herself into Merlina De Novais, a poor illegal Brazilian, to work in several sewing factories and report on sweatshop conditions in the garment industry of Los Angeles. She played this role off and on for eight months in 1980 to produce a sixteen-part series that won at least two national awards besides being a finalist in the 1981 APME and the 1982 Pulitzer Prize public service competitions. She also used conventional interviews with people in the garment industry and public officials.

Wolin says she had to talk her editors into letting her go inside the sewing shops as an illegal alien because they were afraid for her safety and skeptical that a fair-skinned reporter from Cheyenne, Wyoming, could pull it off. She knew she could not pass as a Mexican or Central American, where most of the Spanish-speaking Latins in the garment industry come from, because she speaks Spanish with a blurred French accent, French being her first foreign language. So she decided to pass herself off as an illegal alien from Portuguese-speaking Brazil, because few Brazilians do that kind of work and the fact that Portuguese was supposedly her native tongue would explain her strange Spanish accent. With the help of a Mexican-born colleague, Wolin selected her clothing from a discount department store where many Los Angeles Latins bought their clothes. She figured that her sewing skills, learned at home and in a 4-H club in Cheyenne, would get her by. And they did. When she worked in the shops, she would work nine to ten hours a day and then sneak back to the newspaper to put her notes into the computer.

Wolin believes undercover reporting should not be used for every story and can be abused, but it was the only way she could "find out what the lives of garment workers were like and how they endured." She believes undercover reporting is "controversial, not to the public, but only in the minds of certain newspaper editors who in a way are copping out from not going that extra step to really get the story."[40]

The *Milwaukee Journal.* The *Journal* used five reporters posing as patients to investigate Medicaid in the Milwaukee area in 1977. The reporters first were given medical examinations to assure that they were in good health. One was also given a Medicaid card that the *Journal* had obtained "from a high state official whom the paper took into its confidence," then managing editor Joseph W. Shoquist relates.[41] After Surgical Blue-Shield Care, which administered the Medicaid program, was informed by the *Journal* that the paper would pay all his bills, the reporter with the Medicaid card went to six doctors complaining of a sore throat. Five doctors prescribed medication, including chest and neck X rays, antibiotics, lozenges, aspirin, blood sampling and throat culture, urinalysis, and cough depressants. The sixth doctor, at a Milwaukee clinic, told the *Journal* reporter: "Frankly, I don't see anything wrong with you. If there is soreness, I would only recommend that you go home and gargle with warm salt water. There is no need for medication." The doctor who made the biggest fuss about the first reporter's unsore sore throat was then visited by the other four reporters, one at a time. They all paid cash and at a counter in his office bought the drugs the physician prescribed—an antibiotic for each of them, plus cough syrup with codeine for two, and a cough depressant for a third.

Shoquist says the doctor who told all five of the well reporters they were ill was the only one the paper named and photographed in its stories. "He was running a pill factory," Shoquist explains. "He had fifty people lined up in the street waiting for his office to open at 8 A.M. He'd give them any drug they asked for." After the *Journal* broke its Medicaid story, the State Medical Examining Board investigated all five doctors and went to court to charge the one the *Journal* had identified, who then fled to Cyprus, according to Shoquist. "We did a public service by putting a major drug abuser out of business in Milwaukee," the editor claims.

The now defunct National News Council investigated the *Journal's* stories after the State Medical Society of Wisconsin charged the paper with "unethical conduct." The council unanimously found the complaint unwarranted, hesitating only over the charge in the complaint about the "apparently fraudulent Medicaid card." The council noted on this point that the *Journal* recognized that the possession of the card "was a subterfuge" and "explained publicly that it would pay whatever costs were involved." The reporter did nothing that called for criminal prosecution, the council decision said, quoting an assistant attorney general for the state as saying that no Wisconsin law was broken because no criminal intent, "deceiving with intent to reap personal gain," could be proved. So the council decided the subterfuge was appropriate in this case.[42]

Gannett News Service. Somebody at the Strand Book Store made a terrible mistake sending a letter to the book editor of the *Milwaukee Journal*, inviting him to sell his review books and promising confidentiality. Book editor Robert W. Wells turned the letter over to *Journal* managing editor Shoquist, who was then president of the APME. Shocked by its implications, Shoquist asked Richard B. Tuttle as chairman of APME's Professional Standards Committee to look into the matter. Tuttle, from his position in Gannett's corporate headquarters in Rochester, New York, worked out an arrangement for Michael Cordts, then a reporter for Gannett's morning newspaper in Rochester, the *Democrat and Chronicle*, to investigate the nation's largest used book store, the Strand of New York City. Before Cordts got through and his stories were distributed around the country through the Gannett News Service in 1979, several newspapers were embarrassed to learn that their book editors had been selling complimentary review copies to the Strand and pocketing as much as $1,000 a month. Most newspapers consider such selling by staff members to be an improper use of their positions for personal gain.

How could Cordts be so sure of his facts? He worked for two weeks at the Strand as a $2.85-an-hour clerk, and discovered crates of books from various book editors, with their names on the return address labels. He usually had to mention those crates to the book editors he called before they would admit they had been selling books to Strand. For that reason, Cordts believes his undercover work was justified.

Cordts, who left the Rochester paper to join the *Chicago Sun-Times,* quoted Strand managers in his stories as saying that they had been "buying books from hundreds of newspaper reviewers." Yet Cordts was able to name only ten newspaper book editors who were doing it. Either the book store sources exaggerated or Cordts needed to stay undercover for longer than fourteen days. Incidentally, he donated the $280.84 he was paid by Strand to the Reporters Committee for Freedom of the Press.

Of the ten book editors named in Cordts's stories, two lost their jobs almost immediately. Larry Swindell of the *Philadelphia Inquirer,* who drafted the section of the *Inquirer's* ethics code that prohibited the selling of review books, resigned. Terry Anderson of the *Denver Post* was fired. One of the ten – Nancy Grape, who covers politics and does book reviews on the side for the Lewiston, Maine, *Journal* – came through the crisis of the investigation without a scratch. Cordts quotes her editor, A. Kent Foster, as saying, "If she was paid for reviewing I'd consider the books the property of the newspaper. But she isn't paid so what she does with the books is her own business."

Newspaper editors who are aware of the problem (Cordts said only one of the ten he snared was) see to it that review books for the most part are donated to libraries or charities.[43]

The *Wall Street Journal.* Several times in the last two decades, the distinguished *Wall Street Journal* has sent reporters into the bowels of American business and industry to find out how things work from the inside. They have done this as workers, not as reporters. One famous *Journal* undercover reporting project was done back in 1967 by a student intern from the University of Michigan, Roger Rappaport. He worked for two weeks on an automobile assembly line in a Ford plant in Detroit, producing what *Journal* associate editor Lawrence G. O'Donnell calls "a terrific story that told us all about blue collar blues" long before assembly line problems were generally known and talked about. O'Donnell, who was Rappaport's editor as Detroit bureau manager then, says Ford officials told him later that they found out who Rappaport was three days after he was hired, but they did nothing because they did not want to create an incident in the midst of negotiations with the United Auto Workers.[44]

The most significant undercover reporting project by the *Journal* since then, in O'Donnell's opinion, was a controversial look at a Texas Instruments (TI) plant in Austin in 1978. Reporter Beth Nissen, who left the *Journal* for a reporting job with *Newsweek,* got a job as a $2.93 per hour solderer on an assembly line in the Austin plant to try to find out how TI had warded off unionization. At the time TI was the third largest nonunion company in the United States after International Business Machines and Eastman Kodak. Her article told of the very tight security system in the plant and of the heavy pitch against unions in the company's orientation program for new workers. It also reported pleasant working conditions, but only average pay and benefits, which caused a large turnover that was a natural deterrent to union organizing efforts. Nissen deliberately talked about unions with her fellow employees, which caused most of them to shun her. They called her "that union chick from Detroit," and said the company would find some reason to fire her if she didn't cool it. Nissen reported that she had planned to work a month at the plant, but she was fired after three weeks because she had falsified her application form by omitting the fact that she was a college graduate.[45]

O'Donnell reports that after Nissen was dismissed, she went back to TI officials to tell them that she was a reporter and to get their side of the story, but instead of talking to her, they went to New York to protest to *Journal* editors. They talked to Ed Cony, vice-president for news of Dow Jones and Company, publisher of the *Journal* and other newspapers. Texas Instruments tried to get Cony to kill Nissen's story. "They threatened to sue us for trespassing and perhaps other things," Cony recalls. "I told them I could understand how they would get upset at the methods we used, but that they should not jump to the conclusion that we were out to do an unfair story on them." He urged them to talk to Nissen, which they eventually did.[46] But O'Donnell says that the reporter did not get much from the response of TI officials that was useful in her story. "They were so upset about the way the story was done that they did not respond to the issues raised by the reporter," O'Donnell concludes, noting that Nissen's story reported in the fourth paragraph that the company "strenuously objected to the way in which the story was obtained."

The *Journal* got "lots of letters after the Nissen story expressing a deep sense of outrage that we had given ourselves the right to do something nobody else could do," O'Donnell adds. Among journalists also there was criticism because of the way Nissen openly engaged fellow employees in talk about unions, perhaps jeopardizing their jobs.

The *Journal* has done a few other less significant undercover reports since the TI piece, O'Donnell notes, but the paper has a feeling of caution about the use of that method. "The climate is just all wrong for this kind of reporting," the associate editor explains. "People resent the special privilege that the press assumes for itself, and they really don't like the break-and-enter mentality that a lot of reporters have." He observes that the *Journal* still considers using undercover reporting but with the realization that some serious problems have to be faced. "The biggest problem is entrapment," O'Donnell warns. "People don't know who you really are when they bare their souls to you, and then you smear them by invading their privacy." And "you have to bend over backwards" to give the employers or public officials involved a chance to comment. "A second problem is how honest are you going to be with the readers about how you got the story," O'Donnell suggests. "You've got to tell them how the hell you got in there, and if you lied and cheated, you've got to tell them that. So you'd better be prepared to suffer some loss of prestige."

If the story is significant and there is no other way to do it, the *Journal* might resort to undercover reporting, O'Donnell says, "but the managing editor has to be involved from day one . . . and you have to have confidence in the integrity of your reporter."

Cony is equally cautious. "Deception is an uncomfortable technique to use," he believes. "Maybe sometimes the results are sufficiently in the public interest that you can make peace with your conscience, but as soon as you do, you are aware that throughout history a lot of people thought ends justified the means, and some terrible things happened as a result."

MISREPRESENTATION

Undercover reporting always involves some degree of misrepresentation by journalists to their sources. Even when journalists merely pose as members of the public, their motives are still to get a story, which sets them apart from other members of the public and results in their misrepresenting who they really are to the people they deal with while undercover. But as with most things, there are degrees of misrepresentation. And misrepresentation occurs in some conventional as well as undercover reporting.

The telephone changed news reporting in many ways, speeding up the process but also enlarging opportunities for inaccuracy and making it easier for reporters to misrepresent themselves to sources on the other end of the line. I recall with embarrassment showing my first journalism class a film on reporting that I had not screened, and watching with horror as the reporter picked up the phone in the pressroom to call someone involved in a crime and said, "Hello, this is O'Neill down at police headquarters." Thus was born a healthy caution about the use of audiovisual aids in teaching.

Ethical journalists do not try to make people believe they are cops. That stuff supposedly went out with Harry Romanoff, the legendary reporter for the old *Chicago American* who was called the "Heifetz of the newsroom" for the way he played the telephone. Legend has it that he would pose as a police officer, a coroner, or even a governor to get a story.[47] He once got the mother of mass murderer Richard Speck to talk to him by telling her he was Speck's attorney.[48] But although Romanoff has been dead since 1970, his methods live on. Craig Ammerman, who was New York City bureau chief for the AP when Elvis Presley collapsed, recalls that there was a thirty- to forty-minute period after the singer had been taken from his Memphis mansion in an ambulance when no one was able to get any information from police. "A guy on my staff with a New

York City voice called Memphis police and said he was Sergeant Kelly of the New York Police Department and was curious about what was going on. And they told him," Ammerman says. "We didn't use very much of what they told us, but we used it to confirm that Presley was dead and that he probably died of a drug overdose."[49]

A variation of the Romanoff method is related by Les Whitten, novelist who was senior reporter on the Jack Anderson column for twelve years. Whitten tells of a colleague he heard telephoning from Robert Kennedy's political headquarters to someone in that organization and saying, "I'm calling from Bobby Kennedy's headquarters here in Washington. What the hell's going on with such and such?" Whitten concedes that "the guy got a peach of a story but I thought what he did was very unethical."[50]

Executive editor Roberts of the *Philadelphia Inquirer* believes reporters "have an obligation to get the news out . . . and not passively accept handouts and police rules in emergencies." This can sometimes mean doing things to get across police cordons, "short of falsifying credentials or breaking into an office," Roberts adds. He remembers once when he was covering a murder case as a reporter for the Raleigh *News and Observer* he picked up a stethoscope from a desk in a hospital and walked nonchalantly into the emergency room where police were questioning a suspect. No one stopped him as he went into the interrogation room and heard the suspect confess to police. "I didn't lie to anyone," Roberts says. "We're not obligated to wear a neon sign."[51]

Roberts and other reporters who covered the tense South during the civil rights movement in the late 1950s and the 1960s often did not object to being mistaken for federal agents. It was safer that way. This meant dressing more stylishly than many reporters like to – coat, tie, and a hat – and it didn't hurt to stuff your notebook inside your coat in such a way that it might be taken for a shoulder harness for a gun. Claude Sitton, now editor of the Raleigh *News and Observer* but who, like Roberts, covered civil rights for the *New York Times,* remembers how he and a reporter for *Time* magazine were having a cup of coffee in a little Mississippi town when a fight broke out in the restaurant between some rednecks and a group of freedom riders. They sat there in their Brooks Brothers suits, London Fog raincoats, and hats, and witnessed the whole thing. The next day, Sitton says, the local paper reported that the riot had been witnessed by two FBI agents.[52]

There were times, though, when civil rights movement reporters did not want to look like federal agents. Roberts felt that reporters had a right to report what was going on in high schools that were being desegregated, even though local authorities would not let them in. So he would stash his "FBI clothes" in a bush somewhere, slip on a sweater and "blend in with the students." Editor Tuttle of the Elmira, New York, *Star-Gazette* did the same thing when police blocked reporters from entering the University of Mississippi campus in the turmoil after James Meredith became that school's first black student. Tuttle, who was reporting for the *Miami Herald* then, says "that kind of posing does not bother me."[53] And Sitton recalls that there were times when the only safe thing for a reporter to do was to "take off your shirt, roll it up and stomp on it, put it back on inside out, and go down and sit on the bank and chew grass."

In a more recent life-threatening news situation, Bill Kurtis of WBBM-TV, Chicago, tells of moving through a market in Tehran with a camera crew the day after America's abortive mission to rescue the hostages. Kurtis says his guide and interpreter–after hearing whispers of, "They're Americans. Let's kill them."–suggested that Kurtis pretend to be French. "You bet!" Kurtis told him.[54]

And in a recent replay of a technique and story that have been done by other news organizations in the past, the *Miami Herald* sent two reporters, one black, one white, to check on possible racial discrimination in rental housing. They found lots of it, so much that they could write: "Racial discrimination is widespread in Dade County's rental housing market despite federal and local statutes outlawing such practices."[55]

Reporters Paul Shannon, white, and Larry Bivins, black, created almost identical backgrounds and profiles for themselves, according to Shannon, "that would make us ideal tenants–well-dressed, professional, relatively affluent, and no kids or pets." Then they went from apartment to apartment, using classified ads. The black reporter went in first and the white reporter ten to thirty minutes later so that they were apt to deal with the same rental agent. Both used their own names but fudged their occupations: Bivins said he worked as a minority recruiter for the *Herald,* which was part of his job, and Shannon said he worked in an office for the Knight-Ridder Corporation, owners of the *Herald.* "No one caught on," Shannon said.

They found both overt and subtle discrimination. One rental agent would tell Bivins that some apartment complex was all filled up and twenty minutes later tell Shannon that he could have an apartment there immediately. But sometimes when they compared notes after their visits they would find that the white reporter had been shown such amenities as a swimming pool, sauna, and Jacuzzi, while the black reporter was never told about them.

Herald executive editor at the time, Heath Meriwether, defends the misrepresentation used to get this obviously important story even though he is very cautious about approving any kind of deception. "There are times," he said, "when undercover reporting with very stringent

. . . safeguards, preceded by full discussion, is OK."[56]

Claude Lewis, editorial writer for the *Philadelphia Inquirer*, would not misrepresent himself over the telephone, but he recalls slipping on a white coat a couple of times to get a story. Once he did that to pass as a physician in order to get into a hospital room to interview a patient for the Philadelphia *Bulletin.* He found that the man, who was being held for shooting himself and about eight people in Cherry Hill, New Jersey—killing some and injuring others—was being held in the same recovery room with many of his victims. Another time, working for *Newsweek* in the sixties, he and other reporters were trying to find out what was going on in a New York hotel room in which the owner of a major league baseball franchise was negotiating with some people to sell the team. When the people in the room sent down for some food and a waiter rolled up with a food tray, Lewis talked him into letting him don his jacket and take the food into the room where he got some idea of what was happening. "I just stood around and listened for a while," Lewis recalls. "I was a natural part of the scene—you know, a black guy with a tray."[57]

About thirty police officers were discharged or suspended after Alex Dobish, reporter for the *Milwaukee Journal,* got an interview with a woman who claimed she had been taken out of her jail cell to a police stag party where she was forced to perform sexual acts on the stage with several policemen. Dobish got the interview by putting on a good suit, picking up his briefcase, and striding confidently into the hospital where the woman was being held. He did not say who he was, but hospital officials must have assumed he was a lawyer because they let him go to the woman's room. Dobish's managing editor, Joe Shoquist, says he both "reprimanded and complimented" the reporter.[58]

A good illustration of how opinion divides among journalists on misrepresentation, whether it be active or passive, is provided by Gene Roberts and former *New York Times* executive editor Abe Rosenthal. Both of them once had reporters who donned coveralls to get close to airplanes involved in news stories. Rosenthal chastised a new reporter who tried to pass as an airline mechanic to get near the plane in which the wife of defecting Soviet ballet star Alexander Godunov was being detained.[59] When an enterprising *Inquirer* reporter put on a similar costume and succeeded in getting into a hijacked plane being held at the Philadelphia airport, Roberts not only approved; he gave the reporter a bonus.[60]

Some Lesser Deceptions. Some types of misrepresentation and deception are acceptable even on papers with ironclad "no masquerading" rules such as the *New York Times.* Restaurant reviewers, consumer reporters, and travel writers find it more honest to be a little dishonest sometimes.

Restaurant critics who want to avoid any special treatment they might receive if the restaurant knows it is being reviewed usually hide their identities. If they make reservations, they do so in some other name. David Shaw, media reporter-critic for the *Los Angeles Times,* observes that to avoid being recognized some critics wear funny hats or wigs, eyeglasses one time but not another, go with different people each time, or deliberately show up ten minutes late so that the rest of the party is already seated.[61]

Elaine Tait, restaurant critic for the *Philadelphia Inquirer,* tries hard to keep from being known, but "more important than all that cloak and dagger stuff is knowing what you're doing—being informed, honest, and sober." She never drinks wine with her meals when she is reviewing "because I need to be as sharp as I can." Although most newspapers and magazines never run photographs of their restaurant reviewers, the *Philadelphia Inquirer* and the *Detroit News* run promotion ads with pictures of their reviewers. Tait says she "sort of objects" to her picture being used but she doubts that many people would recognize her because newspaper pictures are "so one dimensional." She says that if she senses she is known in some restaurant, she orders prepared food (such as the soup of the day) and other things that cannot be whipped up at the last minute.[62]

Reporters trying to find out how consumers are treated by various kinds of retail businesses almost invariably do their checking as ordinary customers and not as reporters. Most, however, identify themselves as reporters to get comments from owners and managers after they have done their research. This not only helps balance their stories; it allays any feeling among the retailers who have been checked that they have somehow been taken advantage of.

Responsible travel writers—there are plenty of the other kind as we learned in Chapters 3 and 4—often find it best to travel as ordinary citizens. Alfred S. Borcover, editor of the travel section of the *Chicago Tribune* and a former two-term president of the SATW, has sent writer Kermit Holt on a number of tours incognito. In 1981, for example, Holt signed up for one of those whirlwind budget trips to Europe—nine or ten countries in twelve or fourteen days. His report showed both goods and bads, Borcover says, and the tour company wrote to them later saying that it was trying to correct the problems Holt had noted. A year or so earlier, Holt signed up for one of the first tours of China, not as a travel writer but as just another tourist. "Craig Claiborne may have taken a gourmet tour of China," Borcover notes, "but our man, who traveled the way most Americans will have to travel to China, found the food was not so hot."[63]

GUIDELINES FOR DECEIT

The codes of ethics and standards of national journalism organizations do not specifically deal with undercover reporting, deception, and misrepresentation, but some of the policy statements of individual news organizations do. The Operating Standards of NBC News, for example, state that "misrepresentations by NBC News personnel of their identity or of any other material fact, even though intended solely to expedite an investigation, are generally *not* necessary and should be avoided." It goes on to say that in those "isolated and infrequent situations" in which concealing your identity seems necessary, the president of NBC News should be consulted.

Similarly, ABC News cautions its reporters not to "disguise their identity or pose as someone with another occupation without the prior approval of ABC News management."

CBS News says "misrepresentation should be avoided" because candor by reporters and producers better achieves the purpose. But identity might be withheld, CBS News adds, when "there is clear reason to believe that an improper activity could otherwise not be reported."

"We should avoid impersonation," the code of the Rochester *Times-Union* and *Democrat and Chronicle* states. "Posing as a prisoner or a mental patient or a salesperson or a public employee in order to report authoritatively rarely produces results that are significant to offset the risks that may result." Advising staff members to consult with editors about appropriate ways to report a story, the Rochester code says:

> There are two tests for editors to consider in deciding whether to authorize a covert form of reporting. First, would misrepresentation by a reporter violate the rights of individuals that are guaranteed under the Fourth Amendment? Second, is the information being sought of such overwhelming public importance that a reporter can be allowed to undertake impersonation?

The *Philadelphia Inquirer* also condemns impersonation, contending that it "undermines the trust that should be implicit in our relationship with the public." Admitting that it is difficult to distinguish between enterprise and deception, the *Inquirer* code says, however, that "entrapment or criminal methods to develop a story cannot be condoned." Approval of the executive or managing editor is required in the rare instances when deception may be necessary to get an important story, the *Inquirer* code adds.

That kind of top-level approval also is required by the codes of the *Detroit Free Press* and the Sioux Falls, South Dakota, *Argus Leader.* But "staff members generally should identify themselves as *Free Press* staff members," the Detroit paper says. The *Argus Leader* cautions its staff to "identify themselves by name and tell sources they are from the *Argus Leader.*"

Although only a few news media codes deal with this problem of deception, misrepresentation, impersonation, masquerading, and undercover reporting, the use of covert techniques seems to be on the wane in American journalism. This is linked to a general decline in investigative reporting – the name journalists give to depth inquiries that dig beneath superficial facts – and fewer and fewer of the diminishing number of depth investigations employ undercover methods these days. Even at Pam Zekman's shop, WBBM-TV, Chicago, only about half of the investigative projects done in recent years have involved undercover techniques. Zekman, formerly with the *Chicago Tribune* and *Chicago Sun-Times* and considered by most to be one of the most skillful investigative and undercover reporters in the business, says that undercover means were used in only one of the three stories her station did recently that "have had the most dramatic results." She emphasizes, however, that she still believes undercover reporting "not only is justifiable, it is sometimes the only way to do it."[64]

Zekman believes there are ethical ways to report undercover:

> 1. Don't do anything in an undercover capacity that would be breaking the law, except . . . in situations such as the classic example when you have evidence of gun-running or government agencies not doing what they're supposed to do to stop the free flow of illegal firearms. To prove the point, you go buy a gun. You're breaking the law. To cover yourself you immediately notify and turn the gun over to authorities. There are people who don't agree with this. . . . They're concerned about keeping an arm length's distance (from government). But somewhere along the line you have to balance all that out. . . . As far as I'm concerned the appropriate thing is to show that you don't intend to break the law for personal gain or profit but to make a point and thereby uncover something that needs to be corrected. . . .
>
> 2. Make sure that in the undercover capacity you don't put yourself in a position where you are doing things for which you are not trained and where you may hurt somebody in the process. A doctor, a nurse, for example. If you're trying to prove something about illegal chemical dumping and pose as a truck driver to make a haul of toxic chemicals, what if you get into an accident because you're not really qualified to drive that truck? . . .
>
> 3. Steer away from staying in the undercover capacity too long, and doing the very things that you end up criticizing the people you are investigating for. . . . I worked for a bill collector who liked to scare people by impersonating the police; he'd call up and say,

"There's a warrant out for your arrest." The last thing I was going to do was to get on the phone and do that myself. It got a little sticky when he wanted to get on another phone and listen to me talking to people, and I had to leave. The way you get around that, if you feel you need to stay longer, is to tell the guy you need more training, that you don't feel secure . . . one more day, one more day, and drag it out as long as you can. . . .

4. Another standard: When . . . involved in a situation where . . . undercover work will cost people money, . . . pay for their inconvenience or their services. For example, at the *Sun-Times* we did a series called "The Accidents" about lawyers and doctors who counseled people how to commit insurance fraud, how to fake injuries and get into the hospital. Part of our story involved our people being put into the hospital by these lawyers even though they weren't injured because we wanted to see whether . . . they would treat us or just let us sit there for five days. They let us sit there for five days with no treatment, and that became part of the story. But the hospital, which was not directly involved, was out a bed. We demanded a bill and paid them before the series came out.[65]

A journalism ethicist, Deni Elliott of Utah State University, has developed a six-question method to help journalists decide if the information they are seeking is worth going undercover to get (using what she calls "active misrepresentation" or "masquerading"). She suggests prior consideration of these questions:

1. Why do the readers need this information?

2. Would your readers support your information-gathering technique even if the story you hope to find isn't there? This question is important because you probably have little solid information or you wouldn't be using the deceptive technique in the first place. If you have enough solid information, the story could be written without undercover work. Whether the reporter finds what she/he hopes or not, public response is the most important consequence to consider.

3. Have you exhausted all other means for obtaining the information?

4. What are your arguments against law enforcement officers doing this undercover work rather than reporters? The result of a law enforcement investigation is likely to harm fewer people than a journalistic undercover investigation. Law enforcement officers are only interested in the persons performing criminal acts. Everyone is vulnerable in a journalistic investigation and anyone in the situation may be unwillingly exposed in the resulting story.

5. Does the reporter understand all of the risks of the assignment (to self and to the practice of journalism in general) and has she/he been given the chance to turn the assignment down?

6. If the problem is great enough for higher level deceptive prac-

tices, what changes are likely to occur through exposure? Is the potential change a great enough benefit to offset the certain damage created in the public trust?[66]

Applying her six-question test to two of the cases described earlier in this chapter, Professor Elliott found the infiltration of Camp Lejeune by a team from the Wilmington paper to be a justifiable deception. But she concluded that Leslie Linthicum's masquerading as a high school student was not justifiable. I applied her six questions to those situations and concluded that neither was justifiable. To me, the theatrical raid by reporters dressed up like terrorists was a good example of stunt journalism, a step beyond masquerading or the usual undercover investigation. In fact, there seemed to have been little investigation of the sort that Zekman-like undercover reporters do. The stunt was the main concern, and it produced a splashy story. As for Leslie Linthicum's infiltration of the Albuquerque high school, her principal findings had to do with the methods and competence of the teachers she experienced. I think most thoughtful readers would ask, "What does this twenty-four-year-old Northwestern journalism graduate know about teaching? Why should I trust one who lies so easily?" The fact that Professor Elliott and I draw different conclusions from applying her test to these two cases is not surprising. I'm sure she does not posit her questions as a means for all journalists to arrive at the same decision, but to stimulate them to think more deeply and clearly about serious deception before they employ it.

On the surface, it is difficult – and for some impossible – to condone journalists lying or deceiving to get information. None of us wants to think of ourselves as liars. Yet who among us has never told a lie? As with most things, there are degrees of lying. There are also degrees of deception that journalists have practiced in pursuit of their stories. Hardly anyone in or out of journalism finds fault with the lesser deception of a restaurant reviewer who does not identify herself or himself as such while checking out an eatery. But some of the big guns of journalism have been challenging the use of more serious deception, as in undercover reporting and masquerading, which is the main reason such deception seems to be declining in the field. Yet the best of our undercover reporting has exposed evil, advanced knowledge, and improved civilization. That kind of journalism – when it is done by skilled, ethical, and careful journalists because there is no other way to get at a vital truth – should not be suppressed.

7 Fakery

"You know what you can do with your New Journalism. What I want are straight, factual news stories—and keep 'em short!"

Let's say you are a wire editor on a daily newspaper in California. From one of the wire services you get a news story that begins like this:

> LOS ANGELES—The $100,000 Lamborghini Countach shoots up the on-ramp at 65 mph in first gear, 80 mph in second.
>
> Once in the fast lane, the speedometer inches toward 200 mph. Signs along the deserted freeway flip past in a blur and gentle curves become hairpin turns. Make a mistake at that speed and both car and driver would likely disintegrate in flight.
>
> This is a "banzai run" with an outlaw racer, a man pursuing an illegal, dangerous and expensive hobby that goes beyond the speed limit and even beyond the reach of the law. For these racers, speed is a kind of intoxicant.
>
> "Military jets take off at 200 mph," the driver of the Countach says with a terse laugh. "If this car had wings . . ."
>
> He eyes the Ferrari Boxer and Vector Twinturbo V2 behind him in electronic rearview mirrors. The exotic cars in this high-speed caravan are barely visible out the Lamborghini's tiny back window: "It's the Italian philosophy of driving," he said of his sports car. "You don't have time to look back."
>
> Indeed, looming suddenly ahead is a dreaded black and white cruiser of the California Highway Patrol. The distance eaten up in a

second, the sports cars rocket past in a flash. As seen in the mirrors, the patrol car seems to be hurtling backwards as if shot from a cannon. Are its red lights turned on?

"Doesn't matter—might as well try to catch a Russian spy satellite," sneers the driver, who asks not to be identified. Nevertheless, some banzai runners take no chances—they've installed switches in their cars to flip off their tail lights and make their vehicles more difficult to follow.

By the time the patrol radios for help, the banzai runners will be hiding safely in some small town miles up the coast, slinking down back streets, maybe parking in a dark alley until things cool down.[1]

The rest of the story tells of police surprise that this new "sport" is as organized as it is and describes the banzai drivers as former race car drivers or the "newly rich," such as rock stars, actors, and Middle Eastern princes. Would you publish this story, assuming you had space? Would you question the story? Does it bother you that the writer of the story, who presumably was on the banzai run described, has protected (by not identifying) the drivers who obviously were breaking laws?

When this story was sent out by the AP to its member papers in California and Nevada, many published it. Three weeks later, they had to publish what the AP calls a "corrective." The story was partly phony and partly plagiarized. The reporter who wrote it, Gloria Ohland, had not been on the banzai run she described, or on any run. What she portrayed as if she had been a witness or participant was fabricated. She also had lifted parts of the piece from an article that had appeared nine months earlier in *New West* magazine. In addition, she attributed statements to a California Highway Patrol officer who denied that he had ever talked to her, and who said that the patrol had not had a problem with banzai runners.

When AP president Louis D. Boccardi confronted Ohland, she eventually admitted in the course of several telephone conversations that her story was a misrepresentation. The twenty-nine-year-old reporter decided then and there that she had no future with the AP and she resigned. She had been with the AP in its Los Angeles bureau for two and a quarter years. Before that, Boccardi reports, she had worked briefly in Minnesota as a part-time reporter for the AP. She graduated from St. Olaf College in Minnesota with a degree in English and did graduate work in mass communications at the University of Minnesota in 1977–78, but did not receive a degree.

Boccardi, who wrote the corrective himself, calls the episode "a serious lapse in our standards." Ohland did not fabricate the phenomenon of banzai racing, Boccardi concedes. "But she misrepresented the circumstances under which the story was gathered, she took some material from a magazine without credit, and she inaccurately attributed some quotations."[2]

An editor in the Los Angeles bureau, Steve Loeper, was officially reprimanded for not inserting in Ohland's story the fact that it was what she called a "composite," by which she meant it was her impression of what a banzai run would be like based on taking brief rides and talking to banzai sports car drivers. (Although "composite" in writing means melding people or things into a single entity, journalists have carelessly extended its definition to mean almost any kind of journalistic fabrication.) Loeper found that Ohland considered her story a "composite" when he passed along to her questions about the story that editors in AP headquarters in New York raised when they were considering the story for national transmission. But Loeper said he decided against changing the story because it "was a representative portrayal of a typical banzai run."[3] Boccardi is pleased that his New York editors raised the right questions, but he says what happened in the banzai run story is "easy for a reporter to do and hard for an editor to spot. We are so vulnerable to the integrity of our reporters."

The AP found out about the misleading and plagiarized story from David Shaw, media reporter-critic for the *Los Angeles Times*. Shaw was asked by his editors to look into Ohland's story after another *Times* reporter, Paul Dean, found that her story did not jibe with what he was turning up in his research for an article on the Lamborghini Countach. Shaw talked to Ohland, who told him that her description of the banzai run was a composite. "I just couldn't think of any other way to write the story," Shaw quoted Ohland as saying. Asked why she did not say in her story that she was writing a composite, Ohland told Shaw, "I didn't feel it was necessary." After reading to her similar passages in her story and in a *New West* article by David Barry, Shaw said Ohland told him she had read Barry's article and had gotten her sources from it, but she did not lift phrases from it for her story. However, she said she might have unconsciously taken some material from the *New West* article. Shaw in his report showed that several phrases and sentences that appeared in Barry's article as the author's own observations came out in Ohland's story as statements made by other people. Shaw also said that much of Ohland's story was similar to Barry's "in structure, tone and actual wording."[4]

Besides being an embarrassment, the Ohland story is one of several that have caused questions to be raised about the reporting and writing methods that some journalists use: fabricating news stories, plagiarizing, making up quotations, embellishing the facts so much that a false picture is presented. This kind of fakery is rare, but that it occurs at all is disturbing to those seeking a more ethical journalism.

FABRICATING NEWS

Unfortunately, one of the surviving traditions of American journalism is the manufacturing of news. Hoaxes, they used to be called. Perhaps the most celebrated journalistic hoax was the lengthy account, complete with drawings, of the manlike creatures with wings discovered to be living on the moon. This discovery of the "man-bats" and other lunar life was supposedly made by a Sir John Herschel, employing a giant new telescope. This nineteenth century version of pure baloney published in the *New York Sun* in 1835 helped that paper achieve the largest circulation of any daily in the world.[5]

The hoax did not die with the turn of the century. In the late 1950s when the *San Francisco Examiner* and the *Chronicle* were battling toe to toe for the largest circulation in town, the *Chronicle* started publishing a series of articles by outdoor writer Bud Boyd that put it ahead of its chief competitor. Boyd's articles, called "The Last Man on Earth," told how he and his family were surviving in the wilderness, living off the earth, like modern-day Robinson Crusoes. Lynn Ludlow, veteran reporter for the *Examiner,* recalls that his paper countered Boyd's circulation-winning series by sending its top investigative reporter to check out Boyd's claims. The *Examiner* reporter finally tracked down the Boyd family campsite, where he reportedly found canned food, tools, and other amenities of civilized life. When the *Examiner* published its exposé, the *Chronicle* sued, Ludlow reports, but the suit was dropped when the two papers entered into a joint operating agreement five or six years later.[6]

Broadcast news is not immune from fabricators. The late Jessica Savitch in her book *Anchorwoman* tells of a fellow anchorman at KYW, Philadelphia, who "always came up with cuter, funnier, more interesting closing pads than I did." She couldn't figure out how she was missing those good items in all the newspapers and magazines she scoured each day. "Finally I begged him to tell me where the hell he was getting his information," Savitch wrote. "I make it up," he said. His tenure at KYW was short, Savitch noted.[7]

The *Chicago Sun-Times* recently fired reporter Wade Roberts because he apparently made up a story about some "good ole Texas boys" watching the Chicago Bears thrash the Dallas Cowboys on TV in a bar in Eden, Texas. Although the story was used, some reporters and copy editors didn't like the smell of it. "Some people felt . . . it was just too pat a story," managing editor Kenneth D. Towers said. Towers was also surprised that Roberts had gone to the little town of Eden to do this story when his assignment was to do a Dallas-area color feature on the Bears' game there. Eden is 240 miles from Dallas. So the next weekend, Towers went back to Texas with his reporter to confirm that there really was a

"Bonner's" bar in Eden that was patronized by the characters Roberts had named in his story. Towers found no such bar in Eden and nobody in that area with the names Roberts had written.[8]

Janet Cooke and Jimmy's World. The *Washington Post,* a newspaper that has been a leader in setting higher ethical and professional standards for journalism, sent back a 1981 Pulitzer Prize for feature writing because the reporter admitted she had counterfeited the article that won it. Man-bats from the moon again!

The story that embarrassed the *Post* was a dramatic account of an eight-year-old heroin addict. The writer, Janet Cooke, gave him the name, "Jimmy," and her page one article was headlined, "Jimmy's World: 8-Year-Old Heroin Addict Lives for a Fix." Illustrated by a moving drawing of what *Post* artist Michael Gnatek, Jr., imagined Jimmy would look like as he was getting a fix, Cooke's article began:

> Jimmy is 8 years old and a third-generation heroin addict, a precocious little boy with sandy hair, velvety brown eyes and needle marks freckling the baby-smooth skin of his thin brown arms.

The article went on to paint a dreary and hopeless picture of "Jimmy's world" in Southeast Washington where he lived with his mother, an ex-prostitute, and her lover, Ron, a pusher who got Jimmy hooked on heroin. Jimmy wanted to be a dope dealer like Ron, the article said, and "he doesn't usually go to school, preferring instead to hang with older boys between the ages of 11 and 16 who spend their day getting high on herb or PCP and doing a little dealing to collect spare change." At the end of the article, Cooke described Jimmy being "fired up" with an injection of heroin:

> Ron comes back into the living room, syringe in hand, and calls the little boy over to his chair: "Let me see your arm."
> He grabs Jimmy's left arm just above the elbow, his massive hand tightly encircling the child's small limb. The needle slides into the boy's soft skin like a straw pushed into the center of a freshly baked cake. Liquid ebbs out of the syringe, replaced by bright red blood. The blood is then reinjected into the child.
> Jimmy has closed his eyes during the whole procedure, but now opens them, looking quickly around the room. He climbs into a rocking chair and sits, his head dipping and snapping upright again, in what addicts call "the nod."
> "Pretty soon, man," Ron says, "you got to learn how to do this for yourself."[9]

The story of Jimmy saddened, outraged, angered, and upset many

Washingtonians, including Mayor Marion Barry, who ordered a search for the child. Police Chief Burtell Jefferson threatened to have Cooke and *Post* editors subpoenaed if they did not reveal who Jimmy was. *Post* lawyers replied that the paper had a right under the First Amendment to protect its sources. As Robert U. Woodward, then assistant managing editor-metro, put it, "We went into our Watergate mode: Protect the source and back the reporter."[10]

Cooke had told her editors that the dope pusher in her article, Ron, had threatened to kill her if she told anyone who he was. No editor pressed her to identify Jimmy or his family. Instead they stood by her and succeeded in scaring off Washington officials. But three weeks after the story appeared, then managing editor Howard Simons was still worried about Jimmy. He ordered city editor Milton Coleman—who had shepherded Cooke's story from the moment she said she had heard of an eight-year-old heroin addict until it got into print—to find Jimmy. "Take Janet with you," Simons said. Coleman told Cooke what Simons wanted them to do, but before they got around to it, Cooke informed Coleman that there was no need to go. She said she had revisited the house and found that the family had moved to Baltimore. So that was that. Exit Jimmy.

Two months later, the *Post* entered the Cooke article in the Pulitzer competition for general local reporting. It ended up winning the Pulitzer Prize for feature writing after the Pulitzer advisory board moved it from the general local reporting category where it was about to place second. The jury of editors that had screened the local reporting entries had recommended that the prize in that category go to the Longview, Washington, *Daily News* for that small paper's coverage of the eruption of nearby Mount Saint Helens; it found Cooke's article "gripping and powerful," but put it second to the Longview entry. So the Pulitzer board, as it has done in the past, moved the *Post* entry and awarded it the Pulitzer for feature writing even though that jury of editors had not even seen the Cooke article. The only vocal dissent on the board came from Eugene C. Patterson, editor and publisher of the *St. Petersburg Times,* who said he considered the story "an aberration" that should never have been published.

Cooke, who had been on the *Post* news staff a little more than eight months when her "Jimmy's World" made page one, had herself a Pulitzer at the age of twenty-six. But the imagination that had gotten her the prize also brought her down. She had exaggerated her background and credentials when she applied at the *Post,* and on her biographical material she provided when the paper put her in for the Pulitzer. She claimed when she applied to the *Post* that she had two years on the Toledo *Blade* and was a Phi Beta Kappa graduate of Vassar College; she also said she could speak or read French and Spanish and had won an award from the Ohio Newspaper Women's Association. The biographical form she filled out for the Pulitzer entry claimed that in addition to graduating from Vassar, she had a master's degree from the University of Toledo and had studied at the Sorbonne; she added Portuguese and Italian to the foreign languages she claimed to know and reported six awards from the Ohio association. When the Toledo *Blade* started to do a "local gal makes good" story, it found that the biography transmitted by the AP from the Pulitzer form did not jibe with *Blade* records. Informed of the discrepancies, AP checked with Cooke, who said the biography she had submitted was essentially correct. *Post* editors were then brought into the act and Cooke's house of lies began to tumble. By early the next morning, the young reporter had confessed to her editors that "Jimmy's World" was a fabrication. She said she never encountered or interviewed an eight-year-old heroin addict. He was a "composite" of young addicts social workers had told her about. Most of her biography was also fiction: she had gone to Vassar but only for her freshman year, and then she returned to her home town and got a bachelor's degree in English from the University of Toledo; she had won one award from the Ohio Newspaper Women's Association; she studied French in high school and college but was not fluent in it. Cooke resigned, and the *Post* returned her Pulitzer with apologies.[11]

Why did she do it? At the time her fakery was discovered, Cooke refused to be interviewed, but about nine months later, she allowed Phil Donahue to interview her on NBC's "Today" show for the usual $400 to $500 actor's pay plus expenses. She said to Donahue that after spending about two months looking for the eight-year-old heroin addict her sources told her was out there, her "whole mindset was in the *Washington Post* mentality: He must be there and it's being covered up; I must find him." She decided to make up an eight-year-old addict, she said, because "the last thing I could do was to go to my editor and say, 'I can't do it.'" Cooke said she does not "excuse what happened: It was wrong; I shouldn't have done it. . . . I simply wanted . . . not to fail." Asked why she lied on her job application, Cooke, who is black, said she believed she would not have been hired otherwise and she felt "a need to be perfect."[12]

A *Post* staffer who knew Cooke, reporter-photographer Linda Wheeler, recalls conversations they often had when both would be working late in the newsroom. "She was attractive, but also friendly and nice," Wheeler relates. "I talked to her a lot about the Jimmy story, a story that went way beyond anything I could do. I was very impressed by that story, and I believed it." When Cooke's Pulitzer Prize was announced, Wheeler remembers congratulating her and asking whatever happened to Jimmy. "She looked me straight in the eye and said, 'You know, I was back there a couple of weeks ago and the women who were dealing out in front of the building told me that the mother and kid were still gone and that Ron was looking for me and they told me not to go in.' " Wheeler believes Cooke "lived her lies" and was not conscious of them.[13]

"The ultimate tragedy of the Janet Cooke episode was that it was so predictable," in the view of Lyle Denniston, U.S. Supreme Court reporter for the Baltimore *Sun.* "The power groupie, the fame-driven person runs through this profession now in great numbers. I don't think people respect truth very much: they respect theater and they respect excitement, but truth isn't a driving proposition anymore."[14]

The Case of Michael Daly. While journalism was still reeling from the embarrassment of Janet Cooke, a young columnist for the New York *Daily News* resigned after the London *Daily Mail* attacked him for writing "a pack of lies." The columnist, twenty-nine-year-old Michael Daly, was called back from Ireland by his editors when he could not satisfy their questions about a column he wrote which began:

> BELFAST–Peering over the hood of an armored car, gunner Christopher Spell of the British Army watched a child not yet in his teens fling a gasoline bomb against the front of the Northern Bank of Falls Road. . . . A soldier to Spell's right raised his SLR rifle and fired two shots. A 15-year-old named Johnny McCarten fell. . . . "If I'm lucky, the little Fenian will die," the soldier said.[15]

The column went on to tell in eyewitness detail how the British Army patrol had fired real bullets, instead of the nonlethal rubber or plastic ones. It focused on the soldier, Christopher Spell, reporting that he had watched a comrade shot, and how he saw similarities between himself and the working-class Catholics in Northern Ireland. The *Daily Mail* maintained that although a British trooper had shot a Catholic boy that day, there was no soldier in the British Army named "Christopher Spell." No member of that troop could have seen a comrade shot, the *Mail* claimed, and Daly also erred in reporting the date that the troop had arrived in Ireland and the route it took that day. Daly admitted using a pseudonym for the soldier and recreating scenes that he had not witnessed. One of his supervisors, James Weighart, executive editor of the *News,* said he is not convinced that Daly had ever been with that troop.[16]

Michael J. O'Neill, former editor of the New York *Daily News,* says it was Daly who suggested he resign. "I didn't say a word to him," O'Neill adds. O'Neill admits, however, that he had challenged two previous stories Daly wrote out of Washington. "So when the Irish story blew up," O'Neill reports, "I resolved to act because of public perceptions of the credibility of the paper."[17]

Daly had been with the *News* three years when he resigned and took up free-lance writing, later joining the staff of *New York* magazine. He is a 1974 graduate of Yale, and attended Phillips Academy at Andover, Massachusetts. Before joining the *News,* he had worked as a writer for the *Village Voice* and the Courier-Life newspapers, a chain of weeklies in Brooklyn.

Free-lance Fakery. Another modern-day journalistic faker, a young free-lance writer, sold a fabricated and plagiarized article to the *New York Times Magazine.* The *Times* apologized on the front page when it discovered that twenty-four-year-old Christopher Jones had made up his account of a trip with Khmer Rouge guerrillas to Cambodia that had appeared in its Sunday magazine on 20 December 1981. Jones admitted he had invented the article from his imagination and recollections of two 1980 visits to western Cambodia, according to the *Times.* In fact, he lifted material from an article he wrote about one of those visits that had been published in the Asian edition of *Time* magazine. He also confessed to plagiarizing a passage from André Malraux's *The Royal Way,* a novel set in Cambodia.[18]

It was the plagiarizing that did him in. About two weeks after the Jones article appeared in the *Times Magazine,* Alexander Cockburn wrote in the *Village Voice* that the ending of the article was evidently stolen from a Malraux passage depicting a blind Cambodian minstrel. The *Times* sent off a letter to Jones demanding an explanation and cancelling an assignment he had been given for another *Times Magazine* article, but he never replied. When the *Washington Post* quoted a Khmer Rouge official in Bangkok as saying that Jones had not visited the guerrilla enclaves in 1981, the *Times* executive editor at the time, Abraham M. Rosenthal, put three staffers on Jones's trail. They found him in Calpe, Spain. Jones eventually confessed to Rosenthal's bulldogs that he had intended to return to Cambodia in 1981—he showed them a letter from Khmer Rouge officials authorizing his return visit—but he did not have enough money to pay for the trip. So instead, he holed up for a month in a seafront apartment owned by his parents and a hilltop villa he shared with a fifty-two-year-old German woman, and wrote his fictitious account. When his manuscript was finished, he and the woman drove to Locarno, Switzerland, to mail it to New York, apparently to give the impression that he had flown from Thailand to Switzerland to rest after the rigors of his jungle adventure. Jones also sent in a forged expense account, including a fake bill from a Bangkok hotel.

Rosenthal said that the *Times* had checked on Jones and "was informed by a publication for which he had worked in Asia that he was a reliable journalist." His manuscript was also checked, but apparently not thoroughly enough. Rosenthal said the major mistake was not showing the Jones article to one of the *Times's* specialists on Cambodia. "We do not feel that the fact the writer was a liar and hoaxer removes our responsibility," Rosenthal added. "I regret this whole sad episode and the lapse in our procedures that made it possible."

THE NEW JOURNALISM

Unfairly perhaps, what has come to be known as the New Journalism took a lot of the rap for the explosive fictions crafted by Janet Cooke, Michael Daly, Gloria Ohland, and Christopher Jones. New Journalism is the label that has been put on the technique of writing fact articles as if they were short stories or novels, using the devices and modes of fiction writing to make the articles more dramatic and interesting. Practiced by skillful writers and reporters like Tom Wolfe and Gay Talese, New Journalism has produced some lively articles and books that have also been fairly truthful. Younger writers have imitated the style of Wolfe, Talese, and other New Journalists – and this frequently has brought them applause and promotions from newspaper and magazine editors eager to publish more interesting styles of writing. But a few have practiced their New Journalism without the careful research and reporting – saturation, Wolfe calls it – needed for truthful portrayals. A fabricated piece of journalism is even more harmful when it is so beautifully written that readers are bedeviled into believing it.

One of the early practitioners of the New Journalism was Gail Sheehy whose use of composites stirred much controversy in the field. After doing extensive research on prostitution in New York City, Sheehy described how prostitutes dispense more than pleasure. "These girls swindle, mug, sometimes murder their patrons," she wrote in two articles in *New York* magazine in 1971. The articles detailed the lives and fortunes of a prostitute named "Redpants" and her pimp, "Sugarman." These names were not just pseudonyms, a device journalists sometimes use to protect a news source or subject. They were names that Sheehy made up for the two composites she created from the several prostitutes and pimps she had interviewed. Instead of reporting on what each of her sources said and did, she expressed their words and actions through "Redpants" and "Sugarman."[19]

Many journalists criticized this use of composites when it became known. They didn't find out about it from reading the articles. It came out later when Sheehy was interviewed by other journalists. She had written a paragraph in the article with the composites explaining to her readers what she had done, but *New York* editor Clay Felker edited it out.[20] Sheehy apparently saw the composite technique as a way of protecting the specific identities of her unlawful sources, but also as a way of telling of what she had learned in a more dramatic and interesting way. The use of composites in nonfiction, however, is still not generally accepted in daily journalism as a way to tell stories.

Free-lance writer Teresa Carpenter, who got the 1981 Pulitzer Prize for feature writing that had originally been awarded to Janet Cooke, was chastised by the late National News Council for one of the three articles in *Village Voice* that won her the prize. The council investigated her story about Dennis Sweeney, the young man who was sentenced to a psychiatric center for murdering Representative Allard K. Lowenstein in 1980, and concluded that it was "marred by the over-use of unattributed sources, by a writing style so colored and imaginative as to blur precise meanings, and by such reckless and speculative construction as to result in profound unfairness to the victim of a demented killer."[21] The council was particularly disturbed by this paragraph in Carpenter's article:

> After the shooting, in fact, there were rumors that Lowenstein and Sweeney had fallen out as the result of a lover's quarrel. Everyone simply assumed that Lowenstein had approached Sweeney. (Now, from his cell at Rikers Island, Sweeney denies that they ever had a relationship. Once while he and Lowenstein were traveling through Mississippi together, they checked into a motel. According to Sweeney, Lowenstein made a pass and Sweeney rebuffed it. Sweeney is not angry with Lowenstein, he claims. Nor does he feel any shame. It's just that Lowenstein wasn't always above board.)[22]

Would you assume after reading that paragraph that the writer had interviewed or talked to Sweeney at Rikers Island? The council and many other critics of the article believe most readers would make that assumption. In fact, Carpenter did not talk to Sweeney. Although Carpenter and the *Village Voice,* a New York weekly tabloid, did not cooperate with the council in its investigation, she told the *New York Times* that the statements attributed to Sweeney came from third parties. She noted that none of the statements were in quotation marks. "The reader has to trust me when he or she is reading the piece," Carpenter told the *Times.* "I do not feel compelled to attribute each and every piece of information to its source. I don't mean to sound arrogant, but I do mean to sound confident."[23]

The *Wall Street Journal* also interviewed Carpenter and reported that she had never even met Sweeney. The *Journal* plucked the following passage from her article as representative of the "liberties taken in the name of the so-called New Journalism":

> Sweeney was utterly alone. . . . Lowenstein, he was sure, had willed the murder of San Francisco Mayor George Moscone in 1978, as well as the 1979 DC-10 crash in Chicago. . . . The plan he devised contained a simple and chilling logic. He would confront Lowenstein and demand assurances that in the future he would leave Sweeney, his family, and others alone. If he got those assurances, Sweeney intended to drive home to Oregon. . . . If not, he would have to destroy his tormentor.[24]

Asked how she could write about what Sweeney was thinking without talking to him, Carpenter told the *Journal* she did not mean to imply that she had talked to Sweeney. "It's very cumbersome to say, 'According to sources close to Sweeney,' " she commented. She said the passage above about Sweeney's thoughts was derived from interviews with Sweeney's attorney and another man who talked to Sweeney after the killing and requested anonymity. "I knew in my gut that this is what Sweeney was thinking," Carpenter said. "It's incumbent upon me to make judgments. Otherwise I'm shunting off responsibility and being terribly cautious, and being a clumsy writer in the process." Carpenter said Sweeney wrote to the *Voice* disputing a few points in her story but not its main thrust or the passage quoted above.[25]

Haynes Johnson, reporter-columnist for the *Washington Post*, is turned off by much of what passes for New Journalism. "When Tom Wolfe and the people who call themselves the New Journalists use composite characters and tell us what people are thinking because they've talked to so many of them, well, they're just playing God," Johnson says. "I find that pretentious." He believes there is a need for more polished writing in journalism. "But you don't make up quotes and composite characters and label it as journalism," Johnson says. "It's something else, and should be labeled as something else."[26]

Another tradition in journalism that has contributed to some fakery is the embellishment that once powerful rewrite men added to the bald facts gathered by reporters, some of whom were called legmen. Rewrite men and legmen have all but disappeared in newsrooms today (if they existed, obviously they would have to be called rewrite and legpersons), but the tradition of embellishing stories lives on. "Good editors have to watch for trimmings that writers have added and cut the crap out," says Claude Sitton, editorial director of the Raleigh *Times* and *News and Observer.* "You have to watch your good writers particularly. They don't like rough edges and they'll knock them off everytime."[27] Donald Haskin, associate editor of the *Philadelphia Daily News,* is cheered that newspapers have done away with old-time rewrite men who could hype quotes and embellish stories, but he sighs: "Those crusty old bastards would never dream of doing what Janet Cooke did."[28]

Docudramas. Out of the ashes of the television documentary, the most effective instrument of journalism that TV has developed, has arisen the docudrama, the artful mingling of fact and fiction. How sad. As documentaries have gradually slipped away from the nation's TV screens, fact-based dramas have taken their place, with much higher audience ratings but with unlimited potential for misleading the American public.

For example, the docudrama, "The Atlanta Child Murders," aired by CBS in 1985, was based on the 1982 conviction of Wayne Williams for murdering two young black men and for being implicated in the murder of twenty-three other young blacks in that city. The docudrama made you feel that Williams was innocent. It was apparently intended to do that since its author, Abby Mann, said his film was "definitely a crusade."[29]

That was too much for David Shaw, media reporter-critic for the *Los Angeles Times,* who wrote:

> A crusade? Well, okay. Crusade. That's a legitimate and honorable journalistic exercise. You take a team of reporters to Atlanta; you investigate the murders; you (maybe) uncover evidence the police neglected or concealed. Then you do a documentary showing the new evidence and — if it exists — the cover-up (or the frame-up). But you don't dramatize; you don't invent; you don't create composite characters; you don't put in what you think happened or wish had happened — at least you shouldn't do any of this when you're going into millions of living rooms with a story purportedly based on fact, a story calculatingly based on one of the most sensitive issues of our time.[30]

Shaw and other critics of docudramas fear that many viewers think that they're true. Most of them come right out of yesterday's headlines. But docudrama makers are not reporters or news analysts. Journalism is not their game. They take the facts that help them create a dramatic and appealing story, and they make up the rest of it. "The people who turn these news stories into movies and miniseries don't seem to worry much about telling the full story — or even the true story — as long as they can stay close enough to the truth to exploit viewer interest in the events they are dramatizing," Shaw contends.

Two other docudramas severely criticized for compounding Americans' uncertainty about two major episodes in recent history were put on by ABC in 1977. Daniel Schorr, senior news analyst for National Public Radio and a CBS News correspondent for twenty-five years, said the docudrama "Washington: Behind Closed Doors" gave "a perverted view of Watergate's real drama and tragedy." The script came from a novel by John Ehrlichman, a disaffected former Nixon aide who took up novel writing while in prison for his role in the Watergate scandal. "It created the impression," Schorr said, "that President Nixon, covering up Watergate, and CIA director Richard Helms, covering up a political assassination, may have blackmailed each other into silence."

The second ABC docudrama severely criticized was "The Trial of Lee Harvey Oswald," which suggested, according to Schorr, "that if Oswald had survived to be tried for killing President Kennedy, he would have emerged as the innocent scapegoat for Mafia or CIA assassins." The script also hinted that President Johnson was somehow involved in the assassination, Schorr said.[31]

"I like fiction," Shaw maintains. "I also like facts. . . . What I don't like—what I resent—is the bastardization and confusion of fact and fiction. I don't like newspaper or magazine stories based on composite characters and invented dialogue that are passed off as fact, and I don't like the callous blending of fact and fiction, of documentary and drama, in the horrendous TV hybrid we call docudrama."[32]

Plagiarism. One of the ethical sins that Ohland committed in the "banzai run" story that forced her resignation from the AP was that she plagiarized parts of it. She apparently lifted sections of an article from *New West* magazine and passed them off as her own words. That's serious enough when a college student does it, but it can be career smashing for a professional writer.

Yet anyone who has been in journalism very long knows that a mild form of plagiarism goes on all the time. News organizations and reporters save clips of news stories and articles they may need again, sometimes informally in pockets, drawers, and briefcases, and sometimes formally in news department libraries, traditionally called morgues. When these clips are pulled out for help in doing a story, words, phrases, and whole passages frequently are lifted and repeated. This is no big deal when the stuff being lifted is from your own publication, but it is more serious when the words and ideas are picked up from other writers and publications without credit, as is sometimes the case.

The more serious kind of plagiarism, however, is the kind that the *Washington Post* had to deal with a few years ago. Benjamin C. Bradlee, executive editor, recalls that a new young reporter—"a brilliant Radcliffe graduate"—wrote a story about singles apartments in the area. "The next day someone called us and pointed out that six paragraphs of her story were taken verbatim from Salinger's *Catcher in the Rye*," Bradlee says. "I was stunned. We had to fire the girl." The editor says that the young woman underwent psychiatric care for about six months and then got back into the news business with one of the Detroit papers, but then committed suicide.[33]

When the *Best Newspaper Writing 1982* came out, it brought a call to

Roy Peter Clark, then editor of that annual collection of the winning articles in ASNE's writing contest. One of the stories in the collection was a piece by Tom Archdeacon of the *Miami News* about race car driver Linda Vaughn. That article was unusually interesting to Clark's caller, Jerry Bledsoe of the *Greensboro Daily News and Record,* because he had written a chapter on Vaughn in his 1975 book *The World's Number One, Flat-Out, All-Time-Great Stock Car Racing Book.* In fact, Bledsoe told Clark, he found many of his own words coming up at him out of Archdeacon's article. Clark said Bledsoe sent him "a copy of his chapter, underlining ten instances (about 100 words) in which Archdeacon had borrowed from him without attribution."[34]

Clark reported Bledsoe's complaint to ASNE officers, who first notified the *Miami News* and then set up a special meeting to deal with their problem. When confronted by his editors, Archdeacon explained that because he liked Bledsoe's book, he had turned to it for background on Vaughn. Then in writing under deadline, he got his own notes mixed up with what he had copied in them from Bledsoe and apparently picked up some of Bledsoe's words, thinking they were his own. "I swear to God," Archdeacon wrote in a required mea culpa in the November 1983 *ASNE Bulletin,* "there was no deviousness intended."

The ASNE board chided Archdeacon, but he was allowed to keep his award, and the *News* let him keep his job. "While what happened is a journalistic misdemeanor and not a felony—and appears to be a mistake rather than plagiarism—the board deplores that such gross carelessness and sloppiness could be part of the working procedure of such a talented writer," the ASNE board declared in its wrist slap.[35]

Some newspapers apparently are rougher on plagiarism than the *Miami News* was in the preceding case. The *St. Petersburg Times* obtained a resignation from reporter Julia McKnight after she passed off as her own about a third of an article on credit cards from *Changing Times.* She put a letter on the newsroom bulletin board the day she resigned which read:

> Twelve years of dedicated journalism down the drain because of a stupid mistake. I am writing this public explanation for a selfish reason. It will be easier for me to live with myself knowing that the truth is known. But I hope my mistake will serve as a lesson to others. I have let the *Times* down. I have let myself down. But most of all, I have let the profession down. And for that I am truly sorry.[36]

When Steve Lovelady first joined the *Philadelphia Inquirer* as an associate editor after reporting for the *Wall Street Journal,* he started searching through *Inquirer* clips to determine who the good and not so good writers were.[37] *Inquirer* executive editor Eugene Roberts remembers how impressed Lovelady was with one very well written article he found, but something about it seemed familiar to him. The next day he remembered. No wonder it seemed familiar. It was his article–one he had done for the *Journal*–that an *Inquirer* reporter had plagiarized. Roberts says the reporter was let off with a warning, but had to be dismissed about a year later when *Fortune* magazine informed him that one of its articles had been picked up verbatim by the same writer.[38]

Quote Tampering and Such. Quotation marks are supposed to say to the reader, "What's inside here are the exact words of whoever is being quoted. Verbatim." And most of the time what we read in the press inside quotations marks is a reasonably accurate facsimile of what the source said. Careful writers do not use direct quotation unless they are sure they are presenting the exact or nearly exact words of the speaker; if they are not sure, they use indirect quotation, paraphrasing what the speaker said as accurately as possible and not enclosing any words in quotation marks.

But there is also a convention in journalism of "cleaning up" quotations that are ungrammatical or that contain obscene or offensive language. This is often done merely by changing the offensive words and substituting correct or inoffensive ones, without removing the quotation marks. Some journalists object to such editing because it sometimes conveys a false picture of the speaker. *Dallas Times Herald* columnist Molly Ivins argues that "people stand up on the floor of the Texas legislature and make jackasses of themselves all the time. It is not my responsibility to make them look good." But Eugene C. Patterson, chief executive officer of the *St. Petersburg Times*, believes there are times that journalists have "to use horse sense" and clean up ungrammatical quotations. "I think if you deliberately permit the reader to be confused, you're not working for the person," Patterson contends. "If you ever tried to parse a sentence by President Eisenhower, or even President Reagan, you realize the man needs help. When it is clear what he is trying to say, I don't think it does any harm to try to clear away the obvious underbrush."[39]

Not so often employed or talked about in American journalism is the bad habit of tampering with quotes to make them more exciting and interesting, or making up quotes. Sharp editors who have been around a while recognize and destroy some versions of the exaggerated or made-up quote: Anything said by an unnamed taxi driver is suspect ("As one veteran cab driver put it, 'When you got a mayor who won't tip, you got a city in trouble.'"). Reporters who yearn to summarize or moralize in the manner of essayists or editorial writers have been known to slip their judgments into their news stories through the mouths of such unnamed observers. These brief betrayals of truth that get into print probably do not do much damage to humankind, but they are dishonest and can cause a loss of trust in truthful reporting.

Sometimes the quote tampering gets more serious. Wayne Thompson, associate editor and veteran reporter and editorial writer for the Portland *Oregonian,* was suspended without pay for eight weeks when he fabricated some quotations from an interview with Washington Governor Dixy Lee Ray. The nightmare that occurs to all reporters who use tape recorders became reality for Thompson when his recorder malfunctioned without his knowing it during an hour-long interview with the governor. He could make out parts of the tape when he got back to his office, but feedback from Governor Ray's tape recorder hummed out many of the governor's words on Thompson's tape. Because his paper had already promoted the upcoming interview with Ray to its readers and because he could make out about fifteen quotes clearly, Thompson decided to try to reconstruct other quotes from his notes and the imperfect sound of his tape. That was a mistake. The governor complained, sending the paper a transcript of the interview from her own taping of it to show that twenty statements attributed to her were inaccurate or fabricated. The *Oregonian* ran a lengthy retraction and punished Thompson, who at the time had had twenty-six years of experience in the news business.[40]

Advice columns have been standards in American newspapers for a long time, and almost every daily in the country today carries "Ann Landers" or her sister, "Dear Abby." Many papers in recent years have gone in for action line or hot line columns that try to respond to questions from readers seeking help or advice with almost any problem you could imagine. In most such features, the persons seeking advice are allowed anonymity. That opens the door for various kinds of fabrication, from the silly letters Ann Landers gets from Yale undergraduates pretending to be "Panting Patty from Paducah" or "Swinging Sally from Syracuse," to the more serious manufacturing of letters by staff members of the newspapers publishing the advice columns. Rich Stim, a San Francisco rock musician, confessed in a *Columbia Journalism Review* article that by the time he reached his fifth and last year as editor of the hot line column for the Bloomington, Indiana, *Herald-Telephone* he was creating more than half of the questions he got. As with car thieves who start by shoplifting pencils, Stim started small. He made up two questions once—by turning two facts from the *World Almanac* into readers' queries—in order to leave work early to practice with the rock band he had joined. Nobody said a word. So he was soon making up one or two questions for each of his columns. Stim's editor unconsciously encouraged the practice when he selected the questions for the "best of the Hot Line" column at the end of that year and chose a majority from those Stim had dreamed up.[41]

More recently the *Philadelphia Daily News* started a new advice col-

umn by psychologist David Stein called "Ask David." The column started
out on its first day answering questions from "Frustrated Mom, East
Falls," "Perplexed, S. Phila.," and "Mark, Mt. Airy." As the column
warmed to its task, letters appeared from "Irritated Hubby, Ardmore"
complaining that his wife's "best friend is a lying creep," and from "Carol,
Bala Cynwyd" who was concerned that her husband was too liberal because he told their young daughter details about their lovemaking ("Your
husband's no liberal, he's a pervert," David replied). But when David
printed a letter from "Worried, Kensington," asking advice because after
twenty-two years of marriage her husband "all of a sudden wants to tie
me down to the bed during sex," that was too much for Clark DeLeon,
who writes "The Scene" column for the *Philadelphia Inquirer.* DeLeon
snooped around and reported that all those heavy letters David had received had been written by *Daily News* staff members. *Daily News* editors
said the in-house efforts would end as soon as enough legitimate letters
started rolling in. "Sign us, 'Cynical, South Philly,' " DeLeon concluded.[42]

STANDARDS, WRITTEN AND UNWRITTEN

What was most shocking to many journalists about the fabrications
of Janet Cooke, et al., was that they violated a principle that is so basic to
journalism that you don't have to talk about it and you don't even have to
write it down. Everyone who gets into journalism is supposed to understand that lies and fakery are simply not allowed. Fiction has no place in
journalism.

Because the principle of not lying, not making things up, is so well
understood, the codes of ethics of national news organizations do not deal
with it in any very specific way. There is no provision in any of them that
says simply: "Journalists don't lie!" Perhaps there should be, in view of
the recent resurgence of fakery in journalism.

To most journalists, the accuracy standard means getting your facts
right and presenting them honestly. And it also means being truthful. So
we find in all the national codes some proviso against inaccuracies.

The only code of a national journalistic association that deals specifically with plagiarism, however, is that of the Society of Professional Journalists, which in 1984 added a sentence to its 1973 ethics code condemn-
ing plagiarism as "dishonest and . . . unacceptable."

Some of the codes of individual news organizations also prohibit
plagiarism. The *Washington Post* states that "attribution of material from
other newspapers and media must be total. Plagiarism is one of journalism's unforgivable sins."[43] The *Philadelphia Inquirer* warns its staff to "be

careful not to use someone else's analyses, interpretations or literary devices such as distinctive descriptive phrases unless they are clearly attributed." And the *St. Paul Pioneer Press and Dispatch* attacks the ancient but dishonest practice of lifting stories from other newspapers. "Do not lift a story from other newspapers—including our own—and reprint it," the St. Paul code states. "We should check out all stories and develop our own facts."

Two newspaper codes attempt to define plagiarism in condemning it. "Using the words or the illustrations of others—writers, artists, or the publications in which their work appears—is plagiarism," the Rochester *Times-Union* and *Democrat and Chronicle* says. "It is a form of deception. . . . We should not borrow the work of others unless credit is given to them."

The code of the *Detroit Free Press* states:

> Using someone else's work without attribution—whether deliberately or thoughtlessly—is a serious ethical breach. Staff members should be alert to the potential for even small, unintentional acts of plagiarism, especially in the reporting of complicated stories involving many sources.
>
> Borrowing ideas from elsewhere, however, is considered fair journalistic practice. Problems arise in the gray areas between the acceptable borrowing of inspiration and the unacceptable stealing of another's words. Our standards:
>
> • Words directly quoted from sources other than the writer's own reporting should be attributed. That may mean saying the material came from a previous Free Press story, from a television interview, from a magazine or book or wire service report.
>
> • When other work is used as the source of ideas or stylistic inspiration, the result must be clearly your own work. That is, what is acceptable to learn from another are the elements of style and approach—tone, rhythm, vocabulary, topic ideas—and not specific words, phrases, images.

The *Free Press* also attempts to deal with the problem of news sources who use faulty syntax. "What appears within quotation marks should be what the person said, with ellipses indicating omissions," the *Free Press* code explains. "Indirect quotations or partial quotations often can solve the problems of a speaker's grammatical or syntactical error or the lack of clarity. Quoting in dialect or using a nonstandard spelling will be done only rarely, must be in good taste and must serve an important journalistic purpose. Grammatical errors, when they are not important to the news or when they would make the speaker look foolish or take on undue importance, are to be avoided."

The *Philadelphia Inquirer* code, which outlaws "composite characters" in stories, also tries to deal with the quotation problem:

> We are confronted with two conflicting goals when using direct quotations. Although a person's words should be recorded verbatim insofar as it is humanly possible, it is equally important to refrain from using quotations in a manner that could seem critical or condescending.
>
> Generally, direct quotations are not altered in the editing process. The color of informal speech is one of the reasons for using quotations and should be retained. However, there are occasions when retaining informal and colloquial speech is important for reasons of color and accuracy, and there are occasions when that would be unnecessarily demeaning.
>
> Minor grammatical errors are repaired in those cases when a highly desirable direct quotation would be confusing or would make the speaker look foolish.

As we have seen in this chapter, the mostly unwritten journalistic "law" against fabricating news has been violated an alarming number of times. Writing new rules probably would not have prevented many of the fabrications that have polluted journalism. The only protection seems to be for the news media to hire and retain only people of character. No easy task.

8 Dubious Methods

"Are you sure we want our Debbie to go into journalism?"

Suppose you are president of a large broadcast network news department that is under fire in two major libel suits in which questions have been raised about your ethics and standards. In the course of one of the libel suits it comes out that one of your producers had secretly recorded a telephone interview with a former secretary of defense who is quoted in the *New York Times* as saying that the taping was "entirely unethical." The interview was one of several the producer had conducted in preparing a controversial television documentary that is the subject of one of the libel suits. The producer had not obtained prior approval from you or any of your department's executives as is required for such secret taping in your written operating standards. What would you do?

When this happened at CBS News, in the tense circumstances described, the producer, George Crile, was suspended indefinitely. The suspension was based on his violation of CBS News policy that top brass approval is needed before any of its journalists can tape record a telephone conversation without informing the person on the other end. Crile had recorded a telephone conversation with former Defense Secretary Robert S. McNamara in an attempt to get McNamara to be interviewed on film for the documentary.

Crile's suspension cost him the documentary he was working on then (having to do with the conflict in Nicaragua) but that's about all. He continued on the CBS payroll throughout the suspension, which lasted about a year. He was in court most of that time anyway defending himself against the libel suit that General William C. Westmoreland brought against him, CBS News, and others involved in preparing a documentary Westmoreland objected to. When the general dropped his $120 million libel suit, after a lengthy pretrial and trial, Crile went back to work for CBS as a producer with "60 Minutes," CBS's most popular news program.

The documentary Crile produced that stirred up the general and many of his supporters was aired in 1982 under the title, "The Uncounted Enemy: A Vietnam Deception." It accused General Westmoreland of conspiring to falsify enemy troop strength figures when he was commander of U.S. forces in the Vietnam War.[1]

Just before the Westmoreland suit was tried, CBS had to defend itself against another defamation suit brought against a "60 Minutes" report on insurance fraud by a Los Angeles physician, Dr. Carl A. Galloway. This well-publicized trial raised questions about certain reporting methods used by "60 Minutes," specifically an ambush interview conducted by CBS News star Dan Rather when he and his camera crew converged on a suspect medical clinic with cameras rolling. Although a jury ruled that CBS had not slandered Galloway, the questions about ethics and standards raised in the trial must have affected the mood of CBS News executives when they had to decide what to do about the revelation of Crile's violation.[2]

The tape that brought about Crile's suspension when it became evidence in the Westmoreland trial (and McNamara reacted so strongly to it) was not made to be used in the documentary. It was more of a working tape, Crile explains. "In television you really don't use (audio) tape recordings," he says. "I did it because McNamara had never given an interview on the war to my knowledge . . . and what I was going to be doing was trying to explain to him . . . what we had learned about the order of battle affairs in order to . . . try to get him to allow me to . . . talk to him further to see if he would come on the air."

The producer denies McNamara's later claim that their conversation was off the record. "It was just a conversation in order to set up an interview," Crile claims. "Frankly, I did not think that in a situation in which I had to go through the task of trying to explain what we had and to react to what he was saying that I would be able to take adequate notes. And I suppose, candidly, I did not want to say, 'I'm tape recording you,' when I was in the process of trying to persuade him to come on the air and share with us his history." Although Crile followed up this initial taped telephone conversation with a trip to Washington and another chat with McNamara, he was not able to persuade McNamara to be filmed for the documentary. Crile points out that McNamara was never quoted in any way in the documentary.

Crile, who started in journalism as a legman for muckraking columnist Drew Pearson and who worked as a newspaper reporter and magazine editor before joining CBS in 1976, believes that surreptitious telephone taping is often used by journalists. But he has never used tape recorders much because he finds them bulky and difficult to transcribe afterwards. When he decided to use a recorder for some of the preliminary interviews for the Vietnam War documentary, he says he knew it was not against the law in New York for him to tape record a phone conversation without informing the other party but he did not know then it was against CBS guidelines.

His experience with the McNamara tape has soured him on the tape recorder. "I don't want to use the damned thing," he says. "But I'm not altogether sure ethically what's wrong with recording a conversation if the understanding of the person on the other end is that you're trying to take notes. It seems to me that it is a more accurate way of taking notes."

Is Secret Recording an Ethical Question? Crile is not alone in his view that surreptitious recording by reporters may not be ethically wrong. Jack C. Landau, a journalist with a law degree who served for years as director of the Reporters Committee for Freedom of the Press, has written that the best way to "prove the accuracy of an important interview is to have made a tape recording of the discussion—with or without the consent of the person whose conversation was recorded."[3] Journalism professor Theodore L. Glasser, associate director of the Silha Center for the Study of Media Ethics and Law at the University of Minnesota, has argued that surreptitious recording by a journalist is a "tactical dilemma" rather than an ethical one. It is "no more of an ethical dilemma than choosing between shorthand and verbatim note-taking," he has written.[4]

Andrew Barnes, editor and president of the St. Petersburg Times, is in one of the thirteen states that require consent of all parties before a telephone call can be tape recorded. So that's the policy in his news department. But he sees nothing ethically wrong with taping an interview "if you have announced, as I hope you have, that you are a reporter, and somebody is willing to talk with you." He says the decision to tape is practical rather than ethical, noting that he himself prefers to take notes and not use tape recorders.[5]

Besides Florida, the other twelve states that require consent of all parties before a telephone call may be taped are: California, Delaware, Georgia, Illinois, Maryland, Massachusetts, Michigan, Montana, New Hampshire, Oregon, Pennsylvania, and Washington. Federal law is confusing. The Federal Communications Commission has had a rule since 1947 requiring that phone users have to sound an audible beep tone while taping calls unless the other party consents to being recorded. This rule, which applies only to interstate and not local calls, apparently is rarely enforced. But the FCC does have a rule for broadcasters that forbids airing any live or taped telephone conversation without the consent of all participants. On the other hand, Congress said in passing the 1968 Omnibus Crime Control Act that anyone may secretly record his or her own conversation with anyone else, whether that conversation is by telephone or in person. So much for the law as a guide through this ethical/practical/ tactical thicket.[6]

The *Lexington* (Kentucky) *Herald-Leader* won a 1986 Pulitzer Prize in investigative reporting for a series of articles that were based in part on surreptitious recordings. The series, written by reporters Michael York and Jeff Marx, revealed that boosters had made cash payments to University of Kentucky basketball players and those players had also profited illegally by selling their complimentary tickets at inflated prices. York and Marx used tape recorders for all of their interviews with former players and other sources. Their sources knew they were being taped when the interviews were in person, but they were not told about it when they were interviewed by telephone. York and Marx were given permission to bypass the paper's general policy against taping interviews without letting the source know because "we thought there was a good chance that some players would develop . . . 'amnesia' after the story appeared," York explained.[7]

In his 1983 survey of investigative reporting by the larger TV stations, Charles Burke found that a majority of stations did that kind of reporting, and of those who did, 64 percent used hidden cameras or microphones. Furthermore, Burke said, they had used such covert techniques in an average of 3.8 stories in the previous two years.[8]

If we can believe a 1982 University of Iowa survey, however, most editors of larger newspapers disapprove of surreptitious recording and they see it as an ethical matter. That survey showed that 83 percent of the editors of a cross section of newspapers with a circulation of 25,000 or more oppose journalists using hidden recording devices even if they properly identify themselves beforehand. Of those who disapproved, 85 percent said they based their response on ethics. But while the respondents in this survey as a general principle strongly rejected using hidden recorders (as in surreptitious taping) or cameras, only 22 percent would rule it out completely.[9] Many must realize that there are times when reporters investigating illegal activities might find that secret recording is the only way they can get evidence of wrongdoing. Seeking permission to tape the kind of characters they're dealing with would be futile.

Most of the tape recording being done in journalism today is not in sensitive investigations, but in more routine ways, such as recording interviews, speeches, news conferences, and the like. Most of the time it is obvious to news sources that they are being recorded. But when the telephone is injected between the reporter and the news source, the source has no way of knowing whether he or she is being recorded unless informed by the reporter. Some sources object to having their remarks recorded because they feel that a tape recording can more easily be transferred and perhaps misused by persons other than the reporter who interviewed them. They don't see a reporter's hand-written notes as being that transferable. Other sources, particularly those in politics, object to being recorded because they want to be able to deny what they said and not have a reporter able to refute them with a taped record of what they actually said.

When the tables are turned and journalists become news sources, they seem to have little fear of being tape recorded. At least that was my experience. Almost all of the 170 interviews I did for this book were with working journalists, and all of them were tape recorded, including about 50 that were conducted over the phone. In all cases, the people I interviewed knew I was recording them. Not one – not even George Crile – objected. I did not often use a tape recorder in my reporting days, however, because even the portable ones were heavy and cumbersome back then and the tapes were difficult to transcribe under deadline conditions. I'm sure if I were reporting today, I would make much greater use of the smaller and lighter tape recorders now available because tapes are simply much more accurate than my notes. I would continue to take notes, of course, and use them (as I did for this book) not only as backup in case of recorder malfunction, but as an index for finding material on the tapes. And as for the issue raised by the Crile case, I'm sure that if I were back in news work again, I would continue my practice of letting my sources know that I was recording them. I agree with A. M. Rosenthal, associate editor of the *New York Times,* that "it doesn't sit well in the stomach to tape someone and not tell them you're doing it. It's not honest. It's not fair. Period."[10]

Old-Fashioned Eavesdropping. Although many journalists regard secret recording as unethical, and an even larger number condemn listening in on other people with electronic devices or by tapping their telephones, old-fashioned eavesdropping with the naked ear is not seen as a serious ethical sin.

During the early part of the crisis after the Three Mile Island nuclear power plant breakdown, two *Philadelphia Inquirer* reporters pretended to be a couple of bickering lovers so they could stay in a hotel corridor to eavesdrop on a meeting of public relations executives for the utility. Each time a hotel official or some guest would come by, the two reporters, Julia Cass and Jonathan Neumann, would strike up a lovers' quarrel – which ranks right up there with picking your nose as a surefire way to get other people to look away. Many times reporters use what they hear from eavesdropping only as a lead, but Neumann and Cass did a story on what they heard through the hotel room door. Neumann explained that they had tried for days to talk to the officials inside but were always told that the head of public relations for the utility was too busy discussing the "nuclear question." But the conversation inside "was about the press question," Neumann said. "About how to get us off their tail. They had lied to us."[11]

The *Inquirer* told its readers how Neumann and Cass got their story and got no real public criticism of the method they used, reports executive editor Eugene L. Roberts. "We have to have high standards," Roberts believes, "but we can't get so finicky about ethics that we use them as excuses for not doing our jobs. . . . There's no ethics in being docile and the pawn of whoever wants to prevent you from getting the story."[12]

Robert Giles, executive editor of the *Detroit News,* opposes electronic eavesdropping, but old-fashioned eavesdropping does not bother him as much. He tells of using that technique twice in his reporting days on the *Akron Beacon Journal.* Once he listened at the door after being thrown out of a meeting of the area labor council. Labor officials were furious at him when his story was published. Another time he listened through a basement window of a hospital as police talked to the mother of a kidnapped infant whose body had just been found. Other reporters were "milling about" inside the hospital getting nothing. Giles says he got no flak on the second story. Even though he had those two experiences with the method, he still believes it should be used rarely and "with great caution."[13]

When public officials go behind closed doors, few reporters hesitate to listen in if they can. Jack Severson of the *Philadelphia Inquirer* has done that and he has listened in as lawyers and clients conferred in witness rooms at court houses, but he says he has never gotten anything more than leads to information that might be usable. "I've never based a story merely on what I heard through the door," Severson says, "and I've never eavesdropped except in public buildings."[14]

Getting caught while eavesdropping is embarrassing and not in keeping with the image most journalists like to project. Jack Landau got caught when he was covering negotiations between the port of New York and the longshoremen's union when he was working for the AP. Landau climbed on a chair and put a water glass to an opaque glass panel to hear what was being said in the closed meeting. After he had listened about ten minutes, one of the longshoremen left the meeting to go to the men's room and spotted him on the chair with his ear to the water glass. "All of a sudden I looked down from my chair to see a delegation of burly men rushing at me and screaming, 'The goddam press! We're breaking off negotiations!' " Landau, who had to call in a story that negotiations had broken off because an AP reporter was caught eavesdropping, feared that he was going to be fired, but his editor never said a word to him.[15]

Two reporters for the high-minded Louisville newspapers embarrassed their news bosses when they got caught eavesdropping on a police meeting in 1974. The reporters—Howard Fineman of the *Courier-Journal* and Jerry Hicks of the *Louisville Times*—were arrested as Fineman was lying on the floor while Hicks had his ear to the door of a room in which the local Fraternal Order of Police was holding a closed meeting. The reporters had a tape recorder with them, but they said they had not used it. Charges against both reporters were eventually dropped. What was going on that was important enough for them to take the risk they did? The police wanted to discuss the action of their chief in bugging their squad cars to check on possible police misbehavior.[16]

Michael J. Davies, who was managing editor of the *Louisville Times* when the two reporters were caught, says "the resultant publicity was awful." The publisher, Barry Bingham, Jr., "issued a statement saying that this was a terrible thing to do, but every once in a while we have to do it," Davies recalls, "which didn't sit well with anyone outside the papers." Davies opposes eavesdropping. "We should conduct ourselves the way other people do," he concludes.[17]

Hidden Cameras. A photographic form of eavesdropping is to take pictures of people without their knowing it. The *Chicago Sun-Times* did that in its famous Mirage investigation of bribery and shakedowns by government inspectors. Hiding in a compartment above the toilet rooms of the Mirage Tavern the paper bought for that project, photographers took pictures of police officers and inspectors as they accepted bribes from the reporters posing as owners of the tavern. The principal reporter on that assignment, Pamela Zekman, claims the paper was very careful not to publish any photo that showed ordinary patrons of the bar who were not known to the *Sun-Times* people on the project. "We were concerned about hurting someone who had done nothing wrong, such as someone involved in an affair." She would not support using a hidden news camera in a private home, but Zekman considers it to be an acceptable technique in a public place, like the Mirage.[18]

Although she does not believe the *Washington Post* would allow secret cameras, reporter-photographer Linda Wheeler concedes that her editors permit the use of long lenses that allow photographers to be so far away from their subjects that the subjects do not always know their pictures are being taken. Wheeler used a long lens to photograph a District of Columbia police decoy pretending to be asleep on a doorstep with a portable radio at his feet. From a rooftop across the street, Wheeler photographed a thief stealing the radio and striding confidently down the street into a police ambush, where he was arrested. "If people are in a public place," she says, "they're fair game for photographers."[19]

William Sanders of the Ft. Lauderdale, Florida, *News* and *Sun-Sentinel,* former president of the National Press Photographers Association, agrees with Wheeler about people in public places, but he believes the use of hidden cameras is seldom justifiable. His paper has used that technique occasionally on investigative pieces, such as one recently about "a city official who was using city trucks and work crews for personal jobs." He was photographed without his knowledge, Sanders says, because "in a situation like that, it's acceptable."[20]

Television news has also discovered the hidden camera technique. KPNX-TV in Phoenix used that method to expose insurance salesmen who made fraudulent claims in order to sell policies to old people. Reporter David Page and photographer Bill Timmer worked with the state insurance commissioner and the Grey Panthers to check out information Page got from a dissatisfied insurance salesman. The Grey Panthers put the news team in touch with Winnie Lockwood, who allowed them to build a closet in her home from which they could secretly photograph her living room through a one-way glass. They took videotape pictures of several insurance agents assuring Lockwood that the policies they were selling provided coverage beyond Medicare that they did not actually provide. Then Page interviewed the agents in their offices, where they told him just the opposite of what they had told the elderly woman. After the stories Page and Timmer developed were broadcast, the license of one insurance salesman was revoked, several were suspended, and one insurance company had to make refunds totaling $400,000 to policyholders who bought their policies because of false sales pitches.[21]

ANYTHING TO GET A STORY

Secret tape recording, eavesdropping, and hidden cameras are just some of the methods journalists use to get their stories and pictures that are ethically questionable. Nobody disputes such conventional reporting methods as observing and recording a public event, interviewing people in their work places or homes, or doing library research. But when journalists lie or break laws or use sleazy tactics to get a story, observers wonder whether the ends justify such means, whether their methods do not color or distort the news they produce.

Robert Scheer, who as editor of *Ramparts Magazine* helped develop so-called guerrilla or counterjournalism, has said that "some of the most important stories of recent years have involved theft, burglary, seduction and conning people." Scheer, who has become more conventional as he has progressed from *Ramparts* to the *Los Angeles Times,* makes it clear that he does not believe in using such extreme methods unless you're dealing with a story vital to the public interest. Scheer is not happy with the thought that he'll probably be most remembered for his 1977 comment that when dealing with politicians who are trying to hide things from the public, "the journalist's job is to get the story by breaking into their offices, by bribing, by seducing people, by lying, by anything else to break through that palace guard." During an interview by Ken Auletta shortly after that remark to the A. J. Liebling convention organized by now defunct *More* magazine, Scheer tried to emphasize that he does not support the use of dubious means to get most news stories. He said he does not want to be thought of as a guy whose "main contribution to journalism is to advocate going through the second story. I mean, if I had to make a choice . . . between a young journalist going to the library or breaking into an office, I'd pick the library."[22] Interviewed more than three years after his oft-quoted comment to the *More* convention, Scheer says flatly that he regrets he said it. "I don't believe it's a mark of character or intelligence to stick with things that are dumb," he explains.[23]

James C. Thomson, Jr., former curator of the Nieman Foundation at Harvard, has noted that the ends of journalism "are so patently lofty, yet the means often so tawdry." Thomson concludes from his discussions with nearly a hundred of the country's finest young journalists who have studied at Harvard as Nieman Fellows that in their minds "the clean and beautiful ends" of journalism "can justify virtually any means." Yet the same journalists who believe that anything goes in the pursuit of truth express uncertainty and self-doubt about how far they would or should go or whether they would or should break a law. He also finds "a shrinking from 'playing God'; and a deep-seated cynicism about the purity of the journalist's own craft . . . while seeking out that pure commodity, 'truth.' "[24]

Most Americans tell Gallup Poll researchers that they approve of investigative reporting but not of four principal methods used by investigative reporters. Part of the explanation for this seeming contradiction may be the way Gallup worded its question when it asked 1,508 adults in more than 300 locations:

> As you probably know, the news media—TV, newspapers and magazines—often do "investigative reporting"—uncovering and reporting on corruption and fraud in business, government agencies, and other organizations. In general, do you approve or disapprove of investigative reporting by the news media?

The response showed 79 percent approving, 18 percent disapproving, and 3 percent with no opinion. But how can anybody be opposed to uncovering corruption and fraud?

The question Gallup researchers asked about investigative techniques is probably a better reading of how Americans feel about some of the methods so-called investigative journalists use to get certain kinds of stories. The same adults were asked:

> Now, I am going to read to you a list of techniques the media sometimes use when they are doing investigative reporting. Please tell me whether you approve or disapprove of each technique. . . . Using hidden cameras and microphones? . . . Having reporters not identify themselves as reporters? . . . Running stories that quote an unnamed source rather than giving the person's name? . . . Paying informers for their information or testimony? [Ellipses theirs]

The highest percentage of approval was given to the use of unnamed sources (covered in this book in Chapter 5), a technique 42 percent said they approved of, but 53 percent said they disapproved and 5 percent had no opinion. Using hidden cameras and mikes (discussed earlier in this chapter) was approved of by 38 percent, while 58 percent said they disapproved, and 4 percent had no opinion. Paying informers (to be discussed later in this chapter) was approved of by 36 percent, but 56 percent said they disapproved and 8 percent had no opinion. The lowest percentage of approval was given to reporter misidentification (covered in Chapter 6), a technique only 32 percent said they approved of, while 65 percent said they disapproved and 3 percent expressed no opinion.[25]

Checkbook Journalism. While not a common practice in American journalism, paying for information or exclusive rights to an interview still occurs. It is a method of reporting generally condemned in the United States, but more widely practiced in Great Britain, where even some public officials ask to be paid for granting interviews. The argument against it in this country, in addition to its costliness, is that it tempts informers to lie for cash, to merchandise facts.

The kind of checkbook journalism that has gotten the most attention when it has happened in this country is the payment of large sums of money by big media for exclusive rights to some VIP's story: the $100,000 that CBS paid in 1975 to H. R. Haldeman, Nixon's top White House aide, for two televised interviews; the $500,000 that CBS News paid in 1984 for ninety minutes of a videotaped interview with Nixon conducted by former aide Frank Gannon, who sold the excerpts; the presumably large but undisclosed sums that *Life* magazine paid in the mid 1960s for the exclusive right to the personal stories of the U.S. astronauts, thus covering up blunders in the space program that were not revealed until Tom Wolfe dug back into that material for his 1979 book, *The Right Stuff.*[26] Movie companies and book publishers occasionally pay for exclusive rights to someone's story, but those media are not in the news business and most observers see less harm in their trying to tie down interesting stories that are only peripherally in the public interest.

But most of the paying for information in U.S. journalism occurs at a much lower level than Haldeman and the astronauts, and the money that is passed comes in smaller denominations. When black activist Eldridge Cleaver was in exile, he demanded $2,000 from Claude Lewis for an interview for the Philadelphia *Bulletin.* Lewis talked him down to $200. He says he got a fine interview for his money, but he "felt shaky about it because there is a danger that people will tell you anything for money."[27] When Robert W. Greene, assistant managing editor of *Newsday,* was doing his now-famous investigation of heroin imports to this country, he had to bribe Turkish police for leads. "Nothing is done in Turkey unless you pay bribes." Even though he did it, Greene feels checkbook journalism is a bad practice.[28]

The AP surprised everybody in the news business when it paid a coal miner for his exclusive first-person account of the 122 hours he spent entrapped in a Pennsylvania mine that collapsed in 1977. The AP declined to say at the time what it paid the anything-but-wealthy miner. But James Donna, director of AP's WideWorld Photos, who was the AP editor on the coal mine story by Lee Linder of the Philadelphia bureau, believes the payment was small—something like $2,000.[29]

William F. Thomas, editor of the *Los Angeles Times,* remembers being "lambasted in all the righteous organs across the land" for printing a confession in the Manson trial that he obtained by paying some official of the court. "It was clearly a document I was not supposed to have," Thomas concedes. "I paid quite a bit for it, but you never have to pay as much as people think." Thomas contends he did it because "everybody in the entire community was on edge, wondering whether there were more of those people around and what in hell made them do what they did." But the press could not find out what actually happened and what the Manson gang's motives were because "court officials were trying to protect the court record in order to get a clean conviction." The document Thomas got was a transcript of a taped interrogation of one of the women in the Manson group. "She unburdened herself, and, oh, God, what a story!" Thomas adds. "It was important to everybody."[30]

A dissent from the prevailing feeling against checkbook journalism comes from Jack Landau, a lawyer who directed the Reporters Committee for Freedom of the Press. Landau argues that newspapers buy information all the time when they pay to publish memoirs from important people, such as Dwight Eisenhower and Henry Kissinger, and when they pay for syndicated columns. Newspapers are also willing to pay for photos of some news event they did not cover, but they would not pay for some eyewitness account of the event, Landau notes, adding: "Checkbook journalism may be a bad practice economically, but I can't see the legal distinction between purchasing the kind of information publications do from one category of person but not another."[31]

But Landau is among a very small minority of journalists who have even a slightly kind word to say for checkbook journalism.

The Ambush Interview. Is it fair for a reporter to surprise a news source with tough and sometimes embarrassing questions? That depends, most journalists would reply.

It depends first on who the news source is. If it is a public official who is evading the news media, or someone involved in illegal or questionable practices, then it is all right to use what is coming to be known as the ambush interview—surprising the source by catching him on the street or somewhere away from his or her home or office, or surprising the source by unexpected questions. But many journalists object to ambush interviews of any sort if they are on film or videotape. In other words, it is permissible for a pencil reporter working for print media to ambush a source, but it is not usually acceptable for a television reporter and photographer to do so. Why the distinction?

Fred Friendly, former president of CBS News and a professor at Columbia University, has called ambush interviewing "the dirtiest trick department of broadcast journalism." He believes that when viewers see a TV reporter chasing a source down the street, the impression they get is of "the honest reporter asking the honest question, and the crooked interviewee being unavailable." The truth could be "exactly the opposite," Friendly said, noting that saying no to a television camera is everyone's First Amendment right.[32]

Friendly made that comment in a documentary done by Bill Kurtis, chief anchor at WBBM-TV, Chicago. Kurtis agrees with Friendly's view of the ambush interview if the interviewee is a private person. He maintains that the technique is acceptable if the person being asked questions is a politician used to talking to reporters. His objection to such an interview for private persons is that "you run the risk of not being fair, of making an innocent person look guilty." One alternative method he has used is for the TV reporter to approach the source on the street, with the camera well back, to ask if the source will respond. If the source agrees, then the camera moves in; if the source declines to talk, then you still have film to use to report that the source has declined to comment.[33]

"60 Minutes," CBS News's highly rated investigative reporting program, has not gone in for the kind of ambush interview that shows the interviewee being chased down the street by a reporter and photographer, but it has used the technique. However, Don Hewitt, producer of the show, has come to believe that ambush interviewing "has been abused." In a 1981 program in which "60 Minutes" examined itself with a panel of journalists and media observers, Hewitt agreed with Ellen Goodman, *Boston Globe* columnist, when she said it is impossible for a source to say "no comment" to a TV reporter with the camera on, the way he might with a print reporter. "He always looks bad," Goodman claimed. "The camera is an inherently unfair weapon." Hewitt commented that the ambush interview is, "in effect, asking a man to testify against himself. You shouldn't do that."[34]

Brit Hume of ABC News agrees that some ambush interviews are questionable, but he points out "there are circumstances when you have no real alternative." When he was working for ABC's "Close Up" series, he followed a Department of Agriculture official to Rome and had to put the same question to him fourteen times before he would answer it. "It's fairer to your source if you can notify him in advance that you're going to interview him," Hume concedes, "but if you're dealing with some miscreant, it's legitimate to catch him somewhere and put the question to him. Calling people to account is part of what we do."[35]

William J. Small, former head of NBC News, objects to using the ambush interview just for dramatic effect, but he feels that it is important to allow the "accused" to have his or her say. In Small's view, when "NBC Magazine" showed reporter Jack Perkins running down the street after a portly photographer he had just accused of photographing young girls in the nude, it was the photographer, not Perkins, who turned that into an ambush situation. NBC got no negative reaction from Perkins's losing foot race, according to Small.[36]

Print reporters do not get their pictures in the paper chasing news sources, but they, too, use confrontational tactics on occasion. And quite often, they get interviews with reluctant sources by telling them they want to discuss some unfrightening subject and then once into the interview switching to questions the sources have been trying to duck – getting an interview with a developer, for example, by telling him you want to do a piece on how his housing developments have contributed to the economy of the area and then pulling some "time bomb" questions out of your pocket about some shady deal he was involved in back in Memphis. *Philadelphia Inquirer* editor Severson admits he has used that technique and he sees nothing wrong with it as long as there is no TV camera recording it. "We're not dealing with retardees," he argues. "They can duck the questions."[37]

Sources, like the developer in the preceding example, frequently have reasons for not wanting to talk to reporters. When they have secretaries in their offices to protect them, the reporter's task is all the more difficult. One journalist who is said to have developed a sure-fire way of getting reluctant sources to the telephone is investigative reporter Seymour Hersh, formerly of the *New York Times*. Developing legend has it that after Hersh had been turned away about seventeen times, he would say to the reluctant source's secretary: "You tell him if he doesn't call me back in five minutes, we're going to go with the sodomy story."

Taking and Breaking. Most journalists like to think they would not break a law to get a story, but as a matter of fact, they do it often. Usually, though, the laws they break are not serious ones: exceeding speed limits to get to a fire, parking illegally to be near the scene of a story, trespassing on private property after a fire or some other tragic event, things of that sort. But sometimes journalists have gone beyond minor infractions when the stakes have been high.

Les Whitten, novelist who was the senior investigator on the Jack Anderson column for twelve years, admits that he once committed a felony by taking some papers out of a U.S. senator's files, copying them, and returning them the next day. He had help from a person he would not name who opened the Senate office door for him and gave him the letter of the alphabet he should seek in the files. "It was a hell of a story that helped prevent a multi-million-dollar insurance fraud, and I couldn't resist it," Whitten admits, "and I'd probably do it again." Whitten believes that government documents belong to the people and reporters should not be afraid to "liberate" them in certain serious situations.[38]

A Rochester, New York, *Times-Union* reporter lost his job for stealing evidence, according to his editors then, Larry Beaupre and Robert Giles. The reporter, who had gone to a house where police had rounded up a group of suspects, found two envelopes on the floor, evidence apparently dropped or overlooked by the police. The reporter picked them up and brought them back to his office, where he used material in the envelopes in his story. When the city editor asked him about the unattributed information in the story, the reporter confessed. "He said he'd seen it done that way in the movies," Beaupre recalls. This same reporter had earlier offended his editors when he turned his notes over to a defense attorney in a case he was covering. After the second incident, "his lawyer advised him to take a resignation," Giles adds.[39]

Most journalists draw the line at breaking and entering or stealing, but they would not turn their backs on stolen material that came their way. One of the arguments the U.S. government made when it tried to stop publication of the Pentagon Papers by the *New York Times* and the *Washington Post* was that the papers were stolen property. But the journalists on the *Times, Post,* and other newspapers got those papers not by stealing them but by accepting them from Daniel Ellsberg, who had been a government consultant. *Post* executive editor Ben Bradlee observes, "I still don't know whether Ellsberg stole them or had a right to have them."[40] Ellsberg, an antiwar activist, wanted the papers published because they revealed how the U.S. government had gotten steadily enmeshed in the Vietnam War. He made copies available to a few members of Congress, hoping in vain to get them out to the public that way, before he started slipping copies to newspaper journalists he knew. Once they got hold of the copies, editors of the *New York Times* and the other papers Ellsberg made them available to had to decide whether to defy the convention of not publishing government secrets and whether to publish materials that had probably been stolen. An important related question was: How can we not pass these documents on to the public now that we have them? What right do we as journalists have to suppress material so obviously in the public interest? As you know, the *Times,* the *Post,* and other newspapers decided to publish. That was in 1971. None of the dire predictions of the Nixon administration about what was going to happen to the country if the papers were published has yet materialized.

Would a stolen secret government report as important as the Pentagon Papers be published by most newspapers today? Chances are it would. William E. Deibler, managing editor of the *Pittsburgh Post-Gazette,* seems to speak for many when he says, "If I had a document that showed that Lee Harvey Oswald worked for the CIA, no matter how it got in my hands, it would be printed."[41]

The Scoop Mentality. "Scoop" is an old-fashioned word for beating the competition. And even though competition between separately owned newspapers and journalistic competition in general is falling victim to increasing group and conglomerate ownership of news media, scoops live on. Only today they are usually called "beats" or "exclusives." The passion for beating the other guy, even if that means going on the air or to print before the story is completely checked out, has caused some of journalism's greatest "boo-boos." For example, Washington, D.C., residents heard from their radio and television sets one hot summer night that their mayor, Marion S. Barry, Jr., had been shot. Virtually all of the city's stations broadcast the report, and the UPI put out a bulletin quoting the broadcast reports. But the mayor had not been shot. The false report came from someone who called the television stations, claiming he was calling from the mayor's command center, which handles all city emergencies. The caller provided a telephone number and answered questions when TV reporters called the number, but the number turned out to be a public telephone booth. In their haste to get the news on the air, the TV reporters never thought to look up the correct command center number, which had been provided earlier to every newsroom in town.

The AP Washington bureau did not get taken in on the hoax, despite pressures from members to match the TV and UPI report. Actually, the AP put out a story forty-eight minutes after the first TV station aired its "scoop" saying that the report was false. When AP heard the original report on WRC-TV, its Washington night crew started checking police, the mayor's command center, the mayor's press secretary, and city officials, but no one would confirm the report. People they called simply told AP what they had heard on TV. Finally, AP talked to a police officer who said Barry had not been shot, although there was an accidental shooting of an officer earlier that evening near the mayor's home. Then the mayor's command center confirmed that the mayor had not been shot.[42]

Those D.C. broadcast journalists who rushed the false report to the air must have short memories. Only three months earlier the broadcast networks made the terrible mistake of telling the world that President Reagan's press secretary, James Brady, had died in the attempted assassination of the president. Brady, of course, had not died. In those hectic moments after the shootings and the immediate capture of the accused assassin, NBC reported that Reagan had had open heart surgery; he had not. There is a difference, of course, between a newscaster bursting onto the air with a bulletin that the mayor has been shot and one who passes along a false report in the midst of many factual ones as he or she sits in front of a camera or microphone for hours as the assassination-attempt story is developing. What the networks do when a story as big as that breaks is let the viewers and listeners come into their newsrooms to witness the story being pieced together.

The networks apparently learned from their mistakes. At least they were very careful in the fall of 1981 not to report President Anwar Sadat as dead until he had been officially declared so. First reports after the assassination attempt on the Egyptian president suggested that he was safe. But Dan Rather was in front of his CBS camera in New York when correspondent Scotti Williston phoned in from Cairo and reported that Sadat was dead. Rather was visibly shocked. He questioned Williston about her sources and how reliable her information was. She said her sources were reliable and she believed them. That first report held up, but Rather and other network anchors were very careful to label their reports of Sadat's death as unofficial until the Egyptian government confirmed them hours later.

Competition has many advantages. So does the discipline, bred out of competition, of trying to get the news out to the public as soon as possible: Let historians take care of history; journalism's job is to get the news out. But if that discipline is skewed by a passion to be first and not tempered by the checking that accuracy requires, then the public is apt to get false and misleading reports.

Pack Journalism. While most news organizations seem to have a hard time sparing a few reporters to dig into many subjects of public concern, the news media as a whole send as many as 15,000 staffers to cover a national political party convention, as many as 400 to a presidential press conference, as many as 2,500 to a super bowl, hundreds to a big court trial or to the scene of a major tragedy—so many that journalists frequently become part of the story.

But the principal objection to ganging up on big stories—pack or herd journalism, as it's called—is not in the misuse of human power. It is the tendency for all the reporters in the pack "to get hooked on the same line," as Charles B. Seib, retired ombudsman of the *Washington Post,* puts it.[43] "One interpretation becomes everybody's interpretation," declares Louis D. Boccardi, president of the Associated Press. "And soon you see the attributions disappearing and that single interpretation becomes almost a fact."[44]

So when you have scores or hundreds of different reporters covering the same story, instead of getting scores or hundreds of quite different stories, you tend to get pretty much the same story from all of them. Part of the reason for this lack of diversity lies in the way that sponsors or public officials try to organize (sometimes even orchestrate) the coverage of many big stories. They set up special press rooms, arrange transportation, and schedule news conferences, interviews, and photographic opportunities. Reporters are thrown together, whether they like it or not, and forced to base their stories more or less on the same information made available to all. "Reporters covering a major event get all glued together," comments Nancy J. Woodhull, a senior editor at *USA Today*.[45]

The *Sacramento Bee*'s Art Nauman participated in the herd when he was chief of the state capital bureau for that paper. "Government knows how to play the herd like a violin," Nauman observes.

> A press conference would be called. I'd better be there because if I'm not, our competitor will be and I'll get a call from my desk "Why didn't you have that story?" What I'd like to say is that I decided not to cover the press conference because it's nothing but a self-serving piece of crap and the wire services will cover it anyway. And I'll be able to work on that hard-hitting investigative story on transportation that you've always wanted. But I know that won't fly. The editor back home just isn't going to see it that way.[46]

Leslie H. Whitten, novelist who was senior investigator for the Jack Anderson column for twelve years, has observed pack journalism at work in Washington for years and calls it "a bullshit way of doing things." He believes that most of the reporters in town all work on the same story – Bobby Baker, Watergate, Koreagate, the economy. "Lots of Washington reporters are nothing but titsucks for the administration," Whitten charges. "They follow, they pick up handouts, or they jump into a big story long after everyone else has been in it . . . rather than going their individual ways. The beauty of Jack Anderson's column is that he's Peck's bad boy, an outsider, who's always been willing to tackle the tough stories."[47]

Political and sports reporters seem to run into pack problems more than other kinds of reporters: So many of the events they cover are staged to a degree and it is easy for them to become pawns of the stage managers. They can become very dependent on the people they cover. "They end up using you," says Robert Scheer, *Los Angeles Times* reporter. "You can't say, 'Wait a minute, is this true, and why are you giving this to me now?' You end up being a conduit."[48]

Quote swapping is an offshoot of pack journalism. A number of sports reporters covering a game swarm the winning and losing team locker rooms and then trade quotes and information with other reporters to get a fuller picture. A political reporter covering a closed meeting of the House Judiciary Committee in Washington can grab only one committee member or at the most two as they break for lunch. James Naughton, associate managing editor of the *Philadelphia Inquirer* who was in that situation when he reported for the *New York Times,* maintains: "It became a case of 'I'll give you a Father Drinan if you'll give me a Pete Rodino.' So there are some circumstances in which it is done and usually by people who have enough confidence in one another's integrity that they don't get burned. But I still don't like it."[49]

But David Broder, one of the most respected reporters in the business, does not see any serious problems with quote swapping. Broder, political reporter-columnist for the *Washington Post,* believes "it's a useful device sometimes, such as a situation not uncommon when you're waiting outside a Senate hearing room or the White House for some meeting to break up. Reporters pick up targets of opportunity and then get back together and exchange quotes."[50]

Jack Landau sees some good in pack coverage: "It was advantageous to have twenty-five different reporters all with different contacts working on the Bobby Baker case," concludes Landau, who broke that case as a reporter for the *Washington Post.* He also recalls press conferences at the Justice Department or at regulatory agencies where reporters with many intellects and backgrounds were able to pose questions a single reporter might never think of and to prevent the entire pack from being snowed. "Good reporters also pick up on one another's questions," Landau believes. "There's something to be said for that kind of reporting."[51]

The television networks feel they have no choice but to put up with pack reporting because they have to cover the big stories. They are in the same boat as the two major wire services. "It's easier for the print guys to break out of the pack, do their own stories, and let the wire services cover the principal stuff," comments Brit Hume, Capitol Hill correspondent for ABC News. "But the TV networks assign the top stories each day to the correspondents they want most to have on the air. It's difficult to get away from the major story of the day to which you've been assigned."[52]

None of the journalists interviewed for this study had any solution to the pack journalism problem. No one in the business likes pool reporting – allowing only a handful of reporters to observe an important event and then having them brief the other reporters who weren't there. Editors want the right to decide which stories their reporters should cover each day. It is unfortunate that so many editors choose the same stories to the point that the sheer number of reporters and photographers covering certain stories gets in the way of competent reporting. And it is difficult for observers to understand why so many of the nation's best reporters are so often tied up on the same story when so much significant material is being ignored or handled by less able reporters.

Another kind of pack problem is the tendency of much of American journalism to let the *New York Times,* the *Washington Post,* and the AP set the agenda–decide what journalists should be attending to. When the *Times* and/or the *Post* and/or the AP decide a certain story is important, it automatically becomes important in virtually every news medium in the country. Such sheeplike behavior destroys one of the advantages that is supposed to accrue from freedom–variety, diversity, differences. It also helps explain why some news is overcovered and some is never developed at all.

Posed Photos. Since the invention of the camera, news photographers have occasionally set up their photographs by getting their subjects to pose for them. And there have been times when photographers arriving late for some event have gotten their subjects to reenact whatever it was the photographer missed. Increasingly, such setups and reenactments in news photography are seen as unethical when they result in photos that are untrue or distort reality.

Former NPPA president William Sanders says the policy on his paper, the Ft. Lauderdale, Florida, *News* and *Sun-Sentinel,* is that reenactments of spot news events are prohibited. But posing is occasionally permitted in photographing "an advance on some general kind of event."[53]

But some posing is beginning to trouble journalists. Don Black, assistant managing editor of the *Statesman-Journal* in Salem, Oregon, tells of a photographer at another paper who was sent out to get a shot of young people smoking in the lounge of the local vocational-technical school. The photographer got to school at the wrong time–the lounge was empty. "So he rustled up a couple of kids, gave them some cigarettes and set up the picture he was sent to get," Black recalls. "The paper got into a big hassle, because one of the kids did not smoke and came from a family that felt strongly against smoking."[54]

The *St. Petersburg Times* and *Evening Independent* dismissed a veteran photographer who set up a stunt picture and was photographed doing so by a photographer from the rival *Tampa Tribune.* Attempting to liven up routine picture coverage of a football game between Eckerd College and Florida Southern, the St. Pete photographer, Norman Zeisloft, asked a barefoot student in the stands to print "Yea, Eckerd" on the soles of his feet. The student agreed, his girl friend did the art work, Zeisloft got his picture, and so did the *Tampa Tribune.* "It was a hard call," said Robert Haiman, then *Times* executive editor, but "one of the cardinal sins of a journalist is to tell a lie." "It was just a whimsical little picture," said Zeisloft.[55]

Breaking Embargoes. Certain news sources, particularly in government, have for years given information to reporters with the understanding that it not be published or broadcast until such-and-such time and date. These restrictions are called embargoes, and most of the time they work just fine. They give reporters time to work on complicated news stories, such as the Warren Commission report on President Kennedy's assassination. They give magazines that go to press weeks before they hit the news stands a chance to be newsworthy at the time they are read.

But when the information is hot or the journalists suspect that they are being used by sources imposing the embargoes, the whole system breaks down. The embargo on the president's annual budget message to Congress, for example, has been broken three times in recent years. Despite the fact that this embargo was created to give news people two days to study the budget of more than a trillion dollars, competitive drives among those in the major news organizations caused it to be violated. And once one news medium jumps the gun on an embargo, the others feel free to break it as well.

Editor Bradlee of the *Washington Post* was pleased that the voluminous Warren Commission report was embargoed when it was released, giving him four days to absorb it and do his story for *Newsweek,* for which he was a correspondent in those days. "If information is embargoed for the legitimate purpose of giving reporters more of a chance to adequately prepare themselves, the public is well-served," Bradlee believes.[56]

But another editor, George Blake of the *Cincinnati Enquirer,* decided recently that his public would be better served by ignoring an embargo that was attached to a news release put out by the Catholic Conference of Kentucky. Unlike the embargoes on the president's budget proposal and the Warren report, this one was imposed by the source without the press being asked whether it would accept it. But all of the newspapers in that area honored the embargo, all but the *Enquirer.*

The news release said that Kentucky's three Roman Catholic bishops were going to hold press conferences in Covington, Louisville, and Owensboro to announce their opposition to the death penalty. A lengthy pastoral letter was to be released at the press conference. *Enquirer* reporter Cindy Schroeder got on the phone and found out that the bishops had visited with death-row inmates in Kentucky and that they also planned to send a letter to the governor. She also got comments from other clergy and lawyers. "Her story was solid," Blake reported. "There was no real need to wait for the press conference to release the news, and our metro editors decided to publish the story."

When Schroeder showed up at one of the news conferences, she was turned away. The *Enquirer* had to send another reporter, and it ran another story on the bishops' stance the next day. "We make no apologies for not waiting for the press conference," Blake wrote afterward. "We will continue to avoid any press conferences that give us only information we can share with 'pack journalists' when we can develop better (and sooner) information on our own."[57]

Blake's position on the bishops' embargo was criticized by a religion writer for the *Kentucky Post* in Covington, which honored that embargo. "The notion that news should be published at all costs disregards ethics such as trust and fair play," Debbie Creemers wrote. "When trust between a newspaper and its sources breaks down, it is the reader who ultimately suffers."[58]

Rifling Trash Cans. Not ordinarily taught as a reportorial method, rifling through somebody's trash cans to get news has been known to happen. The technique is usually associated with the schlock press—the colorful tabloids available at supermarket checkouts and other papers and magazines specializing in sleaze. But the technique was used by a couple of orthodox reporters in Alaska recently.

John Lindback, Juneau correspondent for the *Anchorage Daily News,* and Andy Ryan of the independent Alaska News service were covering a grand jury investigation into whether Alaska Governor William Sheffield illegally influenced a $9.1 million state office lease. The jury sessions were closed to the press, of course, and news of what was going on inside must have been hard to get because the two reporters started exploring the grand jury's trash. They found carbon copies of twenty-three pages of handwritten notes taken by the grand jury's clerk.

Their stories based on the notes explained how they had gotten them. Although the *Anchorage Daily News* published Lindback's story, the four papers Ryan represented rejected his story. Lindback's article was then picked up by the AP and used throughout the state, even by the four papers that had rejected Ryan's story.

The papers that rejected the story initially seemed to object to the trash rifling less than they feared jeopardizing the grand jury investigation. As Kent Sturgis, managing editor of the *Fairbanks Daily News-Miner,* explained: "We declined to publish the story because of its questionable and distasteful source, because of our newspaper's respect for the confidentiality of the grand jury process and because we had no reason to believe the grand jury wasn't doing its job properly." Why did they publish the AP story the next day? The reasoning seemed to be that the damage had already been done by the first story in the *Anchorage Daily News.* Journalism works that way a lot.

The governor eventually was impeached because of what the grand jury uncovered. Lindback got a $100 bonus for his trash rifling. Ryan folded his news service and took a reporting job with a warm-climate daily, the *Miami News.*[59]

The dubious methods covered in this chapter are not all of the practices journalists use that cause their ethics to be questioned. Some are covered in other chapters: Secret sources in Chapter 5, deception in Chapter 6, interviewing jurors in Chapter 11, and putting the story ahead of humaneness in Chapter 12 are the most important of these.

FEW CODES HAVE GUIDELINES

The dubious methods that journalists sometimes use to get news are not dealt with in the major national codes of ethics. The national journalistic organizations apparently do not view the use of such methods to be widespread enough to merit attention. This was indicated when, in one of the interviews for this book, Casey Bukro of the *Chicago Tribune,* principal author of the SPJ-SDX code, turned aside a question about checkbook journalism because he said it so rarely occurs in American journalism.[60] However, some of the codes of individual newspapers and broadcast networks do contain advice about methods of gathering news.

The *Philadelphia Daily News* advises that "in gathering the news, staff members should avoid conduct that could reasonably be considered unethical or illegal."

ABC News warns its news people to "not knowingly engage in acts, or encourage others to engage in acts that would constitute a criminal violation of the law." Although ABC News does not want its journalists "inducing" criminal conduct by others, its code allows a reporter to "take a legal step which sets in motion a chain of events that may include illegal acts by others," such as taking "an automobile in good repair to various repair shops in order to determine how much unnecessary and fraudulent work is being performed."

The law-breaking problem is addressed by CBS News in a provision in its code that states CBS News "personnel will not knowingly engage in criminal activity in the gathering or reporting of news, nor will they encourage or induce any person to commit a crime." The provision goes on to discuss exceptions, such as technically violating the law to buy liquor in a dry state or handguns for "reports on how easy it is to acquire these articles." But, the CBS News code adds, there are "acts which cannot be countenanced, no matter how important the subject under investigation, the most obvious example of which would be injury to another person. Between these extremes lie many hard questions."

On surreptitious taping, the *New York Times* operates under a 1984 directive from publisher Arthur Ochs Sulzberger that prohibits all taping of telephone or in-person conversations "unless we have the clear agreement of the other party prior to the conversation."[61] At the *St. Paul Pioneer Press and Dispatch* the simple rule is, "Do not tape a telephone conversation unless you inform the other party that you are recording." The *Detroit Free Press* leaves room for exceptions to its general policy against taping people without their knowledge. Exceptions require a managing editor's OK and "may be made only if we are convinced the recording is necessary to protect us in a legal action or for some other compelling reason, and if other approaches won't work."

The CBS News provision on electronic eavesdropping and hidden cameras expresses great concern about what federal and state laws do and do not allow and prohibits its newspeople from using these methods in any case where they may be illegal. As stated in the opening of this chapter, CBS requires top brass approval for taping telephone conversations without the knowledge of the person on the other end of the line. CBS policy concedes that hidden cameras can be used in public and semi-public places, but not in a private place unless the subject has given permission to do so.

NBC News also sees nothing wrong with using hidden cameras in public places "such as streets and parks." But supervisory approval is required before hidden cameras can be used in private places and "in buildings or locations which are not public, but which the public is invited to enter, such as stores, restaurants and common areas of apartment houses or office buildings."

All three commercial broadcast networks prohibit checkbook journalism in the form of paying people to be interviewed on hard news programs. ABC News also prohibits paying news sources for a story because, among other things, it would "raise suspicion that we bought what we wanted to hear." All three networks recognize some possible exceptions to their rule against paying people to be interviewed. The ABC code, for example, lists these exceptions:

> (1) An author, reporter, commentator, teacher, entertainer or other professional or expert, who appears in his professional or vocational capacity. . . .
> (2) A public figure for participation in a broadcast which is in the nature of an electronic version of the person's memoirs.
> (3) A consultant, who may or may not appear on broadcasts,

who is employed to provide information and expertise that we cannot duplicate by our own efforts. . . .

(4) Persons who own rights to an already completed work (book or movie), or work in progress, that we plan to use.

(5) In foreign countries, persons such as British members of Parliament who customarily receive small honoraria for giving broadcast interviews.

Among the few newspaper codes that face the checkbook journalism problem are those of the *San Jose Mercury News* and the *Detroit Free Press.* "Any attempt to pay for news or for access to news raises serious questions about the validity of the news and the motives of seller and buyer," the *Mercury News* states, warning that approval of the editor is needed for those "extraordinary circumstances" when the paper might pay for news. The *Free Press* allows its managing editors to approve rare exceptions to its rule against paying for information. When that happens, the *Free Press* code says, serious questions can be raised about the credibility of that information and the motives of buyer and seller.

Although the wimpish code of the National Press Photographers Association makes no specific reference to setting up or staging photographs, a few individual news organization codes try to face up to that problem. The *San Jose Mercury News* believes that integrity and fairness command photographers and editors to "exercise caution in the use of 'set-up' photographs. In the same way that reporters do not make up quotes, photographers do not reconstruct scenes or events with the purpose of making them appear as if they were 'found' moments." The Rochester *Times-Union* and *Democrat and Chronicle* prohibit passing off "recreated, staged or posed" photos as representing "a candid situation." Nor does the Rochester code tolerate representing old photos as "fresh and new" or cropping photos "in a way that would misrepresent the situation."

The three network news departments all rule out staging news coverage. "Cover only what is happening," NBC News warns. "Make no effort to influence participants or observers to do or refrain from doing anything." CBS News urges its people to "say nothing and do nothing that may give the viewer or listener an impression of time, place, event or person which varies from the facts actually seen, heard and recorded by our equipment." ABC News bans "various techniques and devices intended to stage, simulate or re-create what actually happened." All three network codes, however, permit simulations or re-creations, fully explained to the audience, in special cases such as an artist's re-creation of the Supreme Court where cameras are not allowed or a simulation of a moon walk.

It is difficult to understand why most of the codes of ethics in journalism pay so little attention to the methods used to get stories and photographs. Some of the methods journalists use are obviously questionable if not unethical. You don't measure the ethics of a piece of journalism just by examining the final product; you have to also look at the methods used to get and produce what was published or aired. To me, digging through someone's trash can be justified only if the information sought is life- or society-threatening in nature. And that goes for electronic eavesdropping or burglarizing to get information for a story. The ethical implications of some of the other methods discussed in this chapter—checkbook journalism, ambush interviews, the drive for scoops, pack journalism, and surreptitious taping—are less clear. But their use can present ethical problems that not enough journalists are talking and thinking about. Ethical standards for news gathering and photography depend way too much on who you are, where you work, and for whom.

9 That's Shocking!

Picture yourself as the managing editor of an afternoon newspaper in a medium-sized city. One of the stories brought to you for decision is a report about a forty-nine-year-old woman who doused herself in gasoline and then set fire to herself on a quiet suburban street this morning. Horrified residents of the area smothered the flames with blankets; firefighters and an ambulance crew treated her there on the street and then took her to a hospital, where she is near death. Your city editor did not know of this unusual incident in time to send out a staff photographer, but one of the residents who helped smother the flames took some photographs and has loaned you his roll of exposed film, from which your photo department has printed up two photographs for possible publication.[1]

What do you tell your news staff to do with this story and pictures?

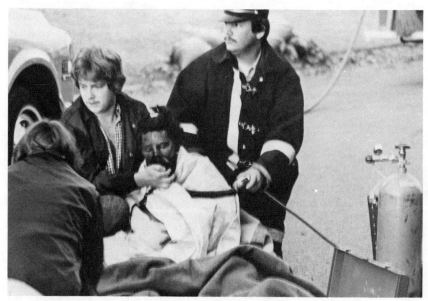

9.1 Rescue workers giving oxygen.

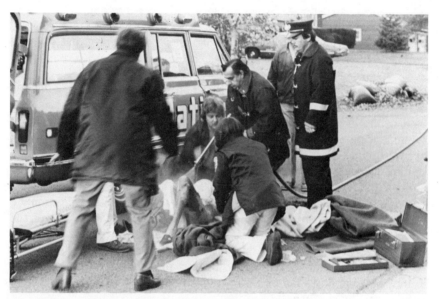

9.2 Victim of suicide by fire. *Firefighters and ambulance crew members fight to save the life of a woman who tried to take her own life by setting fire to herself. Should these pictures have been published?*

Would you be inclined to publish the story and both pictures, or the story and perhaps only one picture, or the story alone, or a picture alone, or nothing at all? If you are squeamish about running either the pictures or story on this incident, what is it that makes you so? Shouldn't people in your town know that one of their neighbors has acted in this highly unusual way?

This is the sort of decision that faced the editors of the Rochester, New York, *Times-Union* when a woman attempted suicide by fire in a surburban community about a mile from her own home, where she had left a suicide note. There was no question in the *Times-Union* newsroom that day that a story on this strange incident had to be published, but the photographs were a different matter. "We thought about it for a long time before deciding to run one picture on the back of the local news section," says Nancy Woodhull, then managing editor of the *Times-Union,* who later rose to senior editor at *USA Today.* The picture that was used (Fig. 9.2) was probably worth page one, Woodhull says, but "you have to be considerate of readers . . . who welcome you into their homes every day and expect you to handle things in a certain way."[2]

The woman who set fire to herself died later that day, after all editions of the *Times-Union* had gone to press. It turned out that she had been under psychiatric care — no surprise, of course — and that she had quit her job as a junior high school teacher only two months earlier. She left a husband, mother, and five children.

The *Times-Union* got a lot of criticism for using the picture, and none of the letters of protest it printed noted that the picture was on the back page of the local section and not in what editors would regard as a more prominent position. The letters, many of which came from friends of the dead woman, concentrated their protests on the picture, which the letter writers saw as tasteless and as compounding the anguish of the surviving family.

Woodhull, who consulted then executive editor Robert Giles, among others, before deciding to run the controversial photograph, believes the critics overlooked the fact that the woman did what she did in a public not private place — "in the middle of the street." Besides, she explains, "the world needs to know this is what happens to a person if pushed to the brink. . . . This is what we're talking about when we talk about mental health facilities and mental health care."

What this case study tells us, among other things, is that pictures usually have more impact on people than written words. Their capacity to shock exceeds that of language. People are shocked by both visuals and words, of course, and editors and television news directors and producers tiptoe when they have to decide whether and how to present news material that might be shocking.

Another word that is used to describe what this discussion is all about is "taste" — the sense of what may be done or said without giving offense or committing an impropriety. All journalists seem to believe that they have to be aware of taste in the material presented to the public, but some do not see taste as an ethical problem. This chapter will try to show that extreme violations of taste — shocking words and visuals — are ethical issues in that they force the journalist to make what is basically a moral decision: If the news is shocking, how much, if any, should be screened from the public?

DISTURBING PHOTOS

Ralph Otwell, former editor of the *Chicago Sun-Times,* recalls the photographs U.S. newspapers ran during the Vietnam War of Buddhist monks burning themselves to death. Those self-immolation pictures were shocking, he admits, "but they were important in telling the story of that war and people's reaction to that war." Otwell does not believe, however, that all such photos should be published automatically. "If an emotionally unstable woman goes down to the civic center plaza and sets herself on fire," he explains, "we would not use that picture."[3]

Otwell's paper and most others in this country published many photographs from the Vietnam War that startled readers. Remember the little Vietnamese girl running naked and screaming down the street after her village was bombed? Or the close-up photo of the Viet Cong prisoner as he was executed with a shot to his head from a pistol being held two inches from his ear by a South Vietnamese officer? Or those TV pictures of South Vietnamese soldiers cutting the ears off the dead Viet Cong soldiers? (Younger readers may need to be told that the South Vietnamese were on our side.)

It should not be surprising that news pictures from a war would be disturbing. War is disturbing. But news photography depicts a lot of violence and tragedy in peacetime as well. A study by photojournalist Lil Junas showed that 56 percent of the winners in the top two news photography competitions in the United States were pictures of violence and tragedy. The Pulitzer Prizes have been particularly partial to such pictures. Junas found that twenty-six of the forty Pulitzer awards for news photography between its beginning in 1942 and through 1981 went to pictures showing violence and tragedy. She discovered that thirty-two of the sixty-three "pictures of the year" recognized by the National Press Photographers Association and the University of Missouri School of Journalism between 1944 and 1982 were photographs of violence or tragedy. In addition to the fifty-eight winning photos that depicted violence or tragedy, Junas said eighteen winners "were related to or results of tragic and violent situations – like refugees fleeing a war area and rescues from fires and accidents."[4]

A news photograph of a family tragedy was entered in the 1986 Pulitzer competition but it failed to win a prize. The fact that it was entered at all surprised many in the business because the managing editor who decided to publish the picture said he wishes he hadn't. The dramatic photo (Fig. 9.3) was taken by John Harte for the Bakersfield, California, *Californian.* Responding to a call he heard on the police scanner, Harte arrived at a lake northeast of Bakersfield as divers were still searching for a drowning victim. After about fifteen minutes, the divers brought up the lifeless body of five-year-old Edward Romero. As the boy's distraught family gathered around the body that had been placed in an open body bag, a sheriff tried to hold back onlookers, including Harte and a local TV crew. The TV crew did not film that moment, but Harte did, by ducking under the sheriff's outstretched arms and shooting eight quick frames with a 24 mm lens and motor drive.[5]

Managing editor Robert Bentley was called into the *Californian* office that Sunday evening to make the decision about whether Harte's moving photo should be run. Apparently persuaded that the picture might remind people to be more careful with kids swimming, Bentley decided to waive his paper's general policy against publishing pictures of dead bodies. In the next two days, the *Californian* got five hundred calls of protest, one of them a bomb threat, some cancelling subscriptions, and later it received more than two hundred irate letters.

"Some claimed the *Californian* showed callous disrespect for the victim," Bentley wrote in his column the next week. "Others felt the photograph had forced their visual intrusion on what should have been a fam-

9.3 A family's anguish. *As the weeping father kneels over the body of Edward Romero, a rescue worker (left) tries to console the drowning victim's brother and other family members. The editor who ran this picture says he wishes he hadn't.* (Photo courtesy of the *Californian*, Bakersfield, Calif.)

ily's private time of shock and grief. Most combined the dual protests."[6]

Syndicated columnist Bob Greene of the *Chicago Tribune* called the picture "pornography." Having seen the Harte photo that was distributed throughout the country by the AP, Greene wrote that "because of journalistic factors they could not control," the Romero family was exposed to the entire country in "the most terrible moment in their lives."[7]

Editor Bentley agrees with Greene that the picture should never have been published. He called a meeting of his news staff while the protests were still pouring in to emphasize that "a serious error of editorial judgment was made." He said the most important lesson his staff should learn from the error "is the stark validation of what readers – and former readers – are saying not just locally but across the country: That the news media are seriously out of touch with their audiences." Yet, Bentley told Greene he was going to nominate Harte's photograph for the Pulitzer, seeing no contradiction. "I think the photograph should never have been published. I also think it should be awarded the Pulitzer Prize," Greene quoted the editor as saying.[8]

Charles B. Seib found a similar difference in the way readers and news editors look at photos when he was ombudsman for the *Washington Post*. When the *Post*, along with most other daily newspapers in the land, prominently displayed photographs of a woman and a little girl falling from the collapsed fifth floor fire escape of a burning Boston tenement, many readers complained. Seib reported he got about seventy such calls the day the photos ran, more than he had ever received as ombudsman. He said many of the callers were more hurt than angry, expressing sorrow that the *Post* had "sunk to pandering to the most morbid instincts." But when he checked about the *Post* newsroom, he found no second thoughts about running the dramatic fall photos, only some discussion of how such photos should be displayed. "It is not too farfetched to suggest that the Boston pictures and the reactions to them shed some light on the strained relations between the press and the public," Seib wrote. "Our professional 'little shells' can diminish our awareness of the human and humane feelings of the reader in matters far beyond picture selection."[9]

The Boston fire photos won a 1976 Pulitzer Prize for Stanley Forman of the *Boston Herald American*. The woman he photographed in her fall from the fire escape balcony was baby-sitting the little girl. The woman was killed. The little girl survived because she landed on the body of her baby-sitter. Forman said he thought he was photographing a dramatic rescue as he stood on the back of a ladder fire truck clicking off shots of a firefighter on the ladder reaching for the woman and child. Just as the firefighter's hand touched the arm of the woman, the metal balcony of the fire escape started falling. Forman was not certain what was happening but he kept his motor-driven camera aimed at the scene. He said he started following the girl down and then he realized what was going on. He completely turned around because he did not want to see her hit the ground.[10]

Tom Kelly, photo department manager for the Pottstown, Pennsylvania, *Mercury*, won a 1979 Pulitzer Prize for some shocking photos of another tragedy. Alerted by the police radio in his car, Kelly was the first journalist to arrive at a home near Pottstown where a young man had barricaded himself after killing his pregnant wife, stabbing his six-year-old daughter in the eye, and seriously injuring his seventy-one-year-old grandmother. The grandmother, lying stabbed on the lawn, was the first to be rescued by the police. They then talked the berserk young father into releasing his daughter. Kelly says he could not stop the tears from his eyes as he photographed the little girl, blood-covered from head to toe and pleading with the police not to hurt her daddy. Then police went in after the man, and as they brought him out he broke free about four feet from Kelly. The photographer believes he must have reacted automati-

9.4 Beserk young murderer. *Blood-stained murderer breaks loose from police. Is this too shocking for your family newspaper?* (Photo courtesy of Tom Kelly, the *Mercury,* Pottstown, Pa.)

cally because he does not remember taking the picture that his paper used to lead off the fifteen photos it published the next day (Fig. 9.4).

The photographs Kelly took that afternoon, which were distributed by the AP and used all over the country, were "shocking and very emotional," he admits. But he does not believe the press should "hide what's going on. It's life. It happened." He said all of the pictures the *Mercury* used to tell this tragic story "may have been shocking or horrifying, but none was distasteful."[11]

Another case that gave editors a decision as to whether news photos justified the shock occurred when the U.S. government sent a mission to Iran in 1980 to rescue the hostages and then had to abort it when a cargo plane and a helicopter in the mission collided and exploded in the desert. Both major wire services transmitted some stark photographs of the charred bodies of U.S. servicemen killed in that collision. Most newspapers ran them, but they got a lot of protests from their readers. Ombudsman George Beveridge, in defending the use of those "ghastly" pictures by his newspaper, the now defunct *Washington Star*, wrote that "newspapers were obliged to print them because they gave readers a dimension of understanding of the situation and the people involved that written words could not possibly convey." The *Boston Globe* received more than 200 calls and letters protesting the use of a picture of a charred body. *Globe* ombudsman S. S. Micciche held that this was a case where the event was so historic that it outweighed all other considerations. "We would have been derelict in our obligation to print the truth and reality if we had banned the use of that picture," Micciche said. But editors of the small daily in Gulfport-Biloxi, Mississippi, the *Sun*, told their readers that they tore up the AP photos of the charred bodies because it would have been "the poorest kind of taste to display those ghastly pictures." The *Sun* said the "decision was based on common decency and simple good taste."[12]

Although its news value was much below that of the charred bodies described above, a shocking AP photo out of Las Vegas was widely used. The picture showed a striking hotel worker being run over by a car driven by a scab hotel guard trying to push his car through a picket line (Fig. 9.5). Amazingly the crushed striker was not killed. The APME Photo and Graphics Committee surveyed 286 daily newspaper managing editors and found that about two out of three (194 yes, 92 no) had used the picture, and only 75 of the 194 who used it received any reader criticism. "The only offensive thing about this photograph is the driver behind the wheel," one managing editor told the committee. Some of the comments from editors who rejected the photo: "The news value . . . did not warrant its use." ". . . too distasteful." ". . . would have caused an uproar." "We're a morning paper and we don't want our readers to upchuck their shredded wheat."

9.5 Striking picket crushed. *Two out of three daily editors thought this photograph was not too shocking for their readers.* (Photo courtesy of the Associated Press.)

"If there is a trend in this little survey, we did not spot it," wrote David E. Halvorsen, former editor of the *San Francisco Examiner.* "Generally we found the editors went through a thoughtful process before accepting or rejecting the photograph. Perhaps, that is the most significant conclusion of all."[13]

Some readers and viewers aim their "poor taste" criticisms at visuals that show presidents and other VIPs in unsightly or embarrassing lights. News photographers in an earlier day were unusually respectful of presidents, as were reporters. Franklin D. Roosevelt, for example, was not often shown in a way that gave readers any clear idea of how difficult it was for him to get around in the braces he had to wear because of polio. Years later President Ford might have yearned for that kind of "protection" as he was photographed slipping on stairs, bumping his head, and doing other things that gave him a reputation for clumsiness. And Governor George Wallace, after the assassination attempt that crippled him, was frequently photographed in his wheel chair or as he was being carried onto an airplane or being helped to a podium.

The FDR treatment was also lacking when President Carter fell while jogging in Georgia, three days after he turned the White House over to President Reagan. Photographer Charles Kelly of the AP was there shooting a jogging picture when Carter tripped over a curb and fell forward to the pavement, slowing his fall with his hands. A single photo and a four-picture sequence were sent out by AP to all its clients, most of whom used at least some of the pictures the next day. Reader reaction was strong, many accusing the AP and newspapers that put the pictures on page one of kicking the man while he was down. Louis D. Boccardi, president of the AP, claims that he understands the reaction the pictures brought from some people, but the photos "were perfectly valid" because it happened in public to "one of the most public persons in the world." Boccardi notes that the AP never heard from Carter personally about the fall photos.[14] Edwin Guthman, editor of the *Philadelphia Inquirer,* which heard from several angry readers after displaying two pictures of the Carter fall on page one, apologized for running the photos in such a prominent position and for the facetious caption, but denied that his paper was trying to rub salt in Carter's wounds. Guthman said he was glad to see in the public reaction "a sense of fairness and humane concern for Carter, a genuine outpouring of sympathy and decency." He added that the paper had learned from the criticism.[15]

Guthman's comments should not be read to mean that news photographers and editors are thinking of retreating to the softer attitude that dictated their depiction of crippled President Roosevelt. Rightly or wrongly and with some exceptions, journalists today keep a fairly consistent heat on presidents, senators, governors, and other top public officials, and if those officials slip or stumble in public they are apt to land on page one.

Another kind of taste problem for editors and television news directors occurs when news includes photographs of nudity. Elizabeth Ray comes to mind. She was the woman who claimed to be the mistress of Ohio Congressman Wayne Hays while she was being paid $14,000 a year to be a secretary on his congressional staff who never had to come to the office. Shortly before she broke the news of her illegal employment by Congressman Hays, Ray had posed for *Playboy* magazine, which provided the AP with a bare-breasted photograph of her. The APME did a survey and found that only 24 of the 138 editors who responded had used the partially nude picture, and 20 of them said they cropped it to avoid showing the woman's breasts. APME Photo Committee chairman Joseph M. Ungaro concluded that "editors don't think the public is ready for nudity in the newspapers."[16]

A student newspaper published at a large university can take greater risks with shocking photos than, say, a newspaper in a small to medium-sized community that tries to appeal to families. Editors presume that the audiences for a college student newspaper and a community newspaper are different. But the *Daily Collegian,* student newspaper at the Pennsylvania State University, still had to defend itself against critics after it published a picture of a young woman winning a wet-T-shirt contest by stripping the shirt (Fig. 9.6). Letter writers and other protesters said the picture was in poor taste and was insulting to women. To which *Collegian* columnist Kathleen Pavelko replied that the wet-T-shirt contest, which had attracted hundreds of people to a local bar, "was like the streaking incidents of 1974; not in its nudity, but as a student phenomenon and a possible trend on American college campuses. The contest was a slice of student life." Pavelko said the editor consulted with many staff members before deciding to run the photo. The photo "did not pander to anyone's prurient interest," she wrote. "In fact . . . it was a strong argument for the women's point of view; the reaction of the men on the left was caught beautifully – tongues out, eyes bulging. I could think of no better way to illustrate the ugly reaction of the crowd that night."[17]

Another kind of nudity problem for editors comes up in pictures of human birth. Don Black sold an interesting set of photographs to *People* magazine after his own newspaper, the Binghamton, New York, *Evening Press,* would not use them. The pictures told a story of an obstetrician in

9.6 Wet T-shirt. *Young college males recognize a winner in a wet T-shirt contest. It was published. Should it have been?* (Photo by Randy L. Woodbury, courtesy of the *Daily Collegian,* University Park, Pa.)

that area who taught fathers how to deliver their own babies, with the OB standing by. Black's photos showed a father delivering his own 9½-pound son and a look of joy on the mother's face seldom seen anywhere. That was in the mid-1970s. Black, now assistant managing editor of the Salem, Oregon, *Statesman-Journal,* believes that public acceptance of such material is much greater now and thinks his paper would publish those photographs today.[18]

While he does not feel newspapers should publish shocking pictures for shock's sake alone, Black sees a danger in journalists being "too timid." He contends that "failing to run an important news picture for fear of reader response is indulging in a form of censorship." But many editors are still timid about publishing shocking pictures, worrying about whether the shock will not get in the way of the message the picture is supposed to communicate. This caution is more noticeable, for understandable reasons, in the smaller newspapers.

OFFENSIVE LANGUAGE

One of the things young reporters quickly learn is that the people they cover sometimes use language their editors will not let them publish. Some solve this problem by cleaning up such language as they write their stories. Others try to keep it in when it is part of the news, arguing that when a source says "horse shit," it is dishonest and misleading to change it to "horse manure."

One such reporter is David Shaw, media critic for the *Los Angeles Times,* who feels strongly that there are no words that should not be used in the newspaper. But he runs into arguments with his editors all the time, he admits, even though the *Times* is more liberal on language than most newspapers. "I remember once having to trade a 'shit' and an 'asshole' for a 'ratshit,'" Shaw says.[19]

Shaw may or may not be typical but many younger writers see their newspapers as being too conservative about the kind of language they will print. AP president Boccardi has felt some pressure from younger AP staffers. Boccardi concedes that standards on offensive words have loosened up in society and the media, but he does not favor "a wholesale letting down of barriers." He wonders whether the younger reporters pressing for more liberal use of language in news stories "will feel that way when they have eight-year-olds reading newspapers."[20]

Boccardi's views are shared by most newspaper editors in this country who see their audiences in terms of families and who worry about what children should or should not read. And the size and location of the newspaper usually make a difference, editors of smaller newspapers tending to block obscenities and other kinds of shocking language that might be permitted in a metropolitan newspaper. Radio and television journalists are even more cautious about allowing offensive language on the air.

Obscenities. The Federal Communications Commission (FCC), which regulates broadcasting in the United States, has a 1978 Supreme Court ruling to back up its right to reprimand broadcasters who use any of seven words the FCC has said are obscene, indecent, or profane. The court decided that the FCC had a right to chastise WBAI, a Pacifica Foundation station in New York City, for broadcasting a monologue by comedian George Carlin, in which he used all seven of the FCC's filthy words—shit, fuck, cocksucker, motherfucker, piss, cunt, and tit. Although this decision sent a shiver through American broadcasting, news departments have continued to air occasional obscenities, banking on the traditional reluctance of the FCC to mess with news and the First Amendment. Many TV stations in 1980, for example, used portions of transcripts from the ABSCAM tapes of conversations between congressmen and undercover FBI agents that were sprinkled with vulgar and obscene words.[21]

Commenting on the Supreme Court's decision in the Pacifica case, Russell Baker wrote in his *New York Times* column that what the court found offensive about the seven words, which refer to bodily wastes or sex, "was not the subject matter they dealt with, but the use of Anglo-Saxon vocabulary to discuss it." Impishly, he continued:

> All seven words have long-winded Latinate synonyms which are commonly used without producing a blush outside the most sheltered backwaters of society. Anyone who undertook court action against a broadcaster for saying "micturition" or "defecation" into a microphone would doubtless be dismissed as a crank or a fool.
>
> But let the same subject be broached in one-syllable Anglo-Saxon words and the Supreme Court assembles to ponder the implications for the future of the Republic. Very few persons, one suspects, would be much offended if, on tuning in their home tubes, they were to hear someone refer to "sexual intercourse," "practitioner of fellatio," "female reproductive canal," "incestuous male issue" or "female mammary glands." . . .
>
> Something about the Anglo-Saxon tongue has the power to make us see red. Or, in the case of the seven unspeakable words, blue. This may go back as far as the Norman invasion of England when the conquerors from France tried to destroy Saxon culture and, in the process, succeeded in stigmatizing the Saxons as crude barbarians.[22]

The respected *Boston Globe* used one of those Anglo-Saxon words in 1986 in reporting on a man sentenced to prison for a racially motivated attack on some Cambodians. As the convicted man was being led away in handcuffs, he turned to the courtroom audience, including many Cambodians, and said, "I won't forget this shit." To the predictable complaints from some readers, *Globe* ombudsman Robert L. Kierstead responded in his column that publishing this story with "expletive deleted" would be inadequate reporting. "Clearly, obscenity must be kept to a minimum in newspapers," the readers' representative wrote. "But I feel the sheer impact of this serious socially and racially oriented case and its implications justified . . . use" of the shocking word.[23]

Publishing another of those Anglo-Saxon words on page one of the Dayton, Ohio, *Journal Herald* in 1975 cost Charles Alexander his job as editor. The word with all that power was used by a U.S. Treasury agent explaining to authorities how it happened that he shot and killed another law enforcement man in a furious quarrel. "Goddamn it, you are fucking with my family," the treasury agent shouted. "You are fucking with my future. . . . I'll kill you first." Five days after that quotation was published and almost a hundred readers complained, the angry owners of the *Journal Herald* forced Alexander to resign.[24]

Writing later about his decision to print the quotation, Alexander said the news story in which it appeared told how the minor argument escalated to "a state of rage that resulted in a struggle for life between two armed law enforcement agents." He said the story "vividly detailed the erosion of all the restraints that characterized civilized beings, finally culminating in the ultimate obscenity—homicide. But homicide is a socially acceptable obscenity in print. Vulgar language, to some, is not." Alexander argued that journalists have to start telling "the whole truth" if they want to be believed, even though that may require indelicacy. "The reality of truth will have to supplant the illusion of propriety," he declared.[25]

The flap in Dayton reminded John McCormally, then editor and publisher of the Burlington, Iowa, *Hawk Eye,* of the time his paper "used that ultimate 12-letter obscenity (in a story attempting to show what caused nice policemen to lose their cool and hit protesting college students on the head)." This upset a woman reader who called his home one evening when he was not there, McCormally revealed in a letter to *Editor and Publisher* magazine, "but my 11-year-old daughter, as she'd been trained to do, asked: 'May I give him a message?' 'Yes,' replied the woman, 'tell him if he doesn't quit printing that filth, I'm gonna quit taking his fucking paper!' "[26]

Newspaper editors and broadcasters dug into their dictionaries of synonyms and thesauruses to report a racist "joke" that caused President Ford to fire the guy who told it, Earl L. Butz, who had been secretary of agriculture for five years. The "joke" not only made use of vulgar barnyard language, which Butz often lapsed into despite his high cabinet position; it slurred blacks. But most Americans never found out exactly what it was he said that so upset his boss, because only a handful of newspapers and magazines and no broadcast stations carried his remarks verbatim. Those who did not ignore the "joke" altogether resorted to euphemisms.

The news media first learned of the Butz "joke" in a report on the 1976 Republican National Convention in *Rolling Stone* written by John Dean, former White House counsel to President Nixon. Dean said that on the plane coming home from the convention he got into a discussion with Pat Boone and Sonny Bono. They were joined shortly by a man Dean did not name in his article but identified as "a distinguished member of Ford's cabinet." Dean asked the unnamed cabinet secretary why convention delegates had given such a cool reception to a speech by their vice presidential nominee, Senator Robert Dole:

> "Oh, hell, John, everybody was worn out by then. You know," he said with a mischievous smile, leaning over the seat in front of Pat and me, "it's like the dog who screwed a skunk for a while, until it finally shouted, 'I've had enough!' "
>
> Pat gulped, then grinned and I laughed. To change the subject Pat posed a question: "John and I were just discussing the appeal of the Republican party. It seems to me that the party of Abraham Lincoln could and should attract more black people. Why can't that be done?" This was a fair question for the secretary, who is also a very capable politician.
>
> "I'll tell you why you can't attract coloreds," the secretary proclaimed as his mischievous smile returned. "Because coloreds only want three things. You know what they want?" he asked Pat.
>
> Pat shook his head no; so did I.
>
> "I'll tell you what coloreds want. It's three things: first, a tight pussy; second, loose shoes; and third, a warm place to shit. That's all!"
>
> Pat gulped twice.[27]

It took some simple sleuthing by the staff of *New Times* magazine to find out who Dean's foul-mouthed storyteller was. The now-defunct magazine reported that it simply checked the traveling schedules of Ford's cabinet members, all eleven of whom had attended the convention, and found that Butz was the only one who flew from Kansas City to Los Angeles on August 20, the day after the convention ended. Dean would not "confirm or deny" that Butz was the storyteller, and Butz refused to comment, but *New Times* got Pat Boone to confirm that it was Butz who told the "joke." "I took it as a joke," Boone was quoted as saying, "but I didn't think it was funny. I felt it was inappropriate language for anyone. He knew he was talking to a reporter, and he may have thought what he said was unprintable. It occurred to me right then that it might be printed. I cringed for him."[28]

The major wire services picked up the story, of course, and editors had to decide how much if any of Butz's remarks would be used. The AP, as it sometimes does, put out two versions of its story, "one you could publish in the church bulletin," AP's Boccardi says. The version that hardly any paper used quoted Butz verbatim. The other version said: "Butz, in his comments, referred to blacks as 'coloreds' and discussed in derogatory terms what he said were their sexual, dress and bathroom preferences." AP's competitor, the UPI, handled the offensive comments with the paraphrasing, "good sex, easy shoes and a warm place to go to the bathroom."[29]

The *New York Times*, which has a reputation as the most bluenosed of major U.S. dailies, reported that Butz had referred to blacks as "colored" and said they wanted only three things that he "listed, in order, in obscene, derogatory and scatological terms." After Butz resigned, the *Times* loosened a bit and used the euphemisms "satisfying sex, loose shoes and a warm place for bodily functions – wishes that were listed by Mr. Butz in obscene and scatological terms." The San Francisco *Examiner and Chronicle* employed the old crossword puzzle trick: ". . . first, a tight p----, second, loose shoes, and third, a warm place to s---."[30]

Some newspapers told their readers that Butz's comments were too raw to publish but adult readers could see them at the office or write in for copies. More than a hundred people visited the Erie, Pennsylvania, *Morning News* to read the "joke" for themselves. About three hundred fifty showed up at the *Lubbock* (Texas) *Avalanche-Journal,* including a farmer and his wife who drove seventy miles to copy the "joke" to show their neighbors.[31] The somewhat larger San Diego *Evening Tribune* got three thousand letters in a week from readers responding to the paper's invitation to write in if they wanted a copy of what Butz really said.[32]

Charles B. Seib pointed out in his *Washington Post* ombudsman's column what can happen when newspapers blue-pencil controversial remarks by public officials. Seib said that Republicans, including then vice-presidential candidate Robert Dole, were putting out the story that Butz's language was no worse than what Jimmy Carter had been quoted as saying in *Playboy* magazine. That was the famous interview in which Carter, who was then running as the Democratic candidate for president, used such words as "screw" and "shack up" and admitted that he had "looked on a lot of women with lust." Seib held that since Butz's exact words were not as widely publicized as those of Carter, the public had no basis on which to make a comparison. "And somehow, I think Carter comes out the loser, even though Butz is the man who lost his job," Seib wrote. "Again I am not arguing that the words Butz used should have been published. Nor am I arguing that Carter's words should not have been published. I do say, though, that the press finds itself in a strange position on the dirty language front."[33] (Seib's paper told its readers what Carter had said but waffled on Butz's more extreme language, reporting that he had said "coloreds" wanted "good sex, loose shoes and a warm place to dispose of bodily wastes.")

That racist revelation to John Dean was not the first time that Butz put his foot in his mouth publicly. During the height of Watergate, he called Senator Sam Ervin "senile." And after Pope Paul VI had criticized birth control as a means of combating world food shortages, Butz quipped to the press – in a mock Italian accent – "He no playa da game, he no maka da rules." Butz got back in the news more recently when he paid a $10,000 fine and served thirty days of a five-year sentence for income tax evasion. He was on probation for the balance of the sentence.

Loose-Mouthed Heroes. Many Americans were surprised and shocked when they read court transcripts of tape recordings President Nixon had made in his White House office during the Watergate scandal. His language was salty, to say the least, employing three of the FCC's seven verboten words as well as some of the milder swear words. Americans saw or heard these because most news executives decided that the revelations on the tapes were too important to doctor. Oh, some used the crossword puzzle technique (f---ing, and the like) but Americans got the idea: Nixon, in private, at least, used a rich vocabulary.

It made a difference to editors that the language they might otherwise paraphrase, disguise, or delete came from the top guy in the government. "If the president of the United States says 'fuck,' I'm going to quote him," observes Benjamin Bradlee, executive editor of the *Washington Post.* Abraham Rosenthal, associate editor of the *New York Times,* put it this way: "We'll take 'shit' from the president of the United States, but from nobody else."[34]

The Bradlee and Rosenthal attitude toward presidential expletives was widely followed by editors and broadcast news directors when President Reagan was heard calling reporters "sons of bitches." It was during a picture-taking session. As reporters continued to question him after the pictures had been taken, Reagan turned to David Packard, chairman of a special committee on defense management, and used the swear words. Newspapers all over the country quoted him the next day and CBS News used a videotape of the incident. White House spokesman Larry Speakes said Reagan did not recall making such a remark. "If he said anything," Speakes told the press, "he said, 'It's sunny, and you're rich.'"[35]

VIPs below the presidential level are not always quoted verbatim when they utter an obscenity or profanity. It depends on the story, the circumstances, and the judgment of the editors involved. When people who figure in the news use obscene or vulgar language, most editors and news directors follow the same general rule: keep the language in if it is essential or germane to the news story; otherwise, delete it. There is obvious disagreement among news executives, however, on what is germane and then on whether the dirty words need to be disguised somehow. So it becomes quite a game.

Many newspapers editors, for example, agreed that when Democratic presidential candidate George McGovern climbed over a fence and told a heckler to "kiss my ass," that had to be reported. David Broder, *Washington Post* reporter-columnist who was covering McGovern then and reported exactly what the candidate said, believes that "any public statement by a president or presidential candidates ought to be quoted as accurately as possible."[36] But James Naughton, who was there for the *New York Times,* could not get that quote in his paper. *Times* editors were not persuaded by Naughton's argument that the comment "exhibited an awful lot about the state of mind of that candidate at that point in his candidacy which was important for the reader to know."[37]

Another presidential candidate, George Wallace, gave Broder "more of a problem with his language," not because of obscenities, but because of grammatical slips. He tried to quote Wallace literally when he'd say "ain't" and "he don't," but that made it seem that he and other reporters were putting a "Dogpatch label on him." So the standard of literal quotation for presidential candidates becomes arbitrary, Broder adds, "because none of us speaks absolutely correct grammatical English in everyday life."

The *New York Times,* which obviously does not believe in Broder's literal quotation standard except perhaps for presidents, decided to change Senator Barry Goldwater's words when he said that "every good Christian should kick Falwell in the ass." The senator was responding to conservative religious leader Jerry Falwell's statement that Christian groups should be mobilized against Justice Sandra O'Connor's appointment to the United States Supreme Court. The *Times* quoted Goldwater as saying that Falwell should be kicked "in the posterior." This caused an interesting little problem for the *San Diego Union,* which used the "posterior" quote in its story from the New York Times New Service, to which it subscribes. At least one reader complained that he had heard what Goldwater actually said on television and wanted to know why the paper felt it had to clean up Goldwater's language.[38] Good question. Other wire services and newspapers quoted Goldwater verbatim or did not put quotation marks around the word "posterior" as if that is what the senator said.

The late Mayor Richard J. Daley of Chicago gave Chicago journalists a somewhat different problem in reporting his expressions. James Hoge, then editor in chief of the *Chicago Sun-Times,* recalls that Daley, who used a "colorful brand of fractured English," would often get upset when he was quoted and would claim that he had been misinterpreted. "Don't quote what I said, quote what I mean," he would insist. Hoge believes Daley had a good point and his paper tried to "quote what he meant" as often as it could, "except in an occasional feature story on his malapropisms."[39]

Sports reporters and editors have a tough time deciding how much if any of the foul language they hear from athletes should get passed on to the public. "You can't quote most pro athletes verbatim because of obscenity," says Bill Lyon, sports reporter and columnist for the *Philadelphia Inquirer.* "You have to launder their words." Lyon believes that in his experience, at least, baseball players have the "filthiest mouths," with hockey players second, and football players third; "basketball players may have the cleanest mouths," he suggests. In addition to heavy profanity and obscenity, many athletes "butcher the English language," Lyon notes, and sports writers have to ask, "How far should we go for the sake of complete accuracy if it makes an athlete appear to be illiterate?"[40]

Rick Starr, sports editor of the *Valley News Dispatch* in New Kensington, Pennsylvania, usually edits out offensive language but he sometimes substitutes the word "bleep" and occasionally he uses an offensive word. One of the times he used a verbatim quote was when Pittsburgh Steeler lineman Joe Greene reacted to new rules that caused a flag to be thrown against Steeler linebacker Jack Lambert for hitting an opposing quarterback. "We play faggot football now," Greene reportedly said. Starr explains that he warned his managing editor that the quote was going to be in his column, and the editor let it stay.[41]

The word "faggot" that Joe Greene used has been a troublesome one for news executives. The first time I saw that word in a news story was in an article by a young sports writer on a university student newspaper. He used it to describe a college wrestler, thinking that it meant someone small and fast like a "leprechaun." (That topped an earlier experience with a high school friend who wrote in the school paper about "row upon row of little yellow concubines," thinking he was describing cottages or small houses.)

The "bleep" technique to which Starr referred is one sports editors often use, although it is not usually seen in other parts of the paper. The *Miami Herald* gave us an example of that device when it reported Clemson football coach Danny Ford's reaction to the news that the NCAA was investigating his program for alleged recruiting violations. "I don't bleeping have to talk about the bleep," the *Herald* quoted Ford as saying. And for readers who did not understand whatingodsname Ford was saying, the *Herald* story elaborated: "I don't give a bleep what nobody thinks."[42]

Stories edited with such skill and a sense of propriety must be what Drake Mabry, former managing editor of the *Des Moines Register* and *Tribune,* had in mind when he told the APME: "It takes a dirty mind to edit a clean newspaper."

Slurs on People. Some news stories that contain no obscene language can still offend some group in the community or society. What would you do, for example, with a news story during a presidential campaign quoting one of the candidates as telling this joke to a group of supporters on his bus:

> How do you tell who the Polish one is at a cockfight?
> He's the one with a duck.
> How do you tell who the Italian is at the cockfight?
> He bets on the duck.
> And how do you know the Mafia was there?
> The duck wins.

That, in case you did not recognize it, is an ethnic joke, possibly offensive to people of Polish or Italian descent. It was told by President Reagan as he campaigned through New Hampshire.[43] Robert Scheer, who studied and interviewed candidate Reagan in depth for the *Los Angeles Times,* would report that particular ethnic joke only in the positive sense: "I tell ethnic jokes. You hear them everywhere. We expect these guys to be human and open, and the minute they show some of that, we slam them. That's a double standard." Besides, Scheer adds, "it's absurd to suggest that Reagan doesn't like Italians or Poles; there is nothing in his history to suggest that."[44]

Scheer was involved in two other flaps about VIPs using words that shocked some people. He was one of the editors of *New Times* when it tracked down Earl Butz as the teller of the racist story that cost him his job as secretary of agriculture. He also did the *Playboy* interview with Jimmy Carter that upset many people. Writing about the Carter interview afterward in *New Times,* Scheer said he had no premonition that Carter's utterance of "screw" and "shack up" would cause a furor. "I just didn't know that they were still dirty words," he said. To illustrate how that part of the interview made Carter come alive, Scheer said his seventy-six-year-old mother told him she found it "reassuring" that "Carter is not an uptight Baptist." Scheer's piece ended with a plea to "reward Carter's honesty with our votes. There must be more of us who 'shack up,' 'screw,' and love it, than those who are still frightened by the words."[45]

A popular column was dropped by the *Dallas Times Herald* because its language offended Dallas blacks. Written by John Bloom, the column is called "Joe Bob Goes to the Drive-In" and is a spoof of beer-swilling rednecks and exploitation movies. The column had already drawn fire from feminist groups because of its references to women as "bimbos" and its emphasis on nudity and violence in the Grade B and below movies it reviewed. But the straw that broke the back for *Times Herald* executives was a column in which the fictional Joe Bob Briggs poked fun at the song "We Are the World," which was recorded by a group of popular entertainers to raise funds for the starving in Ethiopia. In the column Joe Bob reported that drive-in actors were recording a song for charity called "We Are the Weird," which had one verse that read:

> We are the weird,
> We are the starvin'.
> We are the scum of the filthy earth,
> So let's start scarfin'.

In addition to famine victims, funds from the song were to go to "the United Negro College Fund in the United States, cause I think we should be sending as many Negroes to college as we can, especially the stupid Negroes."[46]

After leaders of the Dallas area black community protested, the paper printed a front-page apology. But the protest continued, resulting in a meeting between editor Will Jarrett and about three hundred angry black readers who demanded that "Joe Bob" be cancelled. The *Times Herald* decided to do just that, although Bloom's "Joe Bob" column continues to be syndicated to about fifty other newspapers. Bloom was bewildered. The "We Are Weird" piece "didn't say anything I had not said in the column before," Bloom maintained. "I had said 'stupid Negroes' before, along with 'stupid Meskins' and 'stupid white people' and several other things. No one had complained."

Jarrett's view is that satire just doesn't work in a mass medium. "In my own mind, I'm sure the 'Joe Bob' column was satire," Jarrett said. "But I cannot defend it to my readers on that basis. I don't think we can defend references to 'Meskins' or 'stupid Negroes' in a family newspaper."[47]

Apparently trained in the Earl Butz school of humor, James G. Watt, Reagan's first secretary of the interior, once described an advisory panel he had appointed as being made up of "a black, a woman, two Jews and a cripple." Asked whether his remarks were well-advised, Watt replied that the question "shows that you don't have the ability to laugh at yourself." His use of stereotyping that some might feel expressed bigotry came at a public meeting and was reported in the press. The news stories "disturbed" one member of the panel, Penn State Professor Richard L. Gordon, who has a paralyzed right arm. Two others described the secretary's remarks as "unfortunate." Washington investment counselor Julia Walsh, the woman Watt had appointed to this panel, a special commission on coal leasing practices, resented the implication that she was "a token woman." Watt issued a public apology the next day.[48]

Feminists have demanded that journalists and other public communicators avoid language that stereotypes and insults women or ignores the changing role of women. Newspaper style books have undergone a flurry of changes in recent years as editors tried to meet at least some of these demands. Some, like "chairperson" for "chairman," were resisted stoutly, but news executives found more reasonable, for example, the insistence that firefighter and mail carrier be substituted for fireman and mailman to reflect the entrance of women into those callings. Careful writers now try to avoid language that suggests men are always wage earners and women are always homemakers.

SLIPPERY STANDARDS

Journalists have a very difficult tightrope to walk between prudishness and sensationalism in their selection of words and pictures. Public mores do not stand still: what was shocking to Americans born early in this century does not shock their grandchildren. And what does it mean when 70 people, or 300, call in to protest some picture or some language in an article? Do such protesters represent larger numbers, perhaps a majority, or are they merely the self-appointed censors who make up a small minority of the audience for any news medium?

You would think that the one code of ethics that would deal with the problem of shocking photographs would be that of the National Press Photographers Association. But theirs is a disappointing statement, written in vague and general language that reads more like a pledge for entering some monastic order. Just a sample:

> Our standards of business dealings, ambitions and relations shall have in them a note of sympathy for our common humanity and shall always require us to take into consideration our highest duties as members of society. In every situation in our business life, in every responsibility that comes before us, our chief thought shall be to

fulfill that responsibility and discharge that duty so that when each of us is finished we shall have endeavored to lift the level of human ideals and achievement higher than we found it.

Nor are the codes of other national journalistic organizations of much help in deciding what to do about shocking words and pictures. The Code of the Ethics of the SPJ-SDX declares, "the media should not pander to morbid curiosity about details of vice and crime." The ASNE Statement of Principles advises that journalists should "observe the common standards of decency." The RTNDA code directs that newscasts exclude "sensationalism or misleading emphasis in any form." The only mention of this problem in the APME code is in its definition of a "good newspaper" as being, among other things, "decent."

The wire service that all APME members use does not have a code of ethics as such, but AP president Boccardi issues periodic advisories to his worldwide staff that amount to the same thing. In a statement on obscenity, Boccardi reminded AP staffers:

> We do not use obscenities on the wire unless there is a compelling need. Where there is a way around them, and there *almost* always is, take it. Similarly, we do not want the wire peppered with the "hells" and "damns" that sprinkle the speech of many people. Leave them out. Good writers and reporters don't need cusswords to make their work graphic and effective.

Some of the codes or operating standards of larger newspapers and television networks deal with shocking language in considerable detail. For example, the *Philadelphia Inquirer* code maintains that "our policy on the use of profanity, obscenity and blasphemy is based on the premise that the *Inquirer* should appeal to the widest possible audience . . . and offer a G-rated product every day." The *Inquirer* requires that its staffers must ask, "Is an important journalistic purpose served by the use of the questionable language?" Then it offers its editors these guidelines:

> The use of any questionable language is almost exclusively limited to quoted material. It should be rare indeed that our own writers use it.
>
> Generally, if a news subject utters profanity, obscenity or blasphemy when no one is present but one or two reporters, we will not use it. The decision becomes more difficult when the number of listeners is larger and the personage of the speaker more important. When President Carter said in public of a potential campaign opponent, "I'll whip his ass," that was deemed to be a situation in which the verbatim quotation was justified.
>
> Sometimes language that is not in itself profane, obscene or blasphemous might be objectionable on the ground of taste. On the other

hand, we should not hesitate to write in clinical terms of matters pertaining to the human anatomy, sex and excretory functions when relevant to the news.

In most cases, when language is deleted from a quotation, an ellipsis will be inserted to indicate that something is missing. Occasionally—and on approval of a ranking editor—it is permissible to *suggest* the word or phrase by using the first letter of the word, followed by an em dash. The use of "bleep" and "bleeping" as substitutes for profanity is restricted to the sports pages.

Most decisions concerning the use of questionable language should be resolved by departmental editors and copy chiefs. These line editors may determine when circumstances warrant the use of expletives such as "hell" and "damn." Line editors may also authorize the use of such terms as "goddamn," "son of a bitch," and "bastard" when the speaker is a reasonably important person, the audience is a fairly substantial one, or the quotation is in a long, serious piece in a section of the paper such as Review and Opinion or *Inquirer* magazine. When the circumstances are not clear-cut, or if stronger language or a question of taste is involved, the executive editor or managing editor must be consulted. In the absence of these editors, the editor in charge must be consulted. Hard-core obscenities such as "shit," "fuck," "piss," "cocksucker," "motherfucker" and their variations may be used *only* by express approval of the executive editor or the managing editor.

The *Washington Post* also gives detailed advice on shocking material in its *Deskbook on Style*. Benjamin C. Bradlee, executive editor, wrote a sort of introductory statement on taste that declares: "We shall avoid prurience. We shall avoid profanities and obscenities unless their use is so essential to a story of significance that its meaning is lost without them." One of several guidelines under Profanities and Obscenities further on in the deskbook says the "use of nude pictures can be justified only if they provide significant information or understanding that would otherwise be lacking in the story."[49]

Like the *Inquirer,* the *St. Paul Pioneer Press and Dispatch* requires that supervisory editors approve publishing profanity and obscenities. "Often we can 'tell it like it is' without hitting our readers with every four-letter word uttered or written by those in the news," the St. Paul paper states. "If the word is essential—its elimination would make the story meaningless or distort its significance—use the first letter of the word and dashes to indicate the rest. Exceptions: goddamn, crap, ass, bastard can be used in full if the above criteria are met. Make it s.o.b." The St. Paul code also bans use of photos of "dead bodies (especially local) unless covered," with exceptions needing approval of the managing editor. Another St. Paul code provision says it is "derogatory and in poor taste" to refer to homosexuals, lesbians, or gays as "limp wristed, lavender laddies, faggots or queers."

The *Detroit Free Press* decrees that "the race of a person in the news won't be reported unless it is clearly relevant to the story or is part of a detailed physical description." The *Free Press* code treats "racially and ethnically derogatory terms" as obscenities, meaning that they "should be spelled as an initial followed by hyphens and be used only in quoted material, when it is essential to a story, and with approval of a managing editor." Also outlawed are photos or art work that foster racial stereotypes. "Avoid condescending tone or patronizing descriptions when writing about people or places," the *Free Press* states. "We do not ridicule others' mannerisms, customs or errors in language, no matter how subtly."

In its section on "sexism," the *Detroit Free Press* guidelines say:

> Women and men should not be treated differently. Physical description and familial connections of a woman are appropriate only if a man would be described comparably in similar circumstances. We generally avoid terms that specify gender, e.g., police officer rather than policeman, although such uses as actor/actress and waiter/waitress are acceptable. Phrases that suggest there is something unusual about the gender of someone holding a job (woman lawyer, male nurse) should be avoided. When referring to members of a group, a construction correctly using *their* is generally preferable to one requiring *his* or *her.*

The *Washington Post* also advises its news staff to avoid sexist language. Its code lists several gender-free terms that may be substituted for words and terms that offend many women, such as: business executive or manager for businessman; photographer for cameraman; member of Congress, representative, or legislator for congressman; council member for councilman; supervisor for foreman; reporter or journalist for newsman; flight attendant for steward or stewardess; humanity, humans, or the human race for man or mankind; adulthood for manhood; synthetic or manufactured for manmade; worker or work force for workingman.

In its Operating Standards, NBC News directs that "audio or visual material which is considered coarse or offensive by a substantial portion of the audience must be avoided to the fullest extent feasible." It adds that management may make an exception if the news is significant, if the offensive material is relevant, and if the material is not so offensive that it outweighs the need of the public to know and understand. "And, in no event, may any such material be used for its shock effect or as the basis for humor."

The Production Standards of CBS News are similar. They offer the Nixon Watergate tapes as an example of news in which offensive language had to be used. "It was decided that the anticipated objectionable language would be broadcast because of the historical and journalistic importance of reporting the [congressional impeachment] proceedings as they actually took place," the CBS code states.

The ABC News policy states that "morbid, sensational or alarming details should not be included in broadcasts unless they are essential to the factual report. Obscene, profane or indecent material must also be avoided." ABC requires that problems involving objectionable material "must be resolved in light of contemporary standards of taste, the state of the law and the requirements of newsworthiness."

As journalists wrestle with the genuine problem of how much offensive material should be passed on to the public, the question has to be asked: If journalists routinely hold back or disguise certain words and pictures, is the public getting—and should it get—the most accurate reflection of real life that journalists can provide? Frankly, most news executives seem to view their audiences as less able than journalists are to handle shocking words and pictures. "Our readers aren't ready for that," they claim. No sane observer wants all U.S. journalism to suddenly start imitating the sensationalism of the *New York Post* or the *National Enquirer*, but perhaps it is time for news executives to ask how well they serve us if they treat us all as eight-year-olds.

10 Privacy

"I don't know—using the names of these raped Sabine women might stigmatize them for life."

Suppose you are the managing editor of a metropolitan daily newspaper and you have to decide how far to go in identifying eight men who have died in a fire at a homosexual film club. Most of the men are married. None is well known in your city: one is an aide to a congressman, one is an army major, one is a former pastor; the other five hold ordinary jobs. Six other men were injured seriously enough to require hospitalization, but authorities have withheld their names and other identification. Because flames blocked the front door of the club, the only unlocked exit, firemen had to smash through a locked rear door to reach the dead and injured men, who had been watching all-male, X-rated films on the second floor.

Would you identify the dead men fully—name, age, address, job, and survivors? Would you tell your readers that the death scene was a homosexual club? Would you press authorities to name the injured men?

The editors of the *Washington Post* and the late *Washington Star* had to decide how far they would go in identifying the eight men who perished in just such a fire. Basically, the *Star* decided to identify them fully and the *Post* did not. Both revealed the nature of the film club, the

234

Cinema Follies. Neither paper published the names of the injured.

The ombudsmen for the two competing papers discussed their different approaches to this story in columns about a week after the tragedy. Charles B. Seib of the *Post* said his paper's "main motivation in not using the names was compassion for the wives and children of the men."[1] George Beveridge of the *Star* wrote that "the identity of the victims in a local tragedy as substantial as this one was so vital an element of the story that the printing of the names never arose" as an issue in the minds of *Star* editors who handled the story.[2]

Seib saw something "disquieting" in the *Post*'s decision because, "in effect, *Post* editors said that homosexuality is so shameful that extraordinary steps had to be taken to protect the families of the victims. We will report the tragedy fully, they said, and tell you what we know about the men who died. But we won't tell you who they were." Seib questioned whether the *Post* approach did not underscore "the stigma of homosexuality" just at the time that "efforts are being made to bring it out and address it as a social fact?"[3]

Beveridge used stronger language to question the *Post*'s decision:

> Post editors say two factors figured in their decision: First, a doubt that the fire victims' presence at the gay-oriented establishment conclusively proved anything about their actual sexual preferences; and second, a concern about the identifications' impact on the families of the fire victims, some of whom may have been "secret" homosexuals.
>
> The first of the Post's factors, to my mind, lands with a thud. For while I haven't the slightest idea who at the Cinema Follies that evening was or wasn't a homosexual, the question strikes me as being entirely beside the point.
>
> The purpose of those stories, in The Post and The Star alike, wasn't to disclose or suggest the sexual preferences of anyone. The stories were written solely because eight human beings who happened to be in a certain place at a certain time, tragically died in a fire. That was news. I won't argue that the sexual orientation of the Cinema Follies added no element of additional reader interest to the story. But the point is that eight deaths in a fire at the Kennedy Center, or an uptown X-rated movie, for that matter, would be no less a story. The victims would be no less or no more important to the story in those instances than they were in the Cinema Follies fire. And I can't, for the life of me, imagine a like tragedy in any other location in which the victims should not be identified as a matter of legitimate reader interest.[4]

Seib agreed that the *Post* should have fully identified all of the fire victims. "By all the measures we normally use, the names were news, and the business of a newspaper is to print the news," he wrote. "Any other course results inevitably in confusion and precedents that cause trouble later."[5]

Beveridge also expressed concern about precedent. While "it is hard to imagine that anyone fails to share the Post's compassion for the families of the fire victims," the *Star* ombudsman wrote, the *Post*'s failure to identify the victims of the disaster amounted "to a sort of double standard of press responsibility that is much easier started than stopped."[6]

In his post-mortem on the *Post*'s decision not to fully identify the victims in the homosexual film club fire, Seib said he suspects that if a poll could be taken, "the public would favor the course the *Post* took" because the "public generally feels, I think, that the press is much too insensitive to the harm and pain it can cause innocent people."[7]

The question of whether a journalist should or should not reveal or suggest the sexual proclivity of a person who figures in the news is a privacy question. Although invading the privacy of news subjects is usually thought of as a legal matter – the kind you discuss with your lawyer – it is really more of an ethical question: How much of any person's private or personal life should journalists publicize and under what circumstances? The developing law on privacy – based mostly on court decisions in privacy and libel suits – is better at telling journalists what they cannot do than what they should do.

PRIVACY LAW AND ETHICS

You will not find a right to privacy mentioned in the United States Constitution. But since the early part of this century, the courts in this country have increasingly accepted the legal concept that citizens have a right to be let alone. Various opinion polls indicate widespread public support for this idea. One poll by Louis Harris Associates showed that three out of four people questioned urged a guarantee of privacy, equating the right of privacy with the "unalienable rights" of the Declaration of Independence – "life, liberty and the pursuit of happiness."[8]

News organizations often have to defend themselves against suits alleging both libel and invasion of privacy because those two legal theories overlap. For example, litigants may claim that they were libeled (defamed or suffered injury to their reputations) by the publicizing of private facts about them. But defenses against libel and privacy differ. In libel suits, the oldest major defense is truth. Another is qualified privilege, protecting the news media from libel convictions for truthfully reporting government proceedings and records. A third major defense against libel is fair comment and criticism, designed to protect the news media's right to comment on the public performances of people who voluntarily put themselves in the limelight – politicians, entertainers, athletes, and the like. The best defense against a privacy suit, on the other hand, is newsworthiness. If the defendant news organization can show that the offensive item was news and it was accurate, it usually wins suits brought for publicizing private facts.[9]

So the decision about whether and when journalists should invade someone's privacy is largely an ethical rather than a legal one. If the private facts publicized are legitimate news – and courts have been liberal in defining that – chances are slim that a privacy suit will be successful.

A lot of information published and broadcast in this country is regarded by at least some of the people involved as private information. The question for journalists is not whether to invade privacy but how much. At what point does an invasion of privacy pass from reasonable to unreasonable? Most of us find it reasonable that journalists often publicize some private facts in order to tell us what we need to know to measure political candidates and to assess public officials. But do we find it equally reasonable when journalists invade the privacy of children and relatives of those candidates and public officials? Although some invasion of privacy is necessary if the American public is to be well-informed, the question for journalists – and the public as well – becomes one of where to draw the line. That, I submit, is more an ethical than a legal decision. Yet many news executives continue to look at privacy invasion as purely or mostly a legal matter and the question for them becomes, "How much can I get away with?"

Privacy for VIPs. Because "prominence" has long been a criterion of newsworthiness, journalists see the likes of a Senator Kennedy or a Meryl Streep as being more interesting to the public than John or Jane Doe. This has led the news media to afford less privacy to public officials and personalities than they do to ordinary people.

Public officeholders have traditionally been scrutinized rather diligently by the press, which believes a major reason for its constitutionally guaranteed freedom is so it can serve as a watchdog of government. This vigilance, however, had been mostly a nine-to-five thing. Journalists had taken the view that public officials should be able to lead private lives, just like the rest of us. This tolerance even extended to looking the other way when the bad personal habits of some officeholders surfaced while they were on duty. It was common in an earlier day for journalists not to report drunkenness, philandering, and senility on the part of some members of Congress and other officeholders. Former Congressman Wilbur

Mills, chairman of the House Ways and Means Committee, "was a prime example," observes David R. Jones, national editor of the *New York Times*. "The guy was falling down drunk, but the press in general portrayed him as one of the great legislative leaders in American politics. Now, he himself says that his drinking affected his job."[10]

The tapes of private conversations in President Nixon's White House office and the many books that have been written about him since he resigned the presidency in 1974 were shocking to many people because they revealed a rather foul-mouthed man who had trouble holding his booze and distinguishing right from wrong. That is not at all the picture that the news media in general had projected of him prior to Watergate. Admittedly, reporters covering Nixon were seldom able to get close enough to him to observe habits that might rub off on his public performance, but part of the reason we learned about some of Nixon's unflattering personal qualities only after he left office is that most reporters were reluctant to invade his privacy. When you're covering the president, you do not go snooping around inquiring about his bedroom or bar habits.

But, for better or worse, the press seems to be paying more attention these days to the private lives of public officials and reporting them to the public when they affect the jobs the officials are responsible for. Michael J. Davies, editor and publisher of the *Hartford Courant*, believes that public officials, like everyone else, are entitled to privacy from the press "until their private lives affect their public duties." When he was an editor in Louisville, he reported a private matter involving the mayor of that city. Davies recalls that Louisville firefighters went on strike and no one could find the mayor—who had told everyone he was going to Atlanta to some conference. "The paper tracked him down in New Orleans, where he was having an affair with his secretary," the editor reveals. "We printed that."[11]

John M. Fedders resigned as head of the enforcement division of the Securities and Exchange Commission after news stories appeared suggesting that he was a wife beater. The stories were based on charges made by his wife in a divorce suit. At the *Wall Street Journal*, which was the first news medium to break the story, managing editor Norman Pearlstine said he "agonized a couple of weeks" before deciding to run the piece. What made the decision difficult was that there was little evidence that Fedders' private problems were affecting his job as the nation's top securities law enforcer. "As a general rule, I don't think we should be writing about the private lives of public officials when there is no indication that the behavior in private is affecting their public performance," Pearlstine explained. But the editor chose to go against his general rule in this case because Fedders had publicly admitted beating his wife and "the

White House was aware of the issue of family violence and seemed to be concerned about it."[12]

Although he believes the news media no longer protect the drunkards and letchers who get to Congress and high public office, Brit Hume, Capitol Hill correspondent for ABC News, objects to the way journalism has treated some relatives of public persons. "We ought not make relatives public persons by extension," he suggests. "I have thought for years that we ought to leave certain members of the Kennedy family alone—particularly Jacqueline Onassis, who has sought to be a private person. We ought to leave her the hell alone. And sons and daughters who don't try to take advantage of their special positions, we ought to leave them alone, too." Hume holds that the "governing standard" in invading the privacy of public persons and officials *and* their relatives ought to be whether or not some issue of public policy has been raised.

Hume regrets the story he did back in the early 1970s when he was working for columnist Jack Anderson about Randy Agnew, Vice-President Spiro Agnew's son. Hume tracked down young Agnew in Baltimore and confirmed that he had broken up with his wife and moved in with a male hairdresser. Anderson assigned Hume to get the story and he used it in the column because the vice-president often pontificated about child rearing. Hume says he is "more ashamed of that story than anything I've done in journalism. I'm sorry about it to this day."[13]

Hume strikes a sore spot in his criticism of publicity given by the media to relatives of the mighty. Editors who have given big play to stories involving such relatives argue that they are justified because the stories tell us something about the public persons or officials.

A VIP relative story that raised some eyebrows was the report of the arrest in 1975 of the forty-one-year-old daughter of then Senate Republican Leader Hugh Scott. Marian Concannon was one of twenty persons arrested early one morning in drug raids near Philadelphia. Concannon, divorced mother of eight children who was supporting herself by driving a circulation truck for a Doylestown, Pennsylvania, newspaper, was charged with selling $100 worth of hashish to a state undercover agent. Most of the stories identified Concannon in some detail but did not name any of the other persons arrested in that day's sweep. The *Philadelphia Inquirer* ran a 500-word page-one story on the Concannon arrest, illustrating it with two pictures—one of her modest home and one of Concannon with a sweater over her head being led to arraignment. *Inquirer* editors may have felt that this final paragraph of the story justified the play they gave it: "Her father has been a strong supporter of presidential moves to tighten drug controls, and in 1971 supported President Richard M. Nixon's opposition to the legalization of marijuana."[14]

Steve Lovelady, associate executive editor of the *Inquirer,* was not on the paper when the Concannon arrest story was run, but he sees it as a legitimate news story. He puts it in the same class as a more recent story in the *Inquirer* reporting that the man who was about to marry then Mayor Frank Rizzo's daughter was a convicted bookmaker. "Our phones rang off the hook," Lovelady claims. " 'For chrissake,' they said, 'can't you even leave his daughter alone?' " Lovelady argues that if the daughter of the top editor of the *Inquirer* got arrested or was about to marry a bookmaker, that also would be news and would be reported.[15]

The hounding of the Kennedys that bothers Brit Hume reached a low point in 1984 when David Kennedy died of a drug overdose at the age of twenty-eight. David was the son of Senator Robert F. Kennedy, who was assassinated, as was his brother John, the president. The heavy coverage the press gave to the investigation of David's death, which went on for months, perhaps was justified, but the attention it paid to the family wake and burial seemed ghoulish. It so bothered Eric Schmitt, a young reporter who covered the wake for the *New York Times,* that he later wrote in *Quill* magazine that it made him "ashamed to be a journalist."

Schmitt said "it shocked my sense of civility that the press or the public believed it had a rightful place" lining the border of David Kennedy's family home at Hickory Hill in McLean, Virginia. "Instead of what should have been a private moment for the family, the press declared the sad gathering of Kennedys a newsworthy event."

"Why were three dozen journalists at Hickory Hill chasing hearses, interviewing priests, and cornering family friends as they left the house?" Schmitt asked. "The answers to these questions always seemed to come back to an ill-defined journalistic tradition of covering the Kennedys because they were the Kennedys. . . . They say here in Washington that the Kennedys are America's royal family, and as such are denied the rights of privacy granted to normal citizens."

Schmitt rejects that justification for overcovering the Kennedys. "Who was David Kennedy other than the son of the late United States senator? He may be a 'tragic symbol,' but is his tragedy any more significant than those that befall other families?" Schmitt asked. "At Hickory Hill," he concluded, "we overstepped the boundary between serving the public's right to know and the privacy of the individual, tossing compassion to a distant corner."[16]

Charles B. Seib, retired ombudsman for the *Washington Post,* is critical of allowing the law to set the ethical standards for privacy. He contends that journalists have been handicapped in their thinking about privacy by the stiffer tests that courts require in libel suits brought by public officials or persons. "When we ask ourselves, 'How public is this person whose privacy we're about to invade?' " Seib continues, "what we mean is, 'How far can we go?' " Seib believes that "compassion has to come up occasionally" when journalists try to decide whether and how far to invade someone's privacy.[17]

Privacy of Ordinary People. When ordinary people get caught up in the news somehow, journalists – for that moment at least – tend to treat them like public figures. It does not seem to matter whether the private persons thrust themselves into the news (such as demonstrators for a cause) or fall into the news through no action of their own (such as victims of a public accident). Many journalists worry, however, about hurting people who fall into the news and are not seeking publicity. "I don't want to hurt people unnecessarily," observes Claude Sitton, editorial director of the Raleigh *News and Observer* and *Times*, "but sometimes that may be necessary. I regret it and we don't do it lightly."[18]

A recent incident in Cocoa, Florida, provides us with a good example of the sort of problem created for editors when a private person gets involuntarily involved in a newsworthy event. Anne M. Saul, managing editor of Cocoa *Today* before she moved to *USA Today,* explains that the Cocoa paper had to decide how much coverage to give to a story about a woman who was abducted by her estranged husband and held captive by him for about two and a half hours while police surrounded their former home. The woman was grabbed by her ex-husband, who had a gun, as she left her job at an electronic plant. He pushed her into his car and drove her to their former residence, where he threatened her and made her take off all of her clothes. Sheriff's deputies, called by a co-worker of the kidnapped woman, surrounded the house, keeping the press and spectators behind a roped-off area. Suddenly there were shots inside. The deputies rushed the house and brought out the woman, who had only a small hand towel in front of her. It turned out that the shots had been fired by the husband as he killed himself. The problem for *Today* editors was not whether to publish a story of this unusual event – there was no question about that – but whether to use a photograph of a plainclothesman rushing the woman out of the house with only a hand towel to hide her nudity. The decision was to use the photograph on page one. (Fig. 10.1)[19]

The woman later sued the paper for invasion of privacy, and she won a damage award from a Florida jury of $10,000, much below the more than $7 million she sought. The woman's attorney appealed the judgment, but the Fifth District Court of Appeals decided against the woman, ruling that since what the newspaper reported was newsworthy and true,

10.1 Kidnap victim. *This photo of a woman being escorted by a police officer from the home where her estranged husband had been holding her hostage raised an ethical question for editors of the local newspaper. Although the face is masked here, it was not in the photograph published on the front page of Cocoa Today. (Photo courtesy of Today, Cocoa, Fla.)*

no invasion of privacy had occurred. Her attorney again appealed, but the Florida and U.S. Supreme Courts refused to review the decision, thus letting the appellate court's ruling stand.

In his arguments to the jury, the woman's attorney contended that the paper should have cropped the photo above the woman's waist. In response, the executive editor when *Today* published the photo, Charles Overby, testified that he decided against cutting out the lower portion of the picture because that would have eliminated the motion of the woman and the officer running during a "dramatic rescue attempt." Overby said that if the picture had shown her private parts, "we never would have considered" running it.[20]

News photographers who intrude on the grief of ordinary people are justifiably criticized. It's bad enough when they do that with the Kennedys or other prominent persons, but unless the grief is an essential part of some very public tragedy, photographing ordinary people in that very private moment is intolerable. Yet when that happened recently at the *Orange County Register* in Santa Ana, California, the editors, photographers, and the paper's ombudsman all defended the photo. Taken by a free-lancer, the picture, published on page one in color, showed a grief-stricken wife right after she had come upon a car crash in which her husband had been killed. The wife was driving to work when she noticed a familiar sports car in an accident that had just occurred. She stopped and ran up to a police officer who had to confirm that it was her husband in the wreckage and he was dead. The photo was taken at that moment. Readers protested its use, calling the newspaper insensitive, irresponsible, exploitive, and sensationalistic. But ombudsman Pat Riley wrote in his column afterward that he agreed with the editors who decided to use the photo. Conceding that the picture intruded on personal grief, Riley defended it because "it mirrored emotional reality in a powerful way and aroused our empathy. It did not, in my view, hold the woman up to ridicule. It showed her expressing natural understandable suffering, and we could all feel it."[21]

A privacy decision that puts journalism in a more favorable light was the one that kept the family name of the famous "bubble boy" secret for the more than twelve years that he lived. All of the thousands of news stories about the boy born in Houston with an immune deficiency that forced him to live in a germ-free bubble identified him only as "David" — first "bubble baby" David, later "bubble boy" David. The news media protected the family name merely because they were asked to by David's parents. The parents felt that if the entire world knew David's family name, their lives and their ability to raise David and their daughter properly and safely would be jeopardized. After David died in early 1984, his mother went before a meeting of the Texas Daily Newspaper Association to thank journalists for protecting the family name and for "the way they handled David's passing." She said "there was virtually little or no intrusion and David's death was with much dignity."[22]

SOME SPECIAL PRIVACY PROBLEMS

Some kinds of news and news subjects cause special problems for journalists who have to decide about publicizing private facts. News stories involving homosexuals, rapes and other sex crimes, juveniles in trouble with the law, and suicides are almost always troublesome, but they are merely the most obvious areas of privacy that journalists have learned to be cautious about.

Even something as routine as reporting someone's age in a news story can upset people who see their age as a private matter. Smaller and medium-sized newspapers seem to get the heaviest criticism for this practice. "We don't always use ages, particularly of older women," notes James A. Dunlap, editor of the Sharon, Pennsylvania, *Herald.*[23]

Addresses, another standard way of identifying people in news stories, also seem to some citizens to be a private matter, particularly those whose homes have been burglarized or who have suffered some criminal act that is apt to be repeated. A White House task force urged in 1983 that addresses and telephone numbers of crime victims and witnesses be kept secret unless a court ordered otherwise. "Victims and witnesses share a common, often justified apprehension that they and members of their family will be threatened or harassed as a result of their testimony against violent criminals," the President's Task Force on Victims of Crime declared.[24]

A few newspapers have started to do what the task force recommended. Many more are obfuscating addresses of crime victims by stating them in general terms (5400 block of Elm Street, the Pittsfield area, nearby Barnsville, etc.). But specific addresses of crime victims and witnesses are still widely published.

The *Charlotte* (North Carolina) *Observer* found out that publishing a name and address even in a routine feature story can sometimes spur harassment. The *Observer* ran an interesting but fairly standard photograph on its front page showing a mother strolling her six-year-old daughter to the first day of classes at her elementary school. The picture was taken from the rear so that the schoolhouse could be seen in the background. The caption under the photo identified the mother and daughter and gave their address.

Four days later, the mother called the paper to complain that she had received more than a hundred telephone calls, some obscene, some from men who wanted to meet her, others from men who wanted to meet her daughter. She also got some threatening letters, one from a man in jail for assault with a deadly weapon, armed robbery, and breaking and entering who was due to be released in twenty-two months. "Do you realize that hundreds of sick people know who I am and where I live?" the mother asked city editor Greg Ring. The calls and letters stopped after about two weeks, but the mother's anger continued long after that. "Newspaper editors need to pay attention to what they're doing to innocent people," she said.

Sobered by the unexpected impact of the routine publishing of a name and address, Ring suggested that editors should ask these questions before publishing addresses:

> Is it a vital fact in the news story, i.e., the site of a crime?
> Is it necessary information to identify an individual who might otherwise be confused with someone else? Is there another fact, other than the address, that would serve the same purpose?

Is the exact address necessary? Would just giving the street or neighborhood serve the same purpose? Who can get hurt, and how? Is publishing the address more important than that?[25]

News of mentally retarded people who get in trouble raises a red flag in most newsrooms. Sometimes the problem can be solved simply by not identifying the retarded person as such; some editors have chosen to ignore minor stories about retarded people in trouble if no community interest is involved. But one young editor who apparently had difficulty spotting red flags got run out of Marceline, Missouri, in the late 1970s when residents strenuously objected to his treatment of a local retarded man. Randy Miller, who took over the editorship of the weekly *Marceline Press* when he was fresh out of the University of Missouri journalism school, published a page one story and a full page of photos about a thirty-two-year-old retarded man who had to be subdued by police after he showed up at work with a twenty-gauge shotgun, hit his plant manager, and threatened his foreman. Angry readers protested by phone calls and letters, one accusing Miller of "capitalizing on the infirmities of this young man." Another letter signed by four people said that Miller's article and photos of the retarded man might be acceptable in large cities, "but in a town the size of ours, where everyone is a neighbor to everyone else in the community, such pictures and articles can only cause resentment and dislike." Then Miller reopened the wounds by reprinting one of the photos of the man in his year-end review of memorable local news events. Shortly after that, people in Marceline heard that the retarded man had committed suicide in Colorado. Whether he or his family had seen the year-end photo was not known, but Miller left Marceline on the advice of the police chief, who said he had heard rumors of threats to the young editor's life.[26]

Homosexuals. As we saw in the case study that opened this chapter, the sexual orientation of people who have fallen into the news can become a thorny issue for reporters and editors. Public acceptance of homosexuals and the gay life-style undoubtedly has increased in this country over the past two decades, but sensitive journalists know that hanging a homosexual label on someone can still hurt. The ethical problem for editors is deciding whether the homosexual identification is relevant to the news being reported. It obviously would be in a story about an admittedly homosexual junior high school teacher fired because of his homosexuality. It just as obviously would not be relevant in a story about a local businessman who is homosexual being awarded a prize for beautification of his business site. But in between those rather easy calls lie many news situations in which the decision for editors is far from simple.

Because AIDS (acquired immune deficiency syndrome) is a disease that is associated in the public mind with homosexuality, news executives have been careful not to report specific identities of AIDS victims. The *Boston Globe* and the *Centre Daily Times* in State College, Pennsylvania, handled two recent stories about AIDS victims in a typical manner—by not specifically identifying the victims. The *Globe*'s story was about a patient who was turned away by two doctors at a city hospital because they suspected he had AIDS. The *Globe* named the two physicians but not the patient. "AIDS victims, because of the public's inordinate fear of them, may often require the type of voluntary media protection accorded rape victims," *Globe* ombudsman Robert J. Kierstead wrote in his column.[27] Explaining why the *Centre Daily Times* decided not to identify the first resident of its area to be diagnosed as having AIDS, executive editor William A. Blair wrote: "The stigma of the disease is such that those who contract it often become treated like lepers. They lose jobs. They're kicked out of schools. Friends, relatives and business acquaintances quit associating with them."[28]

AIDS presents another problem for the news media, particularly those that regard themselves as family oriented. As medical researchers have learned more about the disease, they have associated it with anal intercourse. Medical thinking holds that AIDS is a blood-borne disease. In many of the known cases in this country, it strikes males who have participated in anal sex in such a way that the delicate lining of the rectum has torn so that the AIDS virus could enter the body's circulatory system. Prudery about printing or broadcasting terms like "anal intercourse" or "anal sex" has prevented candid reporting about AIDS in all but a few media.[29]

Dr. James O. Mason, acting assistant secretary for health and director of the Center for Disease Control in Atlanta, told the APME in October 1985 that 74 percent of the 14,000 reported cases of AIDS in this country were transmitted sexually among homosexual or bisexual males. Some 15 percent of the cases were transmitted by the sharing of needles among heavy drug abusers. The disease has also been transmitted, but in small percentages of cases, by blood transfusions, by infected mothers passing it on to their paranatal babies, and by sexual intercourse between heterosexual women and infected males. "Although the AIDS virus has been isolated from human saliva and tears, there is no evidence that transmission has occurred through these routes," Dr. Mason reported. "Transmission doesn't even occur in close family situations where children share lollipops or spoons or even a bed."[30]

AIDS was not a factor in the best known recent case of the news media publicizing the private fact of homosexuality—the story of the ex-marine who knocked aside the gun hand of Sara Jane Moore as she aimed a 38-caliber revolver at President Gerald Ford. Moore's shot was deflected, missing the president as he left a San Francisco hotel to get into his limousine. Almost immediately Secret Service agents and police wrestled Moore to the ground and arrested her. And the hefty marine veteran, thirty-three-year-old Oliver W. Sipple, became an instant hero.[31]

Three days later newspaper and broadcast editors in California and around the country had to decide whether to reveal to their publics that hero Sipple was probably homosexual. There was no suggestion that Sipple was gay in any of the news reports published and broadcast in the two days after he apparently saved the president's life. But then Herb Caen, in his widely read *San Francisco Chronicle* column that other news people call a newspaper within a newspaper, reported that two San Francisco gay leaders were "proud" of Sipple's heroism and remarked, "Maybe this will help break the stereotype." Caen identified one of the leaders as "gay politico" Harvey Milk, who had gotten help from Sipple in his later-to-be-successful campaign for city supervisor. Picking up on the Caen item, *Los Angeles Times* reporter Daryl Lembke located Sipple and filed a story noting that although Sipple "declined to characterize his sexual preferences," he admitted that he was a member of the "court" of Mike Caringi, who had been elected "emperor of San Francisco" by the gay community. Lembke's story was carried on the *Washington Post-Los Angeles Times* news wire and picked up by both major wire services.[32]

One of the newspapers that ran Lembke's story was the *News* in Detroit, where Sipple's mother and father lived. The *News* published a follow-up story the next day reporting on how relatives and others who knew Sipple when he was growing up in Detroit reacted to the revelation that he "was a prominent figure in San Francisco's gay community." The story reported that his mother, Mrs. Ethyl Sipple, "said her motherly pride is tarnished by the stories about her hero son," and quoted her as saying, "We were very proud of Oliver, but now I won't be able to walk down the street without somebody saying something." The story also said that Sipple was a high school dropout, and that he was honorably discharged from the marines and placed on 100 percent disability because of mental adjustment problems from Vietnam combat, during which he was wounded twice.[33]

Sipple sued columnist Herb Caen, the *San Francisco Chronicle,* the *Los Angeles Times,* and five out-of-state newspapers for invading his privacy. The suit claimed that the publicity about Sipple's homosexuality brought him "great mental anguish, embarrassment and humiliation" and caused his family to abandon him after learning about his sexual proclivity for the first time through the news stories. Lawyers for the *Los Angeles Times* argued that Sipple, by becoming involved in an event of worldwide importance, had wittingly or unwittingly injected himself into the "vortex of publicity," thus relinquishing "a part of his right of privacy to the extent that the public has a legitimate interest in his activities." To counter Sipple's argument that his homosexuality was not newsworthy, the *Times* maintained that reporting his sexual orientation gave the gay community the favorable publicity it had demanded, because Sipple's action was heroic and helped break the stereotype of homosexuals as effeminate and helpless. The *Times* also said that Sipple's homosexuality was already known by many people, through his participation in well-publicized activities in many cities other than San Francisco.[34]

Although the San Francisco County Superior Court dismissed Sipple's case on a summary judgment without comment in 1980, Sipple's lawyer filed a motion for a new trial, arguing that a jury, not a trial judge alone, should decide whether "reasonable people" were offended by revelation of Sipple's homosexuality. At this writing, that appeal is pending.[35]

A less well-known publication of a private fact occurred in another California newspaper, the Oakland *Tribune*. It concerned Toni Ann Diaz, the first woman student body president at the College of Alameda. She got into the news not only because of her election but by her accusations as student president that college administrators were signing her name to checks and using the money for improper purposes. But the best-read publicity about her came in a *Tribune* column by Sidney Jones, who wrote:

> More education stuff: The students of the College of Alameda will be surprised to learn that their student body president, Toni Diaz, is no lady, but in fact a man whose real name is Antonio.
> Now, I realize, that in these times, such a matter is no big deal, but I suspect his female classmates in P.E. 97 may wish to make other showering arrangements.

Diaz had undergone sex-change therapy three years before and, until the *Tribune* item, had kept the surgery secret from all but her immediate family and closest friends. Diaz sued the *Tribune* for invasion of privacy and won the first round when a jury awarded her $25,000 in compensatory damages and $525,000 in punitive damages. But a California court of appeals overturned that judgment because the lower court judge had improperly instructed the jury.[36]

Publicly identifying homosexuals and transsexuals as such may not be as harmful to them as it once was, but, as we have seen, suits for privacy invasion are still a risk. The ethical argument for not identifying homosexuals unless it is extremely relevant to the story is that the identification can stigmatize the person – cause him or her to lose a job or an apartment, or to be alienated from relatives and friends. But Seib holds to his view that the *Washington Post* carried that reasoning too far in not fully identifying the eight men who died in the homosexual film club fire reported at the opening of this chapter. "We were saying that some things are so stigmatizing that we declared those eight men to be non-persons," Seib observes. "It was demeaning to the men who died."[37]

Rape and Sex Crimes. Another troublesome area of news is that having to do with rape and sex crimes. The convention in U.S. journalism has been to withhold the identification of rape victims unless the victims are well-known persons or unless the victims are also murdered. The reason for such self-censorship is that rape is seen by many as a crime that often stigmatizes its victims so that they become double victims, so to speak. But this convention of protecting the woman who alleges rape is being challenged by some journalists. And the U.S. Supreme Court, in a 1975 case involving a Georgia TV station's broadcast of a young rape victim's name, held that the media cannot be sued for violations of privacy when the victim's name comes from court records.[38]

A 1982–1983 survey of American newspaper editors showed that 67 percent of them believe rape victims should not be named, while 82 percent hold that the accused should be named. Professor Carol Oukrop of Kansas State University, who did the survey, identified several kinds of rape stories in which the victims are generally named, even by those with policies against doing so. These are rape situations in which:

1. The victim was killed.
2. A kidnapping or other serious crime was also involved.
3. The victim/complainant is willing to be identified.
4. The newsworthiness is so extraordinary the full story must be told (victim is a public figure, attack was in a very public place, etc.).
5. The complaint is invalid and complainant is charged with filing false information.[39]

For some news organizations, though, the rules go out the window when the rape case is as spectacular as the one that occurred in New Bedford, Massachusetts, in March 1983. A twenty-two-year-old woman charged that she was gang-raped by six men while she was pinned to a pool table in a tavern. Police initially reported that she had been surrounded by "jeering" men. That picture of a barful of men cheering while a woman was being raped was spread throughout the world by the news media, even after it became known in the trial that there apparently were only nine men in the bar, including the six who were charged with rape. Only one man acknowledged before the court that he had called out "Go for it! Go for it!"

The aspect of press coverage of this rape case that brought the greatest criticism, however, was not the possible false image of the rape itself that made the event appear to be even more horrible than it was. It was the way Cable News Network (CNN), the United Press International, and some newspapers and TV stations identified the rape victim by name during the trial in early 1984. Her name had been protected in the months between her complaint and the trial, but the judge permitted the trial to be photographed by a pool TV camera being shared by CNN and three other electronic news organizations. Although the camera operators agreed not to photograph the victim while she was on the witness stand or in the courtroom, her name was mentioned right off the bat by the judge and prosecuting attorneys. Her name, therefore, was heard not just in the courtroom but throughout the country.

In addition to CNN and UPI, the victim was named by the *Providence Journal* and *Evening Bulletin;* the Fall River, Massachusetts, *Herald News;* Colony Communications, a cable TV system covering New Bedford and Fall River; WLNE-TV, Providence; and a Portuguese-language newspaper, *O Jornal.* Some newspapers and the three major networks, CBS, NBC, and CBS, showed pictures of the woman leaving the courthouse, but with her face covered. Interestingly, CNN did not photograph the woman outside the courthouse and never used her name in its newscasts, only when it was spoken by others in its live coverage of the trial. Despite the broadcast of the name through the cable systems, most news organizations covering the trial did not identify the victim.

Those news organizations that used her name justified it on the grounds that the name was already publicized. But some went beyond that. Charles M. Hauser, executive editor of the Providence papers, said that while he expects his papers will revert in the future to their traditional policy of not naming rape victims, he is bothered by giving rape victims such special treatment. "Any time we are suppressing public information, we are deciding what is good for society, for the public, for an individual," Hauser added. News executives at WLNE-TV and *O Jornal* said the New Bedford case has led them to change to a policy of routinely naming rape victims. WLNE-TV managing editor Dave Layman even intends to use pictures of rape victims if his crews can get them.

The *Standard-Times* in New Bedford did not publish the name of the victim in this case, even though it was obviously known by some people in that city. Editor James R. Ragsdale believes "the stigma faced by rape victims is real. The hate I have heard on radio call-in shows expressed toward that woman is unbelievable." (The hostility Ragsdale sensed helped drive the rape victim out of the community after the trial. She moved with her husband and two young daughters to Miami, where she was killed in a car crash in December 1986 at the age of twenty-five.)

All news organizations covering this rape case named the six accused rapists from the beginning and throughout the trial, which resulted in convictions of four of them, who were sentenced to terms varying from six to twelve years; two were acquitted.[40]

It is the the unevenness of naming accused rapists but not the accusers that worries some editors like Claude Sitton, editorial director of the Raleigh *Times* and *News and Observer.* It has been the policy for many years at his newspaper to identify both the victim and the alleged rapist at the time he is arrested and charged, Sitton reports. Until the arrest, the rape victim is not identified. "But once the charge is made, we do not feel we have a right to decide between the guilt or innocence of the man charged," Sitton explains. "We do not print her name again generally until the case is in court and she is on the stand. . . . If the guy pleads guilty, we don't print her name again. But so long as the matter is an open question before the courts, we print the victim's name."[41]

Sitton can recall three or four cases in recent years in which the alleged rapist was found to be innocent or the charge dropped, "but they suffered damage to their reputations anyway." Another case he feels supports his policy was one in which a black teenage boy was arrested after a white teenage girl charged that he raped her at the state fairgrounds. "We published the names of both and the circumstances," Sitton recalls, and as a result other boys came forward and told police they had had sexual relations with the girl that day and she "had invited it all." Sitton believes the publicity helped calm community emotions in this case, which twenty-five years ago "would have led to a lynching." Sitton admits the "policy causes us a lot of pain, but we don't feel we have a right to play God and say who is guilty and who is innocent."

The Shelton, Washington, *Mason County Journal;* the Manchester (Connecticut) *Journal-Inquirer;* the Arlington, Virginia, *Northern Virginia Sun;* and the *Durham* (North Carolina) *Morning Herald* are among the few daily newspapers in the land with policies similar to Sitton's. The *Herald* in a recent eighteen-part series of editorials defending its policy said: "No one seems concerned that the newspapers, along with the police and courts, could be exploited as a weapon against a man by a woman seeking to ruin him." The *Herald* also argued:

> In any other criminal case, the concern for the rights of the defendant seems paramount; great suspicion is directed at the motives and integrity of the prosecution witnesses, the police, the entire judicial system . . . until it comes to the rape charge. Then . . . suddenly they have faith in the judicial system. Suddenly they don't seem to have ever heard of the idea that a defendant might possibly be innocent—the victim either of honest mistake or malice.[42]

Another who questions the conventional policy is Robert W. Greene, assistant managing editor of *Newsday,* who feels that "in modern society it is not as shameful to be a victim of rape as it used to be." Greene contends that withholding the name is a "holdover from the age when women had to be protected." He can imagine cases in which a man goes on trial for rape and because of newspaper policies the public has no idea who the raped woman is. "Yet somebody may have been with that complainant that night thirty or forty miles away and would have come forward to police if he had known the name of the woman who complained."[43]

But even when news organizations hew to the predominant policy of protecting rape victims in most cases, it does not always work out the way it's supposed to. The 6,300-circulation Winfield, Kansas, *Courier* did not identify two women who testified in court about how they were raped. But the two women were so upset about the *Courier*'s detailed story that they complained to the late National News Council, maintaining that practically everybody in that small community of 12,400 knew they were the two women who testified. The women and most of the writers of the twenty-three letters to the editor the paper published the next three days complained that the story was sensationalized and it would deter future rape victims from testifying. (In this case, after the two women testified at his preliminary hearing, the accused rapist pleaded guilty and was sentenced to more than a hundred years in prison.)[44]

The news council staff found that the rape hearing story was written by a reporter three months out of college and was turned in just at deadline. The publisher, Dave Seaton, who was filling in for his vacationing managing editor, explains that the story struck him as "rough," but two thoughts pushed him toward publishing it. One was his feeling that the paper had often been criticized for being too cautious and protective of the community. The other was a concern that the citizens of Winfield needed "to know how severe rape cases are. I felt the town was very reluctant to face the danger. . . . Both these rapes occurred because of the long habit of keeping doors unlocked. I had not expected so vivid and detailed a story, but since the names were not used it seemed to me then to be justified. I cannot accept the charge of sensationalism. That implies deliberate motivation. Our purpose was totally different. We were trying to alert the community."[45]

Seaton told news council investigators if he had it to do over again he would show the story to other senior staff members and hold it for another day to get an account that would convey the seriousness of the situation, but with more delicacy. "We learn by experience," he said.

The news council rejected the charge that the reporting on this story was sensationalized but noted a *Courier* editorial indicating that future coverage would be handled more cautiously. The council also recommended that leading organizations of journalists make a major study of community attitudes toward sex crimes and the attendant problems of reporting such crimes.[46]

The story of another rape victim who indicts the news media for the way they covered her tragedy even though they never used her name is told to us by her friend, Susan Seliger, in the *Washington Journalism Review*. Seliger wrote that her friend was brutally raped and beaten by a man in Baltimore. For the next six hours, the victim was with police, "dredging up the details, poring over mug shots. The model citizen." She was beginning to feel better by the next day, but the news reports then brought the whole experience back to her. The now defunct *News American* reported her street and the hundred block of her apartment; WBAL radio, using a UPI story, revealed that she was a director at such and such a television station, which clearly identified her for many people since she was the only female director at that station. Because of the address in the newspaper report, she never returned to her apartment except to move. When she went back to work at her TV station, she found she was treated differently. One co-worker said to her, "Gee, you don't look very beaten up." Seliger says her friend feels that the way the media covered her rape stank. "My right to privacy was already stripped from me by that one individual," the rape victim said. "Now it's been totally invaded. And I wasn't the one who did anything wrong."[47]

Prosecutors and people who work with rape victims claim that publicly identifying such victims discourages other raped women from reporting their abuse and from testifying in open court. This problem has been intensified by the increasing numbers of TV cameras being allowed in the nation's courtrooms. In Florida, one of the states that has been most lenient in opening its courts to cameras, WXLT-TV, Sarasota, videotaped the testimony of a woman who had been raped. It was used on the news that night and she was named. Although the man the woman accused of raping her was ultimately convicted, she sued the station for invasion of privacy, claiming that she agreed to testify only because she had been assured by the state that her name and photograph would not be publicized. She lost her suit at both the lower and appellate court levels because the U.S. Supreme Court has ruled that publication of accurate information obtained from public documents, even though it may be embarrassing information, is not actionable. But the Court of Appeals in Lakeland scolded WXLT for its insensitivity. Identifying the woman "added little or nothing to the sordid and unhappy story," the court wrote. "Yet, that brief little-or-nothing addition may well affect her well-being for years to come."[48]

Juvenile Offenders. A sixteen-year-old boy leaves a homemade bomb in his locker, causing the evacuation of 2,800 students from his school. Three elementary school boys, ages ten, eleven, and twelve, are ordered detained for trial for trying to hang an eleven-year-old classmate in the school playground with a jump rope. A fourteen-year-old is arrested for shooting and killing a classmate in the corridor of their junior high school. Should any of these juveniles be fully identified in news stories?

These are all actual cases. All were fully identified in news accounts of their crimes.

The three cases each represent a new trend in American journalism to name juvenile offenders in serious crime cases. Until recent years, journalists went along with the justice system in its belief that juveniles—people under eighteen—should be protected from publicity when they got in trouble with the law. Unless the crime was murder or something so serious that courts would rule that the juvenile had to be tried as an adult in open court, journalists generally withheld names and specific identifications of juvenile offenders. But in the 1970s, things began to change, both in the newsrooms and courtrooms. Many journalists, concerned about the increased incidence of juveniles committing major crimes, such as murder, rape, mugging, and armed robbery, began to challenge laws and tradition calling for confidential treatment of such offenders. And courts also began to question the traditional secrecy of the juvenile justice system.

The changes, of course, mean that journalists soon will not be able to lean on the law for their ethics in deciding whether to name juvenile offenders. For years the easy answer about whether to withhold names of juveniles accused of crime has been, "We do what the courts do." As courts from state to state begin to open juvenile records and proceedings to the public, journalists will no longer be able to follow that simple course, unless they want to go completely to the other side of the pendulum and name juveniles accused of even the most trivial offenses. Most people hope that the media will not go to that harmful extreme, that journalists will continue to recognize that some kids who get in minor trouble might not grow into habitual criminals if they're given a chance to be rehabilitated without publicity.

Even in jurisdictions that cling to secrecy in handling juvenile justice—and that includes most of them as this is written—reporters can usually find out identifications and other details hidden from them by officials. That was the case when a smoking homemade bomb was found in a student locker, causing officials to evacuate 2,800 students from a Cherry Hill, New Jersey, high school. After a Philadelphia police bomb squad removed the bomb and said it had the destructive force of a hand grenade, a sixteen-year-old sophomore was arrested and charged as a juvenile with causing or risking widespread injury or damage and criminal intent. Police under New Jersey law were bound not to release his name, but reporters found out that he was David Bellune, son of Jerry

Bellune, editor of the editorial page of the now defunct Philadelphia *Bulletin.*

The *Bulletin* had never been a newspaper that exploited people in the news, particularly juveniles, and that was still true in its final years under executive editor Craig Ammerman. "If the Cherry Hill bomb had been left there by just another John Doe without any record of offense, we wouldn't have used the name," Ammerman explains, "but we had to do it because it was Jerry Bellune's kid."[49] After the *Bulletin* printed David Bellune's name, Ammerman explained in his Sunday column that his newspaper and its key officials were public figures who had to be treated like other public figures. "If, for instance, the publisher were arrested for drunken driving (which he hasn't been), or was a principal in a divorce suit (which he once was), we would publish a story," the editor wrote. "We do the same thing if the mayor or governor or some other public figure is involved." Ammerman concluded, however, that the way the press treats the offspring of public figures "is not fair to the children." He said David Bellune "didn't get to pick his parents" and "did not ask for notoriety."[50]

"I was in a difficult spot," Jerry Bellune says. "Craig Ammerman called me at home to say that they knew it was David, that they had it from at least two sources, but he'd prefer that I confirm it before the *Bulletin* published David's name." Bellune declined to confirm it on the record. Then he got a call from *Bulletin* publisher, N. S. "Buddy" Hayden, who had been reached in Chicago by Ammerman. Bellune recalls Hayden saying that "our First Amendment concerns have to override. We've got to publish the name and I want you to confirm it." Bellune talked it over with his wife and they decided to release a statement confirming that it was David who was arrested, but that they did not believe he was guilty.[51]

The *Bulletin* was the first to publish David's name, but the Camden *Courier-Post* and the *Philadelphia Inquirer* soon used it also. The *Philadelphia Daily News,* which has a very small circulation in South Jersey, ran the story without naming David. The fourth Philadelphia daily in business then, the *Journal,* which folded shortly before the *Bulletin,* did not report the story at all. James Naughton, associate managing editor of the *Inquirer,* believes his paper would have used the name even if Bellune had not released it and even if the *Inquirer* had been the only paper in the area to do so.[52]

David Bellune was put on probation for a year. It turned out that the Philadelphia police bomb squad had been wrong about the bomb he made. It was only a smoke bomb and badly designed at that, his father points out. "If it had gone off right, everyone would have known it was a smoke bomb." David Bellune told juvenile court that he made the device and ignited it because "it was getting near the end of the year; things started getting monotonous and I thought I'd break up the monotony."[53]

The whole incident "has enormously affected our lives," Jerry Bellune says. He sees himself as a public figure and he believes "it was unfortunate that my son got penalized for that, because it was not his fault. But intelligent people accept that as part of the bitter that comes with the sweet of notoriety. You don't have to like it, but it's part of the price you pay for being who you are."

Bellune, who left dailies to become co-owner and editor of two South Carolina weeklies, claims that what happened to David has changed his views about publicity for juvenile offenders. "I have been sensitized by that experience," Bellune adds.

> I am a hell of a lot more circumspect about what I publish. My feeling about the public's right and need to know has not been changed, but now I weigh that against factors such as: Does this child have a chance to be rehabilitated, and by publishing his name am I going to impair that chance? Does the community really need to know the child's name? I think I may have considered those questions before, but not with the understanding I have now.[54]

The second case mentioned in the opening of this section on juvenile offenders happened in San Jose, California, a state that has let the press and public in on most of its juvenile justice system. Reacting to a 1979 U.S. Supreme Court ruling, California opened juvenile court proceedings for alleged delinquents or minors accused of twenty serious crimes. So the *San Jose Mercury* (now merged into the *Mercury News*) was allowed to cover the first hearing for the three schoolboys arrested for trying to hang a classmate in their elementary school playground. Although the paper had not named the three accused boys, ages ten, eleven, and twelve, or their eleven-year-old victim in their first report of their arrest, five days later it named all four after they went before a juvenile court judge.[55]

The juvenile court judge who presided over this case disagreed with the *Mercury*'s decision. Judge Lawrence Terry said the paper should have weighed the public's right to know against the damage to the boys and their families – and left the names out. And the prosecutor of the case, deputy district attorney Bob Masterson, said that although newspapers had a right to print the names, they shouldn't have.[56]

But the two *Mercury* reporters who used the boys' names argued that the severity of the act dictated that they be fully identified. All three of the accused were found guilty and punished by the law. Testimony showed that the three had made a noose out of a jump rope and formed it around the neck of their eleven-year-old classmate, a heavyset boy. Looping the rope over a six-foot chin bar, they tried to hang their victim, but he frustrated that by squeezing his hand between the rope and his neck.

Then they tied his feet, let him drop, and dragged him around the school ground. Police said the three youngsters told them they were "only fooling around."[57]

The third case in the opening of this section involved a fourteen-year-old boy arrested for killing a schoolmate. Both Charleston, West Virginia, dailies decided to name him in their stories, in defiance of a state law that prohibited newspapers but not other news media from publishing the name of a juvenile charged with crime, unless a judge approved. The *Charleston Daily Mail* and *Charleston Gazette* fought the case to the U.S. Supreme Court, which in 1979 declared the West Virginia law unconstitutional because it infringed on freedom of the press and discriminated against newspapers.[58] The ruling in the Charleston case and some others opening criminal trials to the public have stimulated a gradual change in state-administered juvenile justice systems.

The *San Jose Mercury* to the contrary, many news organizations are not automatically naming juvenile offenders merely because their names are being released under some new rules in juvenile justice. When the Dauphin County, Pennsylvania, juvenile probation office started releasing names and other details of offenders fourteen to seventeen years old who had been convicted of serious crimes, the Harrisburg newspapers did not change their policy. Ronald Minard, editor of the *Patriot* and *Evening News,* said the new county policy certainly will make information gathering easier for his reporters, but the decision about using names will still be made on a case-by-case basis because the offenders are still juveniles who "have a right to make a mistake."[59]

Suicides, Deaths. Most people in this land seem to think it is important that they and their friends and relatives be allowed to die with dignity. No problem for journalism in most cases. Most news stories or obituaries reporting the deaths of people are about as inoffensive as anything that gets printed or broadcast. But every once in a while editors have to decide how much of the circumstances of death are relevant in reporting the death to the public.

Suicides present difficulties. Some newspapers are beginning to not label suicides as such in routine death reports. One editor who is questioning the need to report it in all cases is James A. Dunlap, editor of the Sharon, Pennsylvania, *Herald.* "If someone jumps off a bridge or a public official takes his own life, then we have to report it," Dunlap agrees, "but a newspaper has to be compassionate and be aware of the grief it can cause families." Two recent suicides in that community caused Dunlap to question the need to report suicides in all cases: both involved men in their eighties who took their own lives in the privacy of their homes.[60] Most papers, however, report most suicides because they believe important causes of death are facts that readers should know. Some report suicides in news stories but not in the obituaries, which are usually what people clip to store in their family Bibles.

A few editors who believe in reporting most suicides, particularly when they involve prominent persons or happen in public places, feel uneasy about the possible copycat effect. Some academic studies have shown that national suicide rates increase after front-page stories appeared in the *New York Times* reporting suicides of well-known people. This possibility is particularly worrisome when you have a teenage suicide in your area or suicide in a class of people undergoing hardship, such as middlewestern farmers. Arnold Garson, managing editor of the *Des Moines Register,* which has published reports of both teenage and farmer suicides, thinks about the copycat effect. "But I've never believed that society cures its problems by sweeping them under the carpet," he says. "In fact, the only way to solve problems is to deal with them openly."[61]

Editorial director Sitton of the Raleigh newspapers tells of a difficult exchange of correspondence with a Methodist minister in nearby Goldsboro, North Carolina, who was angered by the way the Raleigh papers reported a suicide. The head of a water and sewer system in the town had been charged with carnal knowledge of three teenage girls, Sitton says. When three deputy sheriffs went to his office to serve the arrest warrants, the man excused himself, went into the bathroom, and shot himself. The minister objected that reporting what the man had been charged with caused great grief to his family. Sitton wrote the minister that "the charges were a factor in the suicide, that the arrest warrants were a matter of public record, that everybody in Goldsboro knew what was going on because it is such a small city, and that it would hurt the paper's credibility to conceal those charges." Sitton claims he "gets more and more mail on subjects of this kind today. People are very sensitive to anything that smacks of an invasion of privacy."[62]

INVADING PRIVACY TO GET THE NEWS

In the process of gathering news, journalists often invade privacy by what the law of privacy calls intrusion. They do this sometimes merely by asking questions of people caught up in the news—not just public figures more accustomed to answering reporters' queries, but ordinary people as well.

"We are by nature invaders of privacy," concedes James Naughton, associate managing editor of the *Philadelphia Inquirer*. Public officials are "fair game" for aggressive reporting, Naughton believes, but ordinary people "often are unsophisticated" and have to be protected. "The press is sometimes too zealous," he adds.[63]

News of tragedies often pushes journalists to invade the privacy of grieving survivors. "Some smart people ask dumb questions when they have to intrude on grief," observes Brian Healy of CBS News, Washington, alluding to broadcast journalists who jam microphones into the faces of people after a tragedy. Print reporters often intrude in much the same way. A Chicago reporter who had imposed on a grieving family to write a story about a child who had choked to death on a Christmas tree ornament was ordered by his editor to call back to ask the family what color the ornament was.[64]

Too many reporters take advantage of people who are unsophisticated about the media, Healy believes. After more than a dozen years in television journalism, he contends that if he personally got involved in something criminal or embarrassing, "I'd tell the members of my family to keep their mouths shut."[65]

During the many years that this country has been involved in wars, reporters have had to interview surviving family members whenever some American serviceman was reported killed. Usually they also had to ask the family to loan them a photograph of their dead son, brother, or husband. The same intrusion occurs when people are killed in domestic accidents and crimes. Reporters who have had to face this unpleasant task express amazement at how often people are kind to them and willing, almost eager, to talk. I recall being assigned to interview parents and borrow a photograph of an eighteen-year-old woman who had been murdered by her nineteen-year-old sweetheart, who then killed himself. The young woman's father, sitting alone on the back porch steps, talked freely about his daughter and loaned me what must have been the family's prize photograph of the daughter, posed in a full-length gown.

Sometimes reporters and photographers enter private property after a fire, or a crime, or some other human tragedy—unless police stop them, which does not always happen. Jerry Thompson, reporter for the Nashville *Tennessean*, once beat the police to the scene of a celebrated Nashville murder case. He went into the house just before police arrived and was inside when he heard a police sergeant order the house sealed so that no journalists would be allowed in. Thompson quickly found a picture of the dead woman in an upstairs room and threw it out the window. Fortunately for him, the picture landed safely on some shrubbery and Thompson was able to retrieve it. He was proud that his paper was the only medium to have a photo of the dead woman for three days.[66]

The press is severely tested in the matter of privacy invasion when it has to cover survivors in a large tragedy, such as the bombing that killed 241 American marines in Beirut in 1983. In that and similar stories, reporters and photographers are sent out to the homes of surviving family members all over this country, which annoys some people. "Here come the ghouls," neighbors shouted at a Baltimore television crew when it arrived to interview the family of one marine victim. In two other Maryland incidents, a TV photographer videotaped marine officers as they delivered news of the death of a marine son to his surviving family, and another TV photographer shot through a sliding glass door as one family got the official news of the death of a brother. But most of the families in Maryland were covered by more sensitive reporters and photographers, according to C. Fraser Smith, a Baltimore *Sun* reporter who did a study of that coverage in his state. "None of the parents we talked to complained about the intrusion of television," Smith wrote, "although some said they found the longer interviews they had with print reporters more satisfying."

Dean Reese Cleghorn of the University of Maryland College of Journalism told Smith that although "we should be outraged" when the press fails "to follow usual amenities, normal civilities," we should remember that "there is a value in portraying the human condition, including misery, including grief about the loss of a son." Cleghorn also sees a value in invading privacy "in some cases to show people what has gone on. It adds a dimension to our understanding of war. . . . People come home dead from war."[67]

Another story of tragedy that involved many privacy invasions by journalists was the coverage given to the families of the fifty-two American hostages in Iran. Ramon Coronado, reporter for the *Fort Collins Coloradoan,* described the mob of journalists who covered the family of Marine Sergeant Billy Gallegos of Pueblo, Colorado, as the family awaited the call, which did finally come, that their son and the other hostages were coming home. "The media camped in the sloped front yard, an area no bigger than two spaces in a parking lot," Coronado wrote. "Electrical cords, telephones, television sets, radios, tape recorders, microphones, cigarette butts, coffee cups and paper from fast-food restaurants blanketed the ground. In the back, the alley was filled with television news trucks manned with technicians." About three dozen of the reporters and photographers were allowed inside the small home, but some had to stay outside. As those inside jostled for better positions, one journalist knocked a ceramic plate off a wall, Coronado reported. Photographers stood on furniture, breaking one table. A reporter from Colorado Springs was caught looking in the family's mail. "There is no question that the press should have been at the Gallegos home," Coronado concluded. "A story like the release of the hostages and how their families have been affected is of concern to us all. But perhaps the press lost sight of the fact that the Gallegoses were not just a story but are people. People with feelings and the need for privacy."[68]

It needs to be said here that many journalists conducted themselves properly in covering the hostage story, and many became close friends of the hostage families, whom they covered off and on for the fourteen months of their ordeal.

Robert Giles, executive editor of the *Detroit News,* once wrote out some ground rules for reporters who have to cover disasters and human tragedies—what he calls "news that nobody likes." With the preface that the one quality he likes to find in a reporter is compassion, Giles suggests these ground rules:

> Say you are sorry, and mean it.
> Show a sense of feeling without abandoning the story.
> Do not ask dumb questions.
> Do not break and enter in search of pictures or a comment.
> Establish a trust with family and friends.
> Make sure they understand that what has happened is news.
> Try not to be part of the story.
> Be prepared to listen. Survivors . . . need to ventilate many kinds of feelings: anger, sorrow, disbelief. Some do this by talking.
> Avoid the temptation to run with the pack.[69]

WHERE ARE THE GUIDELINES?

Guidelines on privacy, such as those suggested by Robert Giles in the preceding section, are few and far between in American journalism. A beginning journalist turning to most written codes and standards would find very little help in deciding how far to go in gathering and writing news involving private matters. Perhaps this paucity can be explained by the heavy reliance that many journalists place on the law to guide them in matters of privacy. But the law of privacy in this country provides an inadequate set of rules that are often difficult to apply to particular news situations.

This is not to say that journalists are unconcerned about privacy. Newsrooms are full of unwritten rules in this area—not publicizing the names of most rape victims or juvenile offenders, for example. But there are many other privacy questions that newsroom folklore usually does not acknowledge, let alone address, except in the most general way.

Paul A. Poorman, Kent State University journalism professor and former editor of the *Akron Beacon Journal,* sees privacy as the foremost ethical issue for journalism in the future. "It's a complex problem because privacy is increasingly a legal concept," Poorman explains.

> But there are some strong moral issues raised by privacy: Why do we run all those pictures of grieving relatives? Why do we delve so deeply into the private lives of public officials? There are often good reasons for doing these things, but we tend to get carried away. And unless the newspaper industry becomes aware of privacy as a simple question of fairness and as a moral issue as well as a legal issue, others will write those laws for us.[70]

The codes of ethics of national organizations of journalists either ignore or say little about what Poorman sees as the field's foremost ethical issue. The APME code states that the newspaper "should respect the individual's right of privacy." The RTNDA urges that "broadcast journalists shall at all times display humane respect for the dignity, privacy and the well-being of persons with whom the news deals." The SPJ-SDX calls on journalists to "show respect for the dignity, privacy, rights and well-being of people encountered in the course of gathering and presenting the news" and calls on the news media to "guard against invading a person's right to privacy."

Somewhat more detailed is the advice in the *Detroit Free Press* code, which reads: "The public's right to know often needs to be weighed vis-à-vis the privacy rights of people in the news. We need to respect not only their legal rights, but also their own and our readers' sensibilities about what is reasonable coverage and what is unfair or intrusive coverage. Generally, we do not identify living victims of sex crimes or persons whose safety would be jeopardized by publishing their names or addresses."

The code of the *Philadelphia Inquirer* is the only one I have seen that deals with virtually all the problems in this chapter. Its general provision on privacy states:

> Most of the people mentioned in the news columns are public officials, whose official activities are legally the subject of scrutiny, or public figures, who often seek out publicity. However, private citizens who have not sought public notice are frequently surprised, and sometimes upset, when they are approached by reporters or find themselves written about. This is especially true in tragic situations. Staff members should approach stories with both a desire to inform the public and compassion for the individuals involved.
>
> A private citizen who is thrust unwittingly and unwillingly into a public situation is likely to be unfamiliar with news-gathering practices. Staff members should clearly identify themselves when approaching such inexperienced people and treat them with courtesy.

Relatives of public officials and public figures are sometimes newsworthy solely because of their family position. Such stories can, however, be overdone. They should be handled thoughtfully and not be simply voyeuristic.

In rape stories, the *Philadelphia Inquirer* says, "the name of a rape victim generally is not published except as determined by" the supervising editor. The *San Jose Mercury News* also provides for exceptions but states that it "is sensitive to the privacy of victims of rape and child molestation, or of subjects who clearly would be in physical danger by publication of their names and addresses." The very clear policy of the *St. Paul Pioneer Press and Dispatch* reads: "We do NOT identify rape victims in news stories. In cases of wives accusing their husbands of rape, we do NOT use the name of the husband in order to protect the identity of the victim. We do not identify victims of incest." The *Argus Leader* of Sioux Falls, South Dakota, admonishes, "We will NOT use the names of rape or incest victims. We will NOT use the names of any person charged with or convicted of incest—man or woman. (Any exceptions, i.e., Nancy Reagan, the mayor's wife, will be discussed with the managing editor and executive editor, who will then discuss it with the publisher.)"

As a leader among news organizations that have started naming serious juvenile offenders, the *Philadelphia Inquirer* code states that because it "customarily covers only crimes of special importance or unusual violence, it is important that the public be informed of the identity of the accused, regardless of age. In crimes of this nature, the service to the community of full coverage far outweighs any realistic expectation that not naming the accused would assist in his or her eventual rehabilitation." However, the addition of zoned neighborhood sections has caused the *Inquirer* to tone down its policy. In those special sections reporting less serious as well as serious news of the neighborhoods covered, juveniles accused of crime are not to be identified in "police blotter" items, but "if an incident is serious enough to warrant a separate story, the juvenile's name should be used."

The *Inquirer* also warns its staff that "a person's mental or physical infirmities, sexual preference or the like generally should not be referred to unless it is directly relevant to the story." On the matter of addresses, the *Inquirer* notes that "victims, witnesses to crimes, accused persons and jurors can be subjected to harassment. Therefore, we do not generally use exact addresses, but use more general references, such as 'Broad Street near Callowhill Street,' 'the 200 block of Pine Street,' or especially for a short street, 'Emery Lane, Phoenixville.' "

The St. Paul paper also shows concern for crime victims. "In reporting crime stories, avoid calling attention to the fact the criminal overlooked some money or goods. It may invite a return visit," the *Pioneer*

Press and Dispatch code says. "We will not use the names of purse snatch or mugging victims except in unusual cases. We will not use the addresses of clerks, tellers, etc. in robberies except in unusual circumstances."

The problem of broadcast journalists who jam microphones in the faces of accident victims or their relatives is faced in the codes of CBS and NBC News. The CBS code directs that such interviews should normally be avoided "except when they are essential for the story" and then they should be conducted with restraint and only after the interviewee has given permission. The NBC code explains that because "there must be sensitivity to the emotional state and physical condition of people who have been involved in tragic or traumatic situations," no interviews will be conducted with such people unless it is "clearly relevant and essential to the story."

It is obvious that most Americans highly value their privacy. It is also obvious that journalists have not given enough thought to how they might best deal with the conflicting pulls of privacy and of public curiosity. Journalists probably never will be able to eliminate their intrusions into private matters because some are necessary to serve the public good, but they must strive to bring them under control. Too often there is no forethought about whether the public interest to be served justifies invading someone's privacy. Restraints are particularly needed in publicity given to the deeds and misdeeds of the children and relatives of public persons. And even the high and mightiest among us—the Kennedys, the Reagans, the Rockefellers—deserve some measure of privacy, especially in moments of family grief or turmoil.

Although the movement toward less protection for serious juvenile offenders is understandable, it is hoped that journalists will be careful in their use of the power of publicity. Kids who get in trouble with the law often need help and sometimes that help can be more effective if the offender has not been humiliated by exposure in the media.

I also understand why some journalists are pushing for equal treatment for the accuser and the accused in rape cases by naming both. But to me, the possible good that results from publicizing the identity of a rape victim hardly offsets the harm, the extra trauma that many women experience when they have to testify in court and be specifically identified in the media. Some women are strong enough, but some obviously are not. That's one of the reasons that only about half the rape victims in the country ever report the crime to the police, according to a Justice Department study.[71] I'd like to see more consultation with the rape victim before editors and broadcast news directors decide to name names, as difficult as that might be in many cases. News executives also ought to spend some time with the people in their communities who work with rape and incest victims. The present lack of intelligence and sensitivity about this particular crime of violence in many newsrooms is a major blemish to journalism.

Intruding on individuals and families suffering tragedy is something most journalists don't like to do and most of them do it with care and reasonable civility. But there are some clods out there – and have you noticed how often they seem to be working for TV – who badger people and poke their cameras through windows and act, as my mother used to say, like they were brought up in a barn. Such brutish tactics might be justified by journalists investigating life- or society-threatening situations, but not when they're covering a wake, or the survivors of a dead marine, or the family of a hostage.

Before barging into private situations or before invading someone's privacy, journalists need to ask themselves some of the questions I posed at the end of Chapter 1: Who will be hurt and who will be helped? Are there better alternatives? Can I look myself in the mirror again? Can I justify this to other people, the public? If the news gathering procedures and the stories they produce don't stand up to such testing, they ought to be abandoned or changed. A journalism of clods serves no one.

11 The Government Watch

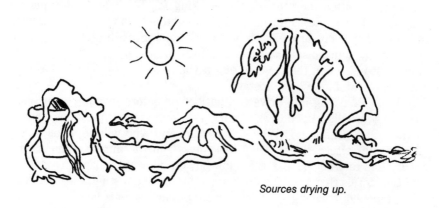

Sources drying up.

As manager and former news director of the only television station in this southern city of about 46,000 residents, you get an urgent call to come to a cabin owned by the U.S. attorney for your area. When you get to the cabin, you are met by the U.S. attorney, the district attorney for your city, and the director of police, all men you know from your days as a reporter for your station. Also present are some police detectives and you are soon joined by the managing editor and the police reporter for the city's only daily newspaper.

The law enforcement authorities tell you that they believe a contract has been put out to murder a local businessman. An undercover police officer posing as the "hit man" has been unable to meet or learn the identities of the person or persons willing to pay $35,000 to have the local businessman killed, but the officer has been told by the "money man" on the telephone that the $35,000 will be paid twenty-four hours after he reads in the news that the "hit" has occurred.

The authorities say they have no choice but to try to persuade the money man that the killing has taken place. They say the intended murder victim is in their custody and is willing to help them stage a hoax. What they intend to do that afternoon is plant the victim's truck somewhere in the area with blood on it. When the abandoned truck is "discovered" by police, they want you and the local newspaper to give the event full coverage as if it actually happened. Authorities will not tell you the name of the intended victim unless you promise them you'll cooperate. They also tell you that once this contract is carried out, the money man has told the undercover officer that he will give him two more names for murder contracts.

Would you cooperate with law enforcement officials in this case? Even if it means airing what you know to be a false report? How does putting out a fake news story stack up against the lives of the local businessman and perhaps two additional persons?

That's the dilemma faced by Cliff Brown, manager of WDAM-TV in Hattiesburg, Mississippi. He decided to cooperate. That evening his TV station showed videotapes of the abandoned pickup truck of local cattleman Oscar Black III. The report suggested that a struggle had taken place on that country road where the truck was found with Black's pistol and other possessions in it. It also implied that Black had disappeared and was probably murdered.[1]

The next afternoon the newspaper, the *Hattiesburg American,* published a one-sentence item in its daily roundup of police news. The sentence read: "Police are seeking information concerning suspected foul play directed toward Oscar Black III."[2]

That sentence was written by the newspaper's publisher, Duane K. McCallister, in an apparent attempt to walk the tightrope between not exposing the police hoax and not lying to the public. McCallister saw that one-sentence report as representing a refusal by his newspaper to participate in the hoax staged by the police. "An important principle was at stake—you just don't lie to your readers," wrote McCallister, who later left Hattiesburg to become publisher of another Gannett daily, the *Times Herald* at Port Huron, Michigan.[3]

Brown says he went along with the authorities in this case because he believed there was a real threat to the lives of one to three people. The U.S. attorney, George Phillips, and most of the other officials who asked him to cooperate were people he had worked with while he was in news. "They had never misled me or used me in any way," Brown recalls. "I had no reason to think that they would mislead me after all the years I had worked with them."

He sees this case as being a clash between the life ethic and the journalistic ethic. He claims that he has always subscribed to the journalistic ethic "of presenting the news so that it is truthful, factual and balanced, . . . but when the value of a person's life hit me square between the eyes, I realized there are few absolutes in this world." Brown also feels he was influenced by his fairly strong religious beliefs.

After he told Phillips he'd cooperate, but only for a week, Brown returned to his station with the intention of *not* informing his news staff, letting them cover the staged murder as if it were for real. As it turned out the news staff was so busy on another big story that it did not immediately send out a crew to cover the police discovery of Black's abandoned truck. So Brown had to lean on the assistant news director to get moving on the Black story, claiming that he had some sort of call that the abandoned truck was important. Later after that first false report was broadcast on the 6 P.M. news, Brown had to reveal the hoax to the assistant news director because the latter had gotten so involved in the story he began to smell something. But the rest of Brown's news staff, including the news director, didn't know they were reporting a false story for three days until police called a news conference to announce that the hoax had failed.

At the news conference, District Attorney Glenn White claimed that police came close to finding out who tried to murder Black, an owner of Custom Cattle Company in Lamar County, Mississippi. But the operation fell apart when the money man sensed somehow that police were involved and called off a rendezvous with the undercover hit man at which the latter was to get his $35,000 for the hit. White commended *Hattiesburg American* reporter Janet Braswell, WDAM-TV, "and the law enforcement officers involved for putting their credibility on the line when it came to a human life and perhaps putting their ethics aside in order to save a human life." He did not commend the newspaper itself.[4] Later Phillips and the Hattiesburg public safety commissioner condemned the *American* for being concerned more about the reaction of the rest of journalism than about human life.[5]

Reporter Braswell put police onto the investigation that spawned the unsuccessful hoax. A longtime police reporter, Braswell got a call one day from a man who said he was "Pete," a private investigator, and he knew there was going to be a hit in Hattiesburg. He said no more. Braswell reported the strange conversation to her managing editor, Frank Sutherland. They decided that the caller must be some kind of nut, but when he called again eight days later, she and Sutherland decided she should inform the police.

"My guiding rule is to let law enforcement enforce the law and let us cover them," Sutherland explains. But "sometimes if a reporter witnesses a murder, you cannot hide behind a journalistic shield and say I'm going to write about it but I'm not going to tell police what I saw." He feels Janet Braswell "was thrust into that same kind of problem. She answered the phone and she was forced to cooperate with police. Somebody calling up and saying I'm going to kill somebody—you don't keep that within the walls of the newsroom, you have to tell authorities. I think she did the responsible thing."[6]

Braswell subsequently persuaded her "private investigator" to deal directly with police. It was on his information that police provided an undercover officer to pose as hit man in an attempt to learn the identities of those who were trying to buy Oscar Black's death. Although the undercover hit man failed to flush out the alleged death buyers and dealers in this initial operation – hoax and all – the same money man tried again to hire a killer a few months later. This time police used an undercover hit man as before but they did not involve the local news media. They ended up arresting and charging two men. One of them – John Hudson, a Purvis, Mississippi, cattleman who had lost $400,000 when Black went bankrupt prior to the alleged contract on him – is serving out a ten-year sentence for attempted murder and a seven-year sentence for retaliating against a witness (Black). The other – John Day, an unemployed butcher who had posed as Pete – was indicted for taking $15,000 from Hudson to hire a hit man. Charges against Day were dropped, however, after the prosecution could not produce an informer it needed to make its case.[7]

Some editors around the country have suggested that the TV station and the newspaper should have at least threatened to blow the whistle on the police hoax at the outset. They reason that the law enforcement people were way out of line when they presented the local news executives with a *fait accompli* – a staged, phony murder that they were supposed to treat as real. Such an unreasonable request should have been rejected because it would compromise the local news media in their responsibility for factual reporting. Although that rejection would seem to have put one to three lives in jeopardy, it probably would have forced police to come up with a different scheme, as they did successfully in their second opportunity to trap the contract killers.

Sutherland, who at the time was president of SPJ-SDX, says he did consider publishing a story that police had staged a hoax, but rejected it because "it would blow the case." His paper was not sure of what was happening at that point – "and we didn't know what we were endangering. . . . If we exposed the hoax, we didn't know what that would do." Sutherland is not happy with what his paper did do in the initial reporting of the Black incident. He recalls that he opposed running the one-sentence report the day after police staged the murder. "I was reluctant to run it the first time and I'd be reluctant to run it again," says Sutherland, who has since become executive editor of the *Jackson* (Tennessee) *Sun,* another Gannett daily.

Although Sutherland represented his paper at that first conference when authorities sought media cooperation in publicizing their hoax, he immediately consulted his publisher, McCallister, who ended up making the final decision about how the paper would handle the situation. The newspaper and television station executives arrived at their differing decisions without conferring with each other. In fact, at that first meeting when authorities asked the TV station manager and the newspaper managing editor to cooperate, Brown turned to Sutherland and asked what the Society of Professional Journalists had to "say about this sort of thing." Sutherland replied that the SPJ-SDX code of ethics "says that we should tell the truth"; then he recalls quickly adding: "But, Cliff, I don't think we should be talking about this together. Whatever decision you make, I am going to make my decision independently." Brown agreed.

This complicated case illustrates how difficult it is for journalists in the American system to decide how far they should go in cooperating with and helping the government they feel they are bound to watch. How can journalists work with government and government officials and still do their jobs as critical observers and reporters of government activities?

Journalists as Watchdogs. American journalists have developed what Peter Braestrup calls a "public theology" in which the press serves as a watchdog of government, representing and providing information to citizens so that they can intelligently participate in democratic government.[8] Government news is a staple of American journalism. Government beats, from the White House to the county courthouse, are among the most important on any editor's assignment sheet.

This ennobling image of journalists as watchdogs protecting the public from abuses of government is rooted in the First Amendment, many journalists believe. They argue that a free press is an essential of democratic government. Without journalists observing and reporting on government actions and inactions, the voters would be ignorant and unable to make intelligent decisions in elections.

"If you look at the history of this country . . . the thing that makes this experiment in government unique among democracies has been the continued independence of the daily newspaper serving as a critic and watchdog of government," says James D. Squires, editor of the *Chicago Tribune*. "It goes hand in hand with us being the forum in which the political debate is played out." Squires also believes that freedom of the press is "most sacred when it is covering government."[9]

The watchdog role, of course, gets interpreted differently from journalist to journalist, from newsroom to newsroom, and from time to time. Some journalists see themselves as representatives, almost champions, of the people, particularly the powerless ones, and they tend to be aggressive watchdogs, sniffing out government wrongdoing at every opportunity. Other journalists are more like lapdogs—"too cozy, too intimidated, and too respectful of people in power," as Les Payne of *Newsday* puts it.[10] Journalistic watchdoggery also seems to wax and wane with the times, showing its more aggressive fangs during the Watergate era and wagging its tail during the Reagan presidency, for example.

Journalists also keep watch on other orders in American life, such as business, sports, and entertainment, but government has traditionally gotten the most intense and vigorous surveillance. "Government can take away your freedom and legislate you into prison, into debt," Squires explains. "Government always operates on tax dollars, on public money. . . . I don't think we have nearly as strong an obligation and an inherent right to look into the personal business of a movie star as we do the mayor of our city, or our city councilmen."

Government officials show less enthusiasm for the idea that journalists are obligated to be their critical observers. Authorities frequently feel the need to do business behind closed doors or to seek the cooperation of individual journalists or their organizations in certain projects or operations. Both of these compulsions of government—to be secret and to involve journalists as partners—threaten the watchdog concept. They also present journalists with difficult ethical decisions about their responsibilities as citizens as well as their functions as reporters and evaluators of their own government.

GOVERNMENT COOPERATION AND SECRECY

American journalists are no longer "on the team." That expression came from a remark that Admiral Harry D. Felt reportedly made when he met Malcolm Browne, one of the early AP correspondents covering the Vietnam War: "So you're Browne," Felt said. "Why don't you get on the team?"[11] The admiral was expressing his anger at Browne and other correspondents who were beginning to defy the official line in their reporting of that war in the early 1960s. American war correspondents had not acted that way in World Wars I and II and in Korea. Their patriotism came out in the positive, morale-boosting stories most filed.

The spirit of cooperation between the press and government that prevailed during America's wars in the first half of this century seemed to carry on for a while after World War II. During that war and for the period after it known as the "Cold War," some U.S. journalists worked or cooperated with the young and still small Central Intelligence Agency (CIA). It was only natural that our spy agency would turn to journalists, many of whom had contacts in and special knowledge of other countries. But the love affair between the CIA and some journalists did not last long because of something that was happening between the press and government in this country.

As the U.S. government grew in size and complexity during and after World War II, it became obvious to government leaders that effective communication with the citizens was required. American business had already discovered this essentiality some years earlier and had turned for help to a new breed of specialist – the public relations expert. Government soon followed suit, adding scores, then hundreds, and finally thousands of such specialists to the public payroll. Today, in both government and the private sector, no major enterprise is without public relations counsel.

With the help of its public relations specialists, government began to find better ways to assemble and package information so it was more apt to be used by the press. It also found other ways of communicating with the public, so that it did not have to depend entirely on independent, nongovernment channels of communication. And somewhere along the line, government discovered that certain kinds of information were better than other kinds, that you did not have to tell the people everything. Image making and manipulating information to certain ends became instruments of government strategy. Even the lie was not out of the question, as the press and the country learned in 1960 when the government said it was not using the U-2 plane to spy on the Soviet Union, and then the Soviets produced the captured pilot of a downed U-2 who said that was just what he was doing. And in 1962 Arthur Sylvester, spokesman for the Pentagon under Presidents Kennedy and Johnson, admitted that the lie had been added to the government's public relations arsenal when he told a meeting of journalists: "I think the inherent right of the government to lie – to lie to save itself when faced with nuclear disaster – is basic, basic."[12]

Well, this was something new. It was one thing for the press to cooperate with government, as it did in World War II, to keep news from the public. But having the government manage the news, even to the extent of lying, to keep information from the press was more than most journalists were willing to take. So in Vietnam, reporters began to ask tougher questions and to go out on their own without military escort to find out what was happening. One reporter, Harrison Salisbury of the *New York Times,* even went to Hanoi, the enemy's capital, to file reports that cast doubts on Pentagon claims that we were not bombing civilian targets in North Vietnam, only military targets. Salisbury's stories in 1966 and the increasingly critical coverage by all reporters and photographers covering Vietnam undoubtedly contributed to the snowballing public disenchantment with that war, which eventually forced the government to disengage us from the conflict without victory.

The more aggressive and less cooperative attitude of the press toward government also was expressed in the publication by the *New York*

Times and other periodicals of the secret Pentagon Papers and by the coverage of the Nixon administration, which brought about the resignation first of Vice-President Spiro Agnew and then of Nixon himself in 1974. Some leaders of journalism believe the press may have overdone its aggression in the period right after Watergate, and the watchdog's growl has tempered a bit of late, but the press is certainly not back on the government's team.

"You Scratch My Back and . . . ." Although the relationship between press and government has become more adversarial, journalists and government officials still find that cooperation pays. Governments at all levels in the United States have traditionally provided the news media with press rooms, press tables, and facilities they need to report on government. Press cards issued by government, particularly police and security agencies, help reporters pass through police lines and other barriers to the general public. Government public information people may not always be truthful in their dealings with the press, but they provide reporters with tons of legitimate information and help them get to the officials who make and carry out government policies. Everywhere government is covered by the news media in this country, there exists a degree of cooperation that serves both interests.

Although he feels strongly that the press should be independent from and not work for government, Andrew Barnes, editor of the *St. Petersburg Times,* sees the need for cooperation. For example, he says, "one of the functions of civil defense in this coastal Florida city is to let people know where to go if a storm is coming. . . . We provide that information to the citizens for government." Another way the press cooperates with government is in "informing citizens when there are open houses at schools." And although he suspects many public officials would not agree with him, Barnes says "we cooperate when we let people know what our elected and appointed officials are doing."[13]

A great deal of cooperation between journalists and officials occurs at ballot-counting time. Spurred by intense public curiosity about the winners, journalists and officials work together, often closely, to get election results out to the public as quickly as possible. In fact, journalists have been criticized in recent years for getting the results out too fast, before many voters in the country have gone to the polls. Television deservedly gets most of this criticism because of the way it has projected winners of some elections while the polls are still open. It does this by interviewing voters as they exit their polling places and then projecting winners through computer analysis. Many political leaders believe that such premature reporting of election results can skew the outcome. Late voters who hear that their candidates are way ahead or behind might decide to skip voting since their votes would not seem to matter. That could affect the outcome not just for those candidates but for other candidates and issues on the ballot as well. Some states have passed laws to prevent reporters from interviewing voters as they leave the polls, but the ethical sin is not in reporters asking voters how they voted and why. That's good journalism that provides information useful in understanding shifts in voting habits, such as union members voting for Reagan, and voting trends. What needs to be stopped, and not by laws but by TV news executives, is using exit interviews to project winners before all the voters have had a chance to vote.

A kind of cooperation that sometimes leads to trouble occurs when public officials, candidates, or other news sources turn to journalists for advice. If the news source is of some importance, such a request can be very flattering and difficult to turn down. Then if friendships develop between the advice seeker and giver, serious conflicts of interest can result for the journalist. That's what happened to George F. Will. He's one of the new breed of newspaper columnists who did not come out of the ranks of reporters but came straight from political employment. Will had been a legislative assistant to a U.S. senator. Similarly, columnist William Safire of the *New York Times* had been a speech writer for President Nixon, columnist Jody Powell was President Carter's press secretary, and Bill Moyers of CBS News was President Johnson's press secretary.

As a participant in conservative politics, Will has many friends among conservative politicians, one of them being President Reagan. When Reagan asked Will to help him prepare for his 1980 debates with President Carter, Will agreed. Later, in his column and as a part-time ABC News commentator, Will praised Reagan's performance in the debates without disclosing his role as one of Reagan's coaches. His involvement came out in 1983 when a House subcommittee investigated Reagan's use of some Carter briefing papers in preparing for the debates. Will defended his aid for Reagan by contending that the relationship columnists have with politicians can be different from that of straight news reporters. But columnist Mary McGrory of the *Washington Post* spoke for many in journalism when she wrote that what Will is saying when "he stoutly maintains he is not a journalist" is that "he is not subject to our rules and conventions, and I find that a bit arrogant." The New York *Daily News* dropped Will's column for what it called his "violation of journalistic ethics." Although none of the four hundred other papers subscribing to his column followed the example of the *News,* Will wrote later that he would "not again come as close to a political campaign" as he did in 1980.[14]

Will may have a point when he separates opinion writers from fact reporters in how much distance should be maintained between them and politicians. But what should journalism then do about the increasing number of fact reporters who go into the government and then come back to the fact side of journalism? Aren't they even more of a threat to journalism's credibility than somebody like George Will?

"Turnstile journalists" is what critics have labeled people like Leslie Gelb of the *New York Times,* who has gone through that government-press turnstile more than once. A former head of the Defense Department's policy planning staff during the Vietnam War, Gelb was working for then U.S. Senator Jacob Javits when the *Times* hired him. He left the *Times* a few years later to direct the State Department's Bureau of Politico-Military Affairs from 1977 to 1979, returning to the paper in 1981 as national security correspondent.

When Gelb wrote an article in 1985 describing American contingency plans to deploy nuclear depth charges in some countries that do not possess them, the director of the bureau Gelb once headed ordered Gelb's photograph removed from the bureau office and ordered his staff not to talk to Gelb. The bureau director, Lt. Gen. John T. Chain, Jr., contended that the article was based on "classified information the release of which is harmful and damaging to the United States." Secretary of State George P. Shultz later conceded that the substance of Gelb's article had been published previously and discussed in the affected countries, but insisted that the *Times* article still did "us a considerable amount of damage." Because Gelb had served in government "in a particularly sensitive post," Shultz argued, his writing took on "special authority." His own feeling about the high government posts he has held, the secretary added, is "that, in a sense, you can't leave them. You have a responsibility to those offices." *Times* editors defended Gelb, noting that he had consulted White House and State Department officials before writing his controversial article. Then managing editor Seymour Topping said Gelb "has fulfilled his duties as a reporter without making use of privileged information that might have been obtained when he was an official, and in full cognizance of all his responsibilities."[15]

"I don't even read Leslie Gelb's stuff," says Steve Lovelady, associate executive editor of the *Philadelphia Inquirer,* "because I don't know if it's the *New York Times* reporter or the State Department spokesman who's talking." Lovelady said what he fears about turnstile journalists is that they might pursue the same policies as reporters that they pursued in government.[16]

Gelb is just one of scores of turnstile journalists in the news business today. Diane Sawyer of CBS News was Nixon's assistant press secretary. John Hughes, former editor of the *Christian Science Monitor,* went into government in 1981, serving in the United States Information Agency and as State Department spokesman until 1984, when he returned to running his weekly newspapers on Cape Cod and writing a column. NBC commentator John Chancellor served for a period as director of the Voice of America. Roger Comstock, executive editor of the Hackensack, New Jersey, *Record,* took a two-year leave to be state director of public information. Even an old government watchdog like Clark Mollenhoff left the Washington bureau of the *Des Moines Register* for a year to work in Nixon's White House. The list could go on and on. Almost every one of the big newsrooms in the country has at least one former government official wearing a journalist's hat.

A perhaps more harmful kind of press-government cooperation occurs when reporters assigned to a particular beat over a period of time tire of being watchdogs. They begin to substitute complacency for vigilance. Some of the reporters covering the space program have confessed to such complacency in the wake of the 1986 explosion of the shuttle Challenger. A panel of such reporters told an Investigative Reporters and Editors (IRE) convention that they had not done a good job prior to the 28 January disaster over Cape Canaveral because they had become lackadaisical and too uncritical of the hype put out by the National Aeronautics and Space Administration. Bob Drogin of the *Los Angeles Times* said the press treated NASA like a "sacred cow," failing to report the agency's waste, fraud, and technical failures, such as the faulty "O" rings later blamed for the explosion. NASA could have lost any of the previous twenty-four shuttle flights because it had known about the booster rocket problems since 1979, Bruce Hall of CBS News charged. But the success of those flights lulled NASA into a complacency that was picked up by journalists, who also knew about the "O" rings, Hall said. Reporters in the early 1980s raised critical questions about NASA, said Olive Talley, space reporter for the *Houston Post.* But as the agency "pulled off more successes," she added, "people began to back off from these questions. NASA said it did work, it can work, it will work." Even though their editors and the public became less interested in the shuttle's technical problems, Talley asserted, reporters can still be blamed "for not properly reporting the internal workings of NASA and failing to cut through its jargon and gobbledegook."[17]

Working with Police. As we saw in the opening of this chapter, police can sometimes lean hard on journalists to cooperate to help them fight crime and criminals. The ethical question is how much cooperation between the news media and law enforcement can be tolerated without its threatening the independence and credibility of the press.

Most journalists seem to believe that at the working level a little cooperation between reporters and police is usually not harmful, but they draw the line at becoming just another arm of law enforcement. There seems to be considerable disagreement, however, about how much cooperation is acceptable.

William F. Thomas, editor and executive vice-president of the *Los Angeles Times,* warns that "you never cooperate with law enforcement in a way that jeopardizes your independence." For example, his paper refused to cooperate with police who wanted staff testimony and photographs of college student riots back in the sixties and early seventies. "Helping police that way would have hurt our effectiveness as journalists." But Thomas believes that if a journalist is walking down a street and sees a crime, there is no reason why he or she should not testify. As a city editor for many years, Thomas concedes that he often cooperated with law enforcement by trading information. "You do this very quietly and it helps you both."[18]

The way Robert W. Greene, assistant managing editor of *Newsday,* sees it:

> All the cops are required to give a police reporter are the basic skeleton details on the blotter report. But they give him more, plenty of background. They volunteer that information. Now there comes a time when the reporter and the police are each working on the same thing, both convinced that the other is working toward the same good end, and so you prime the pump by exchanging information.[19]

Greene, a longtime officer of IRE, says that "a vast majority of reporters I know cooperate with government agencies – senate committees, local police, district attorneys – given certain circumstances." Greene believes journalists do not have a right to withdraw from society. "To say that we will not cooperate when we have seen a crime committed, that because we're reporters we don't have to testify, is to say that we're not citizens, that we're privileged people," he adds.

A considerable degree of press-government cooperation was evident when the *Chicago Sun-Times* bought and operated the Mirage Tavern to expose shakedowns by city inspectors (detailed in Chapter 6). Then editor Ralph Otwell, who believes that journalists witnessing a crime in progress have a duty to report it, points out that the reporters who posed as operators of the tavern made daily reports to the Illinois Department of Law Enforcement. Their memos "summarized their encounters with various inspectors in cases where the inspectors were soliciting bribes."[20] The principal reporter on that undercover reporting project, Pamela Zekman, who later moved to WBBM-TV, Chicago, says the agency "understood that they were not to make arrests while our investigation was still going on, because if you arrest the first inspector in a chain of inspectors, that's the end of the project."[21] The department started making arrests when the investigation was finished but before the *Sun-Times* published its report. Otwell emphasizes that the paper would not have collaborated with law enforcement "if there had not been an actual crime being or about to be committed" because "we don't want to be perceived of as an arm of law enforcement."

Tom Kelly, director of photography for the Pottstown, Pennsylvania, *Mercury,* does not believe in being an arm of law enforcement, but he does not hesitate to supply prints of automobile accidents he has photographed to state and local police when they need them. And he admits he occasionally takes special shots for police who request them for their records. "It's no real big deal," Kelly adds. "We have to have good relations with police. They tip us on stuff and cooperate with us, too."[22]

James A. Dunlap, editor of the Sharon, Pennsylvania, *Herald,* favors cooperating with police if it serves the purpose of better law enforcement. "My feeling is that we're for law enforcement," Dunlap comments. "If we have a picture that will help them catch a criminal, let them have it. I want criminals arrested as much as anybody else. I would cooperate. They don't have to subpoena me."[23]

While he believes the press should avoid being "partners with law enforcement or government," Michael J. O'Neill, former editor of the New York *Daily News,* agrees with Dunlap on photo requests from police. Many newspapers and television stations oppose giving police prints or videotapes of any pictures unless they have been published or broadcast, but O'Neill believes that "if we have a photo that will help the cops solve a murder case and we accidentally didn't run it, there's no crime in giving it to them. We are citizens, too."[24]

William J. Small, former head of NBC News and UPI, would not turn over to police tapes and films that had not been used on the air, but there are times, he concedes, when you try to find ways to cooperate. When he was president of NBC News, Small recalls that "the FBI asked for our outtakes to see if John W. Hinckley, Jr., [charged at that time with trying to assassinate President Reagan] had been at any Carter or Reagan rallies. We culled through our tape files and put the pertinent ones on the air."[25]

Although he wouldn't let himself be recruited by the CIA as some foreign correspondents did in the old days, CBS News producer Brian Healy concedes that he did work with a "guy I knew to be a spook," when covering Iran. Healy, who worked out of London for CBS for several years, believes that in Iran there was a lot of "very informal trading of information" between journalists and government people. Healy adds that if the government wanted to ask him about some place he had been, "I would not refuse."[26]

Behind Closed Doors. "Every government has an interest in concealment; every public, in greater access to information," Sissela Bok writes.
"In this perennial conflict, the risks of secrecy affect even those administrators least disposed at the outset to exploit it. How many leaders have
not come into office determined to work for more open government, only
to end by fretting over leaks, seeking new, safer ways to classify documents, questioning the loyalty of outspoken subordinates."[27]

The drive for secrecy leads government officials who are otherwise
honest and open people to resort to deceptions, half-truths, and even lies.
Often they justify their concealments in the name of national security.
The revelation of some government secrets obviously would jeopardize
the nation's security, but recent history has taught us that our leaders also
invoke national security improperly to cover up embarrassing mistakes,
administrative incompetence, and plans they don't want the public to
know about for strategic reasons.

This systematic lack of candor in government at all levels tests
American journalists every day. When they occasionally pierce the shield
of government concealment—as Bob Woodward and Carl Bernstein did in
uncovering Watergate—the test then becomes one of deciding whether
the secrets uncovered would harm the nation if published. Journalists
lean toward revealing government secrets when they can find them—they
see that as their duty extending from the First Amendment—but they
have often restrained themselves when the possible harm has been obvious. That was the case after the Iranian militants seized the American
embassy in Tehran and captured several hostages in 1979. American reporters and news media were aware for weeks that six members of the
embassy staff escaped being taken hostage and were hidden in the Canadian embassy. The story was suppressed until the Canadians succeeded
in smuggling the six Americans out of Iran.

One way that journalists learn things government officials try to keep
quiet is through "leaks" of information from other government officials.
Howard Simons, former managing editor of the *Washington Post,* says it's
impossible for journalists in Washington to do their daily jobs "without
bumping into a secret." He notes that about four million bureaucrats have
access to classified information and estimates that twenty million government documents are classified as secret each year. "It is a constant wonder how any of" those dealing with secret information "can remember
what is secret and what is not secret," Simons says. He recalls the meeting that *Post* lawyers had with a National Security Agency deputy in
judge's chambers when the U.S. government was trying to get the courts
to stop that newspaper from publishing the Pentagon Papers. The deputy
brought along a top-secret document sealed in several envelopes inside a
double-locked briefcase, claiming that the document was also contained

in the Pentagon Papers, which if published would jeopardize American lives in Vietnam. Ordered to open up the secret, the deputy revealed an intercept from a North Vietnamese radio transmitter, a verbatim quote from a message to their armed forces. Publishing that quote would tell the enemy that we had tapped this valuable source of information, which they could then seal, the deputy contended. Fortunately for the *Post,* the lawyers had brought along George Wilson, respected Pentagon reporter for the paper, who remembered that the quote had been read before an open hearing of the Senate Foreign Relations Committee. And Wilson had the committee transcript with him so that he could point to the quote in the public record. As Simons adds in telling this story, "That clinched that for the *Post.*"[28]

The government, of course, failed in its attempt to keep the *Post,* the *New York Times,* and other papers from publishing the Pentagon Papers, which contained a detailed record of the origins and conduct of the Vietnam War. The papers "should never have been kept secret in the first place," Bok argues. "This information was owed to the people, at home and abroad, who were bearing the costs and the suffering of the war; keeping them in the dark about the reasons for fighting the war was an abuse of secrecy."[29]

Just as the Nixon administration tried to block public knowledge of the Pentagon Papers, the Reagan administration tried to sell the idea that the press has a patriotic duty and a legal obligation to suppress information the government declares off limits. Reagan's chief weapon in pressuring journalists to stay in line is Title 18, Section 798 of the U.S. Code. Passed in 1950 but seldom invoked, that law forbids publication of information about codes, communication intelligence devices, communication intelligence activities, and intercepted communications of foreign governments. Reagan's former CIA director, William J. Casey, threatened to use that law against news organizations that published or aired allegedly secret information.

Casey made such a threat to the *Washington Post* when the *Post* sought comments from him and other high government officials about an article telling of classified intelligence-gathering operations involving American submarines. After a conference with Casey and a telephone call from President Reagan, *Post* editors removed two or three paragraphs from the story. Casey also threatened to seek prosecution, under the 1950 law, of NBC News for airing a story on "Ivy Bells," a submarine eavesdropping program. And he charged that five news organizations had violated the law by reporting on intercepted Libyan communications, naming the five as the *New York Times,* the *Washington Post, Time, Newsweek,* and the *Washington Times.*[30]

As of this writing, no news organization had been prosecuted under

Title 18, Section 798. In fact the statute has never been used against a news organization since its enactment. But the *Columbia Journalism Review* concluded that Casey got what he wanted in that the news organizations he attacked began to censor themselves. "The Casey initiative represents a far more subtle and dangerous threat to the already dubious independence of the press than those posed by more blatant assaults of the Nixon-Agnew era," the *Review* declared.[31]

When the news media break stories involving information the government would like to keep from the public, you can bet that at least some of that information came from leaks. Although governments fight to prevent leaks—even going so far as to tap the phones of reporters—they also leak information themselves to further their own policies. "Although the practice of orchestrated government leaks goes back to Franklin D. Roosevelt," the Reagan "administration has turned the leak into an art," says Jim Anderson, State Department reporter for UPI. "It takes the form of casual tips, institutionalized backgrounders and insider dope sessions, much of it directed at enhancing the image of Reagan as a genial, principled mastermind who not only knows when every sparrow falls but sometimes revives deserving little birdies that catch his benevolent eye."[32]

Journalists were disturbed when the Reagan administration was caught trying to leak false information to the American press in order to scare Libyan dictator Col. Muammar el-Qaddafi. The *Washington Post* in 1986 published a memorandum purportedly written by President Reagan's then national security adviser, Vice Adm. John M. Poindexter, outlining what he called a "disinformation program." The strategy seemed to be to combine "real and illusionary events" to make Qaddafi think, among other things, that the United States was about to make some additional military move against his country. This ploy would be carried out, of course, through leaks to the press. At least one story suggesting that Libya was plotting new terrorist attacks apparently was leaked as part of the "disinformation program" before the *Post* exposed it. Although President Reagan and his press secretary denied that the White House was engaged in any such disinformation campaign, Secretary of State Shultz seemed to confirm such a campaign when he praised the use of deception if it would cause problems for the Libyan leader. Another seeming confirmation came a few days later when a Shultz aide, long-time television journalist Bernard Kalb, resigned as State Department spokesman in protest of "the reported disinformation program."

A. M. Rosenthal, then executive editor of the *New York Times*, expressed the outrage of most journalists about the government's use of deliberate untruths when he said, "We should leave this kind of garbage to the Russians."[33]

Spurred by such brazen tactics by the White House, journalists shortly uncovered the Iran-contra deal, which indicated that President Reagan and his representatives had been trying to conduct a secret foreign policy. How much direct knowledge the president had of secret and illegal deals cut in his name by his aides was not immediately known. But news of secret arms sales to Iran, with some of the profits being diverted to the Nicaraguan contras, obviously embarassed the Reagan administration and hurt the president's standing internationally and in domestic politics. As was the case when Watergate was first exposed to the detriment of the Nixon White House, President Reagan and his supporters tried to blame the press for their troubles. There seemed slight chance, however, that pointing accusing fingers at the messengers would, in the long run, work any better for Reagan than it did for Nixon.

Leaks of information from sources who dared not allow themselves to be named undoubtedly played a part in the unfolding of the Iran-contra affair. Leakers have provided large and small pieces of most of the major exposés of government misconduct in modern times. Why do they do it?

Stephen Hess, who is a student of government-press relations, has identified six reasons why a government employee leaks information to news people: (1) The ego leak that gives the leaker a sense of self-importance; (2) the goodwill leak designed to get favorable treatment from some reporter; (3) the policy leak intended to promote or shoot down a proposal; (4) the animus leak that is aimed at settling a grudge; (5) the trial balloon, an attempt to test public opinion before deciding on some policy; and (6) the whistle blower, who leaks information to try to correct a perceived wrong.[34]

The most noble of leakers would seem to be the whistle blower, who is also the most vulnerable to punishment for going outside the bureaucracy to try to right some wrong. *Chicago Tribune* columnist Mike Royko lamented the lack of a whistle blower in NASA who might have prevented the disastrous explosion of the shuttle Challenger:

> Organizational structures are just people. They might be extremely bright people, with impressive titles and sparkling credentials. But they are people. And there always will be some who make dumb decisions, pass the buck or avoid the buck entirely.
>
> That's where the whistle blower comes in. Somebody decides that the structure can't be trusted to repair or monitor itself. That maybe the rest of us ought to know what's going on.
>
> Whistle blowers have told us about waste in the Pentagon and other governmental agencies; about phony enemy body counts, phony estimates of enemy strength, and phony claims of battles won in Vietnam; about corruption all the way from the rural courthouse to Congress.[35]

Journalists who use information from leakers face some serious ethical problems. The motive of the leaker, not always known to the reporter, might be to use the media for selfish ends, none of which may have anything to do with truth. Many leaks merely distort reality, resulting in news stories that are inaccurate and misleading. And leaked information is almost automatically blind sourced; the public is seldom told who the leaker was.

Secret Wars. American journalists were outraged when they were blocked from covering the U.S. military invasion of the Caribbean island of Grenada in October 1983. It was the first time since the Civil War that the government had denied front-line access to journalists in military engagements. The secrecy of the Grenada operation began to fall apart when Caribbean radio stations and newspapers put out stories saying the United States was about to invade Grenada. When reporters asked about these stories on 24 October, White House press secretary Larry Speakes, after checking with a member of President Reagan's national security staff, labeled the stories "preposterous." The invasion took place the next day.

Within hours after President Reagan announced at a press conference that the landing had occurred, more than 400 American journalists had flown to Barbados, about 160 miles northeast of Grenada. Getting no help from the military and there being no arrangement for a pool of journalists to be taken to the invaded island to report back later to the other journalists in Barbados, some reporters and photographers rented boats or planes and tried to reach Grenada on their own. At least two boats and a plane were turned back by American ships and aircraft.

Two days after the invasion, the military agreed to fly a pool of fifteen journalists to Grenada, but their pool was delayed in returning to Barbados. The reports based on what the pool of observers had seen missed the big network evening newscasts that night. Somehow, though, the films taken by military camera crews made it back in time. This prompted the *Washington Post* to describe the invasion in an editorial as "the first official war in the history of the United States, produced, filmed, and reported by the Pentagon, under the sanctions of the President."

Another press pool was permitted on the island the third day after the landing, and on the fifth day after, the press was given unlimited access. By then the president and the Pentagon had put out a lot of misinformation. The most serious misstatements had to do with the number of Cubans on Grenada and whether they were soldiers or construction workers. President Reagan at first said there was "a military force" of 400 to 600 Cubans on the island. Admiral Wesley L. McDonald made the situation sound even more alarming when he stated the next day that captured documents showed there were at least 1,100 Cubans there, all "well-trained professional soldiers." The Reagan administration claim that the Cubans were about to take over Grenada seemed valid. But it turned out that the number of Cubans on the island had been 784, according to the State Department, and only about 100 of them were soldiers. That figure seems to swing the validity pendulum back to Cuba's claim that the men were there to build an airport and help an ally.

Why did the Pentagon and the White House defy more than a century of military precedent and prevent nonmilitary observers from seeing the Grenada invasion? At first the Pentagon told reporters that secrecy was necessary to insure military success and to avoid the need for military leaders to be concerned with the safety of journalists. But the real reason seems to lie in a later statement by Secretary of State George Shultz. "These days, in the advocacy journalism that's been adopted, it seems as though the reporters are always against us and so they're always trying to screw things up," Shultz said. "And when you're trying to conduct a military operation, you don't need that."[36]

Protests from virtually all major news organizations and journalistic associations apparently pushed the Pentagon to accept a press pool arrangement for future Grenada-type military operations. When military aircraft bombed Libya in retaliation for terrorism in 1986, a pool of eight journalists was allowed on board the USS *America,* an aircraft carrier from which some of the attacking planes were flown.[37]

Very few in journalism are happy with having to rely on press pools to cover events of such significance as the undeclared bombing of Libya. They're also not happy with the aspersions on their patriotism and ability to keep secrets that came from high government officials after Grenada. The record of journalistic performance in the coverage of Vietnam, Korea, and World War II, by and large, does not support the Reagan administration's decision to keep the press out of the Grenada landing. But Grenada and the Libyan bombings were different and more limited kinds of military operations that might have required different kinds of press coverage arrangements. Journalists should not be excluded, though, the way they were in the first two days of Grenada. Independent reporting of such military operations—significant even if limited—is essential to the American people in their need to understand and evaluate what their leaders are up to.

Terrorism. Media-government relations have been strained by the way terrorists and terrorism are covered, particularly by TV. In the aftermath of the 1985 hijacking of a TWA passenger plane by a Shiite Moslem faction in Beirut, for example, government officials in America and Great Britain urged journalists to restrain their coverage of such incidents. Prime Minister Margaret Thatcher said that democracies must "find ways to starve the terrorist and the hijacker of the oxygen of publicity on which they depend." U.S. Attorney General Edwin Meese III suggested that the White House ask news organizations to adopt a voluntary code of restraint. Later a Task Force on Combatting Terrorism, headed by Vice-President George Bush, conceded that government-imposed restraints would violate the First Amendment but called on the news media to "serve as their own watchdog." The task force also urged "close communication between media and government," adding: "The U.S. government should provide the media with timely information during a terrorist crisis. The media, in turn, should ensure that their reporting meets the highest professional and ethical standards."[38]

Most of the terrorism stories that have brought calls for higher reporting standards from some government leaders have occurred abroad in recent years. The FBI found only 7 incidents of domestic terrorism in the United States in 1985 (that compares with 812 around the world in 1985, 177 against U.S. targets). This means that the coverage being criticized is aimed at the three commercial TV networks, the news magazines, the wire services, and the some dozen U.S. newspapers with foreign correspondents. And it is the coverage by TV that has drawn the most fire, and not just from government but from other journalists and media observers as well.

While deploring any attempt by government to control news in an attempt to frustrate terrorists, Ben Bagdikian lashed television in its coverage of the Beirut hijacking. "The frantic rush for exclusive footage went beyond real news to self-serving feeding of ratings and egos," said Bagdikian, veteran journalist who is now journalism dean at the University of California at Berkeley. "Television went wild with its usual hunger for melodrama at the expense of meaning."[39]

In proposing a conference of broadcast and print media to discuss restraint in terrorism coverage, Michael J. Davies, editor and publisher of the *Hartford Courant,* rapped ABC and NBC News for reporting that the Delta antiterrorist force had departed from the United States and NBC for making it clear the strike force was headed for the Mediterranean. Quoting a Pentagon spokesman, Davies claimed that the broadcast reports "may have been responsible for the hijackers' decision to move the hostages off the plane, making a possible rescue more difficult."[40] Davies and other critics also opposed television's allowing the terrorists in the TWA hijacking incident to talk directly to the American audience, without being edited or questioned by reporters as is customary in journalistic interviews.

The news departments of NBC, ABC, and CBS are among the few news organizations in the country with detailed written guidelines on covering terrorism. But in the Beirut hijacking the network journalists either ignored their own guidelines or were allowed to pass through the loopholes that are standard in journalistic guidelines. NBC News president Larry Grossman explained that "when reporting on terrorism, no single set of standards can substitute for common sense, a commitment to professionalism and good judgment each time one of those difficult incidents confronts us." In a talk to a joint regional meeting of SPJ-SDX and RTNDA, Grossman responded to the criticism that television permits itself to become a platform for terrorist propaganda. "I have seen no evidence that audiences are taken in by the propaganda of terrorists who have blackmailed their way onto the television screen," he asserted. "Terrorists are terrible communicators. The brutal actions they must take in order to be seen on television destroys their ability to get their message across." Grossman also argued that "television cameras tend to modify the behavior of terrorists who, as a rule, are not disposed to appear as murderers in full view of the entire world."[41]

Ben Bagdikian believes that controlling the news of terrorist incidents would probably increase political violence, not reduce it. "Forcing news operations to react abnormally, to pretend that these are not frightening, dramatic events with political causes and consequences," Bagdikian said, "not only misleads the American populace, but also can be an invitation for terrorists to escalate their violence until it becomes impossible to withhold or downplay news of their actions."[42]

In the Beirut hijacking all but one of the thirty-nine Americans aboard TWA flight 847 were released alive and largely unharmed after being held hostage for seventeen days. The one exception was navy diver Robert David Stethem, who was murdered by the hijackers. Although the TWA hijacking was not the first terrorism event reported by the news media in the television era, its coverage seemed to arouse more criticism and calls for higher standards in journalism than that of its predecessors. The reaction of television news executives to the criticisms was mostly defensive, but often in the past when that kind of heat has been put on news organizations, reforms have followed.

COURT COVERAGE AND CONFLICTS

The press and the bar have been "dating" heavily in recent years, getting together in numerous conferences to discuss standards, ethics, and procedures in their frequently conflicting callings. The basic issue in these discussions and confrontations is whether media coverage of crime and the legal process does or does not get in the way of justice. At the extremes of the argument are the journalists who want absolute freedom to cover crime the way they see it even if that stirs up the populace, and the lawyers who seek a pure justice through a process that is conducted in a vacuum immune from the stones and shouts from the street. The numerous press-bar discussions seem at least to have given both journalists and lawyers a better understanding of their differing approaches to news versus evidence, charges versus convictions, justice versus advocacy, and a free press versus a fair trial.

Ethical issues are raised by the way the news media cover crime and courts: Should reporters play cop and investigate crimes on their own? Should the media report confessions or prior police records of accused persons when those matters may not always be used as evidence in a trial? Should reporters interview and report statements of people who are apt to be witnesses in the trial? Should the media so emphasize certain very interesting cases that community opinion is aroused against a defendant, making it more difficult to draft an impartial jury? Should reporters interview jurors after they have handed down their verdict? Should the news media allow trial lawyers to try their cases in the news columns and newscasts, to use publicity to affect the outcome in their favor?

There is a community and public interest in reporting crime, of course. Journalists have an obligation to watch the criminal justice system—from arrests to sentencing—in the same way they are supposed to watch the other branches of government. The public is well served when diligent news reporting assures against secret arrests and trials, both contrary to an open and civilized society.

But what bothers many people is the way some segments of the news business publish or broadcast material that seems to jeopardize the Sixth Amendment rights of the accused to a fair trial. Lawyers for news organizations argue that the courts have remedies when they think publicity may get in the way of a fair trial: Trials can be delayed until the impact of publicity has diminished; juries can be sequestered; trials can be moved to other jurisdictions; or juries can be brought in from other places. News media representatives also question whether pretrial publicity has the power to prejudice a jury.

A case that raised the issue of whether publicity affects trials was the John DeLorean trial in Los Angeles. Just as the jury was about to be selected to hear drug conspiracy charges against the auto maker, CBS News and its Los Angeles affiliate, KNXT-TV, aired videotapes taken by the FBI during a sting operation. Among other things, the tapes showed DeLorean beside a suitcase supposedly loaded with cocaine as he toasted a $24 million drug deal with champagne. With him were the other men allegedly in the deal with him who were actually undercover agents. The tapes were slipped to CBS and KNXT by Larry Flynt, publisher of *Hustler* magazine, who claimed he had bought them from an unnamed government official. Hearing that the broadcasters had the tapes, the trial judge, Federal District Court Judge Robert M. Takasugi, asked CBS and KNXT to hold the tapes for a week "in view of an individual's right to a fair trial." When the broadcasters replied that the tapes were too newsworthy to keep off the air, Judge Takasugi ordered them not to use the tapes. A day later, the Ninth Circuit Court of Appeals overturned his decision, calling it an unacceptable prior restraint of the press. The tapes went on the air that evening. Judge Takasugi put off the trial until the next term of court and the next round of jury selection.[43]

Despite the outrageous airing of evidence before it was introduced in court, DeLorean was acquitted in September 1984 by a jury that had been sequestered during his four-month trial. Eight of the twelve jurors answered reporters' questions as a group after the lengthy trial and explained that they felt DeLorean had been entrapped by the FBI.

Another fair trial/free press argument arose after the *Sacramento Bee* broke the story of a local elementary school teacher being arrested on a charge of sexually molesting some of his female pupils. That was what the first-day story reported. On the second day, the *Bee* told how 125 parents and students rallied to support the teacher. The third-day story with picture quoted a twenty-year-old college student as saying that eight years earlier she had been touched by this teacher when she was a student in his sixth-grade class.

A number of *Bee* readers complained to the paper that the third-day story was unfair to the teacher. One attorney called attention to the six-year statute of limitations applying to the offense in this case, which meant that the college student's accusations "will never be decided in court" and the teacher will "never be able to defend himself against them in a legal sense." Another protester said that even if the teacher were exonerated, the college student's accusations would stand virtually unchallenged. "As a result, win or lose, he's finished," the protester contended. "You gave the guy a swift kick while he was down."

When *Bee* ombudsman Art Nauman looked into the *Bee's* coverage, he found that the paper had learned about the college student from police who had interviewed her in their investigation. Metropolitan editor George L. Baker told Nauman the twenty-year-old's statement made under oath to police was news because she was "willing to go public . . . to discuss what many people don't care to talk about in public – child molestation." Baker also pointed out that the third-day article was balanced by statements from the student's mother, who said she thought at the time and still thinks that her daughter had misinterpreted the teacher's actions.

To Nauman the biggest question raised by the *Bee*'s coverage was not its impact on the teacher's right to a fair trial, which he thought the court could still assure by the various devices at its disposal, but whether the *Bee* had been fair in its reporting. He concluded that it had not been fair to the teacher in publishing the college student's recollections.[44]

When the teacher came to trial a year later, he was convicted on two counts of lewdness with children and released under a five-year probation. His teaching credentials were suspended.[45]

These two cases from California are among several that have raised questions about whether journalists are as fair as they should be in their reporting of crime, particularly prior to trials. Although journalism seems to be improving so that fair and evenhanded crime coverage is the rule rather than the exception, the line between responsible reporting and sensationalism still gets crossed.

The Taboo of Testifying. Many journalists are wary of witness stands in court and grand jury rooms. They fear that giving testimony encourages the impression that they are in bed with cops and courts, which would scare off some news sources and cause the public to question the evenhandedness of their reporting on the justice system. Another objection is that some prosecutors and defense attorneys subpoena reporters to testify about matters that police and defense investigators should be digging up.

Journalists can resist subpoenas—and many do—but their success in invoking the reporter's privilege not to testify usually hinges on whether they are being asked to talk about what they learned more or less confidentially in the course of news gathering. If they saw a crime committed while walking their dog, they have no special First Amendment right not to testify. But Jack Landau, former director of the Reporters Committee for Freedom of the Press, tells of a time he advised two reporters to testify even though the murder they witnessed happened while they were on the job. They were doing an undercover reporting project in 1980, posing as derelicts in order to investigate flophouses in their Texas city. In one flophouse they saw a man shot and killed by another man. The reporters called Landau because they wanted to plead First Amendment immunity and not testify as to what they saw. "I told them the whole point of reporter's privilege is that everybody knows you are a reporter, and sources come to you as a reporter, and trust you as a reporter," Landau explains. "You did everything you could to not let them know you were a reporter. So how can you turn around and claim the First Amendment is going to be undermined, when you did everything you could to hide your First Amendment connection?"[46]

The *Washington Post,* which has a long-standing practice of resisting subpoenas directed to its reporters, observes in its deskbook that "testimony by reporters in court cases concerning their news-gathering activities will discourage many persons from talking freely to reporters, because they will be afraid that what they say may end up in litigation." This is true whether the reporter is asked to reveal confidential or nonconfidential information, the *Post* states. "The mere fact that a reporter appears on the witness stand to testify concerning his or her news gathering has a chilling effect on many potential sources of information." The *Post* notes that the First Amendment protection of news gathering has been recognized in a number of cases in which subpoenas have been struck down. "In particular," the deskbook adds, "there has been a tendency by the courts to recognize the First Amendment right of the reporter not to testify in cases where the information sought by the subpoena can be obtained by an alternative means."[47]

A Los Angeles TV reporter was criticized by other journalists when he voluntarily testified in a murder trial. Reporter David Lopez of KNXT, Los Angeles, claimed that William G. Bonin during the course of an interview in the Los Angeles County Jail confessed that he had killed twenty-one young men and boys in 1979 and 1980. But the confession was off the record; Lopez agreed to go off the record with the understanding that Bonin would not tell anybody else "anything we talked about." This was in January 1981 while Bonin was awaiting trial on charges of committing twelve murders. Lopez claimed that Bonin broke his word to him not too long after the "confession" by telling a reporter for the *Orange County Register* some of the things he had told him. Lopez tried to get his station to let him report the "confession" now that Bonin had talked to another reporter, but his bosses told him they felt such a story would jeopardize Bonin's right to a fair trial. In late June, five months after he got his off-the-record interview, Lopez contended that Bonin broke his word again by negotiating for a movie deal. This time the station let Lopez go on the air.[48]

After his story aired, Lopez was called twice to testify. He resisted, claiming the newsman's privilege of confidentiality under the California shield law, which a judge upheld both times. But once the judge had upheld the shield law in his case, Lopez felt he had fulfilled his responsibility as a reporter. "I have two kids and I come from a family of eight," he explained. "If my kid was killed and someone could have done something and didn't come forward, I could never forgive him." Lopez volunteered to testify as a prosecution witness and told the court in great detail what Bonin had said to him eleven months earlier. When Lopez stepped down from the witness chair, he said to reporters: "I'm a citizen first. I feel as though a hundred-pound weight has been taken off me." (Bonin was later convicted of the first degree murder of ten victims and sentenced to death.)

Two reporters who went to jail for resisting court orders to testify, Myron Farber of the *New York Times* and the late William Farr of the *Los Angeles Times*, criticized Lopez. "I would have testified if I were the only witness to see someone kill someone else, but this is not the case" with Lopez, argued Farber, who spent forty days in jail in 1978 for refusing to give a New Jersey court his notes on a story about a doctor standing trial for murder. Farber concluded that Lopez had "injected himself in the case" on behalf of the prosecution. The state ought to try Bonin "on the quality of the evidence it gathered . . . and not on what Lopez, in a purely journalistic attempt, accomplished on his own," Farber added. Farr, who spent forty-seven days in jail for refusing to disclose the source of a story he wrote about the Charles Manson murder trial in 1970, disagreed with Lopez's claim that he was a citizen first and a reporter second. "Bonin talked to him because he was a reporter, not a plain citizen," Farr contended. Farr also criticized Lopez for breaking his pledge of confidentiality to Bonin, maintaining that when reporters break their promises to sources, other sources dry up.

Lopez should not have taken the confession off the record in the first place, in the view of Eugene Patterson, chief executive officer of the *St. Petersburg Times*. But once he did, he was duty-bound to tell authorities, Patterson said. "I don't think journalists can get themselves in the position of using the First Amendment to shield someone for murder."[49]

Chicago investigative reporter Pamela Zekman has never resisted a subpoena to testify, although she has not been subpoenaed often. Zekman says she objects to prosecutors trying to base their cases on her testimony. "We don't want to do their work for them, but if they need us in some small way, I feel we have to help," Zekman says. "We aren't above the obligations of a normal citizen. If you witness a crime, you have an obligation to testify."[50]

Newsday's Greene has testified before numerous congressional and legislative committees and as a witness at more than sixty criminal trials. "Yet I have never encountered a source who avoided me because I did so," maintains Greene, regarded as one of journalism's top investigative reporters. Although he would not disclose a confidential source, he claims he has always been willing to turn over his notes when asked. Greene explains that he has testified because "I believe my craft calls upon me to be a reporter of facts, not a keeper of them."[51]

Greene sees no reason for reporters to refuse to testify about information they have gotten on the record from a source but did not, for space reasons, publish. And even if reporters agree to protect the identity of a source, they have no reason not to testify about the information, Greene believes. "It is not easy for the public to understand why we are withholding information we have not made any contract with our sources to withhold," Greene contends. "We are more and more appearing to the public as some sort of privileged class. The public despises privileged classes."[52]

Jury Privacy. Some trial judges have expressed concern about the increasing tendency of reporters to question jurors after trials have concluded. Seeking explanations for why the jury decided the way it did has produced some revealing stories, some of which have cast doubt on the abilities of some jurors to arrive at reasoned verdicts. By and large the press has not questioned laws and procedures that for years have prevented reporters or any outsiders from talking to jurors while the trial is in progress. But more and more reporters are interviewing jurors after the trial is over. This has led some judges to attempt to extend the privacy that protects jurors during trials to their private lives after the trials. Their argument for these attempts, which have not yet been clearly tested by the U.S. Supreme Court, is that jurors' decisions might be affected by the realization that they will be asked about them by reporters afterward.

After reporters interviewed jurors in a libel trial between John R. Lakian and the *Boston Globe,* Judge George Jacobs of the Massachusetts Superior Court told a courtroom audience:

> I think members of the press at the highest levels ought to think carefully not only in this case, but in every case, about what redeeming value there is in making inquiry of jurors posttrial.
> The press, which is concerned about the chilling effects upon its processes, perhaps ought to think about the chilling effects on the jury process.[53]

Although his staff has chased down jurors after trials, Andrew Barnes, editor of the *St. Petersburg Times,* says "that's one we're still arguing about." He recalls that in 1974 his paper published contents of a note found in the wastebasket of a jury room. "I don't think I'd do that again," Barnes added. "I think that the jury action collectively really probably is all that counts. To go into the components that made it up makes me less and less comfortable."[54]

John H. McMillan, publisher of the *Statesman-Journal* in Salem, Oregon, has called posttrial juror interviews "rotten, lousy and stinky." He said the jury system "should remain sacrosanct" and "jurors should be as insulated from as much potential pressure as they can be."[55]

Many editors obviously do not agree with Barnes and McMillan in their reservations about asking jurors what went on in their closed deliberations. Proponents of the practice cite such enlightening articles as Steven Brill's report of his interviews with the jurors who found for Mobil Oil president William Tavoulareas in his libel suit against the *Washington Post*. Brill's piece in the November 1982 issue of *American Lawyer* concluded that the verdict was nearly the single-handed work of one juror, the foreman, who knew a little law and used it effectively against the *Post*.[56]

SOME CODES HELPFUL

Virtually all of the ethics codes of national journalistic associations recognize the responsibility of the news media to monitor government and the other segments of power in society. "Freedom of the press is to be guarded as an inalienable right of people in a free society," SPJ-SDX declares. "It carries with it the freedom and responsibility to discuss, question and challenge actions and utterances of our government and of our public and private institutions." The APME believes "the newspaper should serve as a constructive critic of all segments of society. It should vigorously expose wrongdoing or misuse of power, public or private. . . . The public's right to know about matters of importance is paramount, and the newspaper should fight vigorously for public access to news of government through open meetings and open records."

In ASNE's view:

> The American press was made free not just to inform or just to serve as a forum for debate but also to bring an independent scrutiny to bear on the forces of power in the society, including the conduct of official power at all levels of government.
>
> Freedom of the press belongs to the people. It must be defended against encroachment or assault from any quarter, public or private.
>
> Journalists must be constantly alert to see that the public's business is conducted in public. They must be vigilant against all who would exploit the press for selfish purposes.

RTNDA also is concerned about open meetings of public bodies. Broadcast news organizations have had a tougher time getting public agencies, including courts, to allow them to record and photograph their proceedings. Although the situation is improving rapidly, pencil reporters have been given much greater access to public proceedings in this country than have radio reporters who want to tape record and photographers who want to take pictures with their still or videotape cameras. RTNDA says in its code that broadcast journalists "shall make constant efforts to open doors closed to the reporting of public proceedings with tools appropriate to broadcasting (including cameras and recorders), consistent with the public interest."

On court coverage and the free press/fair trial issue, RTNDA states that "broadcast journalists shall conduct themselves with dignity, whether the court is in or out of session. They shall keep broadcast equipment as unobtrusive and silent as possible. . . . In reporting matters that are or may be litigated, the journalist should avoid practices which would tend to interfere with the right of an individual to a fair trial."

The NBC, CBS, and ABC news standards on the free press versus fair trial matter are more detailed. NBC notes that "under our judicial system, verdicts must be based on evidence heard in the courtroom. As a consequence, if we report information which would not be legally admissible or available in the courtroom, it may have a prejudicial impact on the judicial proceedings." NBC then offers these general guidelines:

> When reporting news about crimes and criminal proceedings, detailed references to such matters as (1) the existence or content of confessions or (2) prior criminal records or (3) the identity or potential testimony of witnesses have the potential to interfere with the processes of justice. . . .
>
> There are some situations, however, where such information not only may, but should, be reported. If, for example, wrongful behavior by government officials, or a wrongful deprivation of civil rights, or a wrongful imprisonment or any other miscarriage of justice is being investigated or reported, every available and relevant fact must be sought out and reported.

CBS News, after warning in language similar to that in the NBC code about the ways that pretrial publicity can cause miscarriages of justice, explains the kinds of situations in which such publicity might be appropriate:

> We still must fulfill the vital watchdog role of the press, particularly in the administration of justice. Consequently, where there are public policy reasons to do so, we *can* pursue every lead and report it—so long as it relates directly to a story or exposé about the administration or miscarriage of justice and improper action or inaction of officials. Watergate was, of course, a paramount example of this. The Wetumpkta story is a more obscure and less dramatic example: There, a young black was hauled out of his car by the county sheriff

and dragged into jail, and then was found dead in jail – and there was no indictment and no charge against the county officials. After a reasonable time had elapsed and it became apparent that there would be no official pursuit of the case, we reported eyewitness and other evidence that the sheriffs had brutally beaten the black. Here was a case where, indeed, the evidence went to the guilt or innocence of the sheriffs. But it was apparent that nobody was doing anything and hence there seemed clearly to be a miscarriage of justice. In such cases no holds, except careful and responsible reporting, are barred and we go full-speed ahead. So, too, if a seemingly innocent person appears to us to be in the process of being railroaded to jail, we can and ought to report any evidence that we can find.

One other point – where a crime has been committed and there is no warrant or arrest or indictment for any particular person, we certainly can interview eyewitnesses (staying away, as is normally the case, from explicit fingering and identification of the alleged criminal by name) and carry the pictures and description of the suspected fugitive released by the police. Further, where the police themselves or government officials violate the American Bar Association guidelines and publicly announce, in newsworthy circumstances, particular evidence pointing to the guilt of a person including confessions or prior police records, it is not incumbent on us to censor them if our news judgment otherwise indicates that some or all of their statements are worthwhile carrying. An extreme example of the latter is the instance where the Dallas Chief of Police waved a rifle in front of everybody and said that this was the rifle that Oswald had used and that he was clearly guilty. So, also, is the Nixon reference to Manson's guilt before Manson's conviction. These are things that we could not, and should not, suppress. Mr. Nixon and the police official may have been totally wrong, but we cannot put ourselves in the position of playing God and pretending, in these particular circumstances of significant public interest and importance, that the events didn't happen.

ABC News urges that its news people "be sensitive to the accused's right to a fair trial and the potential prejudicial effect of prior publicity." The ABC News guideline on crime reporting also says:

> We should give careful thought on a case-by-case basis before reporting confessions or other detailed "evidence" which directly links a particular individual to a crime. Even if the information comes from the police or prosecutor, it is untested in court and may not be admissible at trial (for example, if a confession is ruled to be not voluntary). On the other hand, if the police hold a news conference to discuss particular evidence, their actions and opinions may be newsworthy and under most circumstances we should feel free to report them.
>
> The dictates of fairness are of particular relevance where indi-

viduals are accused of crimes. While "alleged" is a useful word connoting something unproved, we should also seek out the accused for comment and consider other opinions that run counter to the allegations.

While we wish to proceed with caution in this area, we are not limited to reporting only what the police or prosecutors have done or are about to do. There will be instances where the very point of our story is the failure to prosecute or undue delays in an official investigation, or evidence of miscarriage of justice. In such cases, we may determine that the fullest reporting of facts is justified and necessary.

The *Washington Post* deskbook deals with crime and court coverage. "We should take care to report crime news with caution and accuracy, to bear in mind the rights of the accused and to leave the deciding of guilt or innocence to the courts," the *Post* declares. "Be especially careful about these points:"

1. Guilt of accused or arrested persons must not be conveyed or implied in the stories or headlines. . . .

2. Statements to police officers, reporters or prosecutors are not confessions. The term *confession* should not be used either in headlines or text unless we are dealing with an acknowledgment of guilt given by a defendant in a courtroom. Accused persons *state, relate, report, explain* or otherwise elaborate upon a criminal situation in remarks to the police. We prefer to avoid the use of even such words as *admit* or *acknowledge.*

3. Reports of trials should accurately reflect the proceedings. Reporters and editors should give the prosecution and the defense fair coverage. . . .

6. Persons charged with a violation of the law should be given the opportunity to reply to such charges, if possible.

7. Do not routinely report arrest records of suspects in crime stories. . . . A record (and it should include disposition) may be used only after clearance with a departmental editor. Particular effort should be made to avoid prejudicing a trial by publishing the record of a suspect immediately before trial.

8. We avoid publishing pictures that might prejudice the trial of defendants. . . .

10. As a general rule, we name persons charged with crimes. However, in "trend" or "survey" stories, where one or a few cases are selected as examples, the departmental editor should carefully weigh whether to use those names—particularly if they would not have otherwise seen print. . . .[57]

ABC News is one of the few news organizations that tries in its code to guide its journalists on questions of when and if they should cooperate with government. After stating that it "disapproves of most forms of cooperation with government agencies . . . because it can compromise, or have the appearance of compromising, the First Amendment freedom and independence of the press," ABC News says cooperation might be all right in situations involving threats to human life or national security and in cases where a crime has been, or is about to be, committed. "In such situations, the responsibilities of good citizenship and good journalism must be reconciled," ABC adds, warning, however, that all "invocations of national security" cannot be recognized because "history reveals too many instances where claims of national security have been used wrongly to cover up information that should have been reported." Another kind of cooperation seen as possibly acceptable to ABC News is accompanying police on a narcotics raid or in undercover or "sting" operations. The only specific example in the ABC code of a time when journalists should not cooperate with government is in this prohibition: "A reporter must never use his or her identity as a journalist to ask questions or perform any investigative function on behalf of the police or any other government agency."

Truth telling gets shoved aside when journalists accede to government requests or pressures to hold up or suppress certain information. But sometimes there are good and explainable reasons for the press to cooperate with authorities, as seemed to be the case when officials asked major news organizations to withhold information about the six Americans hiding in the Canadian embassy in Tehran. In the Hattiesburg case that opened this chapter, the reasons that authorities gave for seeking the cooperation of the local news executives may also have seemed good and explainable. But they asked too much. What they sought was not a mere delay in getting some legitimate story out to the public; they wanted the local newspaper and TV station to help them pull off a questionable hoax, to join them in a lie. It may be OK for cops to lie and set deceptive traps to catch criminals (although many disapprove of such techniques), but journalists should report police sting operations, not join them. Knowingly lying to the public destroys the basic trust that people have to have in journalism if it is to do its essential job in a democratic society.

What journalists are supposed to do when government officials deliberately lie to them is difficult to say. Although the increasing use of public relations techniques by government in this country has become acceptable, most government officials stop short of passing out falsehoods to the press. But we learned in the Reagan years that some of his top aides apparently carried out a disinformation campaign to scare Libyan dictator Muammar el-Qaddafi. They did it by leaking false stories to reporters, confident that the competitive juices running through the veins of most journalists would assure dissemination of their lies and half-truths. The credibility of the government suffered more than that of the press when this program of deception was exposed, but journalists were justifiably outraged. It is hoped that the public will support journalists in their efforts to banish intentional lying as a government instrument or policy.

As mentioned earlier in this chapter, all three news departments at ABC, NBC, and CBS have policies on covering terrorism, as well as civil disturbances and disasters. All three call for their news crews to be as unobtrusive as possible covering civil disturbances and disasters, using unmarked cars whenever possible and limiting the use of lights for taking pictures. All three network policies require high brass approval for live coverage of or interviews with terrorists, one of the things NBC News was criticized for in its reporting of the TWA hijacking in Beirut in 1985. Interestingly, the NBC terrorism policy is the only one of the three that does not warn against allowing terrorists to use network TV cameras as an outlet for their propaganda. Another of its guidelines that NBC News seemed to violate in the Beirut hijacking is the one that says it "will not attempt to interview terrorists or hostages until authorities have the situation in control." CBS and ABC also warn their news crews not to tie up telephone lines when they are needed by authorities trying to communicate with terrorists, but NBC makes no mention of this problem.

The intense competition among the three network news departments frequently pressures them to push ethics aside when they are pursuing a story as big as the Beirut hijacking. Their audience ratings vis-à-vis one another are not only a measure of achievement, they determine rates that the networks are able to charge for advertising. The evening newscasts, in particular, are showcases whose ratings impress advertisers.

However, broadcast journalists in general are less intense than their newspaper brethren in monitoring government, especially local and state government. Most newspaper journalists are very serious about their watchdog function. They seem to adhere to a different ethic when exposing government corruption, graft, misuse of funds and power, and other wrongdoing, often exhibiting a mercilessness about exposing erring public officials. Journalists, newspaper people especially, usually justify their no-holds-barred coverage of government by relating it to the traditional responsibility of the press to make democracy work by giving the public the information and the forum it needs to elect competent government officials.

Some scholars scoff at the notion that the press is a watchdog of government and other orders in American life. They see the press as part of the system, not an independent critic of it. Its dependence on advertising for financial survival, it is argued, makes the press an extension of the industrial order. Likewise, many Americans outside the academy often seem unappreciative of journalism's role in a democratic society, particularly when the press goes after one of their political favorites. But some great things have been accomplished in American journalism in the name of that watchdog. Despite its financial moorings, journalism has not only uncovered both large and small abuses of governmental power, it has been about the only check we have had in modern times on the increasingly efficient secrecy of government at all levels. It is hoped that lack of applause will not stop journalists from aggressively pursuing what they see as their watchdog function.

12 Dispassion/ Compassion

Imagine that you are a photographer for a daily newspaper. As you are driving over a bridge on your way to work early one morning, you spot a man and a woman struggling near the railing. You stop your car and get out, instinctively slinging your camera over your shoulder. Now the man is on the outside of the bridge railing and the woman is on the inside, desperately trying to stop the man from jumping into the swirling river nearly one hundred feet below.

What do you do? Take the picture or try to save the man? Maybe you can do both? But is there time to do both? What do you know about jumpers anyway? Why doesn't somebody else stop?

These were the kinds of questions that went whirling through the mind of William T. Murphy, Jr., that morning. This happened to him as he was driving from his home in Vancouver, Washington, to his job at the *Oregon Journal,* the now defunct afternoon daily in Portland. His route took him across the Columbia River. Halfway across the bridge, Murphy saw the struggling couple and stopped his car and got out. "At first they didn't notice me," the photographer said later. "The man was in his mid-40s, I'd guess, a husky guy. His wife was trying to hold onto his arm. She was screaming and pleading with him." Murphy took one picture (Fig. 12.1) and then another one just as some kid on a bicycle pedaled by, passing within two feet of the woman as she struggled to keep her husband from jumping (Fig. 12.2). Other cars crossing the bridge slowed when they reached that point but none stopped at first.[1]

Murphy tried to remember how suicide prevention experts had dealt with jumpers back in Boston where he had worked for the old *Herald-Traveler.* "One thing was for certain," Murphy confided. "I didn't want to try to rush the guy because I thought he'd jump for sure. I got within ten feet when he noticed me. I started talking. 'That's not the right thing to do, pal,' I said. 'Come over here and we'll talk about it.'" The jumper stared at Murphy but said nothing. A van on the bridge stopped and a young woman looked out. Murphy screamed at her to get the state police "at the end of the bridge." Then he remembered something else from Boston: If you insult someone about to jump, he might come back and try to take a poke at you. "Hey, you coward, that's a coward's way out,"

Murphy yelled. "Come on back here, you coward." It didn't work, Murphy added. The guy "leaned out and was gone." The photographer took a picture of the man falling away from the bridge (Fig. 12.3). He took a total of five pictures. About then, Murphy noticed that the young woman from the van had gotten out and was standing fifty feet away watching the man jump to his death.

12.1 A suicide leap. *This is the scene that photojournalist William T. Murphy, Jr., found when he stopped his car on a bridge connecting Washington state and Oregon.*

12.2 "That's not the right thing to do, pal," *photographer Murphy says he shouted at the man struggling to free himself from his wife's weakening grip. The unidentified bicyclist did not stop.*

12.3. The man jumped *to his death in the swirling Columbia River nearly one hundred feet below. The photographer then noticed that the young woman he had asked to go for the police was still there on the bridge, watching the suicide. (Photos courtesy of William T. Murphy, Jr., Portland Oregonian.)*

After his pictures were published in the *Oregon Journal* and in other newspapers across the country that subscribed to the UPI photo service, angry letters and phone calls started coming in. "Don't the ethics of journalism insist that preservation of human life comes first, news second?" asked a woman in Philadelphia. "He let a man die for the sake of a good photograph," a New Yorker wrote.

Murphy was in agony. He had taken his pictures, but he had also tried to help the man. "Why didn't someone else stop?" he asked. "I don't know what I could have done differently. I am a photographer and I did what I have been trained to do. I did all I could."[2]

The uncertainty Bill Murphy felt is not unique to journalism. Any one of us is apt to get caught between the obligations of our jobs and our obligations as human beings. But it seems to be more of a problem for journalists because in some journalists' minds, even humanistic instincts can get in the way of doing their jobs.

The Dispassion of Objectivity. One of the definitions of objective reporting—which most journalists still try to practice despite widespread doubts in the field about its achievability—is that the reporter is a spectator and not a participant in what he or she covers. The discipline of objective reporting, it is said, requires a dispassionate approach to the gathering and presentation of facts. Reporters are not supposed to get involved in their stories; they are not supposed to become part of the story; they are supposed to be neutral observers.

If that conventional wisdom of contemporary journalism is taken literally, then Bill Murphy was foolish to agonize about whether he did the right thing. Of course he did the right thing. He did what he gets paid for doing—taking news pictures. So why did it haunt him for months afterward and why did so many readers rail at him for doing his job? The answer, it would appear, is that both Murphy and his critics believe journalists are human beings even when they are doing the work of journalism, and Bill Murphy the human being was supposed to do something to help another human being in trouble. In this way of thinking, Bill Murphy was no neutral observer on the bridge that morning. He was a human being who makes his living taking news pictures and he was ten feet away from a fellow human being intent on jumping to his death.

It is unfair to suggest that if Murphy had dropped his camera and concentrated on trying to help restrain the suicidal man that he would have succeeded. He apparently felt that if he rushed to the woman's aid, the man would have pulled away from her that much sooner.

(On two occasions after the bridge jump incident, Murphy used his first-aid training to help automobile accident victims. He recalls pulling an older man out of his wrecked car and turning off the engine after a two-car collision near Sandy, Oregon. He bandaged another victim of that crash, using a first-aid kit he carries in his car, and then wrapped her in his coat because she seemed to be going into shock. He took no pictures until the ambulance crew arrived. Another time, because he was in a rented car when he came upon an accident, Murphy had to flag down a passing car to get bandages to wrap around an injured man's head. Murphy remembers with some bitterness that after the second accident, the *Journal*'s chief photographer chewed him out for trying to help because that would expose the paper to a law suit.[3])

The point in telling Bill Murphy's story is not to imply that he should have done anything different or that anyone else would have been able to handle the bridge suicide any better. His experience illustrates the frustrating dilemma that journalists face when they have to decide whether to help people or go for the story or picture. Or to put it another way, when they have to decide whether to substitute compassion for dispassion.

ROOM FOR HUMANENESS?

American newspapers and other news media are well known for their charitable campaigns: Beating the drums for contributions to United Way, to help the needy at Christmas time, to send city kids off to the country for "fresh air" vacations, or to rebuild the fire-damaged home of a local family. One of the awards in the Gannett chain's annual competition for the newspapers and broadcast stations it owns is the Good Neighbor Award, which recently went to the San Bernardino, California, *Sun* for mobilizing the community to help victims of a major forest fire. Second place went to Cocoa, Florida, *Today* for collecting funds for Christmas toys after the Salvation Army's toy locker was burglarized in November.

Although such charitable campaigns represent a sort of institutional compassion, they cannot be read as signs of a growing compassion in the practice of journalism. Journalists are not so sure they can afford to be compassionate in all news situations. "It might be compassionate to suppress a story reporting the arrest of the publisher for drunken driving," says Louis D. Boccardi, president of the AP, "but that might be disastrous for the credibility of the newspaper." Boccardi recalls that when he was a young reporter covering the courts, he was asked many times not to put certain things in the paper. "Compassion might dictate that you not report certain things, but there are other considerations" for journalists, Boccardi believes. Although he's not ready to embrace "compassion" as a prerequisite for work in journalism, Boccardi agrees that journalists should "have a regard for human life."[4]

Diane Benison, managing editor of the Worcester, Massachusetts, *Evening Gazette,* also has trouble seeing a place for compassion in news work. "One of the curses of this business," she argues, "is that you're expected to have your pores open, to be able to feel, to be able to empathize with people, and yet to eviscerate yourself to do your job, just as if you were a machine."[5]

Other journalists more readily accept a place for compassion in journalism. Anthony Casale of *USA Today* tells a story of a police reporter for the Rochester, New York, *Times-Union* who exchanged himself for a woman hostage being held captive by a robber barricaded in a house. The criminal had threatened to kill the woman if he was not allowed to talk to a reporter. After the exchange, the reporter escaped and the robber killed himself. But because "he became part of the story," the reporter was reprimanded by his editor, who put out a memorandum that the next reporter who did anything like that would be fired. Casale is not sure what he would do if that same thing happened to him. "You can't be more objective than you're able to," he reasons. "If it's a matter of saving a life or something that can't be replaced, there's an obligation beyond your professional one."[6]

Reporter Christine Wolff felt she had to step out of her reporter's role when a man intent on suicide started to leap from a bridge right in front of her eyes. Wolff, then with the *Bradenton* (Florida) *Herald,* was driving back to Bradenton from a Tampa assignment one night in October 1982 when she had to pull around a van stopped on the high center peak of the five-mile Sunshine Skyway Bridge over Tampa Bay, a bridge that had been a platform for some forty suicide jumps. It occurred to the twenty-eight-year-old reporter that someone in the van might be planning to jump to the dark water 150 feet below. So she turned her car around and returned to the parked van to find a bridge tollgate supervisor restraining the van's driver who was indeed threatening to jump.[7]

Wolff and the bridge official, who had clamped his large hand on the van driver's forearm to keep him from leaving the vehicle, talked to the would-be jumper for thirty-five minutes until a Florida state trooper arrived. As the bridge official released his grip to start directing traffic, the van driver, who called himself Virgil, lunged out the door on the passenger's side and started toward the bridge rail only a foot or so away.

Wolff ran around the front of the van and grabbed Virgil's arm just as he threw one leg over the rail. "No, no, please, don't, please . . ." she yelled. She held tightly to his arm long enough for the trooper to get there and help pull Virgil back against the van. The two of them—the trooper and the reporter—held onto Virgil for about twenty more minutes until more police arrived and took him off to a St. Petersburg hospital.

Although she believes that in general "reporters should stay as objective as possible," Wolff says that "in this situation, I became a person, a citizen responding." She says she might not have felt compelled to act if the state trooper had been closer to the would-be jumper. But Virgil "had one leg over the rail and was leaning toward the water when I reached him," Wolff adds. "I was maybe five seconds ahead of the trooper and that's long enough for him to go over."

Wolff, who described herself in a telephone interview as an athletic, five-foot-six 140 pounder, recalls that reader reaction to her story about the episode was mostly positive except for a couple of people who told her she should not have interfered with Virgil's right to kill himself. "I could not condone standing there and saying, 'If you want to jump, jump!'" Wolff says. "I have no qualms about what I did."

Her editors also approved of her getting involved in this particular story. She got a bonus, she says, and her city editor, Dan Stober, told her that if she hadn't helped stop the possible suicide, he would not want her on his staff.

Wolff, of course, had an advantage over Bill Murphy. She could help save Virgil and still do her reporter's job (she says she noticed after she had grabbed Virgil and pulled him back from the rail that she had her small reporter's notebook and pen clutched in her left hand). It is more difficult for news photographers to take their photos and do very much about what is going on in front of their lenses.

Two court reporters were still able to do their stories after they put their notebooks aside to administer cardiopulmonary resuscitation (CPR) to a fifty-two-year-old man who collapsed in a Washington, Pennsylvania, courtroom. David Templeton of the *Pittsburgh Press* and Jon Stevens of the local *Observer Reporter* both had had CPR training, which they put to use when the husband of an accused woman slumped to the floor at a preliminary hearing. They administered CPR until paramedics arrived. Unfortunately, the man died in the hospital. Their stories the next day gave more emphasis to the death of the man and their attempt to save him than to the hearing, which was continued indefinitely.[8]

Some people saw a lack of humaneness when *Seattle Times* editors had to decide whether to publish a photograph of a dead boy that was apt to be the first notification to his surviving family that he had been killed. That sort of problem does not arise with most shots of accident or disaster victims because authorities almost invariably notify next of kin before news and photos can be published. But the dead boy in this photograph was unidentified. It was the famous photo of the body of a young boy in the back of a pickup truck after the 1980 eruption of Mount Saint Helens.

Most editors thought that picture, taken from a helicopter by photo-journalist George Wedding of the San Jose *Mercury-News,* was one of the best and most telling news photos to come out of that volcanic eruption in Washington state. But Seattle editors knew there was a good chance that the dead boy's family lived in their circulation area.

The *Seattle Times* ran Wedding's photo, distributed by the AP. "I think we had to run the picture," day picture editor James Heckman explained.

> It made me uncomfortable, especially wrestling with the inevita-
> ble conclusion that family members might well identify the victim.
> But we are chronicling an incredible event and . . . publishing history.
> The photograph in question likely will be the picture – or one of the
> pictures – used in the years ahead when the awesome fury of the
> eruption is detailed.[9]

The dead boy's maternal grandfather was the first of the family to see the photo of his eleven-year-old grandson, Andy. The grandfather had picked up a paper at his motel where he was staying during a visit to his daughter's home in a semirural area southeast of Seattle. What the photo did not show were the bodies of Andy's father and his nine-year-old brother, Mike. All three had been asphyxiated by volcanic ash that carpeted their campsite, four and one-half miles west of the mountain.[10]

National columnist Bob Greene has passed the humaneness test more than once. Back in 1982 when seven people died in Chicago from taking Tylenol capsules that had been poisoned with cyanide, people in Chicago panicked. It didn't help any that police seemed to be getting nowhere in their search for the murderer. (In fact, at this writing, that murderer is still at large.) So it was in that atmosphere that Greene was asked by the FBI to help them capture the killer. John Douglas, a top criminal-behavior analyst for the FBI, told Greene that one of the things multiple murderers had in common was that they became intensely curious about their victims once they were made to think of them in human terms. He asked Greene if he'd considered doing a column on the Tylenol case.

Greene's reply was that he saw a great story in the Kellerman couple whose twelve-year-old daughter – their only child – had been the youngest victim of the Tylenol killer, but Mr. and Mrs. Kellerman had declined to talk to reporters. The agents thought they could persuade the Kellermans to talk to Greene. If the interview worked, the FBI planned to place the Kellerman house and Mary Kellerman's grave under twenty-four-hour surveillance in the hope that Greene's column would attract the killer to take a look at either site.

Greene went along with the plan. The Kellermans also went along, hoping with the FBI that Greene might help smoke out the murderer of their child. The column he wrote about the interview was moving and cleverly baited with the Kellerman's exact address, which copy editors at his home base, the *Chicago Tribune,* kept trying to get him to remove. He couldn't tell them why he wanted the exact address left in. But after some months went by and the FBI trap failed, Greene wrote about what he had done. At one point in his confessional column, he said:

> I have my own questions about the propriety of all this. As jour-
> nalists, we are supposed to be independent agents. If this episode
> were to appear in an ethics of journalism textbook, I do not know how
> I might react to it. It is one thing to say that a reporter should never
> cooperate with a law-enforcement agency; it is quite another, when
> seven people have been poisoned to death in the area where you live,
> to say that no, you will not help.[11]

In another column in *Esquire* magazine, Greene argued for compassionate interviewing. Since almost none of the people he interviews ever asks not to be named, Greene says he suggests it if the topic they discussed is sensitive or potentially embarrassing. The interviewee is often surprised when he suggests not printing his or her name, Greene adds, because one of the tricks he uses is "to make an interview subject feel so comfortable and so warm that he cannot conceive of being betrayed by this nice fellow who is asking the questions and making the notes." Greene continues:

> As often as not, though, the person I'm with has never been
> interviewed before. He is wary at first; it takes a while to make him
> understand that this is not a surgical procedure. There are tricks to
> that, too; I will stumble around in my conversation. I will make my
> questions sound exceedingly dumb; if he is having a few too many
> drinks, I will drink right along with him. I may or may not be a likable
> person in real life, but I can be a likable person in an interview
> situation; it's just another trick I have learned.
> So at the end of our talk, . . . chances are he would willingly give
> the okay to use his name. What he doesn't know is that the sight of
> his words and his world in cold print, in front of hundreds of thou-
> sands of strangers, is going to jar him. . . .
> I decided a long time ago in situations like those, I had the obli-
> gation to help protect a person even if he didn't know enough to
> protect himself.[12]

Mike Feinsilber, Washington news editor for the AP, shares Bob Greene's concern. "Sometimes I'll tell some innocent person I'm interviewing, 'Don't tell me anything you don't want in the newspaper,'" Feinsilber explains. "I don't like to take advantage of someone's inexperience in dealing with reporters." Feinsilber also often "gives news sources a chance to collect their thoughts." When he has to get a reaction comment from someone, he usually calls the person, explains the situation, and then offers to call back in ten minutes or so for a comment. "I find I get better information and better quotes that way, and people appreciate it," Feinsilber adds.[13]

"Compassion is basic to good ethics and good journalism," in the view of Joseph W. Shoquist, journalism dean at the University of South Carolina, who was for years managing editor of the *Milwaukee Journal*. He feels it is important for journalists to have "a regard for people as human beings, not be so hard-nosed about everything, and understand where people are coming from and why they do the things they do."[14]

On Saving Janet's Jimmy. Jimmy lived for almost seven months. He was created on the front page of the *Washington Post* by Janet Cooke — "Jimmy" was what she called the eight-year-old heroin addict she wrote about — and he died almost seven months later when she confessed she had made him up, then turned in her Pulitzer, and left the news business. (An account of this fakery and its aftermath appears in Chapter 7.) The most compelling of the many ethical issues raised by the fabrication, in the minds of some observers, is the issue of whether the *Post* should not have tried to help poor Jimmy instead of turning him into a front-page tearjerker.

The two ethical issues that received the most attention right after the fakery was disclosed had to do with the deception itself and the use of anonymous sources (pseudonyms for fictitious people, as it turned out in this case). But to Charles B. Seib, retired ombudsman for the *Post,* the more serious question was: "Why were the *Post* editors so willing to let Jimmy die?" Seib notes that the massive postmortem *Post* ombudsman William L. Green, Jr., did on the matter after the *Post* returned the 1981 Pulitzer Prize the story had won made no mention of any concern for Jimmy. Green's report had lots to say about "the editors' enthusiasm over the story," Seib wrote in *Presstime*. "There was deep concern for Cooke's safety" after she claimed that Jimmy's dope-dealing guardian had threatened her life. "But not a thought for Jimmy."[15]

Seib said a *Post* editor told him privately, before Cooke admitted the story was phony, that if he had it to do over again, he would handle the story differently. "Before publishing the story, he would put pressure on Jimmy's mother to get the child into treatment," Seib said the editor told him. "The *Post* could have footed the bill, he said. There would have been no need to bring in the authorities." If the *Post* editor had done that, "if he had allowed a humanitarian instinct to rise briefly above his enthusiasm for a smashing story," Seib wrote, "there is a good possibility that he would have uncovered the deception and the story would have died aborning."

Seib is not alone in his feeling that the *Post* should have tried to help Jimmy, assuming that he did exist. Thomas J. Bray, then associate editor of the editorial page of the *Wall Street Journal,* asked, "Why didn't the *Post* scrap the story and insist that the reporter report this pathetic case to the authorities? Was the story in this instance really more important than 'Jimmy'?"[16] John Troan, retired editor of the *Pittsburgh Press,* wondered why somebody at the *Post* had not said, "Hey, let's get this kid out of his horrible predicament, get him the help he needs – and then run the story. That way we might not only win a prize but – even more important – save a life."[17] John Bull, assistant to the executive editor of the *Philadelphia Inquirer,* believes that "the real problem with the Janet Cooke story was the *Post*'s insensitivity to the life of the child. When everybody said please tell us who he is, we want to save his life, the *Post* arrogantly went into its bunker of confidential sources and First Amendment, and . . . the poor kid . . . could have died for all anybody at the *Post* cared."[18]

Bill Green, now back at Duke University after serving a year as *Post* ombudsman, claimed the "*Post* was under siege for four or five days after 'Jimmy's World' was published. It was under siege not because the story was challenged, but because the community was convulsed with feeling about the boy himself. 'Let's save the boy! How dare you play God!' they shouted at us." Green said he tried to explain in a column why the *Post* felt it could not name the boy, why Janet Cooke's promise of anonymity had to be kept.[19]

Benjamin C. Bradlee, executive editor of the *Post,* acknowledges the legitimacy of the question Seib and others have raised, but he says "we talked ourselves into the position that we were focusing on a social problem and we would do the community more good by focusing on it than by going to the cops with a story we thought would put our reporter in physical jeopardy." Bradlee admits he is uncomfortable with case-by-case ethics on when journalists should report crimes they learn about to the police.[20]

In its overall investigation of the *Post*'s counterfeit, the late National News Council looked into the question of whether authorities should or should not have been told who "Jimmy" was. The council report quoted Robert Woodward, then assistant managing editor in charge of the metro staff, as saying that the *Post* had been wrong in deciding to go with the Jimmy story instead of telling authorities about him. The *Post* was in a "morally untenable position," having witnessed a crime and saying "to hell with" the eight-year-old victim, Woodward told council investigators. The council commented on this issue in its report:

> Neither the complaint nor the ombudsman's report addressed what the Council believes to be a pivotal issue in this case: the human concern that a journalist as citizen ought to have for an 8-year-old child whose life is being criminally endangered. The Council's investigation shows that there was no adequate discussion among *Post* editors of a question that admittedly presents an uncomfortable dilemma for news organizations—whether to fulfill their obligations as citizens and report the crime to the police or to stand on the principle that it is the journalist's obligation to publish the story to call attention to a social problem. The Council regrets that even after the story was published, the *Post*'s editors failed to try to help the mortally endangered child they believed to exist.[21]

Journalists seem to have learned many lessons from the "Jimmy's World" case. It might be hoped that one of them is the lesson of compassion—that it is all right to act like a human being even in a business that worships independence, noninvolvement, and dispassion.

When Lives Are at Stake. Most editors in recent years have been willing to cooperate with police when asked to hold up publicity that might put a life or lives in danger. In cases of kidnappings, for example, the news media are often asked to delay their stories so that the kidnappers will assume that police or the FBI have not been called into the case. Authorities believe that if publicity is delayed, they have a better chance of securing the safe release of the kidnapped person or persons.

The famous Patty Hearst kidnapping in 1974 brought just such a request from authorities to news media in the San Francisco Bay area. All of them held off their stories for twelve and one-half hours, except the Oakland *Tribune,* where publisher William F. Knowland insisted on printing the story. He told his editors that this was no ordinary kidnapping, that too many people had heard the gunfire when Hearst was abducted, and that there was no way of keeping such big news quiet. Afterward journalists joined police in condemning the *Tribune* for being the only news medium in that area to print the story during the blackout.[22]

When the APME Professional Standards Committee asked 328 editors if they agreed with San Francisco area media acceding to delay publicity, 260 said they agreed, 40 disagreed, and 28 were not sure. The AP was one of the news organizations that held up its Patty Hearst kidnapping story at the request of police and the FBI, which brought a protest from one of its prominent members, Robert Haiman, then executive editor of the *St. Petersburg Times*. Haiman argued that the press should have "learned a lesson from the *New York Times*'s unfortunate decision to suppress news of the Bay of Pigs at the request of President Kennedy" in the early sixties. "The Kennedy appeal was made to the integrity of the *Times* with a heavy foot on the pedal of responsibility, ethics and concern for the lives of the 'brave invaders,'" Haiman added. "The *Times* weighed that and agreed not to publish. Afterward, both the *Times* and the White House wished they had done otherwise." This brought a reply from AP president Boccardi, who defended what the AP did in the Hearst case as "the ethical, responsible thing to do. To have rushed out in a life be damned headline splurge would have been in my view, nothing short of irresponsibility on our part."[23]

Boccardi's views would have found agreement among several Florida newspaper editors and broadcast news directors who held up the name of a four-year-old kidnap victim for three days. FBI and police credited the news media with helping them save young David Rattray of Vero Beach and capture his kidnapper. When reporters first learned of the kidnapping, police asked them not to run any stories for fear they might spook the kidnapper and perhaps cause him to kill the boy and run. Everybody went along with that request. On the second day, reporters on their own were able to get some details of the abduction and learn that the boy's father was a prominent local physician. The FBI added to what the reporters knew by releasing a photograph of the four-year-old and a description, but agents asked that his name not be used. This was a tough one, being asked to publicize a photo without a name, but authorities persuaded editors and TV news directors that if the name were publicized, every "kook and crazy" in South Florida would make crank calls to the family and interfere with ransom instructions from the kidnapper. So the second-day stories did not specifically identify the kidnapped boy. On the third day, when the kidnapper called the doctor, the call was monitored and a meeting was arranged at a place staked out by the police. The kidnapper was arrested, and the boy was found safe in the kidnapper's car trunk.

Going along with the embargo "was the responsible thing to do," said Bill Dunn, managing editor of the *Orlando Sentinel*. "There seemed to be no public interest . . . in printing the name."[24]

An even tougher embargo was asked of news media in El Paso, Texas, when two boys, ages two and four, were abducted from their townhouse. Because the kidnappers told the family they would kill their children if any stories about them were printed or broadcast in the first thirty-six hours, the FBI asked news media to hold back for a day and a half. All El Paso media, including the Associated Press, which has a bureau there, complied. All local media also went along when the FBI asked to extend the news blackout. Two and a half days after the kidnapping, the embargo was lifted when the kidnappers told the family they could find the two boys in an abandoned car across the river in Juarez, Mexico. They were O.K.

"With the FBI telling us that two lives might be at stake, it was an easy decision not to run the story," Paula Moore, co-managing editor of the *El Paso Times,* told her readers in an article about the media blackout. "We're not accustomed to withholding news from the community for any reason, but people's lives are certainly more important than an immediate story. We knew we could tell the full story later."[25]

A dispassion/compassion decision confronted editors of the *Dallas Times Herald* when a man called one Saturday night to threaten suicide if an exposé about him appeared in Sunday morning's paper. The caller was Norman John Rees, a sixty-nine-year-old retired oil engineer who had lived for a period in Dallas but was now living in Connecticut. The article to which he objected revealed that he had been a Soviet spy for thirty years, the last four of which he was a double agent, spying also for the FBI. The Rees story had been developed from various sources over a three-month period, at the end of which Rees was asked for comment. In interviews by telephone and in person when Rees had voluntarily flown to Dallas and submitted to polygraph tests, he had admitted having spied for the Soviets. That fact was also verified by the FBI.

The day before the exposé was scheduled to be published, Rees called the *Times Herald* and asked if the story was going to be printed and would he be identified. "When he was told that he would be identified, he said that such a disclosure left him no choice but to commit suicide," then executive editor Kenneth P. Johnson reported. "In this instance, it was decided that the story could not be suppressed even in the face of Mr. Rees's threat." The next day, Rees's wife found her husband's body. He had committed suicide by shooting himself in the head.[26]

A similar refusal to give in to compassion is seen in the attitude of many news executives toward journalists becoming mediators in prison uprisings. Although two journalists in recent years have served as mediators in prison riots—Tom Wicker of the *New York Times* at Attica prison in New York State and Chuck Stone of the *Philadelphia Daily News* at the state prison in Graterford, Pennsylvania—many journalists disapprove of that practice. The National News Council surveyed forty-five newspaper editors and broadcast directors on that question and found that only nine had no reservations about journalists serving as peacemakers in prison riots, the holding of hostages, or similar situations. Twenty-seven opposed such participation, and nine had varying degrees of reluctance on the subject.[27]

PITY THE SHOOTERS

News photographers, both still and motion pictures, get a lot of grief for their apparent devotion to a convention that says, "Get the pictures, let editors decide what to do with them later." The basis for this approach is that photographers on the scene ought to be visual information collectors; if they worry too much about the ethics or propriety of taking this picture or that, they are apt to come back with no pictures at all. Another basis of the practice that doesn't get discussed very often is that editors don't trust their photographers.

Despite obvious improvements recently in the status of news photographers – "shooters," as they are sometimes called – they still don't get the respect they deserve in most news organizations. They have a bad image problem, for one thing. The picture of news photographers that many people carry in their heads is one of pushy, uncaring bullies who interrupt public meetings, shove cameras in people's faces, and get in the way of people. The nickname "Animal" assigned to the photographer in the old "Lou Grant" television show seemed appropriate to many observers in and out of journalism. We should understand, however, that it is editors and TV news directors who order those pictures that sometimes require their shooters to be unduly aggressive and disruptive.

Many news photographers like to be called "photojournalists." That word is variously defined as a photographer so skilled that his or her work dominates the words when they are published, as was the case with the stories the great photographers used to tell in the old *Look* and *Life* magazines. It also has been used to mean a news photographer who also writes the news. That latter definition must have been on the minds of scholars who did the two works that have provided us with the statistical population of journalists working for American news media. John W. C. Johnstone, Edward J. Slawski, and William W. Bowman in 1971 and David H. Weaver and G. Cleveland Wilhoit in 1982 counted only those photographers who were also reporters in their surveys of full-time editorial employees of U.S. news media. That leaves out a lot of skilled photographers or photojournalists whose pictures have illuminated and helped make sense out of untold numbers of news situations. It also reflects a view of photographers as being mere technicians, a label that just as aptly describes the work of some newspaper reporters and editors who shovel news into their newspapers with a minimum of thought and care. And many of the people who do what news writing there is at some local TV stations produce work that seems to have been done by technicians rather than journalists. The Johnstone and Weaver studies strike me as unfair and less reliable as statistical studies because of this omission (and the omission of network broadcast journalists, as well).[28]

The real trouble with the convention that says photojournalists are supposed to take pictures, not judge them, is in the way some photographers have interpreted it. Bill Murphy, whose story is told in the opening of this chapter, was adhering to that convention. He, as all good news photographers are supposed to do, jumped from his car with camera in hand. If you take your job seriously in photo news work, you're supposed to all but sleep with your camera. But there are times when the world would be a better place perhaps if photographers did not interpret their charge so narrowly and decided instead *not* to take photographs at a given moment. Two obvious times when photos should not be taken are in moments of private grief, when, for example, a family is around a casket or receiving the news of a dead service man, and in accidents and other tragic situations calling for the photographer to help people rather than photograph them.

Many photographers, of course, do not see themselves as mere robots, shooting whatever some boss has assigned. William Sanders, 1986 president of the National Press Photographers Association, goes along with the general idea that a photographer has to shoot the pictures before any decision about their propriety can be made. "But . . . the editor who made the assignment is not there, and he doesn't know what the situation is and what's happening," Sanders says. "To that extent, the photographer has to use some judgment." Sanders, who is a photo supervisor at the *News* and *Sun-Sentinel* in Ft. Lauderdale, Florida, emphasizes that he "would give up a picture to help somebody in trouble" because "you're a member of the human race first and a journalist second."[29]

Two other photojournalists interviewed for this book said they had taken first-aid training because sometimes they get to accident scenes ahead of everyone else. One is Linda Wheeler, reporter-photographer for the *Washington Post,* who claims she always gets her picture, but she also tries to help people if they need it. "The picture is in the paper only one day," she adds, "and I have to live with myself every day." Wheeler says that when she covers news of accidents, fires, and other tragedies, "I try to turn things around. I try to put myself in the victims' shoes and try to be very gentle."[30]

Bob Gay, a photographer who worked for three different dailies in West Virginia, took paramedic training and instruction in law enforcement and firefighting, "just in case." He explains that at the time he was "working in a remote area" and felt he ought to be "completely prepared." Besides, "if you know what a paramedic has to do to keep someone alive, then you won't get in his way. And if you know what a 357 Magnum will do, you'll have a hell of a lot more respect for an officer when he has to draw one." Gay has never "done anything as dramatic as saving someone's life," but a couple of times at bad accidents he has helped paramedics extricate victims from cars. He has held intravenous bags and helped load people into ambulances. When he did that, of course, he had to put his camera aside. "A human life is a hell of a lot more important than a picture," Gay declares. "Some people can stand there and say, 'It's just not my job,' but I can't."[31]

Photographers covering wars are often witnesses to bloody horrors, many of which they photograph, bringing back pictures that ought to, but don't seem to, end war forever. The best of these visual chroniclers are not without humaneness, however. Liz Nakahara, in a remarkable article in the *Washington Post,* tells of the pictures that some of the top photographers in journalism didn't take. One of these top photographers is Eddie Adams, who covered the Vietnam War for the Associated Press. He recalls pulling his camera away from the face of an eighteen-year-old marine whose "wide, glassy eyes" showed his intense fear. "I'll never forget what was going through my mind – that my face looked exactly like his," Adams said in explaining why he could not bring himself to push his shutter button. "I was just too embarrassed for his sake and mine, plus the picture could have labeled that kid for the rest of his life. I always try to put myself in the other person's place."

Robin Moyer of the Black Star agency told Nakahara of the time he accompanied 150,000 malnourished Cambodian refugees as they listlessly staggered across the Thai border. "I saw people die of malaria in front of my camera," Moyer said. "Bullets killing people is one thing. But watching people die of malnutrition is much more terrible." At one point Moyer put aside his camera to help carry people out of the hills. Don McCullin of the *Sunday Times* in London did the same thing when he was photographing guerrillas in El Salvador. He and a *Newsweek* reporter asked guerrilla leaders, victorious for the moment, for permission to carry wounded government soldiers to a hospital truck. McCullin said he'll never forget the last soldier he picked up that day, one who was bloody and horrendously wounded by a bullet that had shattered his mouth and jaw. The photographer went on the truck with this wounded man and carried him into the hospital when orderlies refused to touch him.

Patrick Chauvel, French free-lancer, described photographers in Beirut in 1982 when Israel invaded Lebanon. "One guy would cry, another would open his camera and throw out his film, another would go on working and still another would walk away." Chauvel is not sure he agrees with the contention that "the professional (photographer) is the guy who works." But "I know I prefer to have as a friend the guy who walks away."[32]

Another problem for photographers, even those with compassion for other people, is their visibility. It is difficult, particularly for TV photographers with their videotape cameras, to hide their identity the way pencil reporters can when covering certain tense situations, such as a civil disturbance. People tend to perform for the cameras when they know they're around and that can result in pictures that don't depict reality. Smart photographers don't let themselves be conned, but TV newscasts still abound with visuals of demonstrators, pickets, and the like who are absent or listless until the cameras come in view. The tendency to attract performers is only part of the visibility problem for photographers, however. Their gear also makes it difficult if not impossible to go to someone's aid – the way reporter Christine Wolff did as described earlier in this chapter – and still take their pictures. They have to put their cameras aside, as many have been willing to do, and that risks not doing their work as photographers. Shooters do not have easy jobs.

Shoot-out in Alabama. A small television station in Alabama shocked the nation when it sent two of its photographers to film a man setting fire to himself. The two photographers for WHMA-TV in Anniston were dispatched to nearby Jacksonville, Alabama, after a man had called the station four times late one evening to say that he was going to torch himself to protest unemployment. The station notified Jacksonville police. The caller, who turned out to be a thirty-seven-year-old out-of-work roofer who had apparently been drinking, asked for a reporter and photographer to come to the town square. WHMA news director Phillip D. Cox says two photographers were sent instead because none of the station's three full-time reporters was working when the calls came in. One of the photographers, Gary Harris, an eighteen-year-old college student, was only a part-timer. He apparently was to play reporter to accompany full-time photographer Ronald Simmons, thirty, who had four to five years experience in news photography, according to Cox. Cox, it must be noted, had a very small news staff.

When the WHMA camera crew climbed out of their car in Jacksonville, the unemployed roofer approached, doused himself with charcoal starter fluid, and applied a lighted match. Simmons filmed the horror for several seconds before his young partner, Harris, rushed forward and tried to beat out the flames with his small reporter's notebook. But the flames got stronger and were not put out until the burning man raced across the square where a volunteer firefighter smothered the fire with an extinguisher. The man survived but he spent eight painful weeks in a hospital being treated for serious burns.

Cox says his photographers tried to stop the apparently drunken man from setting himself afire, but he warned them off. "He said 'Stay back!' several times," Cox maintains. "It's very distinguishable on the audio track of the tape." Interviewed by telephone a few months after the March 1983 incident, Cox is also miffed that much of the criticism of his station was based on the assumption that the station broadcast the full tape taken that night. Actually, no scenes of the man on fire were shown on WHMA, he says, but only scenes of the aftermath of the incident.[33]

The question of whether a TV station should show such shocking scenes is an important one, of course, but it is a small ethical question compared to: Should the photographers have done more to stop the self-immolation even if that meant not getting their pictures? Should the crew have been sent there in the first place—"creating the news," as the *New York Times* put it in a critical editorial?[34]

Cox seems satisfied on both counts. "Our people did what was expected of them," he says. And he has no regrets about dispatching the camera crew that night. The two photographers were not punished. Cox does say that the incident has caused serious discussion at his station and that a copy of CBS News Standards has been distributed to the staff. Although like most TV stations WHMA does not have its own written code of ethics for its news department, Cox claims that he and his staff have become more aware of the ethical guidelines in the recently acquired CBS code as well as in the codes of the Radio-Television News Directors Association and the National Association of Broadcasters.

All three TV networks picked up copies of WHMA's tapes and telecast footage of the man torching himself. Their stories, as well as those in other national news media, were not about the torching incident so much as they were about the ethics of what the Alabama station did that night.

The Alabama incident was widely discussed in the news business, and it gave additional ammunition to critics who decry the low level of sensitivity among TV journalists. There's some evidence as well that the callousness displayed that night in Alabama has helped raise the sensitivity level of news photographers in general. One photographer who helped save the life of a burning man in Middletown, Ohio, specifically mentioned the Alabama case in explaining his own response. What Greg Mahany, photographer for the *Middletown Journal,* did was to ignore his camera and grab a coat when an explosion in an auto body shop instantly engulfed a mechanic in flames. Then he beat out the flames so that the mechanic escaped with only second-degree burns over about 30 percent of his body. The twenty-six-year-old photographer said afterward that when he read about the Alabama incident, he "thought it was pretty weird," adding: "After the situation I was involved in, I don't know how you could continue filming. . . . That's what ethics are—you don't just stand by."[35] And after a *Sante Fe New Mexican* photographer helped rescue a family from a burning semitrailer before he took a single shot, he said his actions were more typical than the stereotype of a news photographer ignoring victims just to get a good shot. "I think that's a stigma we're kind of stuck with," said the photographer, Mike Heller.[36]

What those two Alabama TV photographers did reminded some of the shocking photos that came out of the Vietnam War in 1963, photos of Buddhist monks burning themselves to death as a protest on the streets of Saigon. Two of the photographers who took those photos have defended what they did. Malcolm W. Browne of the AP said shortly after taking the photos that it never occurred to him to try to stop the immolations. "I have always felt that a newsman's duty is to observe and report the news, not try to change it. . . . As a matter of duty, I photographed the whole horrible sequence . . . and relayed the pictures and story as fast as possible into the Associated Press network. It is difficult to conceive of any newsman acting otherwise."[37] Browne's AP colleague, Peter Arnett, admitted in 1971 that he "could have prevented that immolation by rushing at him and kicking the gasoline away," but he added, "As a human being I wanted to, as a reporter I couldn't."[38]

Virtually no one argued with Browne or Arnett in their rationalizations back in the 1960s. Photos of monks committing suicide by fire were widely used in American news media. But that was part of a war and the photos perhaps were important in explaining that terrible conflict. The attitude toward taking and using such photos seems to be changing, however. Today, most journalists probably would question Browne and Arnett about whether the presence of their cameras did not inspire the protesting suicides and whether they should not have tried to stop them; and it is inconceivable that such pictures would get the widespread play they got in the 1960s. Slowly, American journalism is moving away from pure dispassion to an admission of compassion as a basis of journalistic behavior.

STANDARDS HARD TO COME BY

The matter of when and if journalists should show compassion toward the people and the news they deal with is virtually ignored in all of the codes or operating standards examined for this study. That is not surprising. Compassion, in addition to being a word that many macho journalists do not even like to hear, does not easily translate into a standard or a guideline. ("Be compassionate in the following circumstances. . . . Don't be compassionate in the following circumstances. . . .") Also it is hard to legislate a human emotion like compassion, which comes easier to some people than it does to others.

The *Washington Post* touches on the matter of journalists not getting involved in what they are reporting – the dispassion side of the dispassion/compassion issue – in its deskbook guideline on the reporter's role: "Although it has become increasingly difficult for this newspaper and for the press generally to do so since Watergate, reporters should make every effort to remain in the audience, to stay off the stage, to report history, not to make history."[39]

At the same time that there is a lack of written guidelines and standards suggesting that compassion might be acceptable on occasion, there is great concern among journalists about the image of the news business. Various fears about how the press is perceived are often expressed – that the press is arrogant and aloof from people, that journalists try to set themselves up as a privileged class, that journalists do not really care about anyone or anything as they get their stories and move on. Such images may be undeserved, but many journalists believe they already exist in the minds of the public or could be put there quickly by the continuation of certain bad practices in the business.

Although compassion cannot be turned on and off like a faucet, encouraging more of it in news work and presentation might improve the public's perception of the entire enterprise. It also might improve the perception of news work by journalists themselves, many of whom seem to get cynical at an early age. The folklore of the news business is mostly hard nosed, Humphrey Bogart–like. Any feelings of sympathy or tenderness are better expressed off duty.

Perhaps it is time in news work to start honoring compassion more and cynicism less.

13

Responsibility, Accountability

"Don't you think we're carrying our new corrections policy a little far?"

Assume you are a doctor practicing general medicine in a medium-sized city. You enter the doctor's lounge of the hospital just after checking on your patients and are greeted by a fellow general practitioner who says, "Now we know how you can afford that new house!" Then he shows you an article in that morning's local newspaper reporting on fees charged by various medical specialists in the area. Your name is listed at the top of a column of general practitioners for charging $35 for an initial office visit. Your actual fee schedule is $15 for the first office visit, and $12 for each subsequent visit, with slight additional charges for longer revisits.

Does this mistake upset you? Or are you inclined to shrug it off? If you are upset, what do you intend to do about it? Will it do any good to complain to the paper?

When this happened to Dr. Gary A. Hogge, he was angry. He called one of his patients who was an editor of the newspaper, the Louisville *Courier-Journal.* Hogge contends that the editor promised to look into it and get back to him that day, but he did not. When Hogge had not heard from his editor-patient after a week, the doctor called the paper and asked to speak to the reporter whose by-line was on the erroneous article, Robert L. Peirce. Because the reporter was not in just then, Hogge unloaded his complaint on city editor Bill Cox and demanded a retraction. Again he was told that the editor would check into the matter and call him back. But another week passed without a call from the paper. His anger escalating, Hogge called city editor Cox again and was told flatly that no retraction was going to be printed because the article was based on Medicare statistics. Hogge said that after an exchange of some unpleasantries, Cox suggested he talk to reporter Peirce, which Hogge did. The doctor told the reporter that he should have checked the Medicare figures with the doctors—at least those at the top of the price range—because such statistics are "notoriously unreliable." Hogge said Peirce's response "floored me." The reporter "told me (1) he didn't have time to check his figures and (2) even if he had checked with me, he wouldn't have changed anything in the article. It was by now apparent that the *Courier-Journal* was tired of fooling with this insignificant country doc who had the effrontery to challenge its omniscience," Hogge said.[1]

When he asked Peirce whether he had any recourse other than legal action, the doctor said he was surprised when the reporter gave him the name of the then still active National News Council. Nowhere in the *Medical Economics* article he wrote about this experience does Hogge report any cognizance on his part or that of the *Courier-Journal* people he talked to of that newspaper's ombudsman, whose job it is to deal with complaints like his. This despite the regular publication by the Louisville newspapers of the name and address of both their news ombudsman and, at that time, the news council.

The *Courier-Journal*'s news ombudsman then, Frank Hartley, did get involved when Hogge complained to the news council. Hartley investigated the complaint and in his response to the news council supported the article and the two staffers who had dealt with the physician. Hartley found that (1) the paper had hired an outside computer firm to double-check its own study of the Medicare printouts; (2) Peirce had interviewed at random 60 of the 400 physicians listed; and (3) when Peirce found out that charges for an initial visit can vary because of billing inconsistencies, he inserted that explanation at the top of the list of doctors and their charges, directly above Hogge's name.

News council investigators found that Hogge did not deal directly with Medicare and instead asked his patients to file for whatever reimbursement they were due. The council suggested that since Hogge's "billing form was less than ideal," some of his patients might have submitted blanket fees instead of itemized ones, which would have skewed his Medicare "profile." The council report said, however:

The *Courier-Journal* listing was accurate insofar as the Medicare computer records listed Dr. Hogge's charges. What seemed essential was a direct check with Dr. Hogge and all others listed in the top rank of fees recorded, the most sensitive area in the lists. It is clear such a recheck with Dr. Hogge would have brought instant protest and a deeper check. However, the newspaper opted for random checking. Moreover, the newspaper's statement seeking to clarify differentials was not fully informative. The *Courier-Journal*'s motivation was sound and the paper did publish a patient's letter supporting Dr. Hogge's view. Nevertheless, Dr. Hogge was done an inadvertent injustice and the complaint is found warranted.[2]

The *Courier-Journal* reported the council's finding on its front page and then executive editor Paul Janensch apologized to the doctor in his column ten days later. Janensch said he accepted the council's decision "without a quibble" and explained that the error "was a collective one and shouldn't be ascribed to a single individual." Hogge said he "was surprised to get anything near this much redress of injustice. It shows that if you're right – and willing – you *can* fight 'bad press' – and even win."[3]

Hogge might not have fared so well – nor been so gratified by the result – if he practiced in a city whose newspapers cared less about providing channels for complaints and machinery for public accountability. The Louisville *Courier-Journal* and the *Louisville Times,* now defunct, were the first newspapers in the country to set up an ombudsman to deal with readers' complaints and had been longtime supporters of the news council. Yet Hogge's complaint sort of fell through the cracks. Janensch admits that it was not well handled "or it wouldn't have gone as far as it did."[4]

News people make mistakes. ("Doctors bury their mistakes," some editor once said. "We print ours.") But news people are also better at making errors than they are at correcting them. Although newspapers and the broadcast media are making much greater efforts these days to admit and correct their mistakes, many errors still go unnoticed or are deliberately swept under the rug. If an error such as the one in the preceding case study can go uncorrected for five months in a newspaper with the reputation for high standards and ethics that the *Courier-Journal* enjoys, then journalism is a long way from being able to claim that it fully and promptly corrects all its mistakes.

Errors are often caused by incompetence or irresponsibility, or both. Whether journalism has more incompetent and irresponsible people than other orders in American life is impossible to determine, but it certainly has its share. This chapter examines some of the incompetence and irresponsibility that has damaged the news business and looks at methods for making media more accountable to the public.

WHY SO MANY ERRORS?

Pollster George Gallup, Jr., found in 1980 that when people were asked what their own experience has been with newspaper reports of things that they knew about personally, about one in three (34 percent) said the paper had gotten the facts wrong. The 47 percent who said newspaper reports they knew about personally were accurate was much lower than the 70 percent who replied that way in a 1958 poll. Gallup also found that people "who feel the press has been inaccurate in treating news items relating to their own lives are more likely to favor stricter curbs on the press than are those who feel the facts were dealt with accurately."[5]

There are all sorts of explanations for inaccuracies in news reports. Some are caused by carelessness – some reporter or editor not taking that extra step to check a fact or a quote. Some mistakes come out of ignorance – the journalists processing the news report lack the knowledge needed to recognize errors or to prevent themselves from making them. Deadline pressures can cause mistakes. News sources sometimes give out "bum" information and reporters and editors are not sharp enough to challenge or check it. Some subjects journalists have to deal with are so complex and fuzzy that errors can easily occur in the process of simplifying these subjects for mass audiences.

Another cause of errors is the increasing tendency of journalists to isolate themselves physically and personally from their communities. Walking into the offices of the larger newspapers and broadcast stations today is like visiting your cousin in prison. Because of bomb threats and other problems with "crazies," virtually all urban news organizations have hired security guards to protect them. Unfortunately, they also protect them from people who may have news and information but who never get into the fortress. Once while waiting in the lobby of a big TV station for the person with whom I had an appointment to come out and claim me, I listened to an elderly woman trying to explain how a drowning the day before was similar to some previous and suspicious one she had witnessed. The guard patiently discouraged the woman from pursuing the matter and escorted her to the door, apparently judging her, on the basis of his vast news experience, to be just another crazy.

Newspapers and broadcast stations in areas that are less urban can achieve the same isolation from their audiences by locating themselves out in the country where land is usually cheaper. The old-fashioned newspaper office on Main Street is disappearing, for all sorts of economic reasons. Valuable contacts between people and journalists are also being lost.

Isolation has also resulted from tougher conflict-of-interest policies in most news organizations. Most journalists today are supposed to be very careful about the people they hobnob with outside their newsrooms, and some solve that problem by spending most of their leisure time with their families and other journalists. Isolation may prevent conflicts of interest, but it does little to increase journalists' sensitivity, understanding, and knowledge about the people and things they report on.

Carelessness. Carelessness or thoughtlessness causes many errors in the processing of news. Accurately reflecting in a news story what someone said or thought is never easy, and unless it's done with care, serious misinterpretation can result. That's what Colorado Governor Richard D. Lamm thought happened to him when the *Denver Post* broke the widely used story that quoted the governor as saying that elderly people with terminal illnesses had a "duty to die." The remark was the interpretation of a *Post* reporter who covered and taped Lamm as he answered questions at an informal session with lawyers in Denver. The *Denver Post* story said in its opening:

> Elderly people who are terminally ill have a "duty to die and get out of the way" instead of trying to prolong their lives through artificial means, Gov. Dick Lamm said Tuesday.
>
> People who die without having their lives artificially prolonged, Lamm said, are similar to "leaves falling off a tree and forming humus for other plants to grow up."
>
> "You got a duty to die and to get out of the way. Let the other society, our kids, build a reasonable life," the governor told a meeting of the Colorado Health Lawyers Association at St. Joseph's Hospital.

Senior citizens groups and others throughout the country were outraged when they read this story, distributed by the Associated Press without checking out its accuracy. So was the governor, who claimed he was quoting a philosopher and that he did not urge terminally ill oldsters to get out of the way, but instead urged society to take a harder look at life-extending machines. The *Post,* standing by its news story but wanting to be fair to Lamm, loaned him the reporter's tape of the session, the only one made. The transcription of the pertinent section of the tape, made by the governor's office and sent to major news organizations, read:

> The real question gets into, then, high-technology medicine. We have a million and a half heart attacks a year. Every year in the United States we have a million and a half heart attacks. Six hundred thousand of them die. How many Barney Clarks can we afford? You

know we at least ought to be talking about that. . . .

A terrific article that I've read, one of the philosophers of our time, I think, is a guy named Leon Kass. Has anybody seen his stuff? He's just terrific. In *The American Scholar* last year he wrote an article called "The Case for Mortality," where essentially he said we have a duty to die. It's like if leaves fall off a tree, forming the humus for the other plants to grow out. We've got a duty to die and get out of the way with all of our machines and artificial hearts and everything else like that and let the other society, our kids, build a reasonable life.

The *Post* published a correction on its use of "you" instead of the "we" the governor used, but it did not correct the reference to "elderly people" because its reporter said the governor had made several allusions to the aged in his remarks. Over at the rival *Rocky Mountain News,* however, ombudsman Mal Deans wrote that the governor had been treated badly. Deans said the original stories, first in the *Post* and then in his own paper and others throughout the country, erred in reporting that Lamm was talking about the elderly. "Had these remarks received careful attention and been paraphrased accurately, the furor never would have developed," Deans wrote. "The focus on the elderly was strictly a media creation that has continued unabated."[6]

Mechanical problems took the rap when the *Washington Post* failed to run a crucial story in a series of reports from St. Louis on a five-day trial involving Senator Thomas Eagleton. His niece and her attorney were being tried on charges of extortion. The *Post* omitted the story on the day that Eagleton's niece and her attorney admitted that the allegation of homosexuality with which they had threatened the senator was totally false. The omission was blamed on a computer error, compounded by the fact that the *Post* was at the time changing over to a new printing system. But it was also a human error by a makeup editor who should have noticed that the story was "dummied," scheduled to appear on a particular page, according to William L. Green, Jr., *Post* ombudsman at the time. Green later wrote in his column that the omission deprived readers in the city where Eagleton spends most of his professional life "of the words of his accusers that would have documented the Senator's denials. It should not have happened."[7]

The *Post* got egg on its face again when it dug into the background of John W. Hinckley, Jr., the young man accused of trying to assassinate President Reagan in 1981. In its 10,000-word report put together by eight reporters was a 31-word passage, right after a description of Hinckley's purchase of handguns during the eighteen months he was a student at Texas Tech University in Lubbock. The passage read: "A penchant for guns hardly strikes anyone as ominous in free-wheeling Lubbock, where some university students carry guns to class and the pistol-packing frontier tradition runs deep and long."[8]

The good people of Lubbock took exception to that picture. Their complaints spurred ombudsman Green to discover that one of the reporters on the *Post* article, Chip Brown, had based the offensive passage on material he lifted – without independent verification – from a similar article about Hinckley in the *Philadelphia Inquirer* three days earlier.

Donald C. Drake, who wrote the *Inquirer* story that the *Post* reporter used as his source, believes that although his story did say that guns were common in Lubbock, "it didn't give the sense that Lubbock was a wild town, but quite the opposite." Drake calls attention to this section in the *Inquirer* story:

> An official in the Lubbock office of the Federal Bureau of Alcohol, Tobacco and Firearms confirmed yesterday that records showed that Hinckley had purchased at least six handguns over 18 months from various Lubbock pawnshops.
>
> "Should that have raised a warning signal somewhere?"
>
> "Naw," the official said. "We have people that buy a hundred or two hundred a year around here."
>
> Rolf Gordhamer, who directs psychological testing and counseling at Texas Tech, said it was quite common for students to carry weapons at the college."[9]

Drake sees not only a difference in tone between this segment of the *Inquirer* story and that in the *Post,* but "a small but important difference in the actual information reported." Carrying "weapons at the college," as the *Inquirer* said, is substantially different from the *Post* statement that "students carry guns to class," Drake points out. "The thought of a student carrying a pistol in a classroom is much more disturbing to me, as a reader in a northeastern city, than the image of them carrying a gun outside on campus for target shooting or some other sporting activity," Drake adds. The *Inquirer* further quotes Gordhamer as observing:

> "Seriously, this is frontierland. People do have guns. Their grandparents were pioneers. There are a lot of small towns and isolation, and change comes very slowly. People shoot rattlesnakes and coyotes and," he paused to laugh, "trespassers."
>
> "Still," Gordhamer said, "the campus is placid, the calmest, quietest place I've ever seen. Basically, the kids obey authority. They don't protest or march up and down the streets here. They take life pretty easy. They just kind of enjoy it. People out here believe in mother, apple pie and The American Flag."

"As you can see," Drake explains, "the *Inquirer's* picture of Lubbock is much more complex than the one suggested in the segment of the *Post's* story. . . . I think this is a particularly interesting example of how the basic facts in two stories might be the same—Lubbock is a town where guns are common and pioneer independence predominates—but one story, the *Post's*, leaves the impression that Lubbock is the set for a John Wayne movie and the other, the *Inquirer's*, suggests something more like Thornton Wilder's 'Our Town.' "

The *Post* corrected the passage about Lubbock twenty-five days after it ran. The correction said that the article "presented an inaccurate depiction of Texas Tech University and the city in which the university is located, Lubbock. Texas Tech students do not carry guns to class, as the article stated, and the city itself is a quiet town with orderly and law-abiding citizens. There is no 'pistol-packing' tradition in Lubbock, as the article incorrectly implied." The *Post* also carried four letters from Lubbock, all disagreeing with the implications in the *Post* reference to the city and the university.[10]

The Hinckley story also caused an embarrassing error by the AP. The AP's Chicago bureau paid $3,000 to a free-lance photographer for a photograph of "Hinckley" and two other members of the National Socialist Party of America dressed in their neo-Nazi uniforms. The shot was supposedly made at a party demonstration in St. Louis in 1978. But when reporters for the Oklahoma City *Daily Oklahoman* showed the photo to two neo-Nazis they interviewed, the party members said the picture was not of Hinckley. Hinckley's family in Evergreen, Colorado, also said the picture was not of their son. It turned out the uniformed young man in the picture resembled Hinckley but he was really James Gaither Whittom of Shreveport, Louisiana, a former member of the Nazi group. The AP killed the picture two days after it was distributed and had run in many newspapers, and instructed clients to destroy file copies.[11]

Diane Benison, managing editor of the Worcester, Massachusetts, *Evening Gazette,* believes many errors in news reports are caused by "a lack of thought." She tells of one of her reporters, "not an insensitive guy," who wrote in his story about a woman who had been raped that "the woman was not injured." When she questioned him about it, he was not able to see immediately what she objected to. So she asked him to imagine that his wife had been raped and how would he feel if the news story about it said she had not been injured. He got the point.[12]

Ignorance and Inadequate Education. H. L. Mencken took the same dim view of the business that fed him as he did all other orders of American life, with the possible exception of Gibson drinkers. "There are managing editors in the United States, and scores of them," Mencken wrote in the twenties,

> who have never heard of Kant or Johannes Müller and never read the Constitution of the United States; there are city editors who do not know what a symphony is, or a streptococcus, or the Statute of Frauds; there are reporters by the thousand who could not pass the entrance examination for Harvard or Tuskegee, or even Yale. It is this vast and militant ignorance, this widespread and fathomless prejudice against intelligence, that makes American journalism so pathetically feeble and vulgar, and so generally disreputable.[13]

Unfortunately the ignorance Mencken saw in the U.S. journalism of the twenties is still a problem. Errors in news reports, some serious, occur every day because some journalist doesn't have the knowledge or intelligence to get the facts straight. Perhaps it is asking too much of journalists that they have at least above-average knowledge of the many subjects they deal with every working day. But citizens depend on the information they get from the news media to guide them in the decisions they must make at the polling place, the market place, and in their lives in general. Bum information leads to bum decisions.

One important area of journalistic attention that has been unevenly reported because of reporter ignorance is the legal process. David Shaw of the *Los Angeles Times* looked into that problem a few years ago and concluded that such reporting is improving but "media coverage of the nation's legal system is still largely inadequate."[14]

At least some of the blame for inadequate coverage of this important institution has to be placed on lack of knowledge by the reporters covering it. Although an impressive number of top legal system reporters have legal training and even law degrees, the average reporter on the beat has none. Shaw, who interviewed almost 100 attorneys, judges, legal scholars, journalists, and journalism professors, found that most favored some legal training for reporters assigned to this area. Such training "enables a reporter to speak the same, often arcane language as the people he covers, and it also enables him to invite confidences not easily given to non-lawyers—and to provide historical perspective to his daily reportage," Shaw concludes. Several lawyers told Shaw they were "astounded by the number of reporters who accepted what they said—or did not say—without either question or challenge, either out of laziness, ignorance, or a fear of being perceived as ignorant."

Another area in which news sources often complain about journalists' lack of knowledge is business and economics. Although the larger newspapers and network television news departments have beefed up their coverage of business and economics in recent years, "media coverage is often simplistic, careless and cursory," A. Kent MacDougall wrote in the *Los Angeles Times.* But he pointed out that "deliberate distortion" was rare.[15] One of the examples MacDougall used in his prize-winning series on how the media cover business concerned a business story that was interpreted three different ways by three top dailies. It happened when the General Accounting Office (GAO), the investigatory arm of Congress, reported on its investigation into whether American oil producers had deliberately worsened the oil shortage. The *New York Times* headlined its story, "G.A.O. Study Asserts That Oil Companies Worsened Shortage," and reported that American oil companies had aggravated the petroleum shortage in the spring of 1979 by cutting production of crude oil within the United States while imports from Iran were disrupted. But the *Wall Street Journal*'s headline read, "GAO Says Oil Firms Aren't to Be Blamed for Recent Shortage," and its story said GAO had concluded that "there isn't any evidence that the major oil companies created the U.S. oil shortage that occurred after the closing of Iran's oil fields." The *Los Angeles Times* ignored GAO's judgment on oil company culpability; its story emphasized GAO's criticism of Department of Energy actions. Who was right? It was not the *New York Times,* which ran a lengthy correction two days later, saying it had misinterpreted the GAO report.[16]

One explanation for errors in business reporting can be surmised from the experiences of the late Cortland Anderson, who worked as a newspaper journalist and in corporate public relations before becoming director of the School of Journalism at Ohio University. Anderson commented that when he was public relations chief at the New York Telephone Company, "we had to educate reporters seemingly thrown in at the last minute to cover specific complicated rate stories." He recalls how John de Butts, then chairman of American Telephone and Telegraph, terminated an interview with a reporter from "a highly respected publication specializing in business news" when de Butts "discovered the reporter did not know the difference between stocks and bonds." Anderson tells of another case in which a reporter was gathering information from him (as vice-president of the Washington Post Company) to prepare for an interview with Katharine Graham, chairman of the Washington Post Company, for a story on the company's state of business. "In a discussion preceding that interview," Anderson said, "my concern rose and my confidence fell when I learned that this reporter did not understand the implications of a company repurchasing its own stock. That was a process in which the company was deeply involved at the time—a vital part of the story."[17]

One way of assuring more accurate news stories might be to repeal the general taboo against reading back a story to a source. Although not often written down, a policy against such readbacks has existed in most newsrooms for years. The basis for the taboo has to do with giving sources too much control of the news. It is easy to imagine some political and business leaders trying, though denials and claims of being misquoted and the like, to shape readback news stories to their liking. Yet the taboo has been harmful to accuracy, and that's reason enough to consider repealing or at least amending it. In fact, many journalists have already done that.

Reporters and fact checkers at *New Yorker* magazine, which makes a fetish of its credibility, read back portions of articles to sources or show stories to experts to assure their accuracy. The Center for Investigative Reporting, a nonprofit organization that produces in-depth reports for various news media, reads back material to sources. The center checks quotations by reading innocuous ones first, to test the source's reactions before moving on to the controversial ones. Seymour Hersh, former *New York Times* reporter, said that before his book, *The Price of Power,* was published, he "had every chapter read by an expert to avoid stupid mistakes. . . . I think reporters who say they never check stories with sources are nuts."[18]

Jay Mathews, Los Angeles bureau chief for the *Washington Post,* wrote recently about overcoming "twenty years of newsroom conditioning" and reading back a story to a key source. The readback turned up an error that he was able to correct before the story was published. Wondering why he had never done that before and why journalists he knew opposed readbacks, Mathews talked to other editors and reporters and confirmed that the taboo was still firmly entrenched. But he concluded that the journalists he talked to were "defending a rotting corpse." Arguing that reporters should be able to decide when a readback would be appropriate, Mathews wrote:

> Double-checking selected facts is fine. Competent reporters do that. The process catches the vast majority of potential mistakes. What a readback would catch are the unconscious errors, the verbal misunderstandings, the odd misspellings, the mental lapses that occur in communication between human beings and distract readers who should be able to focus on the story's main point.

And as for undue influence by sources, Mathews said, "journalists encounter that whether they read back or not."[19]

A form of reading back stories occurs when journalists, as they are taught to do, call up persons who have been attacked or criticized and ask them to comment. That's known as balancing a story by letting the accused have his or her own say. But the New York AP bureau once gave that practice a ridiculous twist. It happened after an AP reporter stumbled on a report that Congressman Edward I. Koch, then Democratic candidate for mayor of New York, had some years before been found in a car with another man engaging in what police call sodomy. No charges had been filed, so the report went, and the matter was hushed up by politicians. Two reporters were assigned by the AP to check this out, and eventually they came up with a vague story full of qualifications that suggested Koch was gay. One of the reporters was instructed to take copies of the story to Koch and his opponent, Mario Cuomo, Liberal party candidate for mayor, to get their comments. The reporter gave one copy to Koch and left the other with one of Cuomo's aides.

Koch called the AP and demanded that the story not run because it was a lie and he threatened legal action. Cuomo said something to the effect that he intended to continue to campaign "on the issues." The AP decided to hold its story. But soon calls started coming in from people identifying themselves as editors of various New York City news organizations, saying that they had copies of the story and asking when it was going to be put on the wire. The AP determined that these callers were phony: no one by the names the callers gave worked at the news organizations they said they represented. Somebody was trying to pressure the AP into running a story it had spiked. Then copies of the story actually started turning up in newspaper, TV, and radio newsrooms around town, and AP was able to confirm that the copies had been made from the copy of the story given to Cuomo's people.

So the AP, by its clumsy handling of a story that was based on flimsy facts and was of questionable news value, handed ammunition to one side against the other in an important local election. Inexcusable. After the election, which Koch, of course, won, the *New York Post* did a front-page story on rumormongering in that campaign, and specifically mentioned AP's role. When you are justifiably attacked by the *New York Post* for an ethical lapse, you've hit bottom.[20]

Some of the ignorance problems in processing news could be avoided by more preparation—journalists doing their homework before asking questions. Robert Scheer of the *Los Angeles Times* sees library research as the first line of ethical reporting. He believes reporters have to make themselves authorities on the subjects they write about. The ethical question, he says, is "whether you're really going to put out, or whether you're going to surrender to the cynicism and the mentality of shit and just shove it into the paper." Scheer's primary standard is: "I want to be able to pick up the piece two or three years later and say 'God, this holds up!' "[21]

In community news, errors are often caused by what retired *Boston Globe* editor Thomas Winship calls the "highly nomadic" nature of too many young journalists. "They don't live in its neighborhoods, except for the gentrified ones, or care about their community's future," Winship has said.[22] And because these nomads don't care about their communities, they are slow to learn community history, problems, leaders, customs, or even street names.

Although journalists are much more likely to be college graduates than are members of the general population, few have taken advanced education in the specialized areas that journalism has to interpret. A 1982–1983 survey showed that about 70 percent of contemporary journalists have at least a bachelor's degree, more than half of them having majored in journalism or communications as undergraduates. Of the 20 percent who have done graduate work, about half majored in journalism or communications. The fact that about 30 percent of U.S. journalists do not have a college degree, and that almost half of those who have a college degree did not major in journalism or communications, underscores the lack of any single set of requirements for work in this erratic field.[23]

There are several explanations for the dearth in American newsrooms of specialists who have done work beyond the bachelor's degree in legal matters, political science, business and economics, medicine, science, and other fields journalists need to understand. One is that the news business is mostly a business for generalists, reporters and editors who can handle any type of story on any given day. When editors and news directors hire, they usually are not interested in specialists; they want people who can do everything, at least well enough to get by. A second explanation has to do with the abysmally low beginning salaries in news work (discussed in Chapter 2). Although salaries for experienced journalists are quite high, the low pay at the entrance level discourages apprentices from carrying their formal educations beyond the minimum — which is now a bachelor's degree or close to it. There is a third reason: The streak of antiintellectualism that has been part of the history of American journalism from its beginning has not dissipated. There are still news bosses out there who place little or no value on formal education; only what is learned in the newsroom has worth.

Although it may be asking too much for news organizations to start insisting that their recruits have five to seven years of college education and a master's degree or two, journalism must fight ignorance in its ranks. Encouraging staffers to take courses in nearby universities, perhaps through financial support and pay-raise incentives, would be a good first step. Sending more staffers to seminars and workshops, not just in newsroom practices, but in background subjects, would also help. And if there aren't enough conferences on background subjects for journalists, such as those offered by the Washington Journalism Center, news executives should work with their professional associations and universities to get more such programs organized.

Very few journalists are encouraged by their managements to take sabbaticals for advanced study, as is commonly done for faculty in the better universities. And only a relative handful are able to win spots in the few programs, such as the Nieman program at Harvard, that allow journalists to pull out of the front lines for a few months and pursue some special interest of study. More journalists need to be able to do what Walter Lippmann did in the twenties when he was editorial writer and then editorial page editor of the *New York World*–negotiate a contract that allowed him to spend summers in Europe at the paper's expense boning up on his specialty, foreign affairs.[24]

Having made these arguments for more formal and informal education in American journalism, I must add a personal observation as one who has worked many years in both journalism and higher education: Higher education cannot solve all human problems. There are too many Ph.D.'s in our universities who cannot write a clear sentence, too many professors whose vision of the world is as narrow as that of a pet goldfish, too many administrators deficient in humanity and ethics to encourage a faith that more formal education among journalists would necessarily improve journalism. But there is greater competence in the average university than in the average newsroom–a lot more in most cases–and most campuses with reasonably equipped libraries and faculties offer a would-be journalist the opportunity to develop the kind of knowledge needed to combat the ignorance that mars American journalism. Would-be journalists and the universities should be encouraged by the news business to do just that.

Correcting the Record. As we have seen in the specific cases covered so far in this chapter, many news organizations admit and correct their errors. That has been the obvious trend in the country for the past two decades. Not all errors get corrected, of course. Sometimes they slip by unnoticed; nobody complains. And some editors get stubborn and simply decline to correct errors that are dubious in their minds or not completely the fault of the newspaper or broadcast station.

Newspapers as a whole are doing a good job of correcting errors that are called to their attention. The record of broadcast news is less impressive, particularly at local stations. Often errors are never acknowledged on the air even when corrected versions are broadcast later in the day or the day after an error has been made. Sometimes broadcast news directors don't bother to correct their errors at all, apparently assuring themselves that their news reports are not permanent records anyway. It is true, of course, that broadcast stories lack the permanence of printed stories that people can look up and read years and decades later.

That realization of the permanency of the printed word has undoubt-edly spurred some newspaper executives to increase efforts to correct the record. "Newspapers are in a high-risk business," Donald D. (Casey) Jones, ombudsman at the *Kansas City Star* and *Times,* told the 1983 APME convention. "We are going to make errors of fact, errors of judg-ment, errors of taste, errors of omission and commission. The problem comes when we don't correct them, when we become unreasonably de-fensive, overprotective of reporters and editors–'We stand by our story'–when we become abusive with a complainant, or God forbid, threatening."[25]

Another spur are the laws in thirty-one of the fifty states which say that corrections and retractions made within seven to ten days after an error has been published can mitigate damages in a libel suit.[26]

Many newspapers have taken to placing their corrections in a set place in the paper every day. And some have started running clarifica-tions of stories that were not so much incorrect as misleading. The AP has a policy of putting such clarifications on its wires "to clarify or to expand on previous copy which, while factually correct, may be unfair or subject to misinterpretation." The AP clarification is written to be pub-lished by the papers who used the story being clarified, and it is not meant to be a substitute for a correction or a corrective, which is what AP uses to correct factual errors.[27]

The *New York Times,* which has conscientiously sought to correct all errors it can find in recent years, uses an "Editors' Note" to amplify articles or rectify "what the editors consider significant lapses of fairness, balance or perspective." It used such a note in 1984, for example, to explain that President Reagan had at the last minute deleted a sentence in a speech after copies, as is the custom with high public officials, had been distributed to reporters. The *Times* had emphasized the sentence in its story about the president's speech because he seemed to be condemn-ing Americans who support Irish terrorists. The sentence Reagan deleted from his prepared remarks for a toast at a Dublin dinner said: "I can't think of anything more vulgar than Americans providing anyone in Ire-land the means of killing his fellow man."[28]

In a memorandum to his staff explaining the initiation of the "Editors' Note," A. M. Rosenthal, associate editor of the *New York Times,* acknowl-edged that "this will not be a simple policy to carry out, and there will be differences between us and the readers as to whether or not an Editors' Note is called for. And I'm sure there will be differences among editors and reporters. We will not allow the policy to be trivialized or politicized, and we will use our own judgment. But we will carry it out in good faith, and I think it will make most of us happier. It sits well on the stomach."[29]

The *Times*'s tough policy on correcting errors and clarifying stories in Rosenthal's last years as its executive editor contrast with an earlier day when the *Times* and most newspapers simply refused to acknowledge, let alone correct, most errors. I had firsthand experience with the self-righteousness of those earlier *Times* editors in the early sixties when, as director of the School of Journalism at Penn State University, I tried to get that paper to correct an error. The erroneous item in its column on the advertising business said that Penn State was changing the name of all its advertising courses to "paid propaganda" (it was apparently based on the fact that the late Howard Gossage was about to become a visiting lecturer in the school's advertising sequence and planned to teach a special, one-time course entitled, "The Nature of Paid Propaganda"). Phone calls and letters protesting the reported change flooded the school the day of publication. Most came from advertising leaders and practitioners, many of them alumni. Phone calls and letters to the advertising columnist and Turner Catledge, then *Times* managing editor, brought no correction. The letters of protest to the school continued for almost a year as other newspapers and magazines would pick up the item and, because it was from the *Times,* republish it without checking with the university. To the *Times* apparently this was a small error not worth the bother, but it caused great grief and annoyance to the people at Penn State who had to correct the record as best they could without the help of the paper that caused all the trouble in the first place.

The *Times* is better today—not perfect, but better. Recently it corrected a seven-year-old error with a front-page article that said the former U.S. ambassador to Chile, Edward Korry, knew nothing of covert CIA efforts to overthrow Chilean President Salvador Allende Gossens. The 2,300-word corrective was written by former *Times* reporter Seymour Hersh, who also wrote the earlier stories that implied Korry played a major role in an aborted CIA coup against Allende. Other reporters wrote similar stories but Hersh admits he "led the way in trashing" Korry. Hersh discovered he had been wrong about Korry while doing research in the fall of 1980 for a book on Henry Kissinger. When he told Rosenthal that some of the things he had written for the *Times* about Korry were wrong, Rosenthal asked Hersh to write the corrective. "My God, if we were wrong in any way I want to correct it," Rosenthal said. Hersh's article was published on 9 February 1981, seven years after Hersh's first story (apparently based on a Senate subcommittee source) implied that Korry had been involved in the CIA plot. Korry's eight-year diplomatic career was ruined as a result of the story even though no charges of wrongdoing were ever filed against him, and it was not until 1979 that he was able to land a job as visiting professor of international relations at Connecticut College.[30]

One of the more charming *New York Times* corrections appeared recently at the bottom of Flora Lewis's "Foreign Affairs" column on the opposite editorial page. It read:

> NOTE: I've just eaten a large plate of crow. I am now satisfied
> that the document on El Salvador discussed in my column last Friday,
> which I believed was an official paper, was indeed spurious, as the
> State Department later said. Many of the facts checked out, but it
> wasn't a Government paper. I'm abashed.[31]

Before moving on to errors corrected by other news media, it should
be said that it is easy to find examples of slips by the *New York Times*
because it is the country's most visible and written about newspaper.
Errors and the way they are corrected or not corrected in that newspaper
provide fodder for many *Times* watchers who make beer money free-
lancing pratfall pieces to journalism reviews and other publications.

Another constantly watched paper, the *Washington Post,* ran a front-
page apology to former president Carter and his wife, Rosalynn, after the
Carters threatened to sue the *Post* for libel. The Carters were disturbed
about an item in the *Post*'s gossip column, "Ear," which said the Carters
had bugged Blair House to eavesdrop on Ronald and Nancy Reagan when
the Reagans stayed there prior to President Reagan's inaugural. The
column, written by Diana McLellan, offered a "hot new twist" on the
"tired old tale" of how Mrs. Reagan had reportedly said she wished the
Carters would vacate the White House before inauguration day to give
her time to redecorate the living quarters before moving in. "Now word's
around among Rosalynn's close pals about exactly why the Carters were
so sure Nancy wanted them out," McLellan wrote. "They're saying Blair
House, where Nancy was lodging – and chatting up First Decorator Ted
Graber – was bugged. And at least one tattler in the Carter tribe has
described listening in to the tape itself."

McLellan apparently got her "hot new twist" from free-lancer Dotson
Rader, who claimed that there were tape recordings of Mrs. Reagan making such a statement to her decorator, Ted Graber, at Blair House. Somehow in the conversation between McLellan and Rader, "tapes" became
"bugs." After the item was published, and the Carters threatened to sue,
Benjamin C. Bradlee, *Post* executive editor, went up to Princeton, New
Jersey, to talk to Rader and was astounded to learn that Rader had not
meant to suggest that Blair House was bugged but only that there were
tapes of Mrs. Reagan's discussion with her decorator. Bradlee said the
writer did not see any difference between bugged or taped, but Bradlee
saw a big difference: A tape could have been made by a reporter, or
anyone else, with a tape recorder. Bugging means that microphones are
hidden around the place to record conversations surreptitiously. Bradlee
returned to Washington and the *Post* soon retracted the "Ear" item and
apologized to the Carters.[32] (Diana McLellan and her column have since
left the *Post.*)

The Carters then announced they would not sue the *Post,* but the former president lectured the *Post* in a statement which said in part:

> This incident and the newspaper policy which caused it have
> been of considerable concern to us. Fortunately, because of my pre-
> vious position, I had access to the public news media and could draw
> attention to my problem. Many victims of similarly false allegations
> do not enjoy this opportunity, but suffer just as severely.
>
> The decision by the publishers of a nationally and internationally
> influential newspaper like the *Post* to print a regular column which is
> widely known to be based on rumor and gossip adds unwarranted
> credence to its false reports. Even an instant and enthusiastic effort
> by newspaper editors to correct errors can never be completely
> successful in erasing the damage caused by unfounded gossip.[33]

Threatening to sue as the Carters did does not always result in an
apology or retraction, but it usually gets editors to pay attention to your
complaint. In the old days, threatened litigation was about the only way
you could get a newspaper to admit it had erred. It is much less difficult
today to get news organizations to acknowledge and correct their mistakes, but the reluctance to do so still hangs on. There is apparently a
belief that the public will not trust a news medium that errs – and perhaps
that fear is justified in the short run – but if admitting errors and apologiz-
ing for them is seen as a sign of maturity in people, why would it not be
similarly so for news organizations?

Sometimes a news maker is better off not demanding a retraction or
apology. The correction simply calls attention to the original error for
people who missed it. There is also the risk that you will get the kind of
apology that George Papadakis did when he took offense at the *Signal
Hill* (California) *Tribune* for calling him a "Greek orator" in an editorial.
Papadakis, who was a council member in that city, said the reference to
him was a "racial slur." This was too much for editor Ken Mills. "The
Tribune apologizes, George," Mills wrote. "What we meant to call you is a
loquacious asshole, a bore without peer. . . . We've reported your coun-
cilmanic doings accurately and without malice. So stuff it." Mills explained to the AP that he used "Greek orator" to mean that Papadakis was
articulate.[34]

WHO'S WATCHING THE WATCHDOGS?

A responsibility evolving out of the First Amendment that journalists
these days seldom question is the obligation of the news media to be a
watchdog of government. Keeping the press free from government ("Congress shall make no law. . . .") allows the press to help protect citizens

from the abuses of government. In modern times this watchdog role has been extended by most journalists to business, education, sports, and other important institutions of American life.

Many observers believe that the news media also need scrutiny — some watchdog of the watchdogs. Journalism is too important to all of us to be left entirely to journalists. It needs independent and critical monitoring. But journalists (fewer today, fortunately, than in the past) have resisted such appraisals on any systematic basis, mostly out of concern that they might diminish press freedom. So the history of the U.S. journalism in this century has been only lightly spotted with examples of continuing reviews of journalism's performance.

Some of the instruments that have been suggested over the years to monitor news media performance are news councils, ombudsmen, journalism reviews, reporters regularly covering journalism, and university schools of journalism or communications. All of these have been and are being used, but there is no national or regular audit of news media performance. The only watching most of the watchdogs get comes from their own audiences.

Philip Meyer, Kenan professor of journalism at the University of North Carolina, has proposed "an Ethical Audit" that individual newspapers could use to periodically assess their performance on factual errors, staff members' conflicts of interest, audience attitudes, and a number of things that could be learned from various kinds of research. The "centerpiece" of Meyer's audit would be the accuracy measurement. "It will be argued," he admits, "that the ethical problems of journalism go beyond anything that can be measured by such a simple evaluation. But improvement must begin somewhere, and if it cannot begin at that simple and fundamental level, perhaps the newspeople should face the possibility that it cannot be achieved at all. Fairness, balance and objectivity are empty without the basic capacity to gather and report the facts."[35]

The *Hartford Courant* recently took a small but unusual step toward becoming more accountable to its public. Michael J. Davies, its editor and publisher, decided to allow a member of the public to sit on the editorial board that determines what positions the paper takes on its editorial page. The public seat is a revolving one. "Under this program, we will choose a leader from various groups — business, labor, religion, neighborhoods, public service — who will spend two or three months with us," Davies said in announcing the plan. "All will participate fully in editorial board meetings and in the debate, discussion and research that shapes our editorial policies." The first public member was Robert Wiles, outgoing director of the Hartford Institute of Criminal and Social Justice, who joined the editorial board in August 1986.[36]

News Councils. One appraisal method that has had great appeal in this country as well as in Great Britain, Sweden, and other European countries is the news council, a body charged with monitoring the suppliers of news to the public. The idea was first put forth seriously in the United States by the Commission on Freedom of the Press (the "Hutchins Commission"), which recommended in its 1947 report "the establishment of a new and independent agency to appraise and report annually upon the performance of the press." Although the agency proposed was to be nongovernmental, many journalists at the time read veiled threats in the commission's report because of language such as this: "Freedom of the press for the coming period can only continue as an accountable freedom. Its moral right will be conditioned on its acceptance of this accountability. Its legal right will stand unaltered as its moral duty is performed."[37]

The press council recommendation, along with others the commission made, was widely attacked by the press at the time. Many of its critics honed in on the absence of any journalists on the commission – "11 professors, a banker-merchant and a poet-librarian," as the trade magazine *Editor and Publisher* labeled them.[38] This sort of criticism, of course, had to ignore the fact that among the 225 people interviewed by the commission in its study from 1943 through 1945 were 58 journalists. The study was financed by grants of some $200,000 from Time, Inc., and $15,000 from the Encyclopaedia Britannica, Inc. The commission was headed by Robert M. Hutchins, then chancellor of the University of Chicago, who initiated the inquiry into the state of the nation's press at the urging of Henry R. Luce, founder of *Time* magazine and head of Time, Inc. Its membership included ten distinguished faculty members from Harvard, Columbia, Yale, Chicago, University of Pennsylvania, Hunter College, and the Union Theological Seminary, as well as Beardsley Ruml (chairman of the Federal Reserve Bank, New York), and Archibald MacLeish (poet, librarian of the Library of Congress, and former assistant secretary of state).

Although the commission's press council proposal was not immediately cheered by the press, the idea survived. Its supporters were encouraged by the establishment of the British Press Council in 1953. A handful of American publishers and editors began to experiment with local councils made up of representative members of their communities who appraised their local newspapers. In the late 1960s the Mellett Fund for a Free and Responsible Press financed four local press council experiments in California, Oregon, Missouri, and Illinois, but none survived. The press of Minnesota set up a statewide press council in 1971, now called the Minnesota News Council, to indicate its concern with broadcast as well as print media. Some other state press groups, particularly those in Kentucky and Wisconsin, have discussed setting up news councils, but as of this writing, Minnesota's council stands alone. Another survivor is the Honolulu Community-Media Council, founded in 1970. These local and state councils reflected the thinking of many news media appraisal advocates that in a country as vast as the United States with its complicated media system, a national monitoring body would face a virtually impossible task. The more effective way to investigate failures in the news media and improve journalistic performance is through a monitoring system closer to home, they argued.

There were still those, nevertheless, who believed in a national monitoring agency and their thinking dominated a task force put together by the Twentieth Century Fund in the early 1970s. Out of this study came the formation of the National News Council in 1973. Remembering the attacks on the Hutchins Commission, the Twentieth Century Fund put some journalism executives on its task force that recommended "an independent and private national news council be established to receive, to examine and to report on complaints concerning the accuracy and fairness of news reporting in the United States, as well as to initiate studies and report on issues involving freedom of the press."[39]

The National News Council lasted about eleven years before it died of neglect in 1984. Although in its lifetime it investigated 227 complaints and issued several studies of major problems in journalism, its often thoughtful reports were largely ignored by American news media. So the American public, by and large, was ignorant of the council's existence and work. Since the council was nongovernmental and had no power to enforce any of its findings, it had counted on the force of public opinion to bring pressure on erring and irresponsible journalists and news media. But without widespread publicity for its reports and findings, the council was unable even to reach the public at large, let along influence its opinions.

The council received many more complaints from the public than the 227 it investigated. It would first look into the validity of a complaint and, if it seemed legitimate, get the complainant to sign a waiver assuring that the offending news organization would not be sued. Then the council staff would investigate the complaint and prepare a report for the council itself, which would judge the complaint and issue a ruling. The reports of these findings were released to the media and most were published by the council itself in three volumes entitled *In the Public Interest I, II,* and *III,* but they had small readership outside of university journalism and communications faculties.

One serious consequence of the neglect by journalism in general was in the lack of financial support for the council from media companies. The Twentieth Century Fund and the Markle Foundation put up the money to start the council but expected it to find other supporters as it grew. Most of the funds raised by the council in its eleven years came from foundations, and not from media companies, the logical supporters. When the money finally ran out in 1984, the council turned its files over to the Silha Center for the Study of Media Ethics and Law at the University of Minnesota and called it quits.[40]

Why did the great majority of news organizations choose not to support the council either with dollars or publicity? Richard S. Salant, a former head of CBS News who was president of the council when it folded, believes news media opposition to the council "was rooted in the traditional reluctance of the press to have any outside body . . . looking over its shoulder, and in the conviction of the press that each individual news organization could best solve its own problems and in its own way."[41]

Many news executives saw the monitoring agency as a potential threat to First Amendment freedom. That view has been forcefully put forward by Abe Rosenthal, former executive editor of the *New York Times,* which was one of the news organizations that refused to cooperate when the council investigated complaints against it. Calling himself "as close to an absolutist on the First Amendment as you can get," Rosenthal said he feared that the council's decisions would be picked up by judges and used against the press. He argued that no monitoring agency can make publishers spend more money on news, which he sees as the real problem in journalism.[42]

Eugene L. Roberts, executive editor of the *Philadelphia Inquirer,* objected to the council because it emphasized "sins of commission," spending most of its time investigating complaints against the more active and aggressive news organizations, when the real sins of the press are those of omission.[43]

Another reason stated by many journalists for their lack of support for the council was that its nonmedia people were incompetent to judge the work of journalists. The council had always been cognizant of this criticism and had taken care to see that it had members with media experience. Of the seventeen council members in 1983, for example, six had clear media connections, three others had lengthy media experience, and a minority of eight had no media experience to speak of and were there as representatives of the public at large. In addition, the three council staff members who did the investigating had impressive journalistic credentials. In its final days, the council proposed creating a separate body made up entirely of media representatives to rule on complaints, but media organizations refused to suggest names of people to serve for fear such cooperation would be interpreted as approving of the news council.

The death of the National News Council left only Minnesota and Honolulu in this country with instruments, other than the courts, to hear and evaluate public complaints against the news media. People who feel they have been burned can still go to the courts, of course, but lawsuits against news organizations seem more likely to intimidate than to improve journalism.

Giving Readers a Voice. This book is liberally sprinkled with reports and comments from journalists with the strange title of *ombudsman*. About 40 of the some 1,670 U.S. daily newspapers and all three commercial broadcast networks have added such functionaries to their staffs in recent years. The idea came from Sweden, where a government official with that title represents the public in its dealings with the Swedish bureaucracy. American media ombudsmen handle complaints from the public and serve as in-house critics. Most are called ombudsmen, but some are known as reader representatives or some other similar and more understandable term. There's even an Organization of News Ombudsmen (ONO), which they like to call by its initials "Oh, no!" said to describe the ombudsman's typical reaction to the paper's latest goof.

The first newspaper ombudsman in this country was on the *Louisville Times* and *Courier-Journal.* He was appointed in 1967 by Norman Isaacs, then executive editor. Isaacs got the idea from an article he read in the *New York Times* of 11 June 1967, written by A. H. Raskin, then assistant editorial page editor, who became associate director of the news council after retiring from the *Times.*

One of the several newspapers that followed Isaacs's lead in establishing ombudsmen was the *St. Petersburg Times,* but the *Times* later abandoned the idea and its executive editor at the time, Robert Haiman, became a leading critic of newspaper ombudsmen. The press certainly needs criticism, Haiman has argued, but it needs it from outside, not from an employee of the newspaper. "We should not want the press as our principal critic of newspaper performance any more than we want the State Department as our principal critic of foreign policy."

Another problem Haiman sees with newspaper ombudsmen as they have evolved in this country is that they work after the fact. They investigate alleged failures in their newspaper's performance after they have occurred and do not try to prevent the failures from occurring in the first place. He compares ombudsmen with coroners, whose job it is "to do the post-mortem on a disaster, to pick through the tatters of flesh after a terrible crash." The credibility of newspapers would be better improved, he said, if ombudsmen "would have more to do with trying to keep the plane flying, with monitoring the captain and crew who fly it, and with trying to avoid the crash in the first place."[44]

Haiman's criticism aroused Paul Janensch, then executive editor of the Louisville newspapers, to comment: "I think the American newspaper business would be better off if we had fewer executive editors and more ombudsmen."[45]

The Louisville ombudsman does not "go public" with a regular column commenting on the paper's foibles or those of the news media in general, but many ombudsmen, including the one at the *Washington Post,* have that as part of their regular assignment.

The addition of the column-writing role is one of the reasons that Isaacs, who started it all, is disenchanted with the way newspaper ombudsmen have turned out. He believes writing a regular column of media criticism gets in the way of the other more important job of responding to readers' complaints and criticizing the newspaper internally. "You can have a media critic and an ombudsman, but you can't have both in the same person," Isaacs contends. Another reason he has soured on the movement he started is that "in too many cases, the ombudsman is an old, battle-scarred veteran who would have been assigned to the library if he hadn't been named ombudsman. And some of them are purely cosmetic; some guy writing a media column in which all he does is explain the virtues of the newspaper is not answering the need."

Isaacs sees two reasons more newspapers have not appointed ombudsmen. The first is money. He estimates that it would take about $100,000 a year to set up an ombudsman today, counting office space and equipment, a secretary, and all the trappings. Many editors would rather put that kind of money into new reporting positions. A second reason, he believes, is that most news staffs simply do not want an in-house critic looking over their shoulders. "You don't establish an ombudsman with staff consent," Isaacs adds. "You impose it." And that requires an authoritarianism many news executives shy away from.[46]

Two of the nation's most prestigious newspapers, the *New York Times* and the *Los Angeles Times,* have done just that—shied away from appointing ombudsmen. Former executive editor Rosenthal of the *New York Times* believes that newspaper ombudsmen are "a gimmick" and "a cop-out." He maintains that editors have to be responsible for the content of their newspapers and the conduct of their staffs.[47] A less adamant position is taken by editor William F. Thomas of the *Los Angeles Times.* Thomas considered establishing an ombudsman—"some ombudsmen are very good"—but he opted for a full-time reporter covering the news business, about which more will be said later in this chapter. Thomas believes that his reporter's articles, published in the news columns and often starting on page one, have much greater impact than an ombudsman's column "speaking solely for himself and run on a page marked 'opinion.' "[48]

One of the more highly regarded ombudsmen, Art Nauman of the *Sacramento Bee,* does write a regular Sunday column, but he talks about his job in some of the same terms Isaacs uses. Nauman sees himself as the person who makes his paper accountable to its readers, "answering some of their questions and responding to their legitimate complaints." He tries to give readers some voice in the decisions about what gets published and how. "Most of the time we have not been willing to tell our customers how we reach these decisions that have such a terrific impact on so many lives."[49]

Reporting on Yourself. One kind of accountability is provided when the news media turn their spotlights on themselves, report on themselves in the same way they do other important institutions and activities. Many newspapers and a few broadcast stations run occasional pieces on the news business or about some particular incident involving journalists and how they do their work. The coverage that was given to the way the news media reported the Atlanta child murders in 1981 is an example. But only a few news organizations have turned the news business into a regular beat, a full-time assignment for some reporter or critic.

The name that comes to mind whenever coverage of the news business is discussed by people in the business is David Shaw, media reporter and critic for the *Los Angeles Times* since 1974. Shaw reports directly to Thomas, the paper's top editor. That way his reports cannot be kept out or buried in the back of his paper by subeditors upset at what he has written. Shaw often writes about the *Los Angeles Times* when he does an investigation of some national journalistic problem or issue. "If he's going to explain newspaper behavior, he can't leave us out," Thomas observes. Shaw's work evoked a negative reaction in his own newsroom at first, Thomas adds, but "they have accepted him now."[50]

The *New York Times* and the *Washington Post* have reporters regularly covering the news media, as do the *Wall Street Journal* and *Newsday*. *Time* and *Newsweek* magazines also report regularly on the news media. Broadcasting has not done much regular reporting on itself, and media criticism is even scarcer. The Public Broadcasting Service had a media criticism program called "Inside Story" for a while, but it failed to get the funding it needed to survive.

Many newspaper editors write regular columns discussing problems in news and specifically their own paper's approach to some particular story or particular kinds of news. These columns are sometimes self-congratulatory, but most of the time they seem to help readers who want to know more about how journalism works. Broadcast news executives should do more of that.

One forum of media criticism that has evolved in recent years is the journalism review—a periodical devoted to reporting on and criticizing the news media. Chief among them has been the *Columbia Journalism Review,* published by the Columbia University School of Journalism since 1961. Its raison d'étre is "to assess the performance of journalism in all its forms, to call attention to its shortcomings and strengths, and to help define—or redefine—standards of honest responsible service . . . to help stimulate continuing improvement in the profession and to speak out for what is right, fair, and decent."[51]

A more recently founded review striving for the same kind of national circulation as the *Columbia Journalism Review* is the *Washington Journalism Review,* published by the University of Maryland journalism college. Some regional or local reviews—particularly *Feed/back,* a California journalism review published by the Journalism Department of San Francisco State University—have had an influence in their areas.

These reviews, of course, are read mostly by people in news work, so the impact of their explanations and criticisms extends to the public at large only through the journalists who take them seriously.

Most journalists interviewed for this book do not seem to believe that journalism does a very good job of reporting on itself to the public. Ombudsman Nauman of the *Sacramento Bee* puts it more strongly. "The press does an abysmal job of explaining itself," he charges. "We've gotten very big and arrogant; we don't listen to anybody; we don't like dissenting views; we're always right and unwilling to admit our mistakes."[52]

Some, however, question whether the public is all that interested in the news business. Julius Duscha, director of the Washington Journalism Center, agrees that news media do not cover themselves nearly as well as they cover other comparable businesses and activities. But although he feels there is considerable public interest in television, he questions how much people want to know about newspapers. "They certainly want to know about the television stars," he remarks. "You can't write enough about Dan Rather and the local anchor man." He notes that even at National Press Club luncheons, the journalists present are more interested in the TV photographers taking their cut-in shots of audience reaction than they are in the speaker of the day.[53]

Covering yourself is not easy, of course. Many important stories about the news business are embarrassing and reflect negatively on some news organization or executive. That is why, Duscha explains, you did not read much in the *Washington Post* about the many changes in publishers that paper went through at one period; or in the *Chicago Tribune* about the troubles of the paper the Tribune Company owns in New York, the *Daily News;* or in *Time* magazine about the problems of the *Washington Star,* the newspaper it owned and closed in 1981.

"How do we cover ourselves?" asks Paul Poorman, former editor of the *Akron Beacon Journal.* "Like porcupines making love: tenderly, very tenderly."[54]

Academic Critics. Some faculty members in the better schools of journalism and communications see it as their responsibility to be critics of the news media. This feeling is reflected more in their teaching and research than in public forums. When they do go public with their criticisms in writing or in a speech, they are often denounced by working journalists or dismissed as ivory tower know-nothings. But their criticisms continue, because the responsibility of university faculty to provide detached evaluation of everything in society is deeply imbedded and is one of the academy's most useful traditions.

Some people who are concerned about the lack and feebleness of existing watchdogs of the media have suggested that professional schools of journalism and communications ought to provide a more systemized critical evaluation of the news media in their areas. But administrators of those schools have been reluctant to take on that function because they need the support of the news media in their state or region in order to progress and survive in the competition with other schools and disciplines in their universities. Years ago before he became journalism dean at the University of California at Berkeley, media critic Ben Bagdikian suggested, tongue in cheek, that professional schools provide regular criticism of media behavior but of media in some other state. The school at Berkeley, for example, would have responsibility for critically evaluating the news media of Illinois, while the College of Communications at the University of Illinois would criticize the news media of New York state, and so on. The proposal was received by journalism educators as seriously as it had been proferred.

One school of communications, that at the Pennsylvania State University, has recently taken over the only national award given to news media critics. When the Mellett Fund for a Free and Responsible Press folded in 1984, it transferred to Penn State the Lowell Mellett Award for Improving Journalism Through Critical Evaluation. The Mellett Fund had been established in 1966 with a bequest from Lowell Mellett, first editor of the old *Washington Daily News.* The award in his name has gone to such journalists as David Shaw, media reporter-critic for the *Los Angeles Times,* and Norman Isaacs, nationally known retired newspaper editor and journalism professor, for his 1986 book, *Untended Gates: The Mismanaged Press.* (As the last president of the Mellett Fund and as a professor emeritus at Penn State, I influenced the fund's decision to send the Mellett Award to my university, where I hope it will thrive.)

As has already been noted, three of the journalism reviews are published by university journalism units at Columbia, Maryland, and San Francisco State. But the overall record of schools of journalism and communications as media critics has been uneven and often lacking in courage. It is not a record that encourages counting on our universities to be a major watchdog of the watchdogs.

THE IMPORTANCE OF ACCOUNTABILITY

Not all news media proprietors would agree with the major thesis of this chapter that they have an obligation to be accountable to the public. In an earlier day, hardly any newspaper owners thought they had to account for themselves to anybody. They saw themselves as private businesses the public could accept or reject. But more and more news media owners today act as if they accept the need to explain at least some aspects of their publication or station to those who attend to it and depend on it.

What most contemporary news media owners and news executives have a harder time accepting is having some outside agency or group pass judgment on them and the journalism they produce. That kind of monitoring is an anathema to them.

What most leaders of American journalism seem to be saying is: "We'll be responsible in our own way. We'll decide when it's necessary to explain ourselves to the public. We'll decide when it's necessary to correct an error. We'll decide when, if ever, the public needs to know about our finances—how much we spend, how much we make, and how much we send to group headquarters."

As I've indicated earlier in this chapter, many newspapers are doing a good job of explaining themselves through columns written by editors and ombudsmen and through articles about their internal operations. And many more are being conscientious about correcting their errors. Broadcast news organizations lag behind in both of these matters. And with few exceptions, all news media are as secretive as the CIA about their finances.

We might be able to forgive this uneven record of public accountability in the news media if newspapers and broadcast stations were nothing but private businesses. But they are more than private businesses because of the special role that accrues from the constitutionally protected freedom they enjoy in the American system. Drafters of the federal and state constitutions did not extend special guarantees of freedom to newspapers and other news media just so they could make money. The expectation was and is that news organizations should serve the public with information about government and other aspects of life. Serving the public also means being accountable to the public, which has no idea, unless the media explain it to them, why certain events and activities are "newsworthy" and others are not; why their local paper so differs from the *New York Times* and their local TV news so differs from NBC News; how the news staff, whatever its size, is deployed; where all that informational material not produced locally comes from; and how much money the paper or station makes and how much of that profit is reinvested in the local company.

The public would also be better served if it knew more about the ethics policies of the news organizations it supports. The *Wilmington News Journal* publishes its ethics code every year. Not many papers do that, although the relatively few newspapers with ombudsmen usually inform their readers about their ethics guidelines through the ombudsmen's columns. But the huge majority of newspapers, even those with ethics codes, keep their ethics policies to themselves. Most broadcast station news departments don't have written codes of ethics so the problem for them is at a more primitive level.

If most leaders of journalism won't accept news councils, ombudsmen, and other such devices for involving the public in the processing of news that is vital to us, then they must be more accountable to the public. Until that happens, the imperfect media critics we have are essential to provide some check on the power of the media system that has developed in this country.

What the Codes Say. The Society of Professional Journalists has the only code among the major national journalistic associations that addresses public accountability. It says, "Journalists should be accountable to the public for their reports and the public should be encouraged to voice its grievances against the media. Open dialogue with our readers, viewers and listeners should be fostered."

A few codes of individual newspapers touch on accountability. "We want a dialogue with our readers; they, too, have a stake in this newspaper," the *Honolulu Advertiser* states. "It shall be the policy of our editors and staff members to encourage the maximum amount of public participation in bringing all points of view before our readers."

The *Philadelphia Inquirer* believes it "is responsible to its readers for the accuracy and fairness of its work." It adds: "We should, therefore, be as accessible to those readers as humanly possible. In all our contacts with the public, we should strive to let them know that we are seeking the truth, that we are open-minded, and that we want to listen to what they have to say."

The somewhat more detailed statement in the introduction to the code of the *Charlotte Observer* reads:

> A major function of the U.S. daily press is a ceaseless calling-to-account of public officials. That chore is vital in a quite literal sense. Without the press's continuing attention, the muscular but delicate division of American political power would collapse.
>
> But who calls the press to account?
>
> Ultimately, the readers do, but a casual glance through U.S. newspapers will confirm that their stewardship is not rigid. Bad newspapers can prosper. In the short-term economic sense, then, The Observer's ethics policy is unnecessary. A fair number of people will buy the paper whether or not it is written and edited by people who think about the ethical implications of their actions.
>
> So when a newspaper like The Observer adopts an ethics policy, it does so as a matter of self-discipline. The newspaper is powerful; The Observer ethics policy is a way, perhaps awkward, of trying to see that the power is used fairly. Awkward, because that amount of self-consciousness may seem prissy. Awkward, because no policy can cover every situation.
>
> And no policy can supplant the editors' obligation to hire men and women of character. But in the gray areas, where private lives and public responsibilities may meet, a policy can offer some guidelines.

On the more specific matter of correcting errors, all the codes of the major national associations in journalism and virtually all those of individual news organizations say that errors should be corrected promptly.

The codes of the three commercial broadcast networks all deal with different parts of the error-and-correction problem. NBC News dwells on the detection of errors. "Any assertion that a broadcast report by NBC News personnel includes any significant error of fact must be investigated, objectively, promptly and thoroughly," by an appropriate NBC News official, the NBC code holds. Significant fact errors "will be corrected promptly in an appropriate broadcast," NBC says. "The correction must be open, specific and unequivocal."

CBS News is concerned about making it clear that "we are broadcasting a correction." Its code states:

> It is not sufficient merely to report that the statement included in the original broadcast has been denied. The accuracy of the denial must be specifically confirmed. It is not sufficient merely to include the accurate information in the correcting broadcast. The fact that it

is a correction must be specifically noted. It is not sufficient merely to broadcast a letter from a viewer or listener which asserts that we were in error. The accuracy of the assertion must be specifically admitted.

ABC News, after stating that "significant errors of fact must be corrected in a clear and timely manner," sees "another cause for corrective action." Its code notes that "sometimes the error is not one of fact but of balance, when we leave out something important or give too much prominence to the wrong thing. That, too, calls for a report to redress the balance."

The advice on corrections in newspaper codes is usually brief and comes out to something like "mistakes should be corrected promptly and candidly," which is what the *Chicago Sun-Times* code requires. But the *Philadelphia Inquirer* guideline is detailed and specific. "We promptly and forthrightly correct" our errors, the *Inquirer* code states, either in a separate correction under the standing headline "Clearing the record," which usually appears on page two, or in a parenthetical paragraph inserted into a new story on the same subject. The *Inquirer* also uses "Clearing the record" notices to clarify facts that, while technically correct, "might have been confusing or misleading."

When the *Inquirer* publishes one of its standard "Clearing the record" corrections, it includes this policy statement: "It is the intention of The Inquirer that its news reports be fair and correct in every respect. If you have a question or comment about news coverage, write to Ombudsman. . . ." Then it gives an address, phone number, and office hours for its ombudsman.

The *Inquirer* guideline on corrections continues:

> All corrections are approved by the managing editor or, in his absence, by the editor in charge. The assigning editor should always determine the reason for the error; this could result in a refinement in procedure to reduce the possibility that the same mistake will be made again.
>
> When a factual error results in a possibility of libel, the newspaper's attorneys must be consulted in the phrasing of the correction.
>
> These guidelines should be considered in writing corrections:
>
> State the facts as simply as possible. The error should not be repeated unless needed for clarity. If the wrong date for a performance was published, it serves no purpose to repeat the error. On the other hand, it frequently helps explain the correction by stating how the original story was wrong.
>
> Provide enough detail to enable a reader to understand the correction without having read the original story.
>
> Tell when the error was published. Examples: "Yesterday's In-

quirer" or "the May 2 issue of The Inquirer" when the error appeared in the entire press run, or "in an early edition of Friday's Inquirer" if the error appeared only in one edition.

Do not write, "The Inquirer regrets the error." Generally, we prefer to regard an apology as implicit.

Corrections do not attempt to ascribe blame within the Inquirer.

It is encouraging that journalists seem more willing these days to correct their errors. The posture of infallibility that dominated the journalism of an earlier day was ridiculous and harmful to everybody. The time has come, though, for journalists to reduce errors through a more competent and responsible style of journalism.

14 Toward Ethical Journalism

"Don't tell me my newspaper isn't ethical. We haven't offended anybody in this town for years."

The picture this study paints of the state of ethics in the news business in the United States is one of large numbers of obviously intelligent people honestly disagreeing about most ethical standards, goals, and procedures. There is agreement on the goal of accurate and fair reporting and the standard of separating information, opinion, and advertising, but that is about it. Other ethical principles may be adhered to religiously by some or many journalists but ignored by some or many others.

There is even disagreement about what constitutes an ethical or moral issue in the field. Many journalists would not consider all of the quandaries laid out in this study as matters of ethics or morality. Some think of ethics as merely a matter of avoiding freebies and conflicts of interest. The variety of visions about what is or is not an ethical problem has handicapped journalists as they have tried to come to grips with their ethics.

The codes of ethics adopted by national organizations of journalists have a nice ring to them, particularly when read to musical accompaniment by Henry Mancini. But they are of limited help in the day-to-day ethical decisions that journalists have to make. They are statements of ideals and aspirations, which is about the best that can be expected from a field that puts as much stock in freedom and individuality as U.S.

journalism does. As such, the national codes have been useful in getting many journalists to think about the objectives of journalism. But what is needed, it seems to me, is more down-to-earth advice for journalists trying to figure out wrongs and rights in their work lives, the kind of advice found in the more detailed written operating standards of CBS, NBC, and ABC, and of newspapers like the *Philadelphia Inquirer* and the *Washington Post.* Journalists working for such news organizations have few excuses for ethical lapses.

Many news organizations, however, have declined to lay down written codes of ethics for their staffs, sometimes out of fear that such codes will be picked up by outsiders, particularly judges, and applied as standards for all journalists. That fear has been encouraged by the recent history of judicial aggression against the press. But it seems a shame that a fear of something that might never happen (or if it did happen, might not be so bad or might be successfully combatted) has prevented some newspapers from codifying their ethical standards for all to see and follow.

Some editors and news directors shun written ethical standards because they believe that ethical behavior is best learned from others, from models in the newsroom. It is true that many newsrooms have editors and reporters who are good models for learning how to be ethical journalists. But there are also plenty of bad models, and the folklore of journalism in this country teaches unethical as well as ethical practices. Younger journalists need to know in clearly stated terms what their news organizations and journalism in general regard as ethical and unethical. Tough, clear, written standards in every U.S. newsroom would seem to be a step in that direction.

Radio and television news departments lag way behind newspapers in adopting ethical standards. Since so many broadcast news departments are small, it could be argued that standards do not need to be written because they can be communicated by word of mouth. But the facts of unethical behavior cited in this book indicate a lack of standards rather than a failure to communicate. One of the unfortunate consequences of the decline of network news departments that began in the 1980s is that network journalists will have less influence than in the past on the ethics of broadcast journalism. Network journalists like Bill Moyers, Dan Rather, Peter Jennings, Connie Chung, Roger Mudd, John Chancellor, Eric Sevaried, Walter Cronkite, Charles Kuralt, and Edward R. Murrow have been good models.

Even more important than writing down ethical standards is discussing ethics regularly at all levels of the newsroom. A few news organizations do this now through staff meetings and on-the-spot discussions when specific ethical problems arise. But most do not, and that's a shame.

Journalists and the public need to acknowledge that the business nature of American journalism affects its ethics. The need for news media to find audiences they can sell to advertisers limits the freedom of editors to determine content. Almost all U.S. cities today have but one daily newspaper or two owned by the same company: the disappearing competition between separately owned papers demands new responsibilities of journalists and calls into question some of the possibly unethical methods that grew out of competition. Business necessities may bring new delivery systems to newspapers in the future—through television sets hooked up to home printers, for example—and that certainly will demand a rethinking of ethical principles. Likewise, the ethics and standards of television journalists will need to be examined and reexamined as television news continues to be virtually the only source of news for increasing numbers of Americans and as television reaches more and more into the lower economic and social classes of our cities once served by but now being abandoned by many mass circulation newspapers. So the things that news media have to do to survive as businesses are bound to affect not only their technology and procedures, but their ethics as well.

In recognizing the business tugs and pulls that work on journalism, the public should not assume that journalists have lost control of the news process. They certainly have not. Journalists, even those working for corporate giants, seem to have amazing freedom. The philosophy of not interfering in the newsrooms they own seems to dominate the thinking of all but a few news media managers and proprietors, particularly those at the top of the larger organizations. The business environment in which our news media operate has to be a fact of life for editors and broadcast news directors, but it is not a fact that seriously restricts their ability to determine the ethics and quality of news work in their domains.

AN ASSESSMENT

It was impossible to do the research for this book without forming an impression of the people who do the work of journalism in this country. Most of the some 170 journalists interviewed and the scores whose books and articles were studied came across as highly intelligent and interesting people, very much wrapped up in their jobs. Some pomposity and arrogance popped up, but much less than you would find in a comparable exposure to university professors (and no doubt with other groups with which I am less familiar).

The candid opinions and experiences of the journalists interviewed and studied for this book have been melded into an assessment of how journalists are doing, ethically. I realize, of course, that it is presumptuous for a single observer to make such an assessment (a safer but sillier way would be to survey some "scientifically selected sample" of people with questions designed to bring responses that can be squeezed into a computer). But it would also be unfair to you, the reader, *not* to assess the ethics of journalism in a report on its status. In making this evaluation, I have divided the principal ethical problems of U.S. journalism into seven categories: conflicts of interest, freebies, journalists' methods, privacy, compassion, competence, and accountability.

Readers should understand that many if not most of the case studies and anecdotes in this book depict journalism at its worst. Because they are the exception rather than the rule, most of my case studies do not represent journalism as it is most of the time. The day-to-day behavior and output of most journalists is of a much higher quality than many of my case studies indicate. Investigative reporting, for example, has produced many ethical dilemmas for the journalists involved, but it has also exposed wrongs and wrongdoing and accomplished great good for the nation. Journalism at its best often involves ethical risks.

Conflicts of Interest. Conflicts of interest have been a major target of journalism's recent reformers. But there is disagreement about what constitutes a conflict of interest and whether conflicts should be avoided by all who own or work for the news media or just by those who work in news departments.

The prevailing belief in the field is that editors, directors, reporters, photographers, and newscasters–the people involved in news work–have to avoid outside activities and associations that might unduly influence their ability to process the news impartially. Political activity or partisanship of any sort seems to head the list of taboos, but then the list gets fuzzy. Some would even prohibit affiliation with a political party (registering as a Democrat or Republican) or with a conventional church. Others see memberships in local groups as acceptable, even desirable, but draw the line at holding office or directing publicity.

Conflicts are not always a matter of associations and memberships: Reporters who get too cozy or entangle themselves in confidentiality deals with news sources can get caught up in a conflict of interest. So can those who cooperate with the CIA and law enforcement at all levels. This is not to say that a conflict is created every time a reporter gets on a first-name basis with a source, or goes off the record, or trades information with a cop, but the threat is there. Similarly, journalists who take money from outside interests for free-lance material, speeches, or other services risk conflicts of interest.

Different standards seem to be applied to media owners and to executives not directly involved in news. Some media owners still adhere to the Warren G. Harding model and openly seek and hold partisan political office. More commonly, the outside involvements of media proprietors and business managers are in the business and civic arena, rather than the political one (although the line between business and civic projects and politics is often hard to draw). In smaller and medium-sized communities, local news media are usually among the most important businesses in town. A majority of media owners in such communities seem to feel a responsibility to be involved, in varying degrees, in the kinds of community projects that interest business proprietors. Such activities and involvements undoubtedly contribute to the image of the news media being tied up with and generally representative of business interests.

A double standard between the news department and the owners, publishers, and business managers does not exist in all news organizations. On newspapers like the *Washington Post,* top executives take the view that their outside involvements can create conflicts of interest, real or apparent, that threaten the newspaper's credibility just as much as do the conflicts arising from the activities of news people. If anything, the behavior of the top brass is probably more visible than that of most of the news staffers.

Adding to this confused picture of how journalists deal with conflicts of interest is the spouse problem—what to do about spouses of journalists and news executives who, by their occupations or activities, seem to create a possible conflict of interest for the spouse-journalist and his or her news organization. Most news executives feel that about all a news organization can decently do when such conflicts occur is to move the journalist whose spouse is the problem to an assignment that will minimize the conflict. They hope the public will get used to the idea that in this day and age spouses have a right to their own careers and activities that may create conflicts of interest, real or imagined, beyond the power of the affected news medium to correct.

Journalists and news media owners need to do more thinking about real and apparent conflicts of interest. There is a lot of talk in the field about the appearance of a conflict being as damaging to news media credibility as a real conflict. In other words the offending extrajournalistic activity really does not influence the journalist involved in any damaging way, but it looks bad to the public. Yet in most news organizations anything that appears to be a conflict is prohibited just as if it were a real conflict. Perhaps journalists need to consider disclosing and explaining conflicts of interest rather than prohibiting them when it is the appearance not the reality that is bothersome. The public may not be as intolerant of minor conflicts as journalists seem to assume. After all, conflicts of interest are all about us; no one–not even journalists–can avoid all of them. The avoidance of all conflicts of interest that arise in daily life is another way of saying that you are avoiding life itself in that you are removing yourself from the mainstreams of human action and thought. Do we really want journalists who are so aloof from the rest of us that they inevitably fail to understand the rest of us? There are real conflicts for journalists–working on the side for a news source, for example–but there are lots of activities now seen as "apparent conflicts" that need to be reevaluated.

Freebies. Along with conflicts of interest, freebies have gotten the major attention in the comparatively recent effort to improve the ethics of U.S. journalism. And the progress in banning freebies from news work has been noteworthy as journalists increasingly turn their backs on gifts, free meals and drinks, free or cut-rate transportation and lodging, special price discounts on consumer goods, and press perquisites offered by present or potential news sources. The larger news organizations in particular deserve praise for their mostly successful efforts to remove the "For Sale" sign from journalism.

But would-be seducers of journalists are still out there and they still find acceptance in some newsrooms, particularly those in smaller newspapers and broadcast stations. In many cases, owners and operators of smaller media encourage their reporters and editors to take freebies by keeping their news departments on such miserly budgets that some important news cannot be covered unless a free ticket, free ride, or free lodging is provided. It is difficult to believe, in view of the generally good health that media operations enjoy in the U.S. economy, that smaller news operations cannot pay their own way to the essential news events, at least. When managements encourage the acceptance of freebies for their staffs to cover news, it is no wonder that individual staff members have a hard time drawing lines between accepting freebie A to cover an out-of-town football game, freebie B to take the family on a free trip to an amusement park, and freebie C to get a better price on a new car.

It should be said that there has been some silliness in journalism's drive to eliminate freebies. There is a difference between accepting a meal from a news source who insists that lunch in his office is the only time he has to spare for you and accepting a junket from a Hollywood film studio interested in promoting a new movie. Nor does letting a news source buy you a drink once in a while constitute a major ethical sin. Journalists have to be trusted to decide when a freebie is apt to compromise them and when rejecting one would do more harm than good in their primary mission of getting and understanding the news.

Journalists' Methods. Some of the methods journalists use to get news and present it are ethically sleazy. Lying to people, by faking or manufacturing news and plagiarizing, are such flagrant violations of the accuracy standard and so out of place in modern journalism that they should not have to be discussed in a book on journalism ethics. Yet they emerged as two of journalism's thorniest ethical problems in the 1980s. This is not to suggest that our newsrooms are full of liars. But the fact that some writers have recently admitted they made up news stories has stirred up fear in the field that there must have been others who got away with it and still others waiting in the wings to pass off fiction as fact.

Hyping news by the use of exciting language, whether the facts justify it or not, and by taking little shortcuts with the facts, is a more common problem in their field than journalists like to admit. And the hyping is done not just by the reporters trying to make their stories sound better than they are but by editors trying to sell those stories for the front page, or even for prizes.

The various uses of deception and misrepresentation by journalists have raised some bewildering ethical questions. On the surface, deceiving somebody by misrepresenting who you are, passively or actively, seems unethical. Yet some very honorable journalists argue that the only way to get close to the truth about certain vital situations is to get on the inside and watch what is going on, like a fly on the ceiling, or even participate enough to get a feel for what is going on. That is usually called undercover reporting and some leaders in the field oppose its use except in extraordinary circumstances. But there are just as many if not more editors who see nothing wrong with using undercover reporting if the conventional methods of observation, interviewing, and library research do not work on some important investigation.

Most undercover reporting requires reporters to pretend they are somebody other than reporters: auto workers, welders, common laborers, seamstresses, tavern owners, dance instructors, accident victims, convicted wife killers, vagrants, burglars, or nursing home aides, to mention a few of the roles reporters have played in recent newspaper undercover reporting projects. Often when reporters go undercover they do so with the knowledge of some official in the subject area being investigated: for example, the Illinois Department of Law Enforcement was brought in on the deal by the *Chicago Sun-Times* when it bought and operated a tavern to expose shakedowns by city inspectors. Letting some official or agency know what your reporters are doing surreptitiously may make things safer for the reporters and may make editors feel more ethical about it, but such cooperation is not always possible and it does not change the fact that people still are deceived by reporters posing as others.

Reporters also misrepresent themselves in everyday reporting. It is not too serious ethically when they merely pass as members of the public – at a large public meeting or checking on retail prices, for example. But it is disgraceful when reporters lead news sources to believe that they are cops, coroners, or other law enforcement officials to get people to tell them things they might not tell reporters.

The overuse of secret sources in news articles has hurt journalism's credibility. When important sources of information and opinion are not specifically identified, the public is apt to distrust or dismiss what is written. Except in life- or society-threatening situations where source protection is the only way reporters can obtain essential information, journalists ought to close ranks against leakers and news manipulators who insist on anonymity.

Eavesdropping is occasionally resorted to by a reporter who has been barred from some important meeting or event. Eavesdropping with the naked ear is the usual way that reporters try to learn what is going on behind the closed door or wall, and that is probably more undignified than it is unethical. But using electronic listening devices or phone taps is an absolute "no-no" to all of the journalists interviewed for this book. Division exists, however, about surreptitious taping, most journalists feeling squeamish about its use except in extreme situations, but many arguing that taping is no different from note taking. I side with those who believe recording someone without his or her knowledge is dishonest, but I don't see this as a major ethical issue.

More serious ethical problems are raised by pack journalism, assigning so many reporters and photographers to certain "hot" stories that the journalists become part of the story, or get used by the orchestrators of the "hot" event, or both. The overcoverage of some few events is especially sad when you realize how many local situations that need to be exposed get scant or no coverage at all.

The present policy in most newsrooms of protecting the public from many of the shocking photographs and words that often crop up in the news usually results in a distorted picture. We do not need more sensational *National Enquirers* or *New York Posts,* but news executives should test their assumptions about what shocks the public and how much shock the public is willing to accept if the information is essential. More research might lead to more truthful portrayals of certain news now heavily blue-penciled because of fears that people will be shocked.

The ambush interview when used by television journalists can sometimes make the ambushed person appear to be guilty without a fair trial. That may make good theater, but it is unfair. Responsible journalists should reserve that technique for public officials and miscreants who obviously need to be called to account. The ambush interview is also a method that print journalists use, but it is less of an ethical problem when the interviewees are not being photographed as they stumble incoherently or run away from hard questions.

Most news photographers hold that taking pictures of people in public places is fair game regardless of whether the people realize their pictures are being taken. But a published photograph can still be unfairly embarrassing or humiliating to the subjects even if they are in public places. The use of hidden cameras can raise more serious ethical questions. Hiding the camera may be justified if the story being exposed is important and in the interest of the public, such as surreptitiously photographing police officers accepting bribes, but responsible photographers avoid visual eavesdropping in less obviously vital news situations.

It is probably unfair to mention stealing or rifling garbage cans in this list of dubious methods because they occur so rarely, but a few reporters have done such things. And when you add stealing and garbage rifling to the more commonly employed methods of hidden cameras, ambush interviews, eavesdropping, pack reporting, misrepresentation, deception, hyping, plagiarizing, and lying, you get a picture that falls short of an ethical profession.

Privacy. American news media, by and large, have shown sensitivity about protecting the identity of rape victims and juveniles involved in lesser crimes. The changing attitude of journalists and society toward less protection does not detract from the commendable restraint that journalists have often shown in cases in which publicity might have done more harm than good.

Now that law enforcement and the courts are increasing access to records and proceedings in juvenile cases, the responsibility for deciding how much the public needs to know about particular cases is shifting from the law to the newsroom. It is hoped that journalists will handle this new responsibility with sensitivity and continue to protect the identity of juveniles who deserve a second chance. Compared to the opening up of juvenile justice, the trend to identify victims as well as the accused in rape cases is, fortunately, barely visible. But there are strong-minded editors out there who continue to defy the thinking of the majority of journalists by regularly identifying rape victims with little regard for the harm that may be doing to the women involved. Those particular editors, and journalists in general, need to pay more heed to the counselors who work with rape victims and know better than most of us how cruel and uncivil it is in most cases for the media to treat rape the same as they do other crimes of violence.

Invading the privacy of public persons and their families is often justifiable, but just as often overdone. Public officials, particularly at the upper levels, give up some of their privacy when they enter the goldfish bowl of government service, but they don't give up all of it. Journalists have not always recognized the right to and need for some privacy by even the highest ranking public officials—and particularly members of their families. The publicity given to the troubles of the late David Kennedy, Randy Agnew, and Senator Scott's forty-one-year-old daughter in recent years struck an awful lot of people as unfair. Celebrities who lead public lives and depend on publicity for their livelihood invite invasions of their privacy, but the news media have also invaded the privacy of relatives of celebrities who are not public persons seeking publicity.

Another bad practice is the way journalists invade the privacy of ordinary people caught up in the news involuntarily. Barging into private property after a tragedy has occurred or a crime has been committed is inexcusable. So is taking advantage of people who are unsophisticated about dealing with journalists and who may unknowingly, even trustingly, permit invasions of their privacy. Most journalists are not insensitive oafs, but some still act as if they had some God-given right to roll over other people in the name of the public's right to know.

Another troubling tendency in the privacy area is for journalists to rely on law and court decisions to guide their conduct. That cop-out too often results in a newsroom decision based not on what is right or wrong, but on "How far can we go and still win a lawsuit?" Journalists need to think through the ethics of privacy and come up with guidelines that are clearer and more responsible than those derived from the complexities of privacy law.

Compassion. Many journalists will quarrel with compassion as a category of ethical problems in the news business. They either do not see it as a big ethical issue or they fear that the softness implied by that emotion might deter the primary mission of journalism—to get the news out.

But it is treated here as one of the important categories of ethical problems because, in a way, a scarcity of compassion is at the base of many of the troubles journalists have with methods, privacy, and other ethical areas. Failure to feel sympathy for or empathize with the people involved in news—sources and subjects alike—produces a sterile sort of journalism that is superficial at best and grossly misleading at worst.

The lack of compassion displayed by some journalists has also created the impression in the public's mind that journalists and the news media (newspapers, in particular) are arrogant and uncaring. That is the impression many people got of the *Washington Post* when its executives appeared not to care about the life or death of "Jimmy," the eight-year-old heroin addict in Janet Cooke's moving article (assumed then to be true and not the fabrication it later turned out to be).

There seems to be something in the way many journalists interpret their role as neutral observers that makes them come across as cold and uncaring. This impression is conveyed, not just in the few clearcut cases in which journalists turn their backs on human victims in the name of doing their jobs, but in their often uncivil and snobbish treatment of news sources, both on and off camera. The great journalists are people who excel at getting the news out but who also never forget their humanity. Being humble and compassionate in dealing with other human beings involved in the news should be seen as virtues in a news professional.

Journalists have also lost public esteem when they have shunned their responsibilities as citizens and asked for special privileges. There are times, of course, when journalists may have to be uncooperative with government by not testifying about legitimate secret sources, but journalists should argue for that special treatment only in extreme cases, working harder than most do now to get more sources on the record. Constantly insisting that courts and other arms of government exempt them from the responsibilities that all citizens are supposed to bear makes journalists appear to be seeking privileges. That impression coupled with the image of being uncaring in their attitudes toward other people has certainly handicapped journalists in their primary job of getting the news out.

Competence. All the ethics codes and discussions will be for naught if the competence level of journalists is not sufficient to support quality journalism up and down the line. Competence may be the number one ethical problem in the field.

It may be asking too much of journalists that they improve on their knowledge and skills: after all, they already have more formal education than the average person. But journalists are our educators, teaching most of us most of what we know about the world outside of our immediate experiences. Don't we expect our teachers to know more than their students?

Every newsroom in the country has incompetent people. Errors and misinterpretations continue to be a major problem in every news medium we have. There is a great concern among thoughtful journalists about the lack of effective training for news executives: too many editors and broadcast news directors get promoted to those higher-paying positions because they were good reporters. Not many reporters, no matter how good they are, can stop reporting news one day and become good editors the next. Some never become good editors.

Several things would seem to be needed to improve competence in journalism. Despite the occasional whimpers from small-minded publishers and broadcast owners that they want colleges to send them more technicians, the obvious need in all newsrooms is for more depth of education, not less. And something has got to be done about those disgraceful beginning salaries that not only discourage potential journalists from getting more education for news work, but also discourage potential journalists, period. Perhaps news executives could find the money to pay more to beginners by paying less to or culling out the incompetents who now occupy a chair or a video display terminal or two in every newsroom in the country. At the same time, greater efforts need to be made to retain competents who now leave news work for public relations, education, politics and government, and other more lucrative and challenging careers. This flight from news work by competent journalists has left most newsrooms with an overpopulation of people under thirty-five, when a balance of ages and experiences would be more desirable. News organizations ought to run more in-house training programs for their news staffs and send more staffers to good educational programs around the country. And the programs should not be just on the rudiments of cropping photos or laying out pages, but on substantive matters as well.

Most news organizations would elevate their general level of competence by adding more minorities to their staffs. Blacks and other minorities are so underrepresented in American journalism that news reporting and judgment are distorted. In most newsrooms the viewpoints of minorities are simply not a major part of the news process. Many news executives are working hard to correct this failing, but progress has been much too slow. Women were similarly underrepresented in news work in an earlier day, but that picture has changed rapidly in my lifetime. Although women have had a harder time moving into top executive positions in journalism, they have begun to establish themselves as equals in a once male-dominated profession. Journalism has been improved by opening itself up to women and it will be further improved if it will do the same for blacks and other minorities in this country.

Finally, news organizations need to hire and retain more people of character. That's a big order, of course. How do you tell whether a person has character? You can easily find out whether he or she can write reasonably clear English, but there's no quick test for character. Yet, there is no doubt that we could stop worrying about ethical standards, codes, and the like if journalism were populated only with men and women with integrity and a high sense of morality. Hiring and retaining people of character should be a goal at least of every news organization.

Accountability. The news media—newspapers in particular—are doing a more conscientious job of correcting their errors these days. But the overall record of the news media in accounting for themselves to the public is less commendable.

There is first the problem of some media owners not accepting the idea that they need to be accountable to anybody (beyond their stockholders if they are public companies). They see their media properties as private businesses and nothing more, ignoring the responsibility to society that stems from the special constitutional protection afforded the press in our system. Fortunately, these Neanderthal proprietors seem to be fading out.

The second problem with news media accountability is that the various instruments for achieving it have not gained general acceptance in the news business.

Only a handful of news organizations—the three broadcast networks and about 40 of the 1,670 daily newspapers—have ombudsmen, and the movement has spread ever so slowly. Many editors who have not established ombudsmen or readers' representatives argue that they themselves handle readers' complaints and provide internal criticism of their staffs, but the evidence that they do this well is skimpy.

The death in 1984 of the National News Council left the country with only two small news councils—one in Minnesota covering only that state, and the other in Honolulu with jurisdiction only in that city. The news council idea, which has seemed to work in Britain and some European countries, simply has not gained the support of most of American journalism.

Reporters assigned to criticizing the way journalism works are few and far between. David Shaw does that chore for the *Los Angeles Times* but he's almost alone. Some other news media, notably the *New York Times, Wall Street Journal, Washington Post, Newsday, Time,* and *Newsweek,* report regularly on the news business, but are short on sustained criticism. As a whole, journalism does a dismal job of reporting on and criticizing itself.

There aren't many outside critics either. Except for two national journalism reviews and a handful of smaller ones, and except for an occasional university professor, the outside critics of American journalism are mostly ideological. Ideological, in that they represent some special interest group, such as the AFL-CIO or the U.S. Chamber of Commerce, or some special point of view, such as that expressed in the criticism of the conservative Accuracy in Media. Those ideological criticisms may be sincere, but they are too easy for journalists to dismiss as coming from vested interests who are neither independent nor representative of the general public.

Perhaps some new instrument through which the public can call journalists into account needs to be invented. But its invention will be for naught if journalists continue in their stubborn resistance against having anyone outside their own organizations looking over their shoulders. Individual members of the public may have their complaints satisfied by calls or letters to editors or ombudsmen, or through lawsuits, but the kind of accountability that is needed is broader than that. The public needs to be continually assured that the vital role journalism plays in providing independent information and analysis is not being tainted, abused, or handled irresponsibly.

ETHICS THRIVES ON QUALITY

It may seem to the casual reader that some of the better known and most respected news operations in the country have more ethical problems than the lesser known ones. So many examples of questionable behavior in this book came from our most respected media. Part of the explanation for the abundance of ethical violations or marginal practices by the better news organizations lies in their visibility, the attention they get from media watchers. But the other explanation lies in their quality: because they seek out the news aggressively, they take more risks and get into more trouble. News organizations that play it safe and do little more than report what news comes in over the transom or from the wire services do not get into too many conventional ethical problems. But they commit the biggest ethical sin of all: failure to fulfill the primary responsibility of reporting the news fairly, accurately, aggressively, and as comprehensively as possible.

In my judgment, the most ethical journalists in the business are found in quality news operations, large and small. But there are many journalists out there who never get a chance to learn and practice either good or ethical journalism because they work for sleazy news operations that cover the news superficially, cater to the power elements in their communities, and avoid controversy.

If, as it seems, quality and ethics go hand in hand, then journalism will have to get better in many ways to become an ethical calling. As long as there are Thomson newspaper chains and radio stations with one-person news departments and media owners who see themselves as being socially responsible because they never let their news operations rock any boats, U.S. journalism as a whole may never get an A for ethics. But all except the substandard operations can earn top grades if the leaders in the news business want improved ethical practices in the first place and are willing to engage in honest dialogue to get them. The dialogue will have to include all levels of journalism – owners and managers, reporters, editors, photographers, news producers, and directors from both large and small media. And it also ought to include educators in journalism and communications and members of the general public.

And then after the talk, talk, talk has gone far enough, news executives will have to start making the changes that seem called for to bring greater quality and better ethics to the practice of journalism. The dialogue should continue, of course, because so many of the ethical quandaries journalists face do not lend themselves to quick solution by following rule a and principle b. Many times the only solution is the best answer that civilized people reasoning together can come up with at that moment. Civil discourse, that's what's needed.

In their striving for more ethical practices, journalists are well advised to avoid seeking special privileges for themselves and the news media. Freedom of the press and of speech belong to everybody in the American system, not just journalists. And journalists do not stop being citizens or human beings when they go to work. Ethical principles that segregate journalists as a class from the rest of society ill serve either journalism or society. What is needed is a set of principles based on a journalism that serves the public by aggressively seeking and reporting the closest possible truth about events and conditions of concern to people, a journalism that collects and deals with information honestly and fairly and treats the people involved with compassion, a journalism that conscientiously interprets and explains the news so that it makes sense to people. That's all.

Codes of Ethics of Major National Organizations of Journalists in the United States

SOCIETY OF PROFESSIONAL JOURNALISTS, SIGMA DELTA CHI

The Society of Professional Journalists, Sigma Delta Chi, believes the duty of journalists is to serve the truth.

We believe the agencies of mass communication are carriers of public discussion and information, acting on their Constitutional mandate and freedom to learn and report the facts.

We believe in public enlightenment as the forerunner of justice, and in our Constitutional role to seek the truth as part of the public's right to know the truth.

We believe those responsibilities carry obligations that require journalists to perform with intelligence, objectivity, accuracy and fairness.

To these ends, we declare acceptance of the standards of practice here set forth:

Responsibility. The public's right to know of events of public importance and interest is the overriding mission of the mass media. The purpose of distributing news and enlightened opinion is to serve the general welfare. Journalists who use their professional status as representatives of the public for selfish or other unworthy motives violate a high trust.

Freedom of the Press. Freedom of the press is to be guarded as an inalienable right of people in a free society. It carries with it the freedom and the responsibility to discuss, question and challenge actions and utterances of our government and of our public and private institutions. Journalists uphold the right to speak unpopular opinions and the privilege to agree with the majority.

Ethics. Journalists must be free of obligation to any interest other than the public's right to know the truth.

1. Gifts, favors, free travel, special treatment or privileges can compromise the integrity of journalists and their employers. Nothing of value should be accepted.

2. Secondary employment, political involvement, holding public office and service in community organizations should be avoided if it compromises the integrity of journalists and their employers. Journalists and their employers should conduct their personal lives in a manner which protects them from conflict of interest, real or apparent. Their responsibilities to the public are paramount. This is the nature of their profession.

3. So-called news communications from private sources should not be published or broadcast without substantiation of their claims to news value.

4. Journalists will seek news that serves the public interest, despite the obstacles. They will make constant efforts to assure that the public's business is conducted in public and that public records are open to public inspection.

5. Journalists acknowledge the newsman's ethic of protecting confidential sources of information.

6. Plagiarism is dishonest and is unacceptable.

Accuracy and Objectivity. Good faith with the public is the foundation of all worthy journalism.

1. Truth is our ultimate goal.

2. Objectivity in reporting the news is another goal which serves as the mark of an experienced professional. It is a standard of performance toward which we strive. We honor those who achieve it.

3. There is no excuse for inaccuracies or lack of thoroughness.

4. Newspaper headlines should be fully warranted by the contents of the articles they accompany. Photographs and telecasts should give an accurate picture of an event and not highlight a minor incident out of context.

5. Sound practice makes clear distinction between news reports and expressions of opinion. News reports should be free of opinion or bias and represent all sides of an issue.

6. Partisanship in editorial comment which knowingly departs from the truth violates the spirit of American journalism.

7. Journalists recognize their responsibility for offering informed analysis, comment and editorial opinion on public events and issues. They accept the obligation to present such material by individuals whose competence, experience and judgment qualify them for it.

8. Special articles or presentations devoted to advocacy or the writer's own conclusions and interpretations should be labeled as such.

Fair Play. Journalists at all times will show respect for the dignity, privacy, rights and well-being of people encountered in the course of gathering and presenting the news.

1. The news media should not communicate unofficial charges affecting reputation or moral character without giving the accused a chance to reply.

2. The news media must guard against invading a person's right to privacy.

3. The media should not pander to morbid curiosity about details of vice and crime.

4. It is the duty of news media to make prompt and complete correction of their errors.

5. Journalists should be accountable to the public for their reports and the public should be encouraged to voice its grievances against the media. Open dialogue with our readers, viewers and listeners should be fostered.

Pledge. Journalists should actively censure and try to prevent violations of these standards, and they should encourage their observance by all newspeople. Adherence to this code of ethics is intended to preserve the bond of mutual trust and respect between American journalists and the American people.

Adopted 1973. Revised 1984.

AMERICAN SOCIETY OF NEWSPAPER EDITORS: A STATEMENT OF PRINCIPLES

Preamble. The First Amendment, protecting freedom of expression from abridgment by any law, guarantees to the people through their press a constitutional right, and thereby places on newspaper people a particular responsibility.

Thus journalism demands of its practitioners not only industry and knowledge but also the pursuit of a standard of integrity proportionate to the journalist's singular obligation.

To this end the American Society of Newspaper Editors sets forth this Statement of Principles as a standard encouraging the highest ethical and professional performance.

Article I – *Responsibility.* The primary purpose of gathering and distributing news and opinion is to serve the general welfare by informing the people and enabling them to make judgments on the issues of the time. Newspapermen and women who abuse the power of their professional role for selfish motives or unworthy purposes are faithless to that public trust.

The American press was made free not just to inform or just to serve as a forum for debate but also to bring an independent scrutiny to bear on the forces of power in the society, including the conduct of official power at all levels of government.

Article II – *Freedom of the Press.* Freedom of the press belongs to the people. It must be defended against encroachment or assault from any quarter, public or private.

Journalists must be constantly alert to see that the public's business is conducted in public. They must be vigilant against all who would exploit the press for selfish purposes.

Article III – *Independence.* Journalists must avoid impropriety and the appearance of impropriety as well as any conflict of interest or the appearance of conflict. They should neither accept anything nor pursue any activity that might compromise or seem to compromise their integrity.

Article IV – *Truth and Accuracy.* Good faith with the reader is the foundation of good journalism. Every effort must be made to assure that the news content is accurate, free from bias and in context, and that all sides are presented fairly. Editorials, analytical articles and commentary should be held to the same standards of accuracy with respect to facts as news reports.

Significant errors of fact, as well as errors of omission, should be corrected promptly and prominently.

Article V — *Impartiality.* To be impartial does not require the press to be unquestioning or to refrain from editorial expression. Sound practice, however, demands a clear distinction for the reader between news reports and opinion. Articles that contain opinion or personal interpretation should be clearly identified.

Article VI — *Fair Play.* Journalists should respect the rights of people involved in the news, observe the common standards of decency and stand accountable to the public for the fairness and accuracy of their news reports.

Persons publicly accused should be given the earliest opportunity to respond.

Pledges of confidentiality to news sources must be honored at all costs, and therefore should not be given lightly. Unless there is clear and pressing need to maintain confidences, sources of information should be identified.

These principles are intended to preserve, protect and strengthen the bond of trust and respect between American journalists and the American people, a bond that is essential to sustain the grant of freedom entrusted to both by the nation's founders.

Adopted by the ASNE board of directors, October 1975.

RADIO-TELEVISION NEWS DIRECTORS ASSOCIATION

The members of the Radio-Television News Directors Association agree that their prime responsibility as journalists — and that of the broadcasting industry as the collective sponsor of news broadcasting — is to provide to the public they serve a news service as accurate, full and prompt as human integ-

rity and devotion can devise. To that end, they declare their acceptance of the standards of practice here set forth, and their solemn intent to honor them to the limits of their ability.

Article One. The primary purpose of broadcast journalists – to inform the public of events of importance and appropriate interest in a manner that is accurate and comprehensive – shall override all other purposes.

Article Two. Broadcast news presentations shall be designed not only to offer timely and accurate information, but also to present it in the light of relevant circumstances that give it meaning and perspective.

This standard means that news reports, when clarity demands it, will be laid against pertinent factual background; that factors such as race, creed, nationality or prior status will be reported only when they are relevant; that comment or subjective content will be properly identified; and that errors in fact will be promptly acknowledged and corrected.

Article Three. Broadcast journalists shall seek to select material for newscasts solely on their evaluation of its merits as news.

This standard means that news will be selected on the criteria of significance, community and regional relevance, appropriate human interest and service to defined audiences. It excludes sensationalism or misleading emphasis in any form; subservience to external or "interested" efforts to influence news selection and presentation, whether from within the broadcasting industry or from without. It requires that such terms as "bulletin" and "flash" can be used only when the character of the news justifies them; that bombastic or misleading descriptions of newsroom facilities and personnel be rejected, along with undue use of sound and visual effects; and that promotional or publicity material be sharply scrutinized before use and identified by source or otherwise when broadcast.

Article Four. Broadcast journalists shall at all times display humane respect for the dignity, privacy and the well-being of persons with whom the news deals.

Article Five. Broadcast journalists shall govern their personal lives and such nonprofessional associations as may impinge on their professional activities in a manner that will protect them from conflict of interest, real or apparent.

Article Six. Broadcast journalists shall seek to actively present all news, the knowledge of which will serve the public interest, no matter what selfish, uninformed or corrupt efforts attempt to color it, withhold it or prevent its presentation. They shall make constant efforts to open doors closed to the reporting of public proceedings with tools appropriate to broadcasting (including cameras and recorders), consistent with the public interest. They acknowledge the journalist's ethic of protection of confidential information and sources and urge unswerving observation of it except in instances in which it would clearly and unmistakably defy the public interest.

Article Seven. Broadcast journalists recognize the responsibility borne by broadcasting for informed analysis, comment and editorial opinion on public events and issues. They accept the obligation of broadcasters for the presentation of such matters by individuals whose competence, experience and judgment qualify them for it.

Article Eight. In court, broadcast journalists shall conduct themselves with dignity, whether the court is in or out of session. They shall keep broadcast equipment as unobtrusive and silent as possible. Where court facilities are inadequate, pool broadcasts should be arranged.

Article Nine. In reporting matters that are or may be litigated, the journalist shall avoid practices which would tend to interfere with the right of an individual to a fair trial.

Article Ten. Broadcast journalists shall not misrepresent the source of any broadcast news material.

Article Eleven. Broadcast journalists shall actively censure and seek to prevent violations of these standards, and shall actively encourage their observance by all journalists, whether of the Radio-Television News Directors Association or not.

Adopted 1966; Revised 1973.

ASSOCIATED PRESS MANAGING EDITORS ASSOCIATION CODE OF ETHICS FOR NEWSPAPERS AND THEIR STAFFS

This code is a model against which newspaper men and women can measure their performance. It is meant to apply to news and editorial staff members and others who are involved in, or who influence, news coverage and editorial policy. It has been formulated in the belief that newspapers and the people who produce them should adhere to the highest standards of ethical and professional conduct.

Responsibility. A good newspaper is fair, accurate, honest, responsible, independent and decent. Truth is its guiding principle.

It avoids practices that would conflict with the ability to report and present news in a fair and unbiased manner.

The newspaper should serve as a constructive critic of all segments of society. It should vigorously expose wrongdoing or misuse of power, public or private. Editorially, it should advocate needed reform or innovations in the public interest.

News sources should be disclosed unless there is clear reason not to do so. When it is necessary to protect the confidentiality of a source, the reason should be explained.

The newspaper should background, with the facts, public statements that it knows to be inaccurate or misleading. It should uphold the right of free speech and freedom of the press and should respect the individual's right of privacy.

The public's right to know about matters of importance is paramount, and the newspaper should fight vigorously for public access to news of government through open meetings and open records.

Accuracy. The newspaper should guard against inaccuracies, carelessness, bias or distortion through either emphasis or omission.

It should admit all substantive errors and correct them promptly and prominently.

Integrity. The newspaper should strive for impartial treatment of issues and dispassionate handling of controversial subjects. It should provide a forum for the exchange of comment and criticism, especially when such comment is opposed to its editorial positions. Editorials and other expressions of opinion by reporters and editors should be clearly labeled.

The newspaper should report the news without regard for its own interests. It should not give favored news treatment to advertisers or special-interest groups. It should report matters regarding itself or its personnel with the same vigor and candor as it would other institutions or individuals.

Concern for community, business or personal interests should not cause a newspaper to distort or misrepresent the facts.

Conflicts of Interest. The newspaper and its staff should be free of obligations to news sources and special interests. Even the appearance of obligation or conflict of interest should be avoided.

Newspapers should accept nothing of value from news sources or others outside the profession. Gifts and free or reduced-rate travel, entertainment, products and lodging should not be accepted. Expenses in connection with news reporting should be paid by the newspaper. Special favors and special treatment for members of the press should be avoided.

Involvement in such things as politics, community affairs, demonstrations and social causes that could cause a conflict of interest, or the appearance of such conflict, should be avoided.

Outside employment by news sources is an obvious conflict of interest, and employment by potential news sources also should be avoided.

Financial investments by staff members or other outside business interests that could conflict with the newspaper's ability to report the news or that would create the impression of such conflict should be avoided.

Stories should not be written or edited primarily for the purpose of winning awards and prizes. Blatantly commercial journalism contests, or others that reflect unfavorably on the newspaper or the profession, should be avoided.

No code of ethics can prejudge every situation. Common sense and good judgment are required in applying ethical principles to newspaper realities. Individual newspapers are encouraged to augment these APME guidelines with locally produced codes that apply more specifically to their own situations.

A model code for members adopted by the
APME Board of Directors, April 1975.

Notes

1

1. George Bernard Shaw, *Pygmalion and Other Plays* (New York: Dodd, Mead, 1967), 45.

2. Interview by author, 9 Sept. 1981.

3. Interview by author, 25 Nov. 1980.

4. Interview by author, 7 Oct. 1981.

5. Interview by author, 24 Sept. 1981.

6. Interview by author, 5 June 1981.

7. Paul Janensch, "Journalistic Ethics . . . Public Discussion and Private Soul-searching," Louisville *Courier-Journal,* 4 Oct. 1981.

8. Interview by author, 8 Apr. 1981.

9. *A Free and Responsible Press: Report of the Commission on Freedom of the Press,* Robert M. Hutchins, chair. (Chicago: Univ. of Chicago Press, 1947); Fred S. Siebert, Theodore Peterson, Wilbur Schramm, *Four Theories of the Press* (Urbana: Univ. of Illinois Press, 1956), 74–78.

10. Siebert et al., *Four Theories,* 77.

11. Interview by author, 3 Sept. 1981.

12. Clifford G. Christians, "Fifty Years of Scholarship in Media Ethics," *Journal of Communication* 27, no. 4(Autumn 1977):23.

13. John L. Hulteng, *The Messenger's Motives: Ethical Problems of the News Media,* 2d. ed. (Englewood Cliffs, N.J.: Prentice-Hall, 1985), 12.

14. Harold L. Cross, *The People's Right to Know* (New York: Columbia Univ. Press, 1953).

15. Interview by author, 5 June 1981.

16. Walter Lippmann, *Public Opinion* (New York: Macmillan, 1922; Free Press Paperback, 1965), 226.

17. Interview by author, 8 Oct. 1981.

18. Edwin R. Bayley, *Joe McCarthy and the Press* (New York: Pantheon, 1982), 212.

19. Interview by author, 25 Nov. 1980.

20. *Problems of Journalism: Proceedings of the ASNE 1923* (Washington, D.C.: ASNE 1923), 39–52, 118–25.

21. Clifford Christians, "Enforcing Media Codes," *Journal of Mass Media Ethics* 1, no. 1(Fall/Winter 1985–86):14–21.

22. Interview by author, 19 Mar. 1986.

23. Interview by author, 10 Sept. 1981.

24. Interview by author, 2 Sept. 1981.

25. Interview by author, 7 Oct. 1981.

26. Interview by author, 14 Mar. 1986.

27. "Newsroom Ethics: How Tough Is Enforcement?" ASNE Ethics Committee Report, 1986.

28. Interview by author, 28 May 1981.

29. Interview by author, 19 Oct. 1981.

30. Interview by author, 14 Oct. 1981.

31. Estimate provided by David J. Eisen, director of research and information, the Newspaper Guild, Washington, D.C., Apr. 1981; updated by author for 2d ed.

32. Interview by author, 17 Apr. 1981.

33. Interview by author, 18 Apr. 1981.

34. Memorandum to Guild officials from Richard J. Ramsey, executive secretary, contracts committee, the Newspaper Guild, Apr. 13, 1976.

35. Norman E. Isaacs, "Journalism Ethics–1975–2000," lecture at Washington and Lee University; reprinted in *Social Responsibility: Journalism, Law, Medicine* (Lexington, V.: Washington and Lee University, 1975).

36. Interview by author, 7 Oct. 1981.

37. Daniel J. Leab, *A Union of Individuals: The Formation of the American Newspaper Guild, 1933-1936* (New York: Columbia Univ. Press, 1970).

38. Charles Perlik, remarks prepared for panel discussion at Region 5 convention, SPJ-SDX, Muncie, Ind., 9 Apr. 1976.

39. Interviews by author, 17 Apr. 1981.

40. Interview by author, 10 Feb. 1986.

2

1. David H. Weaver and G. Cleveland Wilhoit, *The American Journalist: A Portrait of U.S. News People and Their Work* (Bloomington: Indiana Univ. Press, 1986), 13. Because Weaver and Wilhoit did not include broadcast network journalists or photographers unless they were also reporters in their estimates of a total of 112,072 full-time editorial workers for U.S. news media, the author, based on readings and interviews, added 3,000 broadcast network journalists and 1,000 news photographers to the Weaver and Wilhoit figures.

2. Interview by author, 4 Nov. 1981.

3. Interview by author, 25 Nov. 1980.

4. Interview by author, 4 June 1981.

5. "Journalistic Ethics: Some Probings by a Media Keeper," *Nieman Reports,* Winter/Spring 1978, 9–10.

6. A. Kent MacDougall, "In Reporting Profits, There Are Many Bottom Lines," *Los Angeles Times,* 7 Feb. 1980.

7. The data in the preceding two paragraphs are the author's interpretation of several sources, including "Facts About Newspapers '86," American Newspaper Publishers Association; "Gannett Gets Louisville Papers for 300 Million," *New York Times,* 20 May 1986, A1, D4; and "Groups Now Own 73 Percent of U.S. Dailies," *Presstime* 9, no. 3(Mar. 1987):76.

8. Figures for broadcast stations provided to author by the FCC as of 31 May 1986.

9. Actually, the FCC's 1984 ruling also stipulates that no broadcaster can own so many TV stations that collectively they reach more than 25 percent of the nation's television homes. In this computation, UHF television stations are being assessed for only half of a market's TV homes. And if two AM radio stations, two FM radio stations, and two TV stations in a group are controlled by minorities, that group can go up to fourteen stations and reach up to 30 percent of the nation's TV households. See Harvey J. Levin, "U.S. Broadcast Deregulation: A Case of Dubious Evidence," *Journal of Communication* 36, no. 1(Winter 1986):27.

10. Interview by author, 5 Oct. 1981.

11. Interview by author, 15 Oct. 1981.

12. Interviews by author, 28 May and 15 Sept. 1981.

13. Interview by author, 7 Oct. 1981.

14. Interview by author, 29 Oct. 1981.

15. "General Electric to Acquire RCA in a Deal Valued at $6.28 Billion," *New York Times,* 12 Dec. 1985, A1, D2; "ABC to Be Bought by Capital Cities; Price $3.5 Billion," *New York Times,* 19 Mar. 1985, A1, D24; "Lorimar Purchasing 7 TV Stations," *New York Times,* 22 May 1986, D1; "Tribune Co. to Buy LA TV Station for $510 Million," *Editor & Publisher,* 25 May 1985, 28.

16. "Evening News to Go to Gannett," *New York Times,* 30 Aug. 1985, D1; "Gannett Makes Two Major Acquisitions," *Presstime* 7, no. 3(Mar. 1985):68.

17. "Newspaper Is Sold in Dallas," *New York Times,* 27 June 1986, D1; "Times Mirror Agrees to Buy Baltimore's Sun Newspapers," *New York Times,* 29 May 1986, A1, D8.

18. "Sun-Times Is Sold for $145 Million," *New York Times,* 1 July 1986, D4.

19. "Mr. Murdoch, American," *New York Times,* 5 Sept. 1985, B3.

20. Margaret Genovese, "Hot Newspaper Market Cools Down," *Presstime* 3, no. 5(May 1981):4–7.

21. J. Hart Clinton, "Fate of Independents Is Cause for Alarm," *Presstime* 3, no. 5(May 1981):23.

22. Christopher H. Sterling and Timothy R. Haight, *The Mass Media: Aspen Institute Guide to Communication Industry Trends* (New York: Praeger, 1978), 83.

23. The author has extrapolated these figures from "Group-owned Dailies: 1,186; Independents: 489," *Presstime* 8, no. 3(Mar. 1986):68.

24. Interview by author, 16 Oct. 1981.

25. Clark Newsom, "For Competing Dailies, Disappearing Act Goes On," *Presstime* 3, no. 5(May 1981):8–9.

26. *Facts About Newspapers '86* (Reston, Va.: American Newspaper Publishers Association, 1986), 14.

27. Interview by author, 4 June 1981.

28. "CBS Broadcast Group Says It Will Cut 700 Jobs," *New York Times,* 3 July 1986, C30.

29. "Daily News Tells Staff of Layoffs," *New York Times,* 29 June 1986, 28.

30. *Facts About Newspapers '86,* 9.

31. Interview by author, 7 Oct. 1981.

32. Harrison E. Salisbury, *Without Fear or Favor* (New York: Ballantine Books, 1980), 560–61.

33. Eugene Patterson, remarks to First Amendment Congress quoted in *Editor & Publisher,* 26 Jan. 1980, 15.

34. Interviews by author, 28 May and 15 Sept. 1981.

35. Interview by author, 28 Oct. 1981.

36. "Do Rainy Days and Hyundais Get You Down?" *Wall Street Journal,* 29 June 1986.

37. "What E. B. White Told Xerox," *Columbia Journalism Review* 15, no. 3(Sept./Oct. 1976):52–54.

38. Ibid.

39. "Automobile Dealer Boycotts: How Widespread?" unpublished paper by Charles Brewer, in the possession of the author; "Car Dealers Boycott Tennessee Daily," *Editor & Publisher,* 12 Oct. 1985, 22; Howard Bray, *The Pillars of the Post* (New York: Norton, 1980), 203.

40. Jonathan Friendly, "Trenton Times Journalists Quit over New Policies," *New York Times,* 21 Feb. 1982, 39.

41. "Allbritton Admits Error in Using Press Release," *Editor & Publisher,* 20 Mar. 1982, 16.

42. Interview by author, 28 Oct. 1981.

43. Interview by author, 8 Sept. 1981.

44. John Seigenthaler, remarks prepared for talk at Southern Illinois Univ., Carbondale, Ill., 5 Mar. 1981.

45. Interview by author, 5 June 1981.

46. Interview by author, 22 Oct. 1981.

47. Interview by author, 9 Sept. 1981.

48. Edmund B. Lambeth, *Committed Journalism: An Ethic for the Profession* (Bloomington: Indiana Univ. Press, 1986), 83.

49. James W. Carey, "A Plea for the University Tradition," presidential address to the Association for Education in Journalism, Seattle, Wash., 13 Aug. 1978.

50. See David H. Weaver and G. Cleveland Wilhoit, *The American Journalist: A Portrait of U.S. News People and Their Work* (Bloomington: Indiana Univ. Press, 1986), 45–48.

51. Jack McKinney, "A Matter of Ethics: Learning Write from Wrong," *Philadelphia Daily News,* 11 Dec. 1981.

52. "College Journalism Graduates," *Editor & Publisher,* 2 May 1987, 40, 148–49.

53. Susan Miller, "Measuring Newsroom Salaries: Is the Glass Half Full or Half Empty?" *ASNE Bulletin,* May–June 1986, 4–9.

54. "With an Efficiency, Used Car, Peanut Butter and Byline, What More Could One Want?" *Presstime* 7, no. 4(Apr. 1985).

3

1. "Arbiter Reinstates Reporter," *Presstime* 6, no. 5(May 1984):73; "Reporter Dismissed After Election to School Board," *New York Times,* 15 June 1983, A16.

2. Interview by author, 19 Mar. 1986.

3. "The Reporter," *Philadelphia Magazine,* Apr. 1967, 42–45, 92.

4. "Nightlife Columnist Reassigned," *Philadelphia Inquirer,* 14 Sept. 1978.

5. Interview by author, 28 May 1981.

6. "Winans Conviction Upheld," *New York Times,* 28 May 1986, D1–2; Charles Koshetz, "Winans Case Spotlights Ethics Policies," 1985–86 Report of SPJ-SDX Ethics Committee, 9.

7. "SEC's Inquiry Widens as It Questions Broker, Others in Journal Case," *Wall Street Journal,* 2 Apr. 1984, 1, 18; "Dirty Linen," *Wall Street Journal,* 2 Apr. 1984, 32.

8. Interview by author, 17 Apr. 1981.

9. Richard B. Tuttle, "Invitation Led to Dispute," 1980 report of APME Professional Standards Committee, 9–10.

10. Interview by author, 15 Oct. 1981.

11. Tuttle, "Invitation."

12. "Paper Upheld on Ban against Outside Work," *Presstime* 5, no. 7(July 1983):52.

13. "Columnist Resigns after Paper Learns of His Outside PR Work," *Editor & Publisher,* 9 Nov. 1985, 12.

14. "The Dual News Roles of Hodding Carter 3rd," *New York Times,* 21 Apr. 1984, 38.

15. Randell Beck, "TV Reporter Covers TVA–and Free-lances for It," 1985–86 report of SPJ-SDX Ethics Committee, 22.

16. Interview by author, 8 Apr. 1981.

17. Interviews by author, 28 May and 15 Sept. 1981.

18. "Outside Earnings Rise in Congress," AP dispatch in *New York Times,* 30 June 1986, A17.

19. "A Deadline a Minute Was the Life for Me," *USA Today,* 6 June 1986.

20. Mary T. Schmich, "Granstrom's Progress," *Florida Magazine* section, *Orlando Sentinel,* 18 Nov. 1984, 9–12, 14.

21. "Editor Seeking Political Post Embroils Duluth Papers in Legal Battle," *New York Times,* 17 Nov. 1978, A16.

22. "Councilman's Dual Hats are Front-page News in Tyrone," Johnstown (Pa.) *Tribune-Democrat,* 1 July 1985.

23. "An Editorial Leads to Two Newsmen's Resignations from Public Office," *Quill* 68, no. 5(May 1980):6.

24. Patterson letter to author, 10 Mar. 1982.

25. Interview by author, 14 Nov. 1981.

26. Interview by author, 28 May, 1981.

27. Celeste Huenergard, "No More Cheerleading on the Sports Pages," *Editor & Publisher,* 16 June 1979, 11.

28. Michael York, "Causing a Hoopla in Kentucky," *Washington Journalism Review* 9, no. 1(Jan. 1986):46–49.

29. Interview by author, 8 Sept. 1981.

30. John Consoli, "Pro Baseball Eyes Solution to Official Scorer Problem," *Editor & Publisher,* 3 Nov. 1979, 20: "Baseball Scoring: A Dying Art," 1980 report of APME Professional Standards Committee.

31. Sam Zagoria, "The Ethics of Printing Point Spreads," *Washington Post,* 10 Apr. 1985.

32. "Top Horse-Racing Writers Often Turn Opinions into Profits," *Washington Post,* 17 Feb. 1985.

33. Mike Ryan, "Gambling in the Sports Department—Lack of Guidelines Creates Confusion," 1982 report of APME Sports Committee, 5–7.

34. "National and International Journalism Competitions," *Editor & Publisher,* 28 Dec. 1985, 24J.

35. Richard P. Cunningham, "Of Mice and Mysids," *Quill* 74, no. 6(June 1986):10.

36. "Contests: Which Programs Qualify under Code of Ethics?" 1984–85 report of SPJ-SDX Ethics Committee, 18, 20.

37. "National and International," *Editor & Publisher,* 10J.

38. Interview by author, 8 Apr. 1981.

39. "Can Marriage and Ethics Mix?" 1983–84 report of SPJ-SDX Ethics Committee.

40. Charles W. Bailey, *Conflicts of Interest: A Matter of Journalistic Ethics,* a report to the National News Council, 1984, 10.

41. Jack Anderson, "Why Mike Wallace Axed a Probe," *Centre Daily Times,* State College (Pa.) 27 Feb. 1981; Tony Schwartz, " '60 Minutes' Will Go Ahead with Report on Haiti," *New York Times,* 3 Mar. 1981, C20.

42. Interview by author, 22 Oct. 1981.

43. "Appearances are Deceiving, or So Some Editors Think," *Feed/back,* Summer 1985, 1.

44. "When Is a Reporter in Conflict of Interest?" *Editor & Publisher,* 9 Feb. 1985, 14.

45. Susan Page, " 'Til Deadline Do Us Part," *Washington Journalism Review* 7, no. 3(Mar. 1985):45–48.

46. Don Sneed, "The Editor and Publisher as Public Official: The Ultimate Conflict of Interest," unpublished paper, Association for Education in Journalism and Mass Communication, annual convention, Memphis, Tenn., 3–6 Aug. 1985.

47. "Working for Reagan or for Readers?" *Editor & Publisher,* 29 Sept. 1984, 10–11, 24, 38; "Politics and Publishing—Do They Mix?" *Editor & Publisher,* 2 Mar. 1985, 39.

48. Bill Gloede, "Journalists Examine Ethical Questions," *Editor & Publisher,* 24 Nov. 1979, 14.

49. Interview by author, 12 Nov. 1981.

50. Interview by author, 15 Mar. 1981.

51. Interview by author, 4 June 1981.

52. Interview by author, 5 June 1981.

53. Interview by author, 9 Nov. 1981.

54. Interview by author, 22 Oct. 1981.

55. Bailey, *Conflicts of Interest.*

56. Interview by author, 28 Oct. 1981.

57. Michael Moore, "How to Keep 'em Happy in Flint," *Columbia Journalism Review* 24, no. 3(Sept./Oct. 1985):40–43.

58. Gilbert Cranberg and Elizabeth Bird, "A Prize in Deed: The Miami Herald's 1983 Pulitzer," *Washington Journalism Review* 6, no. 3(Apr. 1984):47–49.

59. Ben Bagdikian, *The Media Monopoly* (Boston: Beacon Press, 1983), xviii, 4–5.

60. Interview by author, 10 Feb. 1986.

61. Ron Dorfman, "Editors, Publishers and Entangling Alliances," *Quill* 73, no. 8(Sept. 1985):11–12.

62. *In the Public Interest—II: A Report by the National News Council, 1975–1978* (New York: National News Council, 1979), 393–414.

63. "An Ethical Question for Newspapers," *Editor & Publisher,* 13 Dec. 1986, 17.

64. See Nelson A. Crawford, *The Ethics of Journalism* (New York: Knopf, 1924).

65. Bailey, *Conflicts of Interest,* 38.

4

1. Interview by author, 23 Oct. 1981.

2. Rick Alm, "Merchants Woo Writers with 'Freebie' Feasts," *Kansas City Star and Times,* 17 Feb. 1980; Bill Norton, "Some Outdoor Writers Accept Gifts, Discounts," Ibid.

3. Interview by author, 14 Oct. 1981.

4. Interview by author, 25 Nov. 1980.

5. Interview by author, 2 June 1981.

6. Interview by author, 29 Nov. 1980.

7. Rhoda Koenig, "Diary of a Freeloader," *Harper's* 264, no. 1585(June 1982):20–26.

8. Quoted by George E. Osgood, Jr., in "Ethics and the One-Reporter, Rural Bureau" (Master's paper, Pennsylvania State University, July 1981), 22–23.

9. Ibid., 25.

10. Jay Mathews, "All the President's Men," *Columbia Journalism Review* 20, no. 4(Nov./ Dec. 1981):5–7.

11. Tom Hritz, "Bottled Gratitude Dies with the Rule," *Pittsburgh Post-Gazette,* 24 Dec. 1960.

12. Interview by author, 5 June 1981.

13. Interview by author, 28 Oct. 1981.

14. Interview by author, 14 Nov. 1981.

15. Interview by author, 28 May 1981.

16. Interview by author, 2 Dec. 1980.

17. John Jacobs, "The National Flackball League," *Feed/back,* Spring 1982, 24–27.

18. Tom Goldstein, *The News at Any Cost: How Journalists Compromise Their Ethics to Shape the News,* (New York: Simon and Schuster, 1985), 169, 171.

19. Richard Benedetto, "The Winter of the 'Freebie Olympics,' " 1980 report of the APME Professional Standards Committee.

20. M. L. Stein, "The Press Takes Advantage of Media Freebies," *Editor & Publisher,* 18 Aug. 1984, 15.

21. "Ethics Survey," 1985 report to APSE convention, 32–35.

22. Interview by author, 9 Nov. 1981.

23. D. David Rambo, "Food Sections," *Presstime* 6, no. 9(Sept. 1984):10–12.

24. Louis Gelfand, "Advice to Newspaper Food Editors from a Huckster Gone Straight," *Editor & Publisher,* 11 Aug. 1984, 44, 20.

25. Rambo, "Food Sections."

26. "Ethics Survey."

27. Perri Foster-Pegg, "Integrity: Not for Sale at Any Price," *Trenton Times,* 10 July 1981; Foster-Pegg letter to author, 27 July 1981.

28. Interview by author, 23 Oct. 1981.

29. Report of the 1979 ASNE Ethics Committee.

30. William A. Davis, "Didja Hear the One About the Traveling Reporter?" *Quill* 73, no. 5(May 1985):20–23.

31. Interview by author, 6 Oct. 1981.

32. Memorandum to active and associate members, SATW, 2 Sept. 1981.

33. Interview by author, 27 May 1981.

34. Interview by author, 25 Nov. 1980.

35. Interview by author, 2 Nov. 1981.

36. Interviews by author, 28 May and 15 Sept. 1981.

37. Interview by author, 2 Nov. 1981.

38. "Travel Editors: Nothing Mickey Mouse about Disney's PR," *Editor & Publisher,* 17 May 1986, 36, 50.

39. Interview by author, 10 Sept. 1981.

40. Judy Flander, "Battlestar Los Angeles: The Networks Meet the Press," *Washington Journalism Review* 1, no. 8(Sept./Oct. 1979):57, 58, 60.

41. Sylvia Lawler, "Chasen's in Walnut Grove?" Allentown (Pa.) *Morning Call,* 27 June 1980.

42. Interview by author, 18 Nov. 1981.

43. Report of 1979 ASNE Ethics Committee.

44. John Harwood and David Finkel, "Disney Birthday a Hit with Media," *St. Petersburg Times,* 5 Oct. 1986, A1 and 4; "Journalists Flock to Birthday Party at Disney World," *New York Times,* 5 Oct. 1986, 26; "The News from Disney World," *New York Times,* 8 Oct. 1986, A34.

45. Interview by author, 3 June 1981.

46. "Ethics Survey."

47. "The High Cost of Foreign Freebies," *Washington Journalism Review* 4, no. 9(Nov. 1982):9–11; interview by author, 29 Oct. 1981.

48. Interview by author, 4 Nov. 1981.

49. Interview by author, 16 Sept. 1981.

50. Interview by author, 24 Sept. 1981.

51. Report of the 1979 APME Professional Standards Committee.

52. Interview by author, 28 May 1981.

53. Interview by author, 23 Oct. 1981.

5

1. "Inquirer Conflict in Cianfrani Case," *Philadelphia Inquirer,* 27 Aug. 1977, 1; "Reporter Linked to a Senator's Gifts," *New York Times,* 28 Aug. 1977, 4. (Laura Foreman worked for the *Philadelphia Inquirer* from September 1973 until January 1977; she was in the Washington bureau of the *New York Times* from January until September 1977.)

2. Interview by author, 7 Oct. 1981.

3. Interview by author, 7 Oct. 1981.

4. Richard Cohen, "For Notorious Woman, 'It Just Ain't Fair,'" *Washington Post,* 2 Oct. 1977.

5. Eleanor Randolph, "Conflict of Interest: A Growing Problem for Couples," *Esquire* 89, no. 2(Feb. 1978):55–59, 124–29.

6. Ibid.

7. Donald L. Barlett and James B. Steele, "The Full Story of Cianfrani and the Reporter," *Philadelphia Inquirer,* 16 Oct. 1977; Jack Tobias, "It's Okay to F____ Elephants, Just Don't Cover the Circus" (Term paper, Pennsylvania State University, Oct. 1980).

8. Laura Foreman, "My Side of the Story," *Washington Monthly* 10, no. 3(May 1978):49–54.

9. "Cianfrani, Ex-reporter Are Married," *Philadelphia Inquirer,* 16 July 1979.

10. Interviews by author, 28 May and 15 Sept. 1981.

11. "Reporter Had Contract with Bouvia for Story," Riverside (Calif.) *Press-Enterprise,* 28 Apr. 1984; Lori Hearn, "Doubts Forced Intervention in Bouvia Struggle," *San Diego Union,* 24 Apr. 1984.

12. "Paralytic Had Book Contract with Reporter," *New York Times,* 4 May 1984, A32.

13. Jack W. Germond and Jules Witcover, *Blue Smoke and Mirrors* (New York: Viking, 1981), 55–75, 77–78.

14. "Greider-Stockman Meetings Were No Secret at the Post," *Editor & Publisher,* 28

Nov. 1981, 36; "Apologetic Stockman Stays," *New York Times,* 13 Nov. 1981, 1, D16.

15. William Greider, "Reporters and Their Sources," *Washington Monthly* 14, no. 8(Oct. 1982):10–19.

16. Interview by author, 23 Sept. 1981.

17. Interview by author, 5 June 1981.

18. Interview by author, 15 Feb. 1981.

19. Interview by author, 12 Nov. 1981.

20. Interview by author, 4 Nov. 1981.

21. Joe Konte, "Ethics of the Police Beat," *Feed/back,* Winter 1983, 16–19; "Glover Story Called 'Serious Disservice,' " *Feed/back,* Summer 1983, 3.

22. Interview by author, 25 Nov. 1980.

23. Interview by author, 4 June 1981.

24. "High Court Refuses Farber Case Review," *New York Times,* 28 Nov. 1978, 1; "Jail Threat Ends for Reporter Farr," *Editor & Publisher,* 26 Dec. 1981, 9.

25. "Source Saves Reporter from Jail Term," *News Media & the Law* 9, no. 2(Summer 1985):26–27.

26. William A. Rusher, "The Press Rampant," *Columbia Journalism Review* 19, no. 4(Nov./Dec. 1979):17–19.

27. James Carey, "A Plea for the University Tradition," presidential address to the Association for Education in Journalism, Seattle, Wash., 13 Aug. 1978; Renata Adler, "Reflections on Political Scandal," *New York Review of Books,* 8 Dec. 1977, 20–23.

28. Interview by author, 4 Nov. 1981.

29. Interview by author, 6 Oct. 1981.

30. Interview by author, 7 Oct. 1981.

31. Interview by author, 5 Oct. 1981.

32. Interview by author, 16 Oct. 1981.

33. Interview by author, 6 Oct. 1981.

34. Interview by author, 5 Oct. 1981.

35. Interview by author, 4 June 1981.

36. Interview by author, 16 Oct. 1981.

37. Interview by author, 9 Nov. 1981.

38. Clark Mollenhoff, "A Lack of Clear Standards for Sound Corroboration," *Bulletin of the American Society of Newspaper Editors,* May/June 1981, 34, 35.

39. "Confidential Sources," *Freedom of Information Annual Report 1979,* APME, 4–5.

40. Interview by author, 5 June 1981.

41. "Who Is 'Deep Throat'? Ben Bradlee Replies," *New York Times,* 7 May 1981.

42. Interview by author, 5 June 1981.

43. Interview by author, 16 Oct. 1981.

44. "No Way to Treat a Tipster," *Columbia Journalism Review* 24, no. 5(Jan./Feb. 1986):10–11.

45. James D. Squires, "When Confidentiality Itself Is Source of Contention," 1985–86 report of SPJ-SDX Ethics Committee, 7.

46. Letter to author, 10 June 1984.

47. Interview by author, 14 Mar. 1986.

48. Interview by author, 25 Nov. 1980.

49. Ron Javers, "Poor Penn-manship," *Washington Journalism Review* 3, no. 7(Sept. 1981):16.

50. Interview by author, 17 Sept. 1981.

51. Interview by author, 25 Feb. 1986.

52. Milton Coleman, "A Reporter's Story: 18 Words, Seven Weeks Later," *Washington Post,* 8 Apr. 1984.

53. Ibid.

54. Interview by author, 25 Feb. 1986.

55. Interview by author, 21 Feb. 1986.

56. Carl Bernstein and Bob Woodward, *All the President's Men* (New York: Simon and Schuster, 1974), 71.

57. Thomas J. Brazaitis, "Background on Covering President," 1985–86 report of SPJ-SDX Ethics Committee.

58. James McCartney, "Perhaps Every Reporter Should Take an Oath to Walk Out on Officials Who Insist on Talking 'Off the Record,'" *ASNE Bulletin,* Oct. 1984, 14–15.

59. Interview by author, 5 June 1981.

60. Brazaitis, "Background."

61. Interview by author, 7 Oct. 1981.

62. Benjamin C. Bradlee, "Standard and Ethics," in *Washington Post Deskbook on Style,* ed. Robert A. Webb (New York: McGraw-Hill, 1978).

6

1. Ben H. Bagdikian, "No. 50061, Inside Maximum Security," *Washington Post,* 31 Jan. 1972.

2. Bagdikian to author, 14 Nov. 1981.

3. David Shaw, "Deception – Honest Tool of Reporting?" *Los Angeles Times,* 20 Sept. 1979.

4. Interview by author, 5 June 1981; letter to author, 8 May 1982.

5. Steve Robinson, "Pulitzers: Was the Mirage a Deception?" *Columbia Journalism Review* 18, no. 2(July/Aug. 1979):14–16.

6. Lina Mainiero, ed., *American Women Writers from Colonial Times to the Present: A Critical Reference Guide* (New York: Frederick Ungar, 1979)1:381–83.

7. Silas Bent, *Newspaper Crusaders: A Neglected Story* (New York: Whittlesey House, 1939), 198.

8. Doug Struck, "Inside Crownsville," Annapolis *Evening Capital,* 6–25 Oct. 1975.

9. Bent, *Newspaper Crusaders,* 47.

10. Frank Luther Mott, *News Stories of 1934* (Iowa City, Ia.: Clio Press, 1935), 258–60, 264–71.

11. Interview by author, 6 Oct. 1981.

12. Robinson, "Pulitzers," 14–16.

13. Interview by author, 8 Sept. 1981.

14. Dennis Holden, "Examiner Prize Lost in the Shuffle," *Washington Journalism Review* 4, no. 5(June 1982):26.

15. Interview by author, 19 Oct. 1981.

16. Interview by author, 8 Sept. 1981.

17. Interview by author, 9 Sept. 1981.

18. "Undercover," research report of the Times Publishing Co., St. Petersburg, Fla., and the Department of Mass Communications, University of South Florida, Summer 1981.

19. Holden, "Examiner Prize," 26.

20. Interview by author, 6 Oct. 1981.

21. Interview by author, 8 Sept. 1981.

22. Interview by author, 24 Feb. 1986.

23. Interview by author, 26 Feb. 1986.

24. Interview by author, 19 Feb. 1986.

25. Interview by author, 19 Oct. 1981.

26. Shaw, "Deception."

27. Interview by author, 4 June 1981.

28. Interview by author, 4 Nov. 1981.

29. Interview by author, 8 Sept. 1981.

30. Interview by author, 25 Nov. 1980.

31. Interview by author, 4 Nov. 1981.

32. Interview by author, 2 Nov. 1981.

33. Neil Henry, "The Black Dispatch," *Washington Post,* 9–14 Oct. 1983.

34. Interview by Donna Shaub in "Undercover Reporting: Is It Always Ethical?" unpublished paper on file with author.

35. Henry, "Black Dispatch."

36. Shaub, "Undercover."

37. William J. Coughlin, "Tell It to the Marines," *Washington Journalism Review* 6, no. 6(July/Aug. 1984):54–55.

38. Ibid.

39. Leslie Linthicum, "When to Go Undercover? As Last Resort to Get Story," 1983–84 report of SPJ-SDX Ethics Committee, 20; Leslie Linthicum, "Undercover Student" series, *Albuquerque Tribune,* 7–14 Mar. 1983; Deni Elliott, "End vs. Means: Comparing Two Cases of Deceptive Practices," 1984–85 report of SPJ-SDX Ethics Committee, 15–16.

40. Interview by author, 16 Nov. 1981.

41. Interview by author, 19 Oct. 1981.

42. *In the Public Interest—II, Report by the National News Council, 1975-1978* (New York: National News Council, 1979), 146–50.

43. "*1 2 3 4 5,*" 1979 report of APME Professional Standards Committee, 2–10.

44. Interview by author, 22 Feb. 1982.

45. Beth Nissen, "An Inside View," *Wall Street Journal,* 28 July 1978.

46. Interview by author, 20 Oct. 1981.

47. Michael Salwen, "Getting the Story by Hook or by Crook," *Quill* 69, no. 1(Jan. 1981):12–14.

48. David Anderson and Peter Benjaminson, *Investigative Reporting* (Bloomington: Indiana Univ. Press, 1976), 109.

49. Interview by author, 27 May 1981.

50. Interview by author, 2 Sept. 1981.

51. Interviews by author, 28 May and 15 Sept. 1981.

52. Interview by author, 4 Nov. 1981.

53. Interview by author, 14 Oct. 1981.

54. Interview by author, 8 Sept. 1981.

55. Paul Shannon, "For Rent or Not For Rent," *IRE Journal,* Fall 1985, 21–22.

56. Interview by author, 21 Feb. 1986.

57. Interview by author, 17 Sept. 1981.

58. Interview by author, 19 Oct. 1981.

59. Shaw, "Deception."

60. Interviews by author, 28 May and 15 Sept. 1981.

61. Interview by author, 25 Nov. 1980.

62. Interview by author, 12 Nov. 1981.

63. Interview by author, 10 Sept. 1981.

64. Interview by author, 24 Feb. 1986.

65. Ibid.

66. Deni Elliott, "The Consequences of Deception: Unwarranted Use Can Damage Public Trust in Journalists," 1984–85 report of SPJ-SDX Ethics Committee, 14–15.

7

1. AP Los Angeles Bureau, 21 Sept. 1981.

2. Interview by author, 8 Oct. 1981.

3. David Shaw, "AP Reporter Resigns over Erroneous 'Banzai Run' Feature," *Los Angeles Times,* 29 Sept. 1981.

4. Ibid.

5. Nelson A. Crawford, *The Ethics of Journalism* (New York: Knopf, 1924), 39–40;

Haynes Johnson, "A Wound That Will Be Long in Healing and Never Forgotten," *Washington Post,* 19 Apr. 1981.

6. Interview by author, 29 Nov. 1980.

7. Jessica Savitch, *Anchorwoman* (New York: G. P. Putnam's Sons, 1982), 172–73.

8. Mark Fitzgerald, "Hoax in Chicago," *Editor & Publisher,* 7 Dec. 1985, 22, 33.

9. Janet Cooke, "Jimmy's World," *Washington Post,* 28 Sept. 1980.

10. *After "Jimmy's World,"* report by National News Council (New York: 1981), 16–22.

11. William Green, "The Confession," *Washington Post* 19 Apr. 1981.

12. NBC "Today" Show, 1 and 2 Feb. 1982; AP, "She Knew She'd Be Caught After Winning Pulitzer," *Leesburg* (Fla.) *Commercial,* 2 Feb. 1982.

13. Interview by author, 24 Sept. 1981.

14. Interview by author, 5 June 1981.

15. Michael Daly, "On the Street of Belfast, the Children's War," New York *Daily News,* 6 May 1981.

16. Mitchell Stephens, "More 'Jimmy' Fallout," *Washington Journalism Review* 3, no. 6(July/Aug. 1981):13.

17. Interview by author, 8 Oct. 1981.

18. James M. Markham, "Writer Admits He Fabricated an Article in Times Magazine," *New York Times,* 22 Feb. 1982, A1, A4.

19. Gail Sheehy, "Wide Open City/Part I: The New Breed," *New York,* 26 July 1971, 22–25; and "Wide Open City/Part II: Redpants and Sugarman," *New York,* 2 Aug. 1971, 26–36.

20. Michiko Kakutani, "Blurring the Lines between Fiction and Nonfiction," *ASNE Bulletin,* July/Aug. 1981, 16.

21. *After "Jimmy's World,"* 82.

22. Teresa Carpenter, "From Heroism to Madness: The Odyssey of the Man Who Shot Al Lowenstein," *Village Voice,* 12 May 1980.

23. Paul L. Montgomery, "Deception Denied by Reporter for Voice," *New York Times,* 11 May 1981, D12.

24. Carpenter, "From Heroism to Madness."

25. Paul Blustein, "Some Journalists Fear Flashy Reporters Let Color Overwhelm Fact," *Wall Street Journal,* 14 May 1981.

26. Interview by author, 4 June 1981.

27. Interview by author, 4 Nov. 1981.

28. Interview by author, 27 May 1981.

29. " 'Child Murders' Sparks Debate on Docudramas," *New York Times,* 4 Feb. 1985, C17.

30. David Shaw, "Docudrama: Where Facts Don't Count," 1985–86 report of the SPJ-SDX Ethics Commmittee, 20.

31. Daniel Schorr, "Harvest of Sham," *Channels,* Mar. 1986, 57–59.

32. Shaw, "Docudrama."

33. Interview by author, 5 June 1981.

34. Roy Peter Clark, "The Unoriginal Sin: How Plagiarism Poisons the Press," *Washington Journalism Review* 5, no. 2(Mar. 1983):43–47.

35. Ibid.

36. Ibid.

37. Interview by author, 16 Sept. 1981.

38. Interviews by author, 28 May and 15 Sept. 1981.

39. Jacques Leslie, "The Pros and Cons of Cleaning Up Quotes," *Washington Journalism Review* 8, no. 5(May 1986):44–46.

40. Ron Lovell, "Wrong Way Stretch: Scoops Vanish, Credibility Remains–As One Reporter Learned after Re-creating Quotes," *Quill* 69, no. 7(July/Aug. 1981):19–20.

41. Rich Stim, "Was Randy Mantooth Ever in the Service?" *Columbia Journalism Review* 19, no. 4(Nov./Dec. 1980):38–40.

42. Clark DeLeon, "The Scene," *Philadelphia Inquirer,* 1 May 1981.

43. Robert A. Webb, ed., *The Washington Post Deskbook on Style* (New York: McGraw-Hill, 1978), 4.

8

1. Interview by author, 26 Mar. 1986; "CBS Producer Suspended for Secret Taping," *New York Times,* 16 June 1983, C27.

2. "The '60 Minutes' Hour of Reckoning," *Washington Journalism Review* 4, no. 7(July/Aug. 1983):13.

3. Jack C. Landau, "Tape Record Important Interviews," *Editor & Publisher,* 21 Jan. 1984, 22.

4. Theodore L. Glasser, "On the Morality of Secretly Taped Interviews," *Nieman Reports* 34, no. 1(Spring 1985):17–20.

5. Interview by author, 14 Mar. 1986.

6. Alan R. Ginsberg, "Secret Taping: A No-no for Nixon–but Okay for Reporters?" *Columbia Journalism Review* 23, no. 2(July/Aug. 1984):16–19.

7. Michael York, "Causing a Hoopla in Kentucky," *Washington Journalism Review* 8, no. 1(Jan. 1986):46–49.

8. Charles Burke, "Sleuthing on Local TV: How Much? How Good?" *Columbia Journalism Review* 12, no. 5(Jan./Feb. 1984):43–45.

9. S. Elizabeth Bird, "Newspaper Editors' Attitudes Reflect Ethical Doubt on Surreptitious Recording," *Journalism Quarterly* 62, no. 2(Summer 1985):284–88.

10. Ginsberg, "Secret Taping."

11. Ann Zimmerman, "By Any Other Name . . . " *Washington Journalism Review* 1, no. 9(Nov./Dec. 1979):32–39.

12. Interviews by author, 28 May and 15 Sept. 1981.

13. Interview by author, 15 Oct. 1981.

14. Interview by author, 18 Sept. 1981.

15. Interview by author, 24 Sept. 1981.

16. "Long Ears in Louisville," *Time,* 14 Oct. 1974.

17. Interview by author, 23 Oct. 1981.

18. Interview by author, 9 Sept. 1981.

19. Interview by author, 24 Sept. 1981.

20. Interview by author, 24 Feb. 1986.

21. From the *Best of Gannett 1980* (Rochester, N.Y.: Gannett Co., 1981), 44–45.

22. Ken Auletta, "Bribe, Seduce, Lie, Steal: Anything to Get the Story?" *More* 7, no. 3(Mar. 1977):14–20.

23. Interview by author, 25 Nov. 1980.

24. James C. Thomson, Jr., "Journalistic Ethics: Some Probings by a Media Keeper," *Nieman Reports* 31, no. 4/32, no. 1(Winter/Spring 1978):7–14.

25. Gallup Poll, "Investigative Reporting Has Broad Public Support," news release, 17 Dec. 1981.

26. Anthony Lewis, "Hire and Salary," *New York Times,* 26 Jan. 1978, A29; John Herbers, "Former Aide Interviews Nixon," *New York Times,* 9 Apr. 1984, C18; Tom Wolfe, *The Right Stuff* (New York: Farrar-Straus-Giroux, 1979), 277–96, 352–79.

27. Interview by author, 17 Sept. 1981.

28. Interview by author, 6 Oct. 1981.

29. Interview by author, 8 Oct. 1981.

30. Interview by author, 2 Nov. 1981.

31. Interview by author, 24 Sept. 1981.

32. Fred Friendly, interviewed on "Watching the Watchdog" documentary, WBBM-TV Chicago, 20 Apr. 1981.

33. Interview by author, 8 Sept. 1981.

34. "60 Minutes," CBS, 27 Sept. 1981.

35. Interview by author, 4 Nov. 1981.

36. Interview by author, 5 Oct. 1981.

37. Interview by author, 18 Sept. 1981.

38. Interview by author, 2 Sept. 1981.

39. Interviews by author, 15 Oct. 1981.

40. Interview by author, 5 June 1981.

41. Interview by author, 22 Oct. 1981.
42. "Mayor Not Shot . . . and That Was the News," *AP Log,* 6 July 1981.
43. Interview by author, 9 Nov. 1981.
44. Interview by author, 8 Oct. 1981.
45. Interview by author, 16 Oct. 1981.
46. Interview by author, 2 Nov. 1981.
47. Interview by author, 2 Sept. 1981.
48. Interview by author, 25 Nov. 1980.
49. Interview by author, 16 Sept. 1981.
50. Interview by author, May 1981.
51. Interview by author, 24 Sept. 1981.
52. Interview by author, 4 Nov. 1981.
53. Interview by author, 24 Feb. 1986.
54. Interview by author, 10 Nov. 1981.
55. Thomas Collins of *Newsday,* "News Photographers under Fire," Orlando (Fla.) *Sentinel-Star,* 12 Dec. 1981.
56. Karen Freifeld, "Embargo: The Rule Not Made to Be Broken," *Washington Journalism Review* 6, no. 10(Dec. 1984):39–40.
57. Debbie Creemers and George Blake, "Are Embargoes Sacrosanct?" *ASNE Bulletin,* Oct. 1984, 18–19.
58. Ibid.
59. "Digging Out the News," *Washington Journalism Review* 7, no. 9(Sept. 1985):12–13.
60. Interview by author, 10 Sept. 1981.
61. Frederick Talbott, "Taping on the Sly," *Quill* 74, no. 6(June 1986):43–46.

9

1. Lewis Regelman is the man who tried to help save the woman's life and then took photographs as firefighters and an ambulance crew worked on her before taking her to the hospital. He gave permission to reproduce his photographs and asked that he be credited only in this way.
2. Interview by author, 16 Oct. 1981.
3. Interview by author, 9 Sept. 1981.
4. Lil Junas, "Tragedy, Violence Photos Dominate in News Prizes," *Editor & Publisher,* 23 Feb. 1980, 17; updated by Junas for this book.
5. "Graphic Excess," *Washington Journalism Review* 8, no. 1(Jan. 1986):10–11.
6. Robert Bentley, "Lessons Sought from Tragic Events," Bakersfield, Calif., *Californian,* 4 Aug. 1985.
7. Bob Greene, "News Business and Right to Privacy Can Be at Odds," 1985–86 report of the SPJ-SDX Ethics Committee, 15.
8. Ibid.
9. Charles B. Seib, "Impact Photos and Reader Sensibilities," *Washington Post,* 3 Aug. 1975.
10. Remarks by Stanley Forman, Region One Conference, SPJ-SDX, Rochester, N.Y., Apr. 1976.
11. Interview by author, 8 Jan. 1982.
12. Jim Gordon, "Judgment Days for Words and Pictures," *News Photographer,* July 1980, 25–29.
13. David E. Halvorsen, "The Perennial Judgment Call: Taste Versus News in Photos," 1984 report of the APME Photo and Graphic Committee.
14. Interview by author, 8 Oct. 1981.
15. Edwin Guthman, "On the Photos of Carter's Fall: The Inquirer Goofed," *Philadelphia Inquirer,* 1 Feb. 1981.
16. Joseph M. Ungaro, "Would You Publish This?" undated APME photo-letter, 1976.

17. Kathleen Pavelko, "Wet T-shirt Photo: The Way the Contest Really Was," *Daily Collegian,* University Park, Pa., 11 Apr. 1977.

18. Interview by author, 10 Nov. 1981.

19. Interview by author, 25 Nov. 1980.

20. Interview by author, 8 Oct. 1981.

21. Mitchell Stephens and Eliot Frankel, "All the Obscenity That's Fit to Print," *Washington Journalism Review* 3, no. 3(Apr. 1981):15–19; Nicholas Von Hoffman, "Nine Justices for Seven Dirty Words," *More* 8, no. 6(June 1978):12–15.

22. Russell Baker, "Anti-Anglo-Saxonism," *New York Times,* 11 July 1978, A17.

23. Richard P. Cunningham, "Of Mice and Mysids," *Quill* 44, no. 6(June 1986):8–13.

24. David Shaw, *Journalism Today* (New York: Harper & Row, Harper's College Press, 1977), 208–9; "Editor's Notes," *Quill* 63, no. 5(May 1975):2.

25. Charles Alexander, "A Word–About Telling the Whole Truth," *Quill* 63, no. 5(May 1975):29–30.

26. John McCormally, letter to the editor, "Over Reacted?" *Editor & Publisher,* 26 Apr. 1975, 7.

27. John Dean, "Rituals of the Herd," *Rolling Stone,* 7 Oct. 1976.

28. Tony Schwartz, "The Insider," *New Times,* 15 Oct. 1976, 27.

29. "Most Papers Bleeped Out Butz's Punch Line," *Editor & Publisher,* 16 Oct. 1976, 13.

30. Ibid.

31. Ibid.

32. Shaw, *Journalism Today,* 211.

33. Charles B. Seib, "Media Influence," *Washington Post,* 7 Oct. 1976.

34. Stephens and Frankel, *All the Obscenity,* 15–19.

35. "There He Goes: Reagan's Mike Tattles on Him," AP dispatch in *Orlando Sentinel,* 1 Mar. 1986.

36. Interview by author, May 1981.

37. Interview by author, 16 Sept. 1981.

38. "Somebody Sanitized, but Not the Union," ONO *Excerpts* 2, no. 5(Aug. 1981):1.

39. Interview by author, May 1981.

40. Interview by author, 28 May 1981.

41. Interview by author, 14 Nov. 1981.

42. Jim Martz, "Now, Tigers' Ford Has Time to Go Fishing," *Miami Herald,* 3 Jan. 1982.

43. John Laurence, "In Politics a Joke Is No Laughing Matter," *Washington Journalism Review* 2, no. 5(June 1980):16–18.

44. Interview by author, 25 Nov. 1980.

45. Robert Scheer, "The Ruling Class: With a Friend Like Me . . . ," *New Times* 7, no. 8(15 Oct. 1976):16–18.

46. Dennis Holder, "Joe Bob Driven Out of Dallas," *Washington Journalism Review* 7, no. 6(June 1985):18–19.

47. Ibid.

48. "Watts Apologizes for Words about Coal Panel," *New York Times,* 22 Sept. 1983, A15.

49. Robert A. Webb, ed., *Washington Post Deskbook on Style* (New York: McGraw-Hill, 1978), 5, 38.

10

1. Charles B. Seib, "How the Papers Covered the Cinema Follies Fire," *Washington Post,* 30 Oct. 1977.

2. George Beveridge, "Identifying the Movie-fire Victims," *Washington Star,* 31 Oct. 1977.

3. Seib, "How the Papers Covered."

4. Beveridge, "Identifying the Movie-fire Victims."

5. Seib, "How the Papers Covered."

6. Beveridge, "Identifying the Movie-fire Victims."

7. Seib, "How the Papers Covered."

8. David Burnham, "Poll Finds Increasing Concern over Threats to Privacy," *New York Times*, 4 May 1979, A19.

9. This very brief description of libel and privacy was drawn from Wayne Overbeck and Rick D. Pullen, *Major Principles of Media Law* (New York: Holt, Rinehart and Winston, 1982), 70–129, 344–45; Paul J. Levine, "Invasion of Privacy and the News Media," in *Reporter's Handbook* (Tallahassee: Florida Bar Association, Florida Press Association and Florida Association of Broadcasters, 1981); Christopher H. Little, "Newspaper Law and Fairness," in Robert A. Webb, ed., *The Washington Post Deskbook on Style* (New York: McGraw-Hill, 1978).

10. Interview by author, 7 Oct. 1981.

11. Interview by author, 23 Oct. 1981.

12. "Life in the Spotlight: Agony of Getting Burned," *New York Times*, 27 Feb. 1985, A16.

13. Interview by author, 4 Nov. 1981.

14. Ellen Karasik, "Sen. Scott's Daughter Is Arrested," *Philadelphia Inquirer*, 31 July 1975.

15. Interview by author, 16 Sept. 1981.

16. Eric Schmitt, "Absence of Pity," *Quill* 42, no. 7(July/Aug. 1984):10–11.

17. Interview by author, 9 Nov. 1981.

18. Interview by author, 4 Nov. 1981.

19. Interview by author, 21 Oct. 1981.

20. "Gannett Daily Fined $10,000 in Invasion of Privacy Case," *Editor & Publisher*, 10 Oct. 1981, 32.

21. Richard P. Cunningham, "Child Photos: Drawing the Line," *Quill* 44, no. 2(Feb. 1986):8–9.

22. "David X," *Washington Journalism Review* 6, no. 4(May 1984):9–10; "A Bouquet for the Press from the Mother of the 'Bubble Boy,' " *ASNE Bulletin*, Oct. 1984, 32.

23. Interview by author, 28 Oct. 1981.

24. "Stop Printing Victims' Addresses: Crime Panel," *Editor & Publisher*, 12 Feb. 1983, 11.

25. Greg Ring, "Are Exact Addresses Always Part of the News?" *ASNE Bulletin*, Feb. 1986, 20–22.

26. Reece Hirsch, "It's a Small Town After All," *Byline*, Spring 1980, 31–33.

27. Richard P. Cunningham, "Names Make News, but Not Always," *Quill* 73, no. 2(Feb. 1985):5.

28. Bill Blair, "Soul-searching Involved in AIDS Decision," *Centre Daily Times*, State College, Pa., 21 Dec. 1985.

29. Edwin Diamond and Christopher M. Bellitto, "The Great Verbal Coverup," *Washington Journalism Review* 8, no. 3(Mar. 1986):38–42.

30. "Health Reporting: AIDS," *APME Red Book*, 1986, 65–66.

31. William Cooney, "Ex-Marine Probably Saved Ford," *San Francisco Chronicle*, 23 Sept. 1975.

32. Daryl Lembke, "Hero in Ford Shooting Active among S.F. Gays," *Los Angeles Times*, 25 Sept. 1975.

33. Pat Murphy, "Ford Hero's Mother Has Misgivings," *Detroit News*, 26 Sept. 1975.

34. R. W. Hollis, "Sipple," research report, School of Journalism, Pennsylvania State University, University Park, Pa., 1981.

35. "Court Dismisses Suit by Homosexual Who Saved Ford's Life," *News Media and the Law* 4, no. 4(Oct./Nov. 1980):28–29.

36. "Oakland *Tribune* Wins Reversal on $550,000 Privacy Judgment," *Feed/back*, Spring 1983, 6; "Diaz Privacy Award Overturned, Judge Erred, Court Rules," *News Media and the Law*, Sept./Oct. 1983, 19.

37. Interview by author, 9 Nov. 1981.

38. Overbeck and Pullen, *Major Principles,* 116–17.

39. Carol Oukrop, "Views of Newspaper Gatekeepers on Rape and Rape Coverage," unpublished paper presented at Association for Education in Journalism and Mass Communication Convention, Corvallis, Oregon, 1983.

40. Bruce DeSilva, "The Gang-rape Story," *Columbia Journalism Review* 23, no. 1(May/ June 1984):42–44; "Press Somehow Failed to Clarify Reports of Cheering in New Bedford Rape," *New York Times,* 11 Apr. 1984, A19.

41. Interview by author, 4 Nov. 1981.

42. *In the Public Interest—III* (New York: National News Council, 1984), 324–32.

43. Interview by author, 16 Oct. 1981.

44. *In the Public Interest—III.*

45. Interview by author, 5 Mar. 1982.

46. *In the Public Interest—III.*

47. Susan Seliger, "Twice Invaded," *Washington Journalism Review* 1, no. 3(Apr./May 1978):50–52.

48. "Rape Trial Tape Privileged: Court," *News Media and the Law,* Jan./Feb. 1984, 43.

49. Interview by author, 27 May 1981.

50. Craig Ammerman, "When Being Professional Hurts Others Badly," Philadelphia *Bulletin,* 10 May 1981.

51. Interview by author, 3 Nov. 1981.

52. Interview by author, 16 Sept. 1981.

53. Julia Cass, "Smoke Bomb Puts Student on Probation," *Philadelphia Inquirer,* 6 Aug. 1981.

54. Interview by author, 3 Nov. 1981.

55. "S.J. Boys Held in Hanging Attempt," *San Jose Mercury,* 19 Nov. 1982; "3 Young Suspects in Hanging Attempt to Be Kept in Custody," *San Jose Mercury,* 24 Nov. 1982.

56. Barbara Bailey Kelley, "Naming Names," *Feed/back,* Spring 1983, 20–23.

57. Ibid.

58. I. William Hill, "Top Court Rules Out Prior Restraint Law," *Editor & Publisher,* 30 June 1979.

59. "Should Juvenile Offenders' Names Be Published?" *Editor & Publisher,* 18 Jan. 1986, 22, 26.

60. Interview by author, 28 Oct. 1981.

61. "The Suicide Syndrome," *Washington Journalism Review* 8, no. 7(July 1986):10–11.

62. Interview by author, 4 Nov. 1981.

63. Interview by author, 16 Sept. 1981.

64. Michael T. Malloy, "Journalistic Ethics," *National Observer,* 26 July 1975.

65. Interview by author, 25 Sept. 1981.

66. Frank Sutherland, "Jerry Thompson: Before and After the Klan Series," *Gannetteer,* Apr. 1981, 10–11.

67. C. Fraser Smith, "Reporting Grief," *Washington Journalism Review* 6, no. 2(Mar. 1984):21–22, 58.

68. Ramon Coronado, "Broken Goblet, Broken Table: The Media Cover a Hostage Family," and "How Far Should the Media Go to Get a Story?" in Editorially Speaking section, *Gannetteer,* May 1981, 2, 4.

69. Robert Giles, "Some Guidelines for Newspeople," *Gannetteer,* May 1981, 12.

70. Interview by author, 8 Apr. 1981.

71. "U.S. Report on Rape Cases Cites Victims' Frustrations with Law," *New York Times,* 25 Mar. 1985, A17.

11

1. Interview by author, 24 Feb. 1986; Cliff Brown, "The Public's Right to Know Can Kill You," unpublished paper in possession of author.

2. "The *American* Did Not Take Part in Hoax," *Hattiesburg* (Miss.) *American,* 11 Dec. 1984.

3. Duane McAllister, "Publisher Goes on Donahue Show to Defend a Tough Ethics Decision," *Gannetteer,* Mar. 1985, 6–7.

4. Janet Braswell, "Police Stage Hoax to Stop Contract 'Hit,'" *Hattiesburg* (Miss.) *American,* 10 Dec. 1984.

5. Frank Sutherland, "A Man Threatens Murder in Hattiesburg–And Debate Rages on Using False Stories," Editorially Speaking section of *Gannetteer* 40, no. 7(Aug. 1986):4–8.

6. Interview by author, 19 Mar. 1986.

7. Sutherland in *Gannetteer,* 8.

8. Peter Braestrup, "Duty, Honor, Country," *Quill* 73, no. 8(Sept. 1985):15–21.

9. Interview by author, 10 Feb. 1986.

10. Interview by author, 21 Feb. 1986.

11. Phillip Knightly, *The First Casualty: From the Crimea to Vietnam–The War Correspondent as Hero, Propagandist, and Myth Maker* (New York: Harvest Book, Harcourt Brace Jovanovich, 1975), 376.

12. Michael Schudson, *Discovering the News: A Social History of American Newspapers* (New York: Basic Books, 1978), 171–72.

13. Interview by author, 14 Mar. 1986.

14. Charles W. Bailey, *Conflicts of Interest: A Matter of Journalistic Ethics,* report to the National News Council, 1984; George F. Will, "A Journalist Is a Citizen Also," *ASNE Bulletin,* Nov. 1983; "N.Y. Daily News Drops Will Column," *Editor & Publisher,* 16 July 1983, 33.

15. "Schultz Calls for 'Crackdown' on Disclosure of Classified Data," *New York Times,* 16 Mar. 1985, 3; "State Dept. Bureau Is Instructed Not to Speak to a Times Reporter," *New York Times,* 28 Feb. 1985, A8; Laura Rehrmann, "Should Watchdogs Go Inside?" 10 Dec. 1984, unpublished paper in possession of author.

16. Rehrmann, "Should Watchdogs," 2.

17. "Could the Media Have Prevented Shuttle Disaster?" *Editor & Publisher,* 12 July 1986, 11, 35.

18. Interview by author, 2 Nov. 1981.

19. Interview by author, 6 Oct. 1981.

20. Interview by author, 9 Sept. 1981.

21. Interview by author, 8 Sept. 1981.

22. Interview by author, 8 Jan. 1982.

23. Interview by author, 28 Oct. 1981.

24. Interview by author, 8 Oct. 1981.

25. Interview by author, 5 Oct. 1981.

26. Interview by author, 25 Sept. 1981.

27. Sissela Bok, *Secrets: On the Ethics of Concealment and Revelation* (New York: Vintage Books, 1984), 177.

28. Howard Simons, "Government and National Security," excerpt from talk to 1986 ASNE convention in *Editor & Publisher,* 26 Apr. 1986, 80, 69.

29. Bok, *Secrets,* 208.

30. "C.I.A. Weighs Action on Washington Post Article," *New York Times,* 22 May 1986, B11; "C.I.A. Director Urges Inquiry on NBC Broadcast," *New York Times,* 20 May 1986, A24; "The Casey Offensive," *Columbia Journalism Review* 25, no. 2(July/Aug. 1986):18–19.

31. *Columbia Journalism Review,* 19.

32. Jim Anderson, "The Pot Calls the Kettle Black," *Washington Post,* 11 May 1986.

33. "Administration Is Accused of Deceiving Press on Libya," "Schultz Justifies Scaring Qaddafi By Use of Press," and "News Executives Express Outrage," *New York Times,* 3 Oct. 1986, A1, 6, 7; "Spokesman Quits State Dept. Post on Deception Issue," *New York Times,* 9 Oct. 1986, A1, 16.

34. "Lesson on Flacking for Government," *New York Times,* 30 Aug. 1984, B10.

35. Mike Royko, "Blowing the Whistle on a Loud Silence at NASA," *Orlando Sentinel,* 11 Mar. 1986.

36. Anthony Marro, "When the Government Tells Lies," *Columbia Journalism Review* 23, no. 6(Mar./Apr. 1985):29–39; Drew Middleton, "Barring Reporters from the Battlefield," *New York Times Magazine,* 5 Feb. 1984, 36–37, 61, 69, 92; "Coverage Efforts Thwarted," *News Media and the Law,* Jan./Feb. 1984, 6.

37. "Pentagon Activates Press Pool to Cover Libya Bombing," *Presstime,* May 1986, 69.

38. John Corry, "Terrorism on Television: Networks Have Journalistic Responsibilities," *New York Times,* 22 July 1985, C14; "Terrorism Coverage Talks Suggested," *Presstime,* Apr. 1986, 47.

39. Ben Bagdikian, "When Less News Is Bad News," *Quill* 73, no. 8(Sept. 1985):26–27.

40. Michael J. Davies, "Assessing Stories on Terrorists," *APME Red Book,* 1985, 9–12.

41. Larry Grossman, "The Face of Television," *Quill* 74, no. 6(June 1986):38–41.

42. Bagdikian, "When Less News," 26.

43. Jonathan Friendly, "Just When Is Pretrial Publicity Unfair?" *New York Times,* 30 Oct. 1983; Lyle Denniston, "How Flynt Hustled CBS," *Washington Journalism Review* 6, no. 1(Jan./Feb. 1984):14.

44. Richard P. Cunningham, "Fairness of Student's Story Questioned," *Editor & Publisher,* 4 June 1983, 7.

45. Interview with Nauman by author, 29 Aug. 1986.

46. Interview by author, 24 Sept. 1981.

47. Christopher H. Little, "Newspaper Law and Fairness," in Robert A. Webb, ed., *The Washington Post Deskbook on Style* (New York: McGraw-Hill, 1978), 24–25.

48. David Shaw, "Newsmen Generally Criticize Lopez Decision to Testify in Bonin Case," *Los Angeles Times,* 18 Dec. 1981.

49. Ibid.

50. Interview by author, 8 Sept. 1981.

51. "IRE Leader Feels Reporters Should Surrender Notes," *Editor & Publisher,* 3 Mar. 1979.

52. Interview by author, 6 Oct. 1981.

53. Lisa J. Mullins, "The *Globe* on Trial," *Quill* 73, no. 10(Nov. 1985):39–44.

54. Interview by author, 14 Mar. 1986.

55. "After the Trial Is Over, Are Jurors Fair Game for Press Interviews?" *Presstime,* Apr. 1983, 22–23.

56. Lyle Denniston, "Jury Privacy: An Emerging Battleground," *Quill* 72, no. 5(May 1984):13–16.

57. Christopher H. Little, "Newspaper Law and Fairness," 16–18.

12

1. Interview by author, 27 Mar. 1982.

2. H. L. Stevenson, "Bill Murphy and the Bridge Jumper," *Editor & Publisher,* 12 Nov. 1977, 34.

3. Interview.

4. Interview by author, 8 Oct. 1981.

5. Interview by author, 19 Oct. 1981.

6. Interview by author, 16 Oct. 1981.

7. Interview by author, 17 Jan. 1983.

8. "Husband Has Fatal Heart Attack during Wife's Hearing," Washington (Pa.) *Observer Reporter,* 12 July 1984.

9. Jim Gordon, "Judgment Days for Words and Pictures," *News Photographer,* July 1980, 25–29.

10. "A Public Photo, but Boy's Mother Grieves Privately," *Philadelphia Inquirer,* 6 July 1980.

11. Bob Greene, "Trying to Trap the Tylenol Killer: A Columnist's Conscience," *ASNE Bulletin,* Mar. 1983, 20–22.

12. Bob Greene, "By Any Other Name," *Esquire* 96, no. 3(Sept. 1981):23–24.

13. Interview by author, 23 Sept. 1981.

14. Interview by author, 19 Oct. 1981.

15. Charles B. Seib, "Could a Little Caring Have Prevented Hoax?" *Presstime* 3, no. 6(June 1981):35.

16. Thomas J. Bray, "What if the 'Jimmy' Story Had Been True?" *Wall Street Journal,* 17 Apr. 1981.

17. John Troan, "The Lesson in the Janet Cooke Case," *Pittsburgh Press,* 3 May 1981.

18. Interview by author, 27 May 1981.

19. Interview by author, 3 June 1981.

20. Interview by author, 5 June 1981.

21. *After "Jimmy's World": Tightening Up in Editing* (New York: National News Council, 1981), 61.

22. Bill Boyarsky, "Motives Sought in Suicide of Oakland Publisher Knowland," *Los Angeles Times,* 25 Feb. 1974.

23. Joe Shoquist, "When Not to Print the News," 1974 report of APME Professional Standards Committee.

24. Thomas Collins, "When the Press Restrains Itself," *Newsday,* 30 Mar. 1983.

25. Paula Moore, "Two Boys Are Kidnapped in El Paso—and the Media Weigh Withholding the Story," Editorially Speaking section of *Gannetteer,* Aug. 1986, 2–3.

26. "Soviet Spy Worked for 4 Years in Dallas," *Dallas Times Herald,* 2 Mar. 1976.

27. *Covering Crime: How Much Press-Police Cooperation? How Little?* (New York: National News Council, 1981), 20–21.

28. See David H. Weaver and G. Cleveland Wilhoit, *The American Journalist: A Portrait of U.S. News People and Their Work* (Bloomington: Indiana Univ. Press, 1986); and John W. C. Johnstone, Edward J. Slawski, and William Bowman, *The News People: A Sociological Portrait of American Journalists and Their Work* (Urbana: Univ. of Illinois Press, 1976). The figure of 116,000 I used in Chapter 2 of this book to describe the estimated total number of full-time journalists in this country is based on the Weaver-Wilhoit statistics plus my own estimates of the number of journalists working as news photographers and for the news departments of CBS, ABC, and NBC networks, and for National Public Radio.

29. Interview by author, 24 Feb. 1986.

30. Interview by author, 24 Sept. 1981.

31. Interview by author, 16 Nov. 1981.

32. Liz Nakahara, "In the Eye of the Storm," *Washington Post,* 6 Nov. 1983, K1, 6, 7.

33. Interview by author, 27 July 1983.

34. "The Double Fire," *New York Times,* 13 Mar. 1983.

35. "Ethics Led Photog to Miss News Shot," *Editor & Publisher,* 28 Apr. 1984, 44.

36. "Photographer Helps Rescue Family—Then Snaps His Pictures," *Editor & Publisher,* 3 Aug. 1985, 55.

37. John Hohenberg, *The News Media: A Journalist Looks at His Profession* (New York: Holt, Rinehart and Winston, 1968), 214–15.

38. Phillip Knightley, *The First Casualty: From the Crimea to Vietnam: The War Correspondent as Hero, Propagandist and Myth Maker* (New York: Harcourt Brace Jovanovich, 1975), 406.

39. Benjamin C. Bradlee, "Standards and Ethics," in Robert A. Webb, ed., *The Washington Post Deskbook on Style* (New York: McGraw-Hill, 1978), 3.

13

1. Gary A. Hogge, M.D., "You Can Fight City Hall: Even When It's a Newspaper," *Medical Economics,* 21 July 1980, 69–72.

2. National News Council Report, "Random Check Left Out Doctor at Top of Fee Listing," *Columbia Journalism Review* 19, no. 2(July/Aug. 1980):86–87.

3. Hogge, "You Can Fight."

4. Interview by author, 19 Oct. 1981.

5. George Gallup, Jr., "Americans Favor Tougher Controls on the Press," *Editor & Publisher,* 19 Jan. 1980, 7.

6. Richard P. Cunningham, "Gov. Lamm and the 'Duty to Die,' " *Editor & Publisher,* 19 May 1986, 18.

7. *After "Jimmy's World": Tightening Up in Editing* (New York: National News Council, 1981), 114.

8. Ibid., 124–25.

9. Drake to Professor R. Thomas Berner, Pennsylvania State University, 30 Nov. 1981, excerpted with letter writer's permission.

10. *After "Jimmy's World,"* 124–25.

11. "Associated Press Moves Erroneous Hinckley Photo," *Editor & Publisher,* 11 Apr. 1981, 48.

12. Interview by author, 19 Oct. 1981.

13. H. L. Mencken, *Prejudices: Sixth Series* (New York: Knopf, 1927), 15.

14. David Shaw, "Legal Issues: Press Still Falls Short," *Los Angeles Times,* 11 Nov. 1980.

15. A. Kent MacDougal, "Flaws in Press Coverage Plus Business Sensitivity Stir Bitter Debate," *Los Angeles Times,* 3 Feb. 1980.

16. A. Kent MacDougal, "When Press Errs on Business, It's Usually Muddled, Not Malicious," *Los Angeles Times,* 4 Feb. 1980.

17. Cortland Anderson, remarks to APME Convention, Toronto, 21 Oct. 1981.

18. David Johnston, "The Wrong Stuff: How Errors Get to the Printed Page," *Washington Journalism Review* 6, no. 6(June 1984):24–28.

19. Jay Mathews, "When In Doubt, Read It Back," *Washington Journalism Review* 7, no. 9(Sept. 1985):33–35.

20. The author cannot identify the reliable source for this tale without harming him or her.

21. Interview by author, 25 Nov. 1980.

22. Thomas Winship, "How Newspapers Can Become a More Vital Force in Everyday Life," speech to National Association of Black Journalists, Baltimore, 31 July–4 Aug. 1985.

23. David H. Weaver and G. Cleveland Wilhoit, *The American Journalist: A Portrait of U.S. News People and Their Work* (Bloomington: Indiana Univ. Press, 1986), 45–60.

24. Ronald Steel, *Walter Lippmann and the American Century* (Boston: Little, Brown, 1980), 200.

25. Donald D. Jones, "Credibility," *APME Red Book,* 1983, 97.

26. Sharon Geltner, "1 Cup Mayo, Hold the Cherries," *Washington Journalism Review* 6, no. 6(June 1984):27.

27. *AP Log,* 10 Sept. 1984.

28. "Editors' Note," *New York Times,* 15 June 1984, B1.

29. Letter to author, 27 July 1983.

30. "The 2,300-word Times Correction," *Time,* 23 Feb. 1981, 84; Andrew Radolf, "New York Times Clears Ex-envoy's Name," *Editor & Publisher,* 28 Feb. 1981, 42–43.

31. Flora Lewis, "The Meanest Way," *New York Times,* 9 Mar. 1981, A23.

32. Phil Gailey, "The Trail of the Rumor on Blair House's 'Bug,' " *New York Times,* 18 Nov. 1981, A24; Gailey, "Carters Threaten to Sue for Libel," *New York Times,* 9 Oct. 1981, A25; Paul Taylor, "Post Apologizes to Carter for Gossip Column Item," *Washington Post,* 23 Oct. 1981.

33. "Text of Carter Statement on Paper's Apology," *New York Times,* 25 Oct. 1981, A27.

34. "So There: Editor's Apology in No Uncertain Terms," AP unpublished file copy, 22 Dec. 1980.

35. Philip Meyer, "An Ethical Audit," Occasional Paper No. 3, Gannett Center for Media Studies (undated).

36. Michael J. Davies, "Hartford Courant Creates Public Seat on Editorial Board," *Editor & Publisher,* 16 Aug. 1986, 48, 33.

37. *A Free and Responsible Press: Report of the Commission on Freedom of the Press,* Robert M. Hutchins, chair. (Chicago: Univ. of Chicago Press, 1947).

38. Jerry Walker, "The Commission Alleges: 'Press Fails to Meet Needs of Society,' " *Editor & Publisher,* 29 Mar. 1947, 7, 60, 61.

39. *A Free and Responsive Press: The Twentieth Century Fund Task Force Report for a National News Council* (New York: Twentieth Century Fund, 1973), 3.

40. See Patrick Brogan, *Spiked: The Short Life and Death of the National News Council,* Twentieth Century Fund, 1985; *In the Public Interest—I* (1973-1975), *In the Public Interest—II* (1975-1978), and *In the Public Interest—III* (1979-1983), published by the National News Council, now available at the Silha Center for the Study of Media Ethics and Law, Univ. of Minnesota, Minneapolis.

41. "News Council Closes, Gives Files to Minnesota," *Quill* 72, no. 5(May 1984):44.

42. Interview by author, 7 Oct. 1981.

43. Interviews by author, 28 May and 15 Sept. 1981.

44. Robert Haiman, talk prepared for convention of ASNE, 22 Apr. 1981.

45. *Problems of Journalism: Proceedings of the ASNE 1981* (Washington, D.C.: ASNE 1981), 65.

46. Interview by author, 7 Oct. 1981.

47. Interview by author, 7 Oct. 1981.

48. Interview by author, 2 Nov. 1981.

49. Interview by author, 2 Nov. 1981.

50. Interview by author, 2 Nov. 1981.

51. Published regularly in the masthead, *Columbia Journalism Review.*

52. Interview by author, 2 Nov. 1981.

53. Interview by author, 5 June 1981.

54. Interview by author, 8 Apr. 1981.

SELECTED BIBLIOGRAPHY

Bagdikian, Ben H. *The Media Monopoly: A Startling Report on the 50 Corporations That Control What America Sees, Hears and Reads.* Boston: Beacon Press, 1983.

Bailey, Charles W. *Conflicts of Interest: A Matter of Journalistic Ethics.* New York: National News Council, 1984.

Balk, Alfred. *A Free and Responsive Press.* New York: Twentieth Century Fund, 1973.

Bayley, Edwin R. *Joe McCarthy and the Press.* Madison: Univ. of Wisconsin Press, 1981.

Bernstein, Carl, and Bob Woodward. *All the President's Men.* New York: Simon and Schuster, 1974.

_____. *The Final Days.* New York: Simon and Schuster, 1976.

Bok, Sissela. *Lying: Moral Choice in Public and Private Life.* New York: Random House, Vintage Books, 1978.

_____. *Secrets: On the Ethics of Concealment and Revelation.* New York: Random House, Vintage Books, 1984.

Bowie, Norman E. *Making Ethical Decisions.* New York: McGraw-Hill, 1985.

Brogan, Patrick. *Spiked: The Short Life and Death of the National News Council.* New York: Twentieth Century Fund, 1985.

Christians, Clifford G., William L. Rivers, and Wilbur Schramm. *Responsibility in Mass Communication.* 3d ed. New York: Harper and Row, 1980.

Christians, Clifford G., Kim B. Rotzoll, and Mark Fackler. *Media Ethics: Cases and Moral Reasoning.* New York: Longman, 1983.

Commission on Freedom of the Press. *A Free and Responsible Press.* Chicago: Univ. of Chicago Press, 1947.

Crawford, Nelson A. *The Ethics of Journalism.* New York: Knopf, 1924.

Goldstein, Tom. *The News At Any Cost: How Journalists Compromise Their Ethics to Shape the News.* New York: Simon and Schuster, 1985.

Hohenberg, John. *The News Media: A Journalist Looks At His Profession.* New York: Holt, Rinehart and Winston, 1968.

_____. *The Professional Journalist.* New York: Holt, Rinehart and Winston, 1983.

Hulteng, John L. *The Messenger's Motives: Ethical Problems of the News Media.* 2d ed. Englewood Cliffs, N.J.: Prentice Hall, 1985.

_____. *Playing It Straight: A Practical Discussion of the Ethical Principles of the American Society of Newspaper Editors.* Chester, Conn.: Globe Pequot Press, 1981.

Isaacs, Norman E. *Untended Gates: The Mismanaged Press.* New York: Columbia Univ. Press, 1986.

Johnstone, John W. C., Edward J. Slawski, and William W. Bowman. *The News People: A Sociological Portrait of American Journalists and Their Work.* Urbana: Univ. of Illinois Press, 1976.

Knightley, Phillip. *The First Casualty: From the Crimea to Vietnam, The War Correspondent as Hero, Propagandist and Myth Maker.* New York: Harcourt Brace Jovanovich, Harvest Book, 1975.

Lambeth, Edmund B. *Committed Journalism: An Ethic for the Profession.* Bloomington: Indiana Univ. Press, 1986.

McCulloch, Frank, ed. *Drawing the Line: How 31 Editors Solved Their Toughest Ethical Dilemmas.* Washington, D.C.: American Society of Newspaper Editors, 1984.

Merrill, John C. *Existential Journalism.* New York: Hastings House, 1977.

_____. *The Imperative of Freedom: A Philosophy of Journalistic Autonomy.* New York: Hastings House, 1974.

Merrill, John C., and S. Jack Odell. *Philosophy and Journalism.* New York: Longman, 1983.

Meyer, Philip. *Editors, Publishers and Newspaper Ethics: A Report to the American Society of Newspaper Editors.* Washington, D.C.: American Society of Newspaper Editors, 1983.

National News Council. *After Jimmy's World: Tightening Up in Editing.* New York: National News Council, 1981.

_____. *Covering Crime: How Much Press-Police Cooperation—How Little?* New York: National News Council, 1981.

_____. *In the Public Interest—I* (1973–1975). New York: National News Council, 1976.

_____. *In the Public Interest—II* (1975–1978). New York: National News Council, 1979.

_____. *In the Public Interest—III* (1979–1983). New York: National News Council, 1984.

_____. *Who Said That? Use of Unidentified Sources.* New York: National News Council, 1983.

Schudson, Michael. *Discovering the News: A Social History of American Newspapers.* New York: Basic Books, 1978.

Siebert, Fred S., Theodore Peterson, and Wilbur Schramm. *Four Theories of the Press.* Urbana: Univ. of Illinois Press, 1963.

Swain, Bruce M. *Reporters' Ethics.* Ames: Iowa State Univ. Press, 1978.

Thayer, Lee, ed. *Ethics, Morality and the Media.* New York: Hastings House, 1980.

Weaver, David H., and G. Cleveland Wilhoit. *The American Journalist: A Portrait of U.S. News People and Their Work.* Bloomington: Indiana Univ. Press, 1986.

Wicker, Tom. *On Press: A Top Reporter's Life in, and Reflections on American Journalism.* New York: Viking, 1978.

INDEX